EXPERIENCING
TESS OF THE D'URBERVILLES

A Deweyan Account

VIBS

Volume 162

Robert Ginsberg
Founding Editor

Peter A. Redpath
Executive Editor

Associate Editors

a volume in
Studies in Pragmatism and Values
SPV
John R. Shook, Editor

EXPERIENCING
TESS OF THE D'URBERVILLES

A Deweyan Account

Arthur Efron

Amsterdam - New York, NY 2005

Cover Design: Studio Pollmann

The paper on which this book is printed meets the requirements of "ISO 9706:1994, Information and documentation - Paper for documents - Requirements for permanence".

ISBN: 90-420-1694-9
©Editions Rodopi B.V., Amsterdam - New York, NY 2005
Printed in the Netherlands

Studies in Pragmatism and Values
SPV

John R. Shook
Editor

Other Titles in SPV

John Shook. *Pragmatism: An Annotated Bibliography, 1898-1940*. 1998. VIBS 66

Phyllis Chiasson. *Peirce's Pragmatism: A Dialogue for Educators*. 2001. VIBS 107

Paul C. Bube and Jeffrey L. Geller, eds. *Conversations with Pragmatism: A Multi-Disciplinary Study*. 2002. VIBS 129

Richard Rumana. *Richard Rorty: An Annotated Bibliography of Secondary Literature*. 2002. VIBS 130

Guy Debrock, ed. *Process Pragmatism: Essays on a Quiet Philosophical Revolution*. 2003. VIBS 137

John Ryder and Emil Višňovský, eds. *Pragmatism and Values: The Central European Pragmatist Forum, Volume One*. 2004. VIBS 152

John Ryder and Krystyna Wilkoszewska, eds. *Deconstruction and Reconstruction: The Central European Pragmatist Forum, Volume Two*. 2004. VIBS 156

Arthur Efron. *Experiencing **Tess of the D'Urbervilles**: A Deweyan Account*. 2004. VIBS 162

To Ruth, whose help has been immeasurable.

CONTENTS

Foreword by Michael Irwin   ix

Preface and Acknowledgements   xiii

ONE   Clearing the Foreground for Experiencing *Tess*   1

TWO   The Body-Mind of Young Tess   29

THREE   Toward Recovery   59

FOUR   Beyond Frustration to Experiential Disaster   79

FIVE   From Confusing Movement to Integral Restoration   109

SIX   Consummations   141

SEVEN   Experience Goes Further   157

Notes   195

Bibliography   223

About the Author   239

Index   241

FOREWORD

Professor Efron refers to the danger of "the theorist or working critic…applying his or her scheme of recognition—his or her governing theory—to the literary work in the manner of using a 'stencil'". He might have gone further. In the majority of cases that "stencil" tends to isolate either those details that might make the text appear merely the product of its age—effectively an authorless ideological exudation—or those that seem censurable in the light of our own favoured contemporary orthodoxies, concerning, for example, race or gender. The work of art as such is eliminated, save insofar as it provides the necessary "evidence".

Such an approach overrides the very factor that gave rise to the term "literature"—the assumption that certain writers can go beyond the ideological confines of their own age to speak with seeming directness to readers from another. The "theorist or working critic" who rejects that assumption no longer has a subject, having sawn off the branch on which he or she was perched. Moreover that essential perversity produces several depressing side-effects. A study in this mode characteristically operates at a level of abstraction remote from the workings of any individual text. It exudes condescension in implicitly asserting superiority to the work or author under discussion, and to the reaction of the lay reader. It is impervious to the idea that a novel or poem can be a thing of wonder. It tends to be written in opaque, formulaic language, inadvertently advertising its incapacity to engage with the literary forms it purports to discuss: the swimmer-instructor is incongruously clad in lead boots.

Professor Efron's book could not be further removed from these limitations. It is a personal account of a particular work. Dewey is invoked to dilate the personal response, not to subsume it into a "theory". The student is informed throughout by Efron's admiration for the work he is discussing and by his own involvement with it. His language is everywhere clear because he is concerned to make things clear to himself.

The activity involved here is precisely the study of literature. Efron resolutely resists deflection into any fashionable meta-discipline. This is very much the work of a teacher accustomed to direct involvement with students. With an admirable willingness to risk naivety or embarrassing self-disclosure, Efron offers his own carefully-considered responses to the text and invites us to cross-relate them with our own. He isn't afraid to make bold generalizations on the basis of his personal reactions: "This section…seems to me to be the most extended immersion of the reader…in the context of sensuous-sensual-sexual nature anywhere in literature"; or again: "Hardy's profoundly realized vision in these chapters of a long-drawn-out conflict between a man and a woman over their married, sexual relationship is probably unmatched by anything in earlier novels by any author." To me these are strong, true claims of a kind which most contemporary criticism could not make and would not risk.

I was innocent of Dewey until reading this manuscript, but found the quoted extracts from his work everywhere relevant to the kind of analysis Efron attempts—certainly as it applies to Hardy. Dewey's emphasis on the experiential and the visceral would seem to be inappropriate to the novels of, say, Jane Austen or Henry James, but bears very directly on the physical and sensual aspects of *Tess*. Efron is often at his best on seemingly incidental passages, as when he comments on Hardy's description of Tess's mouth, and his related reference to the predominance of the "UR" sound in the local dialect:

> ...I can say that Hardy proposes a *fusion* of qualities from two ordinarily unrelated things, Tess's mouth, described sensuously and with loving detail, and a quality in language that the novel seems to want me to stop and try in my own mouth. The UR cannot just be "read through" like any other word... If I want to experience the way this novel is starting to feel, I must hear/sound/feel it at least minimally.

This seems to me a persuasive and original observation, of a kind specifically made possible by the Deweyan context within which Efron has chosen to work. Yes: Hardy's novel does indeed call for this sort of quasi-participatory response. Not every subjective comment of this kind in Efron's book rings true for me; but most do—and there is everywhere an escape-clause in his appeal to the reader's own experience. He proposes and leads a collective enterprise in comparing notes.

There do seem to be some disadvantages, or limitations, in Efron's approach. He has read Tess often and intensively, but the very strength of concentration on the particular novel seems to tune out some contextual considerations. For example, there is no reference to the technical problems faced by the writer of a serial, nor to the differences in reader-response that that mode of publication might have elicited. A substantial question left unanswered is how far a knowledge of Hardy's other work might reasonably condition the reading of this one. A couple of the passages analysed by Efron seem to descend directly from the early sonnet "She, to Him II" and the prose paraphrase of it worked into Hardy's first novel, *Desperate Remedies*. Is not that genealogy worth a mention, as suggesting a sustained theme? Again, a passage concerning the dissociation of Tess's "living will" from her body, which she allows "to drift, like a corpse upon the current" echoes similar comments in earlier novels—most obviously *The Mayor of Casterbridge*, in which the "self-alienated" Henchard seems literally to view his own body floating in the river below him. What further insight, if any, might such lateral knowledge confer? What sort of reciprocity should there be between reading a particular novel and reading the oeuvre as a whole?

Everything Efron does attempt, however, is carried through with seriousness, conviction and a likeable gusto. The reader can agree or disagree with equal relish, and learn something either way. This is a book to stimulate the student and to refresh the teacher.

Michael Irwin
University of Kent
Canterbury, UK

PREFACE

In a project of this size, dealing with one work of literature, it is almost futile to give the reader an explanation of how it came to be. The sources for my decades-long re-reading and teaching of *Tess* are rooted deeply in my need for exactly the kind of profound experience this novel offers, and in the richness of Thomas Hardy's imagination.

It is likewise difficult to explain my nearly lifelong interest in the philosophy of John Dewey. I recall sheltering his book *Reconstruction in Philosophy* under my army jacket and sneaking peeks at it as I walked about the barracks, while being subjected to some "Basic Training." That happened before I had entered college. Decades later, when I had an opportunity to teach that book in a course on Literature and Society, I found it flawed and its arguments not as exciting as I had first thought. But by then, Dewey had taken hold: *Art as Experience*, the book he published when he was 75 years old, had become the Dewey text I could not do without. In the present book on *Tess*, I hope to have shown why *Art as Experience* can be of great value for anyone interested in experiencing a work of literature.

A turning point in my experience of *Tess* occurred in 1967, when I asked an artist to design a cover for an issue of my journal, *Paunch*. This issue (#28) contained my newly-written essay on "The Tale, the Teller and Sexuality in *Tess*." The artist, Priscilla Bowen, decided to read the novel before she went to work. When I received the cover, I saw that it consisted of a non-representational gray background design; well below the middle, appearing within an uneven white space that broke roughly into the design, stood a single sentence from the novel:

> She was not an existence, an experience, a passion,
> a structure of sensations, to anybody but herself.

I liked this cover at once, as soon as I saw it, but I am afraid it struck me as, well, as idiosyncratic. I had a vague feeling of the artist approaching the novel in some inexplicable manner. Only looking back, years later, did I realize that she was telling me something I could not hear as yet: that what Hardy writes as narrator and as a person involved in his own novel, is utterly worthwhile for having an experience of *Tess*. To some extent, I had known this because of my own unaccountably poignant feeling upon first noticing Hardy's question, near the beginning of *Tess*, of "a body's cry of Where?" But locked as I was in the false security of D. H. Lawrence's advice to trust the tale and not the teller, I could not conceive of a fresh and open approach toward the narrator's voice.

Later, as I myself developed, and as I re-read and re-taught *Tess* (and Hardy's other novels), I gradually gave in and allowed myself to hear and feel what was waiting for me in the text, in the voice of the author, and in the ways that his voice fused with and sometimes departed from the lives of his characters. I found not only that Hardy as narrator is vital to the book, but that most of his critical readers for more than a century have been distressed to admit it. When they have admitted it, many (though not all) of these readers have been quite unhappy with what he has to say, and have treated Hardy's voice as if it were one of the most hazardous and misleading factors imaginable in any novel. I hope to persuade Hardy's readers that they must take a new attitude on this problem if they wish to experience *Tess*.

The narrator, all the same, is not as important as the story of the woman. Just after finishing the present book, I was amazed to find in one of the older studies of Hardy a statement that is so accurate and so impossible to imagine anyone saying today, that it almost hurt to encounter it. I immediately felt it to be exactly appropriate for someone reading *Tess*. It may remind us of an ability to respond to a novel that is quite missing from critical writings of our own age. For Joseph Warren Beach, in his book entitled *The Technique of Thomas Hardy* (first published in 1922), *Tess* is primarily a work of emotional experience. There are parts of the story, Beach exclaims, where the reader "can scarcely read for tears, and where he cannot possibly read aloud for very shame of his choking voice."[1] That is an unforgettable admission. It reminds us that this novel, when read with our humanly vulnerable selves, is not safe territory to get through. Hardy's best critics and readers have always known this. It is Dewey, I believe, who best provides an understanding of how an emotionally charged work of literature like *Tess* can be talked about in ways that will deepen and expand rather than detract from and inhibit the reader's experience.

Acknowledgements: For more than four decades, friends who are dedicated readers of Thomas Hardy's novels have sustained a discussion that has gone on largely unnoticed in the most-cited criticism. To them, especially to John Doheny, Michael Steig, Jerry Zaslove, and above all, to Wayne Burns, I am immensely indebted. Others who have helped form my views on Hardy include Paul Green, Bernard Paris, F. R. Southerington, Jimmie Gilliam, Mary Childers, Carol Siegel, Jonathan Pitts, the late Bob Lawyer, and especially, John Herold. Jacqueline George read an earlier version of this book in manuscript and gave me valuable comments. Many of the Hardy critics with whose approaches I now may find fault have provided invaluable challenges, and I would not wish to imply that because I disagree with several of them I thereby find no value in their explorations into Hardy. On the contrary, the challenges remain active in my reading. I am indebted as well to those who have encouraged my interest in Dewey, particularly Peter Hare, who urged me to write what I really thought about Dewey and published my essay in *Transactions of the Charles S. Peirce Society: A Quarterly Journal in American Philosophy*. Some of the points made there are expanded in chapter 1 of the present book. John Shook, the editor of the Studies in Pragmatism and Values series, has been ever supportive in seeing me through the process of publication. To an anonymous critical reader who usefully delayed the book's acceptance, I also am grateful. There is also a wider indebtedness: the freedom afforded for some 40 years by my Department of English of the University at Buffalo gave me many chances to venture into new regions of literary experience. When I became ready to write this book, I was supported with a Research Leave from the University at Buffalo, awarded by the Dean of Arts and Sciences, Kerry S. Grant; for that help I am indeed grateful. To the students in my graduate and undergraduate courses who read *Tess* critically as well as passionately, I can only offer a most inadequate thanks. Finally, the many acts of editorial assistance by Leslie Graff have put the book into presentable form.

I thank Southern Illinois University Press for kind permission to quote from *The Collected Works of John* Dewey, edited by Jo Ann Boydston, especially *Art as Experience* (*Later Works*, volume 10, 1934, copyright 1987); *Experience and Nature* (*Later Works*, volume 1, 1925, copyright 1981), *Ethics* (*Later Works*, volume 7, 1932, copyright 1985), and *Human Nature and Conduct* (*Middle Works*, volume 14, 1922, copyright 1985).

Oxford University Press is hereby acknowledged for generous permission to quote from *Tess of the d'Urbervilles* by Thomas Hardy, edited by Juliet Grindle and Simon Gatrell, Oxford World's Classics, copyright 1998.

Abbreviations:

EN John Dewey, *Experience and Nature*. (*The Later Works*, vol. 1). Edited by Jo Ann Boydston. Carbondale, Illinois: Southern Illinois University Press, 1981.

AE John Dewey, *Art as Experience*. (*The Later Works*, vol. 10). Edited by Jo Ann Boydston. Carbondale, Illinois: Southern Illinois University Press, 1987.

One

CLEARING THE FOREGROUND FOR EXPERIENCING *TESS*

I start with what is simple, with what everyone knows. The power of *Tess of the d'Urbervilles* comes from the depth of its vision of the life of a woman, unique and yet typical, who remains "the same, but not the same" (94)[1] in the course of her experience. Tess's life is a narrative of sexual- and love-relationships, placed integrally within Hardy's evocation of Nature. There are two more essential elements in the novel: one is Hardy's portrayal of two most unsatisfactory men. The other, strangely enough, is the flavor or quality of this novel stemming not only from the narrative but from the intermixture of the author's commentary, a voice sounding in several modes: philosophical, sociological, historical, sexological, and above all personal in Hardy's relationship with the character Tess. Even when Hardy for the most part ceases from such commentary, after chapter 41 (there are 59 chapters in all), the novel seems to reverberate with his voices, so much has he already said. The effects of his comments are felt beyond the points of their occurrence in the text.

There are of course novels in which the narrators are patently different from the selves of their creating authors, but it never has felt to me that *Tess* is one of these, despite the truism that a narrator is not the same as an author. Possibly the well-known critical doctrine that a fictional narrator must not be mistaken for the author's own voice is premised on an error that John Dewey would not have allowed, namely the presupposition that the every day voice of a person is the real self's voice, and the literary one is not. The self (which I do not dismiss as an un-real figment) can have several modes of expression, and several varieties of voice. With Hardy, a man who in *Tess* was writing his thirteenth novel, the narrative voice (or voices) had become an integral part of his self. In Dewey's terms, narrating novels had become a deeply engrained creative "habit" of Hardy's self. By the time he wrote *Tess*, the act of narration would have "left an enduring impress" upon him. A habit of this caliber, Dewey maintains, reaches

> down into the very structure of the self: it signifies a building up and a solidifying of certain desires; an increased sensitiveness and responsiveness to certain stimuli, a confirmed or an impaired capacity to attend to and think about certain things. Habit covers in other words the very make-up of desire, intent, choice, disposition which gives an act its voluntary quality.[2]

Such an all-inclusive claim is not extravagant when considered as a description of what it means for an artist to function as a narrator in novel after novel.

In *Tess*, Hardy comments far more than he had in any previous work; he is taking his narration to new experimental levels. His habit was in a process of change. Dewey's concept of habit is not a closed one. In the same paragraph from which I have quoted, he goes on to say that impulse plays a central role in the growth of habits:

> If one surrenders to a momentary impulse, the significant thing is...the strengthening of the power of that impulse—this strengthening is the reality of that which we call habit. In giving way, the person in so far commits himself not just to *that* isolated act but to a *course* of action, to a line of behavior. [3]

I can feel Hardy giving way at several points in *Tess* to the impulse to comment, and to comment quite freely, using the fullest resources of his mind. As Ian Gregor put it, in *Tess*, we feel "the world of the author" and "the world of his creation ...as transparently close to one another." [4] Once Hardy had begun doing this in the writing of the novel, I can well imagine that he became committed to going on with the process wherever it might lead him.

After many readings, I have therefore come to the position of flatly rejecting J. Hillis Miller's idea that the narrator is a device by which Hardy can safely distance himself. [5] We now realize that he actually monograms the narrative with little designs pointing to his personal experience. The epigraph from Shakespeare indicates this at once: "...Poor wounded name! My bosom as a bed/ Shall lodge thee." Situated on the title page with the author's name, it is his own bosom that I think of first. Then mine. Notice the remark on the quality of Tess's voice, "when her heart was in her speech, which will never be forgotten by those who knew her" (99). This is as much as saying that Tess, in some way, is constructed from memories of a certain woman's voice. Hardy does not have another sentence of this kind anywhere in the novel. It is absurd to think that he just injected this strongly felt assertion to gain additional realistic illusion, when the novel has long before this point created the vivid character of Tess. Notice too the inconspicuous reference to "Phena" (61), the familiar name of a woman he had once loved, a woman he called, in a poem, "my lost prize." [6] And notice his reference in *Tess* to "the Hardys," an old landholding family (131), like the old Le Hardy family, who dated back to the fifteenth century, and from which he thought he was descended. In his autobiography, Hardy wrote: "They had dwelt for many generations in or near the valley of the river Froom or Frome," which is where much of *Tess* is set. [7] He also has the long central part of his narrative take place at a dairy-farm he named Talbothays. That is the name of a piece of land still owned by Hardy's father at the time the novelist was writing *Tess*, and one on which Hardy himself in the early 1890s was designing a house in preparation for his brother Henry's marriage.[8] At one point, Hardy seems to have been thinking of entitling the book *Tess of the Hardys*.[9]

I do not suppose that Hardy implanted these elements in the novel as elements of a crypto-autobiography to be decoded long afterward by scholars. His reason I infer is to place himself into the process of telling the novel at a personal, intimate level. At least that is the effect. In the same vein, his avoidance throughout the body of the novel of any use of the first person within his commentaries allows for his protective anonymity within the conventional narrator role, while having the effect in this novel not of distancing his voice but of taking a personal form of telling that moves along with the story itself. Had he used the "I," he would have signaled a formal separation of teller and tale that would have had the opposite effect.

This is not to pretend that the narrative voice in *Tess* is a simple one, nor is it to deny the various functions of aesthetic distancing. I do not deny that many passages in the narrator's voice describe what is going on in the minds of Tess or Angel, and are not simply expressions of Hardy's views. But I stand with Dewey in his view that the creative value of aesthetic distancing is finally to allow for better contact with the immediate experience, rather than to serve as a safe defense from it. To those who misunderstand this idea, Dewey offers a joke told by Dr. Samuel Johnson: a small boy says to an adult, "Pins have saved a great many person's lives." When asked how that could be, the boy answers, "on account of their not swallowing them" (*AE* 102). The formalist argument on distancing, Dewey holds, runs parallel to this small boy's claim. This little joke points to an important feature of pragmatist criticism, or "contextualistic criticism," as it is called by the philosopher and aesthetician Stephen C. Pepper. For Pepper, as for a contextualist like myself, the point of "psychical distance" is not simply to assure the continuity of aesthetic experience by avoiding a practical response. In works calling on the reader's emotions, the value is almost "the reverse of this idea, which is much more interesting [:] that in proportion as these conflicts do touch you (to the point of not precipitating action) the aesthetic value of the experience is increased."[10]

In my readings of *Tess*, I have found myself challenged to integrate the Hardy-as-author (narrator) commentaries with the experience of the situation. Despite his various lapses, Hardy often is a penetrating thinker; he is a sociologist and philosopher and theorist of love relationships and nature poet, all in close relation to his story and especially to Tess herself. As for Hardy's psychological insight, perhaps this comment by Sigmund Freud will suffice: "*He knew psychoanalysis.*" Freud said this in 1923, as he looked up from the copy of *Tess of the d'Urbervilles* that he was reading.[11] Hardy continued to educate himself through his own study all of his life. He had no university degree, but he was a consistently explorative student on his own. As Paul Turner, one of his most recent biographers notes, Hardy even on the day he died was trying to read a speculative work by the scientist J.B.S. Haldane.[12] The time of writing *Tess* was one in which Hardy had been learning more than ever; he had a "richer reservoir" of ideas to draw from than he had had in his eleven previously published novels.[13]

Not all of his new resources were in the realm of ideas: Hardy's greatly enhanced interest in the landscape painting and watercolors of J. M. W. Turner, and his theoretical insights into Turner's genius for conveying impressions of the natural world through a painting technique that was anything but naturalistic, occurred just prior to his beginning on *Tess*. He enjoyed a new burst of interest in Turner in 1889, while he was hard at work on the new novel. Turner must have spurred Hardy's nature writing in *Tess*, helping to give it the extraordinary lyrical and evocative quality that is quite different from the feeling of the many nature descriptions in *The Woodlanders*, the novel Hardy had all but finished at the time of his involvement with Turner's paintings. From his study of Turner, Hardy was taken with the artist's "strange mixtures" that allowed him to "have upon the spectator an approximative effect to that of the real." Turner, Hardy said, "first recognizes the impossibility of really reproducing on canvas all that is in a landscape," but creates an impression that captures the effect of the real. Hardy concluded this entry in his notebook: "Hence, one may say, Art is the secret of how to produce by a false thing the effect of a true...".[14] Such thinking is genuinely theoretical. The Turner paintings in the 1889 show were in fact most challenging to the late Victorian imagination: they were considered aberrations.[15] Even today, Turner's work is still regarded as not well understood.[16] But Hardy took to these works, and saw into their artistry. It would require Hardy's own creative transformation to use such insights in writing the landscapes in *Tess*.

But the landscape descriptions are not set-pieces to be enjoyed in their isolation. Not only are they integral to the novel's subject-matter of sexual love, but when they are experienced, they project so much feeling that Hardy's personal involvement is palpable.

I think it disastrous for the potential experience of this novel to dismiss Hardy's empathy with Tess as a "familiar narrative pose" and to regard the narrator's voice as primarily "reflexively ironic," as a recent Introduction to the novel declares.[17] I have noticed in fact that many of the novel's critics have made irresponsible use of the concept of the narrator: they seem to feel that since the narrator is not Hardy, they have a warrant to approach his(?) comments with immediate suspicion or contempt, acting as if the narrator is injecting patently biased thoughts requiring nothing more from the reader than condemnation.

Others are not so constrained: they simply trash Hardy. This counter-experiential tactic seems to have begun with Lionel Johnson's early book on Hardy, published in 1894.[18] Johnson offers an instance of Dewey's point that the most common and damaging error made in intellectual work is the fallacy of ignoring context.[19] Johnson gathered together indiscriminately Hardy's various comments about Nature, religion, God, the gods, and justice in *Tess*, and then pronounced judgment upon the hash he had produced: he could understand none of it. Furthermore—in a revealing contradiction—he also could refute all the pessimism about God and religion that he certainly did understand, by bringing to bear upon it the writings of the great Christian thinkers. Johnson justified his method by claiming that Hardy in this book was inviting a response that would require "the rigor of a treatise."[20] But the difference between the coherence of a treatise and whatever unifying quality is needed in a novel—in this particular novel—he did not consider. Johnson, a recent convert to Catholicism, was obviously disturbed by Hardy's thinking, and yet was very moved by the book. His solution was to discredit the thinking, maintaining that all of the commentary should be excised from the reader's experience. The novel, he thought, would then be a better work. At least it would not threaten his own beliefs.

While I feel free to take a critical stance toward Hardy's or the narrator's comments, my main response to them is to try to understand what they can give to the experience. This may take considerable initial tolerance while reading, but I find that it does make the experience richer than it would otherwise be—and certainly richer than it was for me, back in my days of trying to apply D. H. Lawrence's advice to trust the tale but not the teller. This was advice that provided too powerful a critical instrument, one whose pragmatic value in deepening the experience of the novel was eventually overshadowed by its tendency to short-circuit my responsive attention. There are places, I think, where Hardy makes comments that seem to be seriously misleading or imperceptive, but these are not many, and only on a few occasions do such comments interfere with the experiencing of *Tess*. When Hardy's comments are read sympathetically in their contexts, it becomes clear that while he does not attain nor attempt to attain the coherence of a treatise, by no means does he create an incoherent artistic work.

1. A Deweyan Approach

The question arises, at this date, is there anything in *Tess* in need of further discussion? My answer is Yes, virtually the whole novel needs reconsideration, because nowhere is there an exploration of how this novel feels when it is undergone as an experience. There are remarks made about experiencing *Tess*, but few efforts to focus on the long process of reading it as an experience. In fact, recent decades of critical commentary provide few instances of even brief remarks on what the experience is like. We are as a culture eons away, I am afraid, from anything like this statement by J.I.M. Stewart, made in 1971: "*Tess of the d'Urbervilles* is not only an emotional novel; it is one of the greatest distillations of emotion into art that English literature can show."[21] Emotion, affect, feeling—these overlapping qualities of human experience are not the strength of current critical theory. But without them, there is no experience. Dewey in *Art as Experience* knows this well, and writes his aesthetics in such a way as to show its importance.

Such is my project. It will have nothing to do with searching for innovative or radical interpretations of the book. As the Deweyan aesthetician Richard Shusterman has argued, that sort of searching is exactly what makes professional criticism a competitive endeavor that loses touch with the experience it is supposed to clarify. It thus becomes some of the worst criticism imaginable.[22] But I do find that when the novel is approached from the perspective of the experience of its reader—myself—almost everything in it appears in a different, sometimes very different, light. I will be doing plenty of interpreting, but from a different approach, that of the experience I am undergoing. Because *Tess* is dense with potential meaning and rich in its experiential offerings, I sometimes may seem to be merely "explicating" the text. To some degree explication is unavoidable, so closely is meaning woven into feeling, but in no part of what follows is it my aim. In fact there are some meanings in the novel that can be hermeneutically specified (as for example, some of Hardy's allusions to paintings he has seen in museums) but which have little value in the experience.

What I propose to do is my own type of Pragmatist Criticism, developed in this book only for bringing out the experience of this one novel. To do it, I will not hesitate to use any tools of understanding that I may find pragmatically valuable. Given my many readings of *Tess* and my extraordinary interest in it, I may be thought to be setting myself up as the "ideal reader," which would be someone who thinks he can "realize in full the meaning potential of the fictional text."[23] That would be an impossible mission, if for no other reason than that any proposed fullness of meaning would change in its varying emphases with every reading and every reader. But I do not see anything wrong with trying to give the novel its fullest experiential scope, always bearing in mind that my individual perceptions are involved, and that these are humanly fallible. I will use several critical methods in the task, depending on what I think is called for in the novel's many contexts. I may linger over a key passage in a manner that resembles a phenomenological investigation, I will often use my personal response to the text, I may use elements of Hardy's biography and of my own life experiences, I will pay attention to the historical context in which Hardy's novel appeared, and I will do close reading in the manner of the New Criticism. From my Deweyan perspective, I will make many connections between experiencing the novel and furthering that experience by showing its connections with culture as it exists today—and how those connections remain personal as well as social. Indeed the connections are part of the experience. As Philip W. Jackson has put it, Dewey's conception of a work of art is that it is an "art-centered experience," not an experience limited to consideration of an art-object in isolation from aesthetic (or non-aesthetic) experience in general.[24] We can use many approaches to this art-centered experience, and remain within the spirit of pragmatist thought. I accept Richard Shusterman's view of the interface between pragmatism and other philosophies:

With pragmatism's inclusive stance, we should presume that alternative theories or values can somehow be reconciled until we are given good reasons why they are mutually exclusive. That seems to be the best way to keep the path of inquiry open and to maximize our goods.[25]

2. Dewey's Aesthetics, With an Aid from Stephen C. Pepper

I may be asked, why Dewey? Why of all thinkers have I chosen him as my theoretical underpinning? That is a question of over-determination, of course; I have been a Deweyan for decades and I cannot know all the reasons for this preference. I can only say that *Art as Experience* is the only work of aesthetics I know that would give priority to such a project as mine.[26] Without the elements of the novel working with my own reading processes to create an experience, there is no novel. The "work of art is what the product does with and in experience," Dewey wrote, in the opening paragraph of *Art as Experience*.

To this, to what seems to me to be Dewey's perfect statement on the matter, I would add a factor he all but states, but does not. It is the factor of the "perceptive series," formulated in the aesthetics of Stephen C. Pepper (1891-1972) whose work I have already cited. In works of art having complexity, "an experience" cannot be had all in one sitting, viewing, or reading: there is a series of perceptual events.[27] I have gone through a series of readings and re-re-readings (and teaching experiences) with *Tess*, cumulatively re-envisioning and constructing the experience as these went on. In most of the perceptions in this series, I was also revising and sometimes rejecting parts of earlier readings. This process has not come to an end, and as Pepper points out in Contextualism (his name for pragmatism), there can be no "final or complete analysis of anything."[28] But the cumulative process does seem to have occurred. It will not be the same as anyone else's process, and may even differ significantly from that of everyone else. As Dewey put it—and Pepper quotes him on this,

> A new poem is created by everyone who reads poetically....[E]very individual brings with him ...a way of seeing and feeling that in its interaction with old material creates something new, something previously not existing in experience. (*AE* 113)

A. C. Bradley, quoted on this page by Dewey, had already introduced the idea of an individualized perceptual series: "an actual poem is a succession of experiences....A poem, exists in innumerable degrees."[29] In reading *Tess*, readers commonly create something powerful immediately; a threshold of experience is readily crossed. The book "grabs you." But as Bradley realized, there are degrees and degrees beyond that first reading impression. That is why people go on, and on, in reading this book.

In this model, responding to *Tess of the d'Urbervilles* is not exactly a question of "reader response." The experience is undeniably personal. Because of its felt quality, it must be characterized as "immediate." But it is far removed from what in academia has been taken for a response, which is usually a reaction to the first, or the first few readings of a work, and usually to passages or works much shorter than this novel. And while reader response criticism fully allows for the reader's interests and preferences to enter the literary experience, it does not have Dewey's essential sense of bringing about some shift or change or overturning of these pre-held views in the course of the experience.[30]

Everyone's experience is different, but as Pepper pointed out, there is also an undeniable "control object," namely the text itself.[31] An experience comes out of the "interaction" with it, not out of the whole cloth of personal fabulation, else it would not be a response. I am creating my own *Tess* from my relation with its text, but so is everyone else. And the text, when it is brought into our lives by being read, has major features which can hardly be denied.[32] In my experiential commentary, I will make use at times of an editorial "we," speaking for what "we" experience. I do so knowing that this cannot possibly meet with everyone's assent on every occasion, but based on my long experience (over 40 years) of reading, teaching, and analyzing this novel (and engaging its critics), I am convinced that such a "we" is sometimes warranted.

3. Assumptions of a Deweyan Approach to Aesthetic Experience

Aesthetic experience is part of experience. Throughout *Art as Experience* Dewey stresses the continuity of aesthetic experience with the basic rhythms of experience in general. Each great work of art does something unique "with and in experience" (*AE* 9), but it does not exist in a realm of its own. The great work may seem to be comparable to a magnificent mountain peak, but even the mountain peak is part of the landscape (*AE* 9). So Dewey declares on the opening page of *Art as Experience*. No matter how refined or complicated his discussion becomes, he never forgets this starting point. At the conclusion of the three far-reaching introductory chapters, Dewey introduces his descriptive formulation of what an aesthetic work of art is:

> An object is peculiarly and dominantly esthetic, yielding the enjoyment characteristic of esthetic perception, when the factors that determine anything which can be called *an* experience are lifted high above the threshold of perception and are made manifest for their own sake. (*AE* 63, Dewey's emphasis)

This is an important statement, but it is hardly self-explanatory. To begin to tell what it involves, I would point first to the conspicuous refusal to say that there can be a fully aesthetic object: there can be one that is "peculiarly and dominantly esthetic," but that is as special as it can get.

The "enjoyment" is strictly a function of the perception that goes into having the experience. "Perception" is one of the essential terms in Dewey's aesthetic. The factors that can make any event into "*an* experience" are not specified here, but perception is necessary to have such an experience. How do we go about insuring that we do have sufficient perception to have it? Dewey has several striking ideas about that question, and I will take some of them up shortly. For the critic of a work, capable perception is the one thing that cannot be lacking. Dewey even entitles a chapter of his book "Criticism and Perception." We can go "high above the threshold of perception," but we do not leave perception behind us. It is even correct to say that perception is synonymous with the experience itself: thus Dewey writes, "an esthetic experience, the work of art in its actuality, is *perception*" (*AE* 167, Dewey's emphasis). Dewey's central position is that there are times when experience becomes so completely felt and explored, so fully perceived, that it becomes a memorable event in itself, one that is marked off from the flow of experience in general, but never cut off from its connections with further experience. This can happen in any area of life, but it is especially likely to happen when we experience works of art. That is one of the great values of works of art: they show us what the potential of an experience may be; in ordinary living, under conditions that are subject to all sorts of limitations, we are not so likely to find out what an experience is.

The word "perception," upon which I seem to have lighted as I try to explain Dewey's statement, might seem obvious. In some ways, it is: everyone has it, and there usually is nothing remarkable about this fact. Had Dewey wished, he could have given a technical, philosophical exposition of his beliefs about perception. He might have drawn on William James's "radical empiricism," with which he had long been in sympathy. He might also have given his own version of C. S. Peirce's theory of "quality." But in *Art as Experience*, Dewey chose to keep closer to an un-specialized, more democratic appeal to his readers' own sense of their ability to have perceptions. For someone who is skeptical enough to declare, as Jacques Derrida did in 1970, "Now I don't know what perception is, and I don't think anything like perception exists....I don't believe there is any perception"[33]—for anyone with resistance of this kind, Dewey's aesthetics must be based on a hopeless error. But for those of us who are not willing to denigrate our experience before it even occurs, Dewey is making sense when he emphasizes perception. *Art as Experience*, according to Dewey's very recent biographer Jay Martin, is the only work of the 1920s and 1930s in which Dewey "treated the qualities of perception as central."[34]

In Dewey's aesthetics, perception is a critical issue because it contrasts with another element that we also have in abundance: the capacity for "recognition." For my commitment to Dewey, the most important passage in *Art as Experience* is exactly that one in which the difference between perception and recognition is vividly described (*AE* 58-61). Dewey maintains that the perceiver of the work of art, or the reader of a work of literature, must be receptive enough to "*take* in" what the work has to offer. This is a genuine receptivity, not a mere passivity: aesthetic perceiving is "a process" like that which the creative artist has carried out in writing the work. It therefore consists in "a series of responsive acts that accumulate toward objective fulfillment" (*AE* 58). Aesthetic perception for Dewey is a kind of action carried out by the human organism, having the scope of many related or relate-able parts. It is not instantaneous, but goes on over a period of time. Through perception, the perceiver constructs the experience. This process has no resemblance to the narrowly analytic or stereotypical "empirical" perception of a discrete stimulus such as a viewing of the color red. But if no such series of responsive acts occurs, "there is not perception" at all; there is only "recognition. *The difference between the two is immense*" (*AE* 58, my emphasis). In recognition, we merely identify whatever it is we are perceiving, place it within its pre-learned category, and pass on to whatever else is at hand. It is cursorily recognizing someone in the hallway at work or school, and moving on without taking heed of that person's qualities. Recognition is necessary for maneuvering through the world, but we allow our lives to exist too much at this level. Recognition does not have to be all that prevalent: there are encounters which we have all had in which that person whom we usually just pass in the hall suddenly takes on some of the felt qualities of a live human being with individual qualities. "We realize," Dewey writes, "that we never knew the person before; we had not seen him in any pregnant sense" (*AE* 59). When that happens, recognition begins to be transformed into perception.

At the level of critical perception in aesthetic experience, this issue of perception versus recognition has huge consequences. In Dewey's elaboration of how recognition works, I seem to hear the shouts and cries of nearly every critical approach in use in literary theory today. In current theory, the problem is not the simple one of noting someone passing in the street "in order to greet or to avoid him," rather than seeing him "for the sake of seeing what is there," as Dewey puts it (*AE* 59). That sort of by-passing seems to be largely unavoidable in modern social living. But what could be avoided, what *must* be avoided, in reading literature, is the habit of taking "some detail or arrangement of details as a cue for bare identification." Whenever that is done, the theorist or working critic is applying his or her scheme of recognition—his or her governing theory—to the literary work in the manner of using a "stencil." From what I have observed in literary theory for the past several decades, the reign of "theory" over experience has been characterized as just this: the application of a stencil, although usually quite an elaborate stencil, to the literary work. Whatever details can be recognized through the stencil are then considered to be the work. In the critical discussions of *Tess*, there are plenty of examples of this kind, but these are often combined with an older and more pervasive habit of falling back on stereotypical and heavily "loaded" beliefs about sex and sexual love, which is the subject-matter of

Tess. As for the attempt to experience "what is there" in the work, that is almost ignored.

Recognition cannot work to make "*an* experience," even if the theorist who falls into it does so with much affect: there can be "genuine, emotional excitation," Dewey says, but it will be a confused state, because it has not issued from a perceptual act of "comprehension," a term Dewey uses "in its literal signification" to mean "a gathering together of details and particulars physically scattered into an experienced whole" (*AE* 60). The stencil may seem to be doing exactly that for the reader who uses it, but in practice, it will prevent any experienced wholeness from happening. In my observation it is exactly that prevention that is habitually sought for in today's most prominent theories of literature. To be sure, the gathering of details and particulars is assured by the use of the theoretical stencil; indeed such gathering could probably be done by a computer program designed to ferret out instances of whatever the theory is looking for. But the experienced whole will not be formed, since the very act of shielding oneself behind the stencil will produce only a pre-selected entity. Dewey's writing assumes a tone of committed hostility as he states unequivocally why recognition is too easy to do, when having an experience is at stake: "Recognition is too easy to arouse vivid consciousness. There is not enough resistance between new and old to secure consciousness of the experience that is had" (*AE* 59). Even a dog barking and wagging its tail, when it sees its "master return is more fully alive …than is a human being who is content with mere recognition" (*AE* 59).

While "emotional excitation" not based on perception is a miserable substitute for experiencing the work of art, Dewey insists on the essential role of emotion in having an experience. He is describing not what emotion is, but what it does, "with and in experience." But Dewey does not maintain that emotion is "expressed" as emotion alone, or that the author of the work expresses his or her emotion (*AE* 88). As David Granger has argued, Dewey is not a Romantic in that sense.[35] "Just because emotion is essential to that act of expression which produces a work of art," Dewey points out, "it is easy for inaccurate analysis to misconceive its mode of operation and conclude that the work of art has emotion for its significant content" (*AE* 74). Dewey is so un-Romantic as to maintain that some of Van Gogh's paintings are filled with emotion that is too uncontrolled to make for a balance of "undergoing" and "doing" by the receptive observer (*AE* 75). That example troubles me, and I cannot agree with him, but I realize Dewey is explaining his theory of artistic expression, and not laying down some rule for denigrating Van Gogh. The important principle is the manner in which emotion operates within the creative process, whether it is the process of the writer or that of the reader. If the work contains some tragic incident within its imagined world, that is not because the author feels tragic, nor that we as readers have simply supplied that quality: "The emotion of the author and that aroused in us are occasioned by scenes in that world and they blend with the subject matter" (*AE* 74). For the author, if the work is going to become an experience, there is "personally felt emotion guiding the selecting and assembling of the materials presented" (*AE* 74). The writer's emotion "leads" him "to gather material that is affiliated to the mood which is aroused…" (*AE* 74). For the reader, and here I am thinking of any reader of *Tess*, the emotions felt in the most powerful scenes or passages of the novel tend to spread their quality to other scenes and passages that are less intense. It is the most affecting scenes that get us involved enough to make the novel into an experience; without them it would be a series of evenly toned essays with no clue for our perception of what is important and what is less so.

The selecting and arranging that emotion does, according to Dewey's theory, has been described by Philip W. Jackson as a kind of filter: "emotion works like a filter through which perceptions are screened. It allows some features of the environment to stand out, and others to fade away…".[36] This is right, as far as it goes, but the metaphor of the filter leaves me in doubt. For one thing, it sounds a little too much like the term "stencil," which is such a negative one. Rather than filtering, and without denying that emotion operates by selecting from among possible materials or details, I choose the metaphor of spreading. This has the advantage of suggesting a sense of contact with the experience as it is happening. It seems to intimate that any given spreading of an emotion becomes less intense as it moves out from its center of energy, but it can maintain some of its force, enough to be effective in giving quality to passages and scenes that are adjacent or (more problematically) at least related somewhere in the text, to the source of the emotion. "Spreading" also has another feature that I think Dewey definitely implies in his discussion of emotion. "An emotion," he writes, "reaches out tentacles for that which is cognate, for things which feed it and carry it to completion" (*AE* 73). To this, I want to add that an emotional quality can spread not only forward in the reading process to what we are about to read, but backward, retroactively coloring passages we have already read but about which we have not yet become aware of how we feel. On this model of an experience, "The perceived object or scene is emotionally pervaded throughout" (*AE* 59), even if many parts of the long reading experience anyone has in reading a novel are not going to maintain uniform intensity from the first page to the end.

For explaining this process, I must revert once more to Pepper's philosophical thinking. In Pepper's discussion of the experience of an event, according to Contextualist (pragmatist) principles, the event occurs in a "spread" of time, which is never simply linear: as the event goes on, its qualities become clear and what had seemed to have a certain meaning (or lack of it), acquires a different meaning as we go along. "Spread" in fact is a basic category of Contextualism.[37] This is fully compatible with Dewey's theory of emotion, and he all but explicitly says it. In my account of experiencing *Tess*, I find several instances where emotional quality operates retroactively through a sequence of passages. In the opening chapter of the novel, to take an easy example, an amateur researcher into local history tells Tess's somewhat inebriated father that he is descended from a once-powerful family named d'Urberville. The tone of the writing is fairly light, and the episode seems to involve very little emotional energy when it is first read, or even when it is re-read after some time has passed and I have come back to the novel. But when we go on to read about Tess herself and begin to realize how this piece of family information—or misinformation—is going to be used to change her whole life, then the first chapter feels much heavier than it did. A retroactive revaluation of the first chapter occurs, and this happens effortlessly, so far as I can determine.

Not everything in having this experience is so effortless. As the reader of this novel, even though I have been the reader of it many times before, there are certain demands put upon me by a Deweyan approach to an experience that are just as valid as they were the first time I read the book. In an elementary sense, I simply have to do the work if I am to get anything significant out of reading it. Dewey is also un-Romantic enough to say that "There is work done on the part of the percipient as there is on the part of the artist." The person "who is too lazy, idle, or indurated in convention to perform this work will not see or hear" (*AE* 60-1). I have probably over-fulfilled this demand, as far a *Tess* goes. But for me, this and the other demands made upon me by the act of having the experience are not so much demands but privileges, given by the nature of a work of art.

Besides being willing to do the work, I have to be able to approach this novel openly. What is wanted is a "consciousness that becomes fresh and alive," which will take some reconstructive doing, since I have been through this novel before (*AE* 59). In a startling declaration in *Experience and Nature*, Dewey says that we can make ourselves innocent enough to perceive freshly: "there is attainable a cultivated naiveté of eye, ear and thought, one that can be acquired only through the discipline of severe thought" (*EN* 40). But in *Art as Experience*, his emphasis changes; severe thought is less the problem than nurturing a general receptivity to life. That is something that becomes necessary for anyone working in such a profession as that of literary critic: "Every professional person is subject to the influence of custom and inertia, and has to protect himself from its influences by *a deliberate openness to life itself*" (*AE* 308, my emphasis). Dewey's insistence upon the value in aesthetic experience of a sense of immediacy insures the necessity of such openness. Aesthetic experience, Dewey writes, necessarily has a quality of immediacy: "It cannot be asserted too strongly that what is not immediate is not esthetic" (*AE* 123). Reading with emotional quality will cause a "stir of the organism"—my organism and that of anyone else who takes on this book. There will be some "inner commotion" (*AE* 59). If it is an "act of perception" in Dewey's sense, then it will move through my whole bodily self: "[An] act of perception proceeds by waves that extend serially throughout the entire organism" (*AE* 59). And what I will have to do, not all at once but many times as I go through this novel, is "summon energy and pitch it at a responsive key in order to *take* in" (*AE* 60, Dewey's emphasis). For in Dewey's view,

"Perception is an act of the going-out of energy in order to receive, not a withholding of energy" (*AE* 60). This concept of an act has no resemblance to the usual assumption that perception is just something done by a mind that looks out onto an object and perceives it.

In these specifications, Dewey is thinking seriously about energy; he is regarding it not as some one-dimensional force that underlies bodily movement, but as a flexible source of involvement for the emotionally permeated experience that is being had. To be sure, the body is implicated in even the quietest experience, if it is an experience: Dewey specifies that in a perception, "motor elements" work in cooperation with "all funded ideas that may serve to complete the new picture that is forming" (*AE* 59). Such motor elements "remain implicit and do not become overt" (*AE* 59). But the very notion that one does not simply churn up a lot of energy, but must "pitch it at a responsive key in order to *take* in" calls for delicacy in the use of this fundamental capacity of the human organism.

I believe Dewey is emphasizing the concept of energy in *Art as Experience* to a greater degree and with more insistence than he had ever done in his writings before, or for that matter, than he was ever to do in his later writings. There is a clue in the very process of his writing this book, as to why this emphasis on energy could have occurred. As he found his way through the topics of aesthetic experience in every context from that of ordinary events like consuming a good meal in the company of a friend, to the complex operations of creating and appreciating a work of art, he must have found that he needed the notion of energy more and more. Energy, which appears as the focal point of a whole chapter, "The Organization of Energies," might not have been very much on Dewey's mind when he began delivering the lectures that became *Art as Experience*. There is no mention of energy in the list of lectures that Dewey mailed to his friend Albert Barnes on 18 February 1931, a day before the first one was given.[38] Nor is energy mentioned in the titles announced for all ten lectures, in a notice printed at their beginning (*AE* 381-2). But Dewey "was still writing his lectures as he delivered them" (*AE* 382). After completing his revisions in September 1933, however, the chapter title "Organization of Energy" appears in the table of contents he sent to Barnes (*AE* 386). In this sense, the "end-in-view" of writing the book had shifted or changed, as a function of Dewey's experiment of delving much more deeply than he had ever ventured before into a discussion of aesthetic experience. Even this late in his composing of the book, Energy is still a singular; evidently Dewey realized that it ought to become a plural, Energies, in order to reflect the actual effect within aesthetic experiences. In his discussion of his experiencing of a single painting, Dewey located four different types of organic energy at work (*AE* 178).

It is some few pages later, and at about half way through the printed version, that Dewey inscribes a defense of the importance of the term "energy," noting that it "has been used many times in this discussion" (*AE* 189). Dewey admits openly that we cannot settle by mere argument the issue of whether art moves us because of the energy it embodies or because some "transcendent essence (usually called 'beauty') descends upon esthetic experience from without" (*AE* 189). He writes here in an unusually personal voice, as if he is taking a deep breath and drawing himself up to make a statement that he feels he has to utter: "Taking my stand upon the connection of aesthetic effect with the qualities of all experience as far as any experience is unified...," he asks rhetorically how else could art be expressive except by "selecting and ordering the energies in virtue of which things act upon us and interest us?" The "fact of energy" must "be made central: its power to move and stir, to calm and tranquillize" (*AE* 189). Terms that other theories of aesthetics have traditionally emphasized as abstract formal qualities are actually functions of energy. To use the terms "*Order, rhythm and balance*, simply means that energies significant for experience are acting at their best" (*AE* 189, my emphasis). When Dewey deploys "the central role of energy" in aesthetic theory—and he puts the matter unmistakably by saying that an understanding of this role is the "*only*" thing such theory can be based on *(AE* 165, Dewey's emphasis)—he is referring in the very same sentence to all these energy functions:

> that interaction of energies which institutes opposition in company with accumulation, conservation, suspense and interval, and cooperative movement toward fulfillment in an ordered, or rhythmical experience. (*AE* 165)

This is energy going somewhere, making the work of art into what it is. When energy is used aesthetically, "it does real work; it accomplishes something." It takes "memories, images [and] observations and works them into *a whole toned throughout by immediate emotional feeling*" (*AE* 160, my emphasis).

My aim in re-presenting Dewey's comments on energy is not to prepare for some systematic reading of *Tess* in which I dutifully point out where the energy is and what kinds of energies there are. System is not what a Deweyan aesthetic would be looking for. I offer this preliminary view, as I do of all of Dewey's major theoretical tenets on aesthetics, with the understanding that the reader will assume that I am taking heed of them throughout; they have become part of my reading habits. I stress the importance of energy, perception, and emotion, as my own construction of Dewey's views, without pretending to give a full and unbiased explication of *Art as Experience*. (Much fuller expositions of his position, each with quite different emphases than my own, are to be found in the books by Thomas M. Alexander, Richard Shusterman, and Philip W. Jackson; see bibliography). There is one further major claim by Dewey which appeals to me enormously, and which I must discuss here, before launching into the experience of Hardy's novel. It is the claim that aesthetic experience is bodily experience.

4. Dewey's Bodily Aesthetic

Probably I have already signaled my emphasis on the body when I quoted Dewey's extraordinary statement that an "act of perception proceeds by waves that extend serially throughout the entire organism" (*AE* 59). This has to mean that it goes on in the body, and the body will include the mind. As Dewey insisted in *Experience and Nature*, we have got to learn "[to] see the organism *in* nature, the nervous system in the organism, the brain in the nervous system, the cortex in the brain," and at the same time realize that all of these exist in "a moving, growing never finished process" (*EN* 224, Dewey's emphasis). This adjustment in our perspective is not just good intellectual practice; it is what our "recovery of sanity" requires in a world that "seems mad in preoccupation with what is specific, particular, disconnected in medicine, politics, science, industry, education" (*EN* 224). Even those experts who "talk most of the organism" often show very little sense of "the intimate, delicate and subtle interdependence of all organic processes and structures with one another" (*EN* 224). Dewey is probably the only writer on aesthetics who would think it wise and important to declare, as he does in his chapter on "Substance and Form," "The action of any one sense includes attitudes and dispositions that are due to the whole organism. The energies belonging to the sense-organs themselves enter causally into the perceived thing" (*AE* 127). These are statements by someone who has thought long and deeply about the human body, and who has the highest regard for it. The claims made are far from the vague ones that might be suggested by the term, now in frequent use, "embodied." Here we have reference to a normal cooperative interweaving of the senses within the organism "in the action of any one sense." Thus synesthesia is a normal, healthy, underlying function of the body, and not a poetic specialty. "Unless these various sensory-motor energies are coordinated with one another there is no perceived scene or object" (*AE* 180). The sense organs not only play a part in the all-important process of perception, they "enter causally into the perceived thing."

This is not the discussion of the abstract topics of "Substance and Form" that anyone would expect to find in a work on aesthetics. It is the view of a man who is unafraid to say that we have to get back to the animal in ourselves in order to understand aesthetic experience. "To grasp the sources of esthetic experience it is …necessary to have recourse to animal life below the human scale" (*AE* 24)—a formulation that plainly regards human life itself as part of that animal life. In fact, the animal level is there with us no matter how advanced our thinking: "Even 'the greatest philosopher' excercizes an animal-like preference to guide his thinking to its conclusions" (*AE* 40). The quotation marks around "the greatest philosopher" give a satiric edge to the tone: nobody, no matter how adulated, should pretend to be beyond the animal. This and several other references to animal life in *Art as Experience* give the book an underlying tone of association with the primitive, the body and Nature. It is unusual in Dewey's work; in

Experience and Nature, for example, animals are mentioned as creatures for whom "acts have no meaning" (*EN* 276).

The animal in us is almost unavoidably associated with our bodies. Dewey is doing body thinking. To me it is a marvel that he can do this. Where did he get it? How did he develop it? It obviously is rooted so deeply within him that it is useless to look for a definitive source. But it is uncanny that in 1930, in a rare autobiographical essay written only one year prior to delivering the lectures that became *Art as Experience*, Dewey started off with an account of his philosophical awakening, and told of how it took the form of a breakthrough that centered on the body. This event happened even earlier than his encounter with the works of Hegel. It centered on the body not as a concept only, but as a virtually utopian model for what life ought to be. In his junior year at the University of Vermont, Dewey read for a course on physiology a textbook by Thomas H. Huxley entitled *The Elements of Physiology and Hygiene: A Textbook for Educational Institutions*. Huxley did not turn out to be a writer Dewey particularly wanted to follow; as Larry Hickman has shown, the young Dewey was to raise serious criticisms of Huxley's mind-body dualism.[39] But what Huxley had written in this book, Dewey in 1877-78 took in to himself in a creative manner of his own. Indeed Dewey says as much: "I have an impression that there was derived from this study a sense of interdependence and interrelated unity" that drew together his previous inchoate "intellectual stirrings," and this in turn:

> created a kind of type or model of a view of things to which material in any field ought to conform. *Subconsciously, at least, I was led to desire a world and a life that would have the same properties as had the human organism* in the picture of it derived from study of Huxley's treatment.[40]

To have this desire, a person has to admire the human organism as something more than an object for study. I think it no exaggeration to say that Dewey had a basic love of the human body. Richard Shusterman may be right in referring to Dewey's philosophy as "somatic naturalism".[41]

If this is not always evident in Dewey's writings, it is implicit at least in *Art as Experience*, a work composed more than 50 years after his reading of the Huxley book, but only one year after having written about that initial formative experience. Dewey's love of the body is a quality I intuit to be present throughout the work. I also find it in overt expression in such statements that even in doing mathematics, the body is involved. The body is in fact at work in a most interesting way: "the motor mechanism is linked up with reservoirs of energy in the sympathetic and endocrine system" (*AE* 161). That statement is part of Dewey's chapter on "The Natural History of Form." In "The Expressive Object" chapter, Dewey maintains that "the mechanism of motor imagery" is at work in our "movement of attention, backwards and forwards," and that in fact "our motor imagery" is what "reenacts the *relations* embodied in an object" (*AE* 107,

Dewey's emphasis). Later, in the course of fending off the unfortunate connotations for aesthetics of the term "contemplation," Dewey reiterates that "motor elements" are necessary as part of "an organized body of activities," in order to have "full perception" (*AE* 261.) And while perception that operates only in the service of "instinctive need" is "at its lowest and its most obscure" level, "[N]evertheless instinctive demands and responses" continue to function in more than one way as we perceive aesthetically (*AE* 260). Basically, when we become very interested in the aesthetic object, the work of art, we had best understand that we are doing something that has a primal base: "primitive need is the source of attachment to objects" (*AE* 260).

Thomas Alexander's long chapter on the role of "The Embodied Mind" in Dewey's thought[42] provides the philosophical framework and historical context for theorizing these varied remarks on the body that I have selected from *Art as Experience*. There is a direction that I want to take with Dewey's bodily aesthetic however, that has not been sufficiently noted. The body as a valued and indeed cherished component inevitably becomes a critical instrument for deflating the claims of all moral systems that have an investment in denigrating it or taking control over it. The first several pages of the second chapter, "The Live Creature and 'Ethereal Things'," are taken up with Dewey's eloquent protest against the culturally ingrained habit of condemning any attempt "to connect the higher and ideal things of experience with their vital roots" (*AE* 27). Why can we not connect the fine arts with "common life, the life that we share with all living creatures?" Why is life itself so frequently assumed to be "an affair of low appetite" that is always ready to sink to the "level of lust and harsh cruelty?"

> A complete answer to the question would involve the writing of a history of morals that would set forth the conditions that have brought about contempt for the body, fear of the senses, and the opposition of flesh and spirit. (*AE* 26)

Examples of Dewey's long commitment to the correction of dualism are available throughout his works. But in *Art as Experience* I can hear them rise to a new, more acute and more personalized tone. It is a book that insistently, unequivocally makes the case for the value of the senses in perception, in experience in general, in the creation of aesthetic works of art, and in aesthetic experience itself. And people are afraid of that. Moralists must realize that when a perception is had, it does not in itself provide any valuation of good or evil; it is primarily something that is just "had," and it is much more closely connected with the life of human emotion and the functions of aesthetic experience than it is with analysis or valuation. In *Experience and Nature*, Dewey states this clearly:

> Empirically…the characteristic thing about *perceptions in their natural estate*, apart from subjection to an art of knowing, is *their irrelevance to*

both truth and error; they exist for the most part in another dimension, whose nature may be suggested by reference to *imagination, fancy, reverie, affection, love and hate, desire, happiness, and misery.* (*EN* 235, my emphases)

There is a danger therefore that those who have perceptions will escape the control of the culture's moral codes, or those of the moralist. Indeed if the codes are in themselves built around the suppression of sense, sensuality or sex—if they are behind the cultural bias by which "sense and flesh get a bad name" (*AE* 27), then these moralists have good reason to be afraid.

Dewey recognizes that the moralist who is quick to denounce "the lust of the eye as part of the surrender of spirit to flesh" at least understands something that is deeply integral to experience. "The moralist knows that sense is allied with emotion, impulse, appetition" (*AE* 27). But people who are not consciously moralistic could easily have the greater, more generalized fear that Dewey phrases simply and memorably: "fear of what life may bring forth." That fear is the origin, Dewey says, of the most damaging cultural dualisms: "Oppositions of mind and body, soul and matter, spirit and flesh all have their origin, fundamentally, in fear of what life may bring forth" (*AE* 28). This is a fear not simply of sense in itself, but of the new experiences that might come out of the perceptions of sense. And Dewey is clear that perception when it is allowed to develop to the limit of the energies that fuel and form it, will always involve some risk. The "experience" of aesthetic consummation is almost sure to partake most fully of the experimental character of experience itself. Experience is not what we know ahead of having it: it involves risking entry into the unknown. We avoid that risk only by avoiding life itself: "The need of life itself," Dewey writes, "pushes us out into the unknown" (*AE* 173). There is a need for something new, for variety. We do not satisfy that need when "we are cowed by fear or dulled by routine" (*AE* 173). Routine, of course, is one of the two great enemies of the aesthetic explicitly named by Dewey, along with those habits of rushing along in life with "a slackness of loose ends" (*AE* 47). But experience, when it forms out of perception and is not blocked by constriction within the realm of recognition, will always break out of routine. Good teaching and criticism, philosophy directed toward human needs, and intelligent sympathy in relationships can overcome routine. The perceiver just has to arrange for a decent context in which to allow the experience to happen. We can often overcome the forces of aimless rush and dulling routine, at least long enough to have an experience. Moral codes, however, with their apparently generic opposition to the free operation of human senses and of the functioning of perception, are major blockers of experience. When Dewey says that "[r]igid abstinence, coerced submission, tightness" (*AE* 47) are the routines that prevent an experience, I think he is referring to the effect of such codes. *Art as Experience* is devoted to overcoming that blockage.

Enough has been said, perhaps, to convey what I mean by my heading, Dewey's Bodily Aesthetic. Let me now turn to my project of giving an account of experiencing Hardy's *Tess of the d'Urbervilles*. Years of reading and teaching the novel have shown me that experience in fact can easily "go wrong," by which I mean that it can take a turn toward blockage. *Tess* is susceptible to experiential blockage because, ironically enough, its main events tend to flood its reader's sensory capacities and allow the illusion that intense responses to a few powerful scenes are enough to qualify the experience, while further thought is unnecessary. Consider in this light the main elements of the story: a beautiful, responsible, intelligent 16-year-old woman (or girl) is drawn into having sex with a rich young man; possibly she is raped by him. She later leaves him, but has his child, who dies in early infancy. She then meets a man who seems to be extremely appreciative and loving, only to have him cruelly reject her when, on their wedding night, she confesses her sexual past. After long suffering, she realizes the cruelty of her abandonment, and, partly to receive help for her destitute family, returns to the arms of her lover-seducer-(?)rapist. When her husband unexpectedly does return, she stabs and kills the lover, runs away with her husband, and is captured and executed for murder.

5. On Sex as Subject-Matter

It is apparent that this is a story in which sex is extremely important. That may be obvious enough—except for the fact that many of the novel's professional readers have sought to evade or deny it.[43] And even those who have discussed sex in *Tess* have greatly underestimated its pervasiveness and (as I will argue) its implications.

I imagine that most of my "Deweyan" readers are already somewhat uncomfortable with the direction I am taking. They might rightly wonder, what has a Deweyan approach got to do with sex? But that is perhaps a question that reverts back to a relative lack in Dewey's many writings. In the world he deals with, much is included: aesthetics, psychology, metaphysics, education, ethics, politics, religious faith, the theory of inquiry, and the whole theory of experience. Sex figures very little. There is nothing surprising about this; few philosophers even in our own time write about sex. But neither have Dewey's successors in pragmatist thought done much with this subject. And some of Dewey's own remarks about it, as in *Human Nature and Conduct*, seem to show little interest in giving it serious consideration. Even his remark on romantic love, which is very much the subject-matter in *Tess*, takes the form of an analogy that nearly depletes it of its emotional dimension:

> Romantic love as it exists today, with all of the varying perturbations it
> occasions, is as definitely a sign of specific historic conditions as are big

battle ships with turbines, internal-combustion engines, and electrically driven machines.[44]

The act of sex itself, Dewey says in this same discussion, is like hunger, one of the "simpler acts." But how anyhow is hunger an "act"? From what follows in his text, Dewey clearly is talking about sex, rather than hunger. But is the sex act usefully described as being "simpler" than others? I doubt as well that in the sex act, the most important "perceptible changes" the person senses will be "external to the organism," rather than "intra-organic," as Dewey asserts.[45] I find this a disconcerting though only momentary tangent into dualism, on Dewey's part, and his reason for his emphasizing the environmental I find arbitrary:

> [T]hese [external] consequences are more important than the intra-organic ones for determining the quality of the act. For they are consequences in which others are concerned and which evoke reactions of favor and disfavor as well as cooperative and resisting activities of a more direct sort. [46]

Dewey in this brief comment shows that he does consider the sex act as no simple thing. He does know that it is important to determine "the quality of the act," not just to note its occurrence. But I do not see how he can assert so readily the dominance of the environmental over the "intra-organic" aspects. At the least it would seem that Dewey would have allowed for the problematic qualities of sex, and that if he were being consistent with his own philosophical contextualism, he would have tilted the balance of interests neither to the extra- nor the intra-organic aspects of sexual experience.

A similar uncharacteristic suggestion of mind-body dualism seems to invade one of Dewey's comments on sex in *Art as Experience*. He makes it in the context of explaining why T. E. Hulme was wrong to suggest that "an arrested impulse" that accounts for the beauty in a work of art should have been allowed to "reach its natural end." Now as I read the statement quoted from Hulme, such a suggestion does not occur to me; Dewey seems to be going out of his way to find what he terms a "veiled intimation" here. And it is human sexuality that he chooses as his example:

> If the emotion of love between the sexes had not been celebrated by means of diversion into material emotionally cognate but practically irrelevant to its direct object and end, there is every reason to suppose it would still remain on the animal plane. (*AE* 83)

We can grant the truism that procreation in itself is not "celebrated" by non-human animals, although ethology would tell us that there is so much courting behavior among animal species that there probably are few observable instances of the sexual impulse being limited to its "direct object and end." But Dewey's statement does not simply ignore courting behavior. I would say that if we want to suppose that there is an "emotion of love" in sex, even at the animal level, then the imaginative elaboration of this emotion was not a "diversion" of that emotion. The example Dewey gives here rings false in the context of his book, where he finds much in the life of non-human animals that is comparable with what we do in our own existence as "the live creature." An example is the case of the movements of a hawk "who wants a mate," as described by Keats, which provides Dewey with a vivid passage near the end of chapter 2, "The Live Creature and 'Ethereal Things'" (*AE* 38-9). But here, in refuting Hulme, the "animal plane" seems reduced to "body" while the imaginative activity of the human mind is assumed to be needed in order to make sex into something higher.

Let me then say the obvious: sex is a major part of experience; the problems of sexual love form an immense sea of desire in literature and in the last several centuries of Western history. My hope for what can be done with my experiential account of *Tess* is that some adjustment in meeting this reality can be made in the minds of present-day readers of Dewey. For Dewey, or rather for our present day understanding of Dewey's aesthetic, the inclusion of the sexual within the thinking would be a most natural addition. For a bodily aesthetic, it has got to be let in.

At the more mundane level of extant criticism, the problem is not so much a refusal to allow for the reality of sex as a willingness to deny it any experiential complexity. I have found that readers and critics tend to feel licensed by such a narrative as *Tess* to respond prejudicially, applying their already held value judgments concerning rape, the double standard, and romantically justified homicide. I find for example, this view by Mary Jacobus, an engaged and perceptive critic, of Tess's killing of Alec, one of her two lovers: a "triumphant" feeling in response to this event is "surely ours...it repays the injustice to which Tess has been subjected throughout the book". But why would this feeling be "ours," when Jacobus herself has argued that Alec has been developed into an unlikely villain? [47] Would we not feel something out of kilter at this point, rather than a justified relief? We may have a great deal of feeling when Alec is killed (although I will question the occurrence of that feeling later on), but sheer intensity of response cannot be equated with the depth and meaning of "an experience"; if it were so equated, any sensational tale would become a great experience. But even granting that Tess killing Alec is experienced as highly emotional, the significance of the event is still to be understood if experience is to be had. And this argues against simplifications such as Jacobus's claim of Tess taking her generalized revenge on all that has oppressed her.

From a Deweyan perspective, the novel's dramatic events can be given their full importance, but they are taken in as part of a context developed over the course of the entire novel, a context without which they cannot be experienced.

6. The Manuscript: A Dubious Triumph

The word *triumphant*, which I have just mentioned as Tess's expression (she has "a *triumphant* smile") when she announces that she has killed Alec, does not actually occur in *Tess*, but in its manuscript. This points to a special problem for experiencing the novel. The extent to which manuscript and other later revisions by Hardy can be taken into account while reading the novel as it stands is difficult to determine. An interference with continuity of experience is risked with diverting attention to these revisions. Yet there can be formidable reasons to interfere. For example, "*triumphant*": it is Hardy's own italicized word-choice, in the manuscript of the novel. And Mary Jacobus much prefers it. There are issues here of whether Hardy was aesthetically justified in revising his text as he did several times over, and whether the concept of "repaying injustice" does justice to the experiencing of this event. My eventual answer to the latter question is that it does not. But there are a whole series of revisions, from the printed text of 1891, to the one-volume edition of 1892, and extending even to later dates. Substantial revision ended with the edition of 1912; a very few additional revisions were made as late as 1919. All of these changes have been studied exhaustively. In 1998, Penguin Books went so far as to issue the 1891 rather than the 1892 version of *Tess* as its own choice for worldwide distribution in its Penguin Classics series. The 1891 version had been out of print since it was first issued. Plainly there is more than ordinary concern over the text of *Tess*.

Perhaps one should seek out the extant version of the manuscript of the novel and read through it, if the claims made by some scholars on the gravity of the revisions are warranted. Then the manuscript (supplemented with such patches as would have to be affixed to fill in its gaps, by selecting as necessary from all the versions of the text) would lead to an aesthetic work of art different from the *Tess* that has been in print for about 90 years. But I will be dealing with the revised text as Hardy intended it. I say this not out of some faith in the virtues of authorial intention, but from a willingness born of my experience with works of literature that tells me to at least try to trust to the author's judgment of when the work is finished. As Dewey understands this process, the way the author reaches this judgment is by imagining his or her book as if it were being read and taken in experientially by another person. "He observes and understands as a third person might note and interpret" (*AE* 111). As I reconstruct as best I can Hardy's process of writing *Tess*, I see him doing a lot of such putting himself in the role of the reader. But in this process, Hardy finally decides that his writing of the novel has reached completion.

My own conclusion from my study of the revisions is that the text as it stands can lead to a great and valid work; most of Hardy's revisions have enhanced it, and to some extent may have re-shaped it into a different work than the one Hardy began writing in 1888. Some few probably were ill-considered.

I find myself more seriously distracted by Hardy's efforts to guide the reader away from any sharp condemnation of Angel. One of the worst of these occurs in chapter 49, where Hardy, after elaborating on Angel's horribly costly moralistic judgments of Tess's human worth, continues thus:

> But the reasoning is somewhat musty; lovers and husbands have gone over the ground before to-day. Clare had been harsh towards her; there is no doubt of it. Men are too often harsh with women they love or have loved; women with men. And yet these harshnesses are tenderness itself when compared with the universal harshness out of which they grow; the harshness of the position towards the temperament, of the means towards the aims, of to-day towards yesterday, of hereafter towards to-day. (330)

On a recent reading, I wrote "TH waxes too grandly" in my margin here. The passage, in other words, rings false. Had I stopped to analyze it, I would have brought out its irrelevancies (such as the harshness of "women toward men," which is certainly not the problem), its implausibly vague terms ("the position towards the temperament"), the cosmic apologetics ("these harshnesses are tenderness itself when compared with the universal harshness"), the vapid gesture at timelessness: "of to-day towards yesterday, or hereafter towards to-day." And so on. Despite these authorial false notes, however, the intention is not dismissable: Hardy is trying to guide his readers and probably himself away from a response that would be limited to the single response of condemnation.

The passage, I hasten to say, is not one done in revision of the manuscript. But it has all the marks of a writer trying to alter the impression given by what he has just written. Considered from an experiential perspective, this sort of change counts as a revision.

Among the criticisms of Angel that Hardy had given in the preceding paragraphs, one is so bald as to make Angel out to be almost stupid: Angel did not realize that Tess's failure to get in touch with him was a result of her adherence "with literal exactness *to orders which he had given and forgotten...*" (329, my emphasis). At least Hardy did not erase or retract this. Once I succeed in discounting Hardy's apologetics, this and the other criticisms of Angel can be experienced. But could Hardy not have given me a less convoluted text? From my understanding of Hardy, gained through my readings outside of this novel, I suspect that it is the apologetic lines which allowed Hardy to retain the whole passage, thus striking a creative "deal" or transaction within his own ego.

Although no choice here can be entirely risk-free, I find it best to accept the text as it now stands as "the work of art" I will be working with, even though I attempt no formal analytic definition of that term. I will go ahead and see what this work "does with and in experience."

Experience easily can be ruined by adopting a stance of over-seeing the author's work and describing what might have been if he or she had only written otherwise. We have to find a better way than that to relate to Hardy's creative effort, a way that would be compatible with Dewey's belief that the reader of a work of art retraces in some (not literal) sense the pathways taken by the artist as the work is fashioned (*AE* 50). There is room for questioning the author's decisions, of course, but that cannot be the main attitude toward the experience of a work of literature. I am especially concerned to avoid any indication of having found knowledge superior to that of the author by means of studying the revisions. Often the scholar seems to assume that if Hardy revised a passage sometime between the manuscript version and the last fully revised edition of 1912,[48] he must have been trying to fudge some issue in the novel. Jacobus assumes throughout her study that Hardy was caving in to pressure when he altered his original conception. This is simply not a fair way to deal with a writer who said of his career as a novelist working under the restrictions of the Victorian era, "From the very beginning I determined to speak out."[49] In his dealing with four different potential publishers for Tess as he was beginning to write the novel, Hardy seems to have courted their moralist's rejection as a way of sharpening his own hostility to such censorship.[50] While all this was going on, he revised—or developed—his manuscript. Jacobus would have preferred that he stayed with what he had.

For me, as a Deweyan reader, the issue can best be decided as a matter of fictional quality. The early manuscript version of *Tess* is not attractive to me as a guide to what the novel should have been. For example, Jacobus would have liked Hardy to have left in the suggestion from the manuscript that Tess could have chosen to have sex with Angel without marrying him.[51] This intriguing idea is certainly in the manuscript, but the actual wording is disappointing:

> As a path out of her trying strait poor Tess might even have accepted another kind of union with him, purely for his own sake, had he urged it upon her; that he might have retreated if discontented with her on learning her story. To be a cloud in his life was so cruel to him that her own standing seemed unimportant beside it; and she could not master herself sufficiently to give him up altogether.[52]

But how would this passage, had it been included in the novel, really work? I would not welcome a Tess who would go to bed with Angel in order to avoid being cruel to him, and in conscious devaluation of "her own standing." This is a "poor Tess" indeed. And, to anticipate what I will be saying later, there is much to be had in the experiencing of the relationship of Tess and Angel that is far more erotic in its suggestiveness than what is afforded by this cancelled passage.

Nor can I agree with Jacobus that Hardy was compromising his vision when he wrote, of Tess's response to Angel's embrace: "her lips parted, and she sank upon him in her momentary joy, with something very like an ecstatic cry" (153). Jacobus would have had Hardy keep this earlier version: "[Tess] yielded to Angel's embrace as unreflectingly as a child. Having seen that it was really her lover, and no one else, her lips parted, she panted in her impressionability, and burst into a succession of sobs".[53] This would make Tess both a child, unready for adult sex, and a hysterical woman. That is definitely not an improvement—not even stylistically, considering the ponderous word "impressionability."

A more workable assumption, adopted in the spirit of Dewey's appreciation of the artist's creative process, is that Hardy came to a fuller realization of what his novel was doing—or what it was moving toward getting done "with and in experience"—and revised accordingly. There could even have been a major change of focus during Hardy's writing the novel. Or, as some scholars have suggested, he made changes after the early reviewers of *Tess* had pointed to problems. This need not be taken as an act of cowardice or of craven patchwork, but as evidence of a creative mind at work, capable of learning from what his audience had begun to experience. In Dewey's terms, the "end-in-view" for which Hardy might have been striving when he began *Tess* may have changed as he creatively worked within the "means" of his writing, with "means" understood here as his total imaginative involvement with his subject-matter. As one Dewey scholar has formulated such a change, "the projected end may ...fade into insignificance as the risk-laden experiment with processes and materials leads to novel yet fruitful end results".[54] I am saying this not to defend Hardy, but to open the way to the experience.

7. On Having This Experience

It is an experience in which at least a few major qualities are practically undeniable. After the intense opening of Tess's involvement with Alec, and its confusing, depressing sequel, I must make the great shift to experiencing what Hardy calls the "Recovery" and "Consequence" Phases. This section has a different quality: it seems to me to be the most extended immersion of the reader (or of "us" or of "me") in the context of sensuous-sensual-sexual Nature anywhere in literature.

There is also the problem of staying with Tess's qualitative change from a very intelligent and interesting-thinking young person, to a woman with an influx of disturbed, even irrational thinking. This is never a total transformation; her perceptiveness is always at least potentially there in the situations that she lives through. For anyone having the experience, the need is to deal receptively with her thinking and not fall into simplistic categorizing (such as "masochistic") when she thinks, as it were, against herself.

As for the men, the questions are also difficult, but not insoluble. To read with attention to Tess alone, with her men regarded as simple stock types, produces a truncated, much reduced experience. To help clear away this prejudice, it might be well to recall D. H. Lawrence's basic sympathy: that "in Alec d'Urberville there is good stuff gone wrong. Just as in Angel Clare there is good stuff gone wrong in the other direction".[55] Some would deny this, I am sure—but at a cost to their own sensitivity toward other people. The cost to their experiencing *Tess* (or anything else, I am afraid) would be prohibitive. Dewey wakes us up to the relation of sympathy and perception in another statement in his 1932 *Ethics*: "A person entirely lacking in sympathetic response might have a keen calculating intellect, but he would have no spontaneous sense of the claims of others for satisfactions of their desires".[56] Satisfaction of desires, or their frustration, is very much what *Tess* is about.

Hardy provides enough context to understand Angel's character; this is not a great problem. The problem with Angel is the way he confounds and torments Tess within her feelings for this man. Those are feelings with which we are bound to empathize, unless we simply fail to relate to her. But as early as the 1892 review of *Tess* by William Watson, some readers have recognized the complexity in Angel's character.[57] The reason this complexity has not been widely recognized is well explained by Rosemary Sumner, who almost alone among critics, has shown that Angel is a full-scale psychological character creation, and one not entirely unworthy of sympathy. Tess is the center, of course, but

> for a full apprehension of Hardy's art, we must be...capable of entering into Angel's experience, even though this demands of us an emotional response which is in direct contradiction to the feelings evoked by our sympathy for Tess.[58]

The problem, in other words, is one of undergoing the experience even if it is necessary to do more with one's perception of Angel than become contemptuous or enraged at him. Easier said than done. But what about the possibility that Angel undergoes a change by the end of the novel? That, as I shall show, is a problematical yet unavoidable question. It would be unapproachable if the reader had already become locked into the notion that Angel is hopelessly fixed in his ways.

With Alec, an experience of *Tess* requires seeing him as more than a stock figure of the shallow seducer ("Now, my beauty..."); for if that is all he is, the novel itself inevitably becomes shallow. To say this is not to propose artificially magnifying the complexity in his character. We can only have what is there, but there is more there than one dimension. Possibly Hardy himself caused some of this problem for experiencing the novel. Hardy's revisions of the early manuscript version of Alec seem to have coarsened and simplified his character.[59] But was this "character assassination," as Mary Jacobus has claimed? The effect is overcome as the novel goes on, but it is in itself one of the pitfalls in literary experience that I have come to call an "experience blocker." It can block experience by encouraging readers to see nothing but a stilted melodramatic villain in Alec. As late as 1991, a highly trained reader dismisses Alec as a "cardboard villain" even more so at the end of the novel than at the beginning.[60] Yet to the extent that the revised Alec *at the beginning of the novel* becomes a lustful sexual male, that crude effect may make for the kind of discomfort the novel needs. If Tess is attracted to a man whose main characteristic is sexual conquest, can readers allow themselves to experience this fact?

Alec is developed to a lesser extent than Angel, but there are complicating aspects of his self that Hardy hints at with just enough narrative interest to create an uneven, rather "chunky" portrait, one that stays within the bounds of a novel in which Tess is the main character. It is possible moreover, with careful listening and responding, to hear something deeper in Alec, especially in his later speeches and actions. It is the later Alec, after all, who tells Tess, in terms that are grounded in his knowledge of how he feels, exactly why he is not going to abide by religion's precepts of "loving-kindness and purity." He says:

> If there's nobody to say "Do this, and it will be a good thing for you after you are dead; do that, and it will be a bad thing for you," I can't warm up. Hang it, I am not going to feel responsible for my deeds and passions if there's nobody to be responsible to; and if I were you, my dear, I wouldn't either! (319)

This is no mean speech in Victorian England—or even in our own era. A few pages further on, it is this later Alec, not Angel nor Tess herself nor Hardy who sounds this central value of the novel: "by all that's tender and strong between man and woman…" (324).

We have enough: enough in Alec, in Angel, in Hardy, in his book as he decided it was completed, in Tess herself, and enough capability in ourselves to respond to this novel's subject-matter of sexual love, enough to enter into the novel unhampered by "stencils" that would cause experience to be blocked.

Two

THE BODY-MIND OF YOUNG TESS

In chapter 2, presenting the first appearance of Tess, the three centers of energy seem to me to be, first, the young women, outdoors, in what I must call Nature, all of them moving in a faded but still touching ancient ceremony of the harvest season. Within their description I find a sudden increase in intensity with this phrase: "under whose bodices the life throbbed quick and warm" (19). Tess is not yet singled out. Second, soon she is made the focus, although not yet named by the narrator: "She was a fine and handsome girl--not handsomer than some others, possibly—but her mobile peony mouth and large innocent eyes added eloquence to colour and shape" (20). Her description is quickly broken off, to reappear a few paragraphs later in the extraordinary context of the deep sensuousness of the language of the region:

> The dialect was on her tongue to some extent, despite the village school: the characteristic intonation of that dialect, for this district, being the voicing approximately rendered by the syllable UR, probably as rich an utterance as any to be found in human speech. The pouted-up deep-red mouth to which this syllable was native had hardly as yet settled into its definite shape, and her lower lip had a way of thrusting the middle of her top one upward, when they closed together after a word. (21)

This plainly is a passage to savor—I use the term deliberately. It will not do to reduce it cynically, to a mere excuse to dwell lasciviously on Tess's lips, as does the one critic who has written a book on Hardy and the erotic.[1] From a pragmatist philosophical point of view, I can say that Hardy proposes a *fusion*[2] of qualities from two ordinarily unrelated things, Tess's mouth, described sensuously and with loving detail, and a quality in language that the novel seems to want me to stop and try in my own mouth. The UR cannot just be "read through" like any other word: it is not even a word, and besides these two letters "render" only an approximate indication of this "voicing", this process. If I want to experience the way this novel is starting to feel, I must hear/sound/feel it at least minimally. I perceive her mouth as if it were a physical presence in this writing. It is teasingly suggestive of meanings, which it is obviously too early to try to specify (it "had not as yet settled into its definite shape") except that there is a strong perceptual interest focusing on the sensuous qualities of Tess as a person with a body. And obviously, both her name, Durbeyfield, and the name made prominent by its inclusion in the novel's title, d'Urbervilles, have this sound. (So does my own first name, which may have helped me to tune in to this sound in the novel.) Yet at the same time, Tess is contextualized within a whole tradition of speech. Hardy places unmistakable positive emphasis here: "UR, probably as rich an utterance as to be found in human speech." I realize that I must listen for more than the usual tonal quality in a character's speech, and for more than the meanings of words, when Tess begins to speak. Here I am reminded of Dewey's remarks, in his discussion of the function of sound in aesthetic experience, that "Sound agitates directly as a commotion of the organism itself...the intellectual range of hearing though enormous is acquired; in itself the ear is the emotional sense" (*AE* 242).

Third, there is Angel. I find that he comes across with intensity only at this point: "he felt he had acted stupidly" (23). He had not taken notice of Tess until he had been about to leave. Impressed with this segment, I linger to absorb its immediate context. Angel shows and then dismisses a quality of sensitiveness toward Tess:

> Trifling as the matter was, he yet felt instinctively that she was hurt by his oversight. He wished that he had asked her; he wished that he had inquired her name. She was so modest, so expressive, she had looked so soft in her thin white gown that he felt he had acted stupidly.
>
> However, it could not be helped, and turning, and bending himself to a rapid walk, he dismissed the subject from his mind. (23)

These three centers of energy are important in immediately focusing the subject matter on the relations of woman and man. The description of Tess herself is not left as a fixed portrait; it leads into her yearning to have been asked to dance by Angel. In terms of its felt quality, the novel opens with these relations, and immediately places them in a kind of natural context: outdoors, agricultural, and with the remnants of the pagan rites of Cerealia that the women celebrate. Moreover it is the nubile women who count in this scene, even though factually they are not the only women present. To strain out what is not relevant, Hardy overtly directs me to forget about the older women in this ceremony, although he is quite aware of their human worth, and thus allows for, and insists upon, my own awareness of their presence. In a remarkable instance of an author providing guidance that may be freely taken (or not), Hardy admits that for purposes of a truthful account, the older women would indeed be important. But for purposes of having the experience, we tacitly agree to ignore them. All readers and critics of whom I have knowledge take his cue, and before long have forgotten about the

> few middle-aged and even elderly women in the train, their silver-wiry hair and wrinkled faces, scourged by time and trouble, having almost a grotesque, certainly a pathetic, appearance in such a jaunty situation. In a

true view, perhaps, there was more to be gathered and told of each anxious and experienced one, to whom the years were drawing nigh when she should say, "I have no pleasure in them," than of her juvenile comrades. But let the elder be passed over here for those under whose bodices the life throbbed quick and warm. (19)

Which is not to say that the passage has no effect: in experiencing the novel, I find that this passage becomes part of a deep pessimism about the relation of the sexes, a feeling that is both confirmed and resisted.

1. The Unnameable Sex Scene

Several chapters later (in chapter 11), we come to the major center of emotional energy for this part of the novel. It is a scene that has drawn the attention of virtually all readers and critics, including myself. It has also proven to be a notorious stumbling-block for experiencing the novel. It is necessary to deal with it in its highly involved, even involuted, context. Consider the quality of this fragment:

> D'Urberville stooped, and heard a gentle, regular breathing. He knelt and bent lower, till her breath warmed his face, and in a moment his cheek was in contact with hers. She was sleeping soundly, and upon her eyelashes there lingered tears. (77)

Here, just prior to the novel's most famous sex act, there is no suggestion of physical violence; quite the contrary. Many readers assume that this is a rape scene. Others have called it a seduction, and several have settled for calling it a rape/seduction. One has even argued that this is rape in a legal sense, and that seduction, as a separate event, follows upon it as a result and then inexplicably becomes the main focus of Hardy's interest.[3] It may be rape, and everyone will consider this. I know that I have. Even if I had wanted to avoid this problem— and at times I have—students reading the novel with me over many years of teaching would have insisted on dealing with it. I have concluded (for reasons I think will become clear) that invoking the term "rape" would be a serious mistake. But I will have to defer any explanation at this point. The more immediate qualitative impression is that in this situation there is something very wrong. Perhaps it stems from the fact that Alec is choosing to have sex with the virgin Tess, but she very well may not be choosing to have it, or at least not choosing freely, at least not this first time. There is a lot of pressure put on her. She comes from a poor family but is in the arms of a rich man: the possibilities for his taking advantage of her are built into the situation, and at this point he cares nothing about this unfairness. I have learned, just in the previous chapter, that he has made it his practice to have sex with a series of women who are his social inferiors. Much as I might like to approve of Alec's sexual desire for Tess, for which I as a man do not blame him, and can even fantasize along with him, I cannot avoid being troubled by his manipulations of the situation in which Tess has come to work. He has been pretty dirty. Yet there is also something right: Tess is a sexual woman, and there is some evidence of her attraction to Alec. It is far from evident, thus far, that Alec is simply "the wrong man" for her, as Hardy shortly will state. We cannot know that so soon in the story, and perhaps we never do know it. In any case, there is nothing wrong, in itself, with their having sex. If I allow myself to focus on them as a male and female couple, and forget about the class difference, with all the pressures this brings upon Tess in this situation, practically everything in this narrative concerning the two of them leads me to a wish for a consummation—although not the one that they have. This is not merely Alec's stereotypical male wish but, in an uncertain solution of desire and avoidance, it is Tess's wish.

Then I read the description again, and tell myself that Alec, having knelt down and bent over Tess, placing his cheek in touch with her cheek—did what? Did he immediately seize her and assault her? Or was there an interval? Did she wake up immediately to the utterly new sensation of an adult man in this intimate position? When she did wake up, did some of her passivity allow her to consent to have sex with this man to whom she had been attracted? Did she even welcome it? Was her response one of shock? Or, was she simply, brutally, violated? It is clear that if I try to deal with these questions under the legal rubric of "consent" that has been developed since the time of this story's setting. Tess could not have given any meaningful consent.[4] In context, considering all that had occurred between Tess and Alec, what Tess had given was a refusal to give consent or to outright refuse it. This is of little value for understanding the quality of the scene, although it would at least tell me that as far as Alec was concerned, he had taken her ambivalent and mixed responses as a signal to go ahead. But there is no telling, since the immediate moment following the description of her gentle breathing while being sound asleep is not given. The scene, as all readers have realized, is deliberately not rendered by Hardy.

There is a perplexity to be dealt with here. Should we insist on clearing it up, faulting its very existence in the text, or eliminating it? The temptation to clear away the contradictory aspects of experience has long afflicted philosophy, and of critical thinking in general. So Dewey wrote in 1925, in *Experience and Nature*.

> [P]hilosophers...have constantly held that the traits which are characteristic of thinking, namely, uncertainty, ambiguity, alternatives, inquiring, search, selection, experimental reshaping of external conditions, do not possess the same existential character as do the objects of valid knowledge. They have denied that these traits are evidential of the character of the world within which thinking occurs. (*EN* 62)

Genuine perplexity is a frequent enough quality of experience—certainly of sexual experience—and should be credited as being quite as "real" as anything more settled and unambiguous, rather than boiled down analytically to its clearer elements in the hope of making it seem unreal. The notion of the "real" is doubly pertinent here, inasmuch as Dewey, in the context of the passage just quoted, chides the "realists" for their allergic reaction to the uncertain and ambiguous aspects of reality, those that require selection and search. In this instance, Dewey's recognition that a perplexing situation will call for "selection" and "search" can be a pragmatic guideline for experiencing *Tess*. But beyond this guideline is a deeper pragmatist principle, namely that doubt is a driving force for inquiry in any topic that matters. As Jim Garrison has phrased it, "Doubt for Dewey is a living, embodied and impassioned condition."[5] I *feel* that it does matter whether Tess was raped or not. At this point in reading the novel, I just do not know if I will ever have an answer. To the reader, Hardy is saying: You will have to get on without knowing. But you cannot just skip over the difficulty of the scene.

You can still get mad, feel maddened. Reading freshly (today, October 12, 1999, the day I am beginning this book) Hardy's allusive commenting as this sexual event occurs in the text (a comment nominally concerning the prophet Elijah, "the ironical Tishbite"[6]) I perceive a tone and feeling of Hardy being personally aggravated, bitterly witnessing a desecration of this woman:

> ...where was Tess's guardian angel? where was the Providence of her simple faith? Perhaps, like that other god of whom the ironical Tishbite spoke, he was talking, or he was pursuing, or he was in a journey, or he was sleeping and not to be awaked. (77)

I hear now the rising aggravation, Hardy's own ironical bitterness, with the 4 items in the series—or really 5, with the "not to be awaked." The weight of this phrase is heavily meaningful in its context of Hardy's figure of a pathetic, sleeping god who ought to DO SOMETHING ON HER BEHALF. It is an angry series. The word "Perhaps" in this context is not calming or qualifying; it seems to convey a vicious neutrality.

Anger however is not the only strong quality in Hardy's commentary. There is a confusing blend. Hardy, for one thing, evokes the concept of fate: "It was to be." That is what "Tess's own people" would say. This is easy to remember. But less easy is the feeling quality Hardy appends: "There lay the pity of it." It is not so easy to register this feeling: it is not such an impersonal notion as "fate." Still more difficult to relate to, as far as I can find in my multiple readings, is Hardy's packing-in of an analogy between this scene and the plight of some "peasant girls" who were "even more ruthlessly" dealt with, back in the era of the feudal d'Urbervilles. There is something confusing here. I would never have thought, myself, of inveighing at this point as Hardy does, against the view that "the sins of the fathers shall be" visited upon "the children." In a sensitive reading of the passage, H. M. Daleski takes this sentence to mean that Hardy is saying that Tess was raped—although in Hardy's contrasting mode of narration in the same passage, he is not implying that at all. Daleski thus honors the perplexing quality of the passage as few critics have done; many instead have complained about it or have quickly resolved it.[7] But is the meaning of even this sentence on the sins of the fathers as clear as Daleski finds it? Hardy's phrasing, that the d'Urberville ancestors "had dealt the same measure even more ruthlessly towards peasant girls of their time" (77) is inconclusive: what did Alec do? How could he have raped Tess without being completely ruthless? Or is Hardy suggesting that relatively little coercion was involved? And if so, what would that mean for the quality of their relationship? That would be the real question for experiencing the novel.

Hardy rejects the Biblical adage, which he seems to have needlessly introjected, in the name of "average human nature" (77). But the sentence is about "sins"; and as the following chapters make me see, the concept of "sin" itself, as it affects Tess and the other characters, is thematically unavoidable. And it really *is* a confusing concept, confounding the sense of human responsibility with irrational guilt over sexual acts.

There is a part of the commentary that hits me very hard. I am not embarrassed to say so, even though some of Hardy's language, as well as his sentiments, might be dismissed out of hand by anyone who does not care very much about the scene:

> Why it was that upon this beautiful feminine tissue, sensitive as gossamer, and practically blank as snow as yet, there should have been traced such a coarse pattern as it was doomed to receive; why so often the coarse appropriates the finer thus, the wrong man the woman, the wrong woman the man, many thousand years of analytic philosophy have failed to explain to our sense of order. (77)

To experience this, I (and I believe most readers) have to be less "literary" than most of us have been trained to be. You have to retain some innocence to respond to what Hardy is saying: to be able to summon from your own experience a realization of the incredible frequency in which women and men are grievously mis-matched in the sexual relations of our own time. The evocative wording, however, can at least help you to feel your way toward this. This passage furthermore calls for a realization of the woman's initial vulnerability, prior to entering on adult sexual experience: in this sense, it is possible to regard Tess's body as "beautiful feminine tissue, sensitive as gossamer, blank as snow as yet…" (You could choose to take the expression as hopelessly sentimental, or— at the other extreme—as referring only to Tess's hymen. But these choices are not forced upon you, and they surely would lead to a slighting of the possible experience.) Along with this sensitiveness, there is the sheer beauty of the young woman, or rather of any young woman. In some respects, the scope of Hardy's unanswered question reaches as well to any young man ("the wrong woman, the man").

Hardy's writing in this scene may be approached in ways that bring out, or restrict, its potential for experience. To construct a Deweyan account, the reader would have to renounce some habits of explication which have worked their way into *Tess* criticism over the years. You would also have to fend off some trivializing connections—such as between Angel the name and "guardian angel"—a dumb mechanical matching; or linking Tess who is asleep and no doubt *is* awakened by Alec before very long—versus the "not to be awaked" god of the Biblical account. That would be a silly contrast to get hung up on, but not much worse than the many merely verbal connections long performed by the novel's critics. I call such connections merely verbal, since they are made in disregard for their experienced quality, or rather, *qualities*, in the shifting *contexts* of the novel, where repeated words take on changing meanings. The red of Tess's ribbon in her opening scene, the red of the blood pouring from her fatally wounded horse, and the red of Alec's blood blotting the ceiling in Mrs. Brooks's lodging house long after, are reds with very different contexts and meanings. I envision them as having quite different color-tones, as well. I would certainly avoid anything like J. Hillis Miller's compiling of a host of these occurrences of reds, and then commenting "All these red things are marks made by that creative and destructive energy underlying events to which Hardy gave the name 'Immanent Will.'"[8] This makes short work of the problems of experience.

Remarkably, virtually none of the novel's critics attempt to say what the repeated red colors would have meant to Tess herself as she undergoes all the experiences in which the color occurs. So far as I know, there is only a short, unpublished paper on this, by Paul Green, who does try to understand this function of reds. Green makes the reasonable assumption that Tess is a sensitive person who would have been affected by the red color in some of the intense scenes, even if there is no report of what she made of it.[9] I would imagine that her guilt feeling over the death of her family's horse, Prince, would have been considerably less intense if she had not been splattered with the huge gush of blood pouring from the animal. But I do not see any basis for connecting her plausible regarding of herself as a "murderess" in this episode (38) with her murder of Alec, 51 chapters later. That is much too mechanical a way to derive meaning in this novel. Nor do I leap to the notion that the terrible puncturing of the horse is emblematic or prophetic of Tess's loss of virginity. The horse's demise has no quality in common with the "beautiful feminine tissue, sensitive as gossamer," which Hardy describes lyrically, grievously, as being violated, at the point of her first having sex with Alec. The contexts are different, as are the details: she does not gush gallons of blood, nor die on the spot.

For most critics of *Tess*, the red colors exist neither for Tess's experience nor their own; instead they are taken as clues to meaning that can be decoded without undergoing experience.[10] And when, on rare occasion, a red color simply does not fit their scheme, they ignore it. Thus the detail of Tess wearing a "pale pink jacket" as she works in the field has been taken as part of Hardy's symbolic redness, but the fact that another woman alongside her has "a petticoat as red as the arms of the reaping-machine" (93) is never mentioned.

In my own experiential commentary, I have not been led to discuss the sequence of reds, because in the local contexts, I never find that the color alone is an adequate basis for comprehension. In a Deweyan reading, it would be most unlikely that a string of rather dissimilar instances of color spaced unevenly through a novel could be experienced distinctly as a unit in itself. Instead, each of the reds that has emotional quality would participate in energizing the scene or episode in which it occurred. (Some seem not to arouse any emotional quality: think of the red-brick color of the building at Trantridge.) As the experience ultimately develops, there indeed could be a symbolic connection suggested and felt among all or most of these rednesses. But as soon as this connection is delved into, attention turns to the events of the novel rather than to the structural framings or to single details in themselves.

A Deweyan method would insist on considering the perplexing scene in its context. What is the effective context for Hardy's extensive impassioned comment in the scene of Tess and Alec's love-making? Is it the scene alone? The scene is not injected into the novel as a total surprise. We do have one earlier instance of this mode of commentary, one that does not cause the narrative to slow down as much as this scene does for the purpose of complex reflection, but is almost as intense and complicated. In this earlier passage, Hardy initiates us into his intention to involve us in his tragic philosophy of love-relationships. This happens when Alec backs off, for the time being, from his impulse to kiss Tess, as they walk on his family's estate, "between the tall rhododendrons and conifers..." For a moment, "he inclined his face towards her as if—. But no: he thought better of it; and let her go" (45). Hardy now writes his two paragraphs of love-philosophy. The most affecting part, the part that I think gives this meditation on love its emotional force in its context, is this:

> ...the call seldom produces the comer, the man to love rarely coincides with the hour for loving. Nature does not often say 'See!' to her poor creature at a time when seeing can lead to happy doing; or reply 'Here' to a body's cry of 'Where?' till the hide-and-seek has become an irksome, outworn game. (46)

This happens, Hardy writes, not just to Tess but to "millions" of people; the utopian longing for "the two halves of a perfect whole that confronted each other at the perfect moment" typically goes unsatisfied. To this reflection, which is not hard to credit, Hardy adds a further element, one that seems to resonate from something in his own experience, and one that he asserts is especially applicable to what is happening to Tess: one of the pair of lovers who would make up "a perfect whole" is absent when this sexual relationship is consummated:

> a missing counterpart wandered independently about the earth waiting in crass obtuseness until the late time came. [From this] maladroit delay sprang anxieties, disappointments, shocks, catastrophes, and passing-strange destinies. (46)

In Dewey's terms, I must "summon energy and pitch it at a responsive key in order to *take* in" what this scene is about (*AE* 60, Dewey's emphasis). Obviously it is very emotional. But it is also personal: as I hear this passage, there is an appeal to my own intimate experience of love and its unavoidable catastrophes. There is as well a broadening of scope to include all the "millions" of people in modern times who undergo some of these same shocks and disappointments. Their destinies are, as most readers must know, "passing-strange," all right: crazy things seem to happen in modern love relationships, but they are not interesting merely as stories about other people at other times. The stories are in the final sense ours: they are either our own or of others we have known well enough to learn of such things, or both.

But what if we simply resist this love-philosophy of Hardy? D. H. Lawrence no doubt did so in his critical re-write of *Tess*, his "Study of Thomas Hardy." That is a whole other way of experience. Although I will think critically about the great issues of love in *Tess*, I see no point to fighting this passage. The fact is, Hardy's language does affect me deeply. I could fight it off on principle but I do not have that need, as some readers seem to have.

To experience the sex scene itself, between Alec and Tess, I find that I first have to credit Hardy's powerful commentary. It has the effect of temporarily blotting out the sex that this un-seen scene is about. But only for a while. The quality of their love-making or (if this is a better term) sex-making is not specified. But I do not want to play dumb, as so many commentators have done: I can vividly imagine that they engage in sex, that his erect penis enters her vagina. These crude and insufficient words (or something like them) need to be thought. Who indeed could not imagine this at this point? Sex here is genital: that is a point now customarily ignored in comment on the novel. But it would seem that some image of genital contact must be imagined in experiencing this scene, unless it is simply barred by inhibition. The ratio of coercion to voluntary sexual surrender I cannot know. There is an unclear mixing of the crude fact that he penetrates her, combined with the complexities of her own motivation and of the author's comment. The qualities do not form into a "fusion," in Pepper's sense of the word. I can neither complete the scene nor let it pass, since so much of the book will turn upon it. Perhaps the problem can be stated: the scene is left with no overt details given, and yet it is deeply marked, so that its quality—if it is to have any—must be intuited with the retroactive use of any pertinent passages of the novel. We will have to do a great deal of careful listening to the rest of the book, especially the Alec-Tess interactions. This will call for a certain amount of patience and an aversion to categorizing or easily encapsulating the scene. Those would be ways to not-experience.

The novel provides a method for intuiting at least partially what this sex-making means to Tess and to Alec. It is the obvious method of just attending carefully whenever they speak about their relationship at later points in the novel. It is surprising that anyone would want not to engage in such an inquiry, but some have substituted an instant judgment of rape (or not), while others have declared that there is nothing there to intuit, simply because nothing is specified at this point. These are steps that would curtail the experience.

There are conditions for which an inquiry would have to allow. We will have to wean ourselves of any demand that Hardy provide sexually explicit details, for example; those may not even be what he thinks are important, nor, given his era and personality, what he could possibly write out. Thus, I find it necessary to avoid those approaches (many but not all of them by feminist readers) which direct a knowing disapproval upon Hardy's artistic decision not to provide Tess's thoughts and feelings in the very occurrence of this episode. I might retort that Hardy does not tell us what Alec's inner thoughts are either, and the author could as well be accused of dehumanizing the man as well as the woman. There is no aesthetic "law" requiring him to render either person's subjective process at this juncture. Even if there were, he would be justified in ignoring it in order to create the novel according to his own imaginative vision. "It is hardly possible," writes Dewey, "to overstate the relativity of technique" (*AE* 148). "Artists always have used and always will use all kinds of techniques." The artist is "born an experimenter." Listening to Dewey, I realize that in writing this scene, Hardy would almost have had to be experimental: "The artist is compelled to be an experimenter because he has to express an intensely individualized experience through means and materials that belong to the common and public world" (*AE* 148). This scene would have been almost impossible for an English author in 1891 to write about in sexually explicit terms. He could have used vague, sentimental, or melodramatic terms. But Hardy chose to experiment by leaving out the sexual description, and at the same time allowing it to feel as if it is happening, as if it is "there." This certainly affects the quality of the experience, and puts an unusual burden on the reader. But to say that Hardy fails to express the quality of sex in this scene simply on the grounds that he is inexplicit is only a way of needlessly short-circuiting the experience.

Despite the lack of representational phrasing, the scene does have one important implication that I have not yet mentioned. It is this: Tess, by having sex at this juncture with Alec, is in effect sabotaging her family's plan. I say "in effect" since I cannot discern her motives. But she is not using her sexuality in a clever way so as to draw Alec into marriage. The way this episode "was to be" could not include such planning. Neither is it a spontaneous occurrence of boy meeting girl and making love. There is a quality of haphazardness to it that is pitiable, as Hardy suggests: pitiable because in human, emotional, terms, this is an important event and the participants handle it as if it were not.

2. Tess as Body-Mind

The scene also has had a build-up, an experiential preparation, through the depiction of Tess's character, and of her interactions with Alec. We know by this point that a lot about Tess can be understood as an individual "Body-Mind"—to use Dewey's term, from his major work, *Experience and Nature* (*EN* 217). Fittingly enough for the present study of *Tess*, it is a key term in his chapter entitled "Nature, Life and Body-Mind." The term, however, has been largely ignored by Dewey scholars. Dewey's use of it has been defended by Thomas M. Alexander, in the context of a superb vindication of Dewey's philosophy,[11] and another Dewey scholar, Bruce Wilshire, has discussed the term as part of his case for a serious correction of Dewey's philosophy,[12] but the term itself has not caught on. Dewey fashioned it in order to overcome a semantic trap: "Our language is so permeated with consequences of theories which have divided the body and mind from each other, making separate existential realms out of them, that we lack words to designate the existential fact" (*EN* 217). Dewey himself had been forced to employ various "circumlocutions" to get around this difficulty, but at this point he makes a carefully phrased attempt to dispose of such "circuitous arrangements":

> …body-mind simply designates what actually takes place when a living body is implicated in situations of discourse, communication, and participation. In the hyphenated phrase body-mind, "body" designates the continued and conserved, the registered and cumulative operation of factors continuous with the rest of nature, inanimate as well as animate; while "mind" designates the characters and consequences which are differential, indicative of features which emerge when "body" is engaged in a wider, more complex and interdependent situation. (*EN* 217)

The many components of this "naming," with the varied problems that they might easily cause for the precise philosophical thinker, would perhaps account for the failure of Dewey scholars to take up the term "body-mind" and put it to use. Dewey does seem to have a rather elevated expectation of what it means to say that something "simply designates"! But I suspect that "body-mind" has also been ignored because of its frank positioning of "body-" first, and because of his understanding of the term "-mind" to include all those qualities that "emerge" when the body is involved in "a complex and interdependent" cultural situation. And Dewey, notwithstanding his studiously neutral phrasing in the passage quoted, later on in the chapter shows an unguarded admiration for the human body: there are "in actual existence," Dewey writes, "properties of sensitivity and of marvelously comprehensive and delicate participative response characterizing living bodies…" (223). Dewey's apparent priority of "body-" preceding "-mind" may be fitting for *Tess*, and perhaps for many novels, a genre in which the body is arguably of prime importance. It is not without reason that Elaine Scarry has said that Thomas Hardy's subject "is not the passage of persons through the world but the passage of embodied persons through the world, and he is, on this subject, without peer in the three centuries of the English novel."[13] Peter Brooks has made a similar claim:

> One might…maintain that it is Thomas Hardy who finally unveils the body in the English novel, most particularly in *Tess of the d'Urbervilles*, facing at last, in relative nakedness, the presence and power of Eros, and making the next step—to D. H. Lawrence—merely inevitable.[14]

But to focus first on the body in *Tess* is not to suggest that there is nothing else there: "body-mind" implies both terms, together in their unity, but separable for purposes of inquiry. Hardy ultimately imagined them that way. As the critic Elliot Gose put it 40 years ago, though Hardy "tends to make a dichotomy between mind and body, he always ties them together, always makes us aware that Tess cannot separate" the two.[15]

Let me first take up the quality of Tess's "-mind," which early in the novel is still in good functional relationship with her "body-". Later in this narrative it increasingly will not be. But her mind is strong to begin with, well capable of thinking feelingly about her family's habits, and verbalizing what she thinks. To her mother's ridiculous excuse for her father being out drinking, to "get up his strength" for a journey he will have to make at midnight, Tess retorts: "Get up his strength!...Oh my God! Go to a public house to get up his strength! And you as well agreed as he, mother!" This she says "impetuously" and with "tears welling to her eyes" (27). Her emotions are in alignment with her thinking. Later, that night, as she and her little brother drive the family horse and cart to deliver the bees her father should have taken care of, she elaborates a cosmic vision of existence. I consider it both her own vision and Thomas Hardy's. If the stars are "worlds," as she has previously told her younger brother, they also "sometimes seem to be like the apples on our stubbard-tree. Most of them splendid and sound—a few blighted" (35). Theirs is blighted. And to Abraham's question, supposing we had "pitched on a sound one?" her answer is critically exact. "Well, father wouldn't have coughed and creeped about as he does, and wouldn't have got too tipsy to go on this journey; and mother wouldn't have been always washing, and never getting finished" (36). This is Tess thinking. Her words, if they are allowed to linger in the reader's mind, must make the reader wonder whether the problem is that of being on the wrong planet, or of being in the wrong family, or rather (as Hardy has urged a few pages earlier), whether the institution of the family is itself like a badly constructed ship upon which the children are unprotected and trapped (28). It must eventually strike anyone that there is no cosmic necessity for a man to be habitually "tipsy," nor for a woman to have always to toil at housework.

An "experience blocker" could be imposed here by a reader who has predetermined that no 16 year-old girl/woman could have such refined thoughts. Such an assumption would go far beyond the empirical knowledge of that reader, and would fly in the face of innumerable instances of highly imaginative thinking by children even younger than Tess. Hardy, it should be noted, does not suggest that this discussion of blighted and sound worlds just pops out of nowhere: little Abraham precipitates the topic only after Tess has refused to talk about the family's fantasies of marrying her off to a fine d'Urberville gentleman. It is clear that Tess has talked with him about the concept of stars as worlds at an earlier time: "Did you say the stars were worlds, Tess?" (35). But until now, she has never told him that some worlds are "blighted." She may never have realized it until now. As in almost any creative thinking, part of the material is taken from prior learning and part is invented within the situation at hand.

One of Hardy's most perceptive modern readers, John Bayley—who is acutely skeptical about the validity of the strategies Hardy used in writing *Tess*— affirms that "The fantasy about the stars is not Hardy's [even if Hardy wrote the words]. It belongs to Tess."[16]

Inasmuch as Tess engages in critical, analytical and philosophical topics in these early chapters, her mind shows a capacity for traditionally masculine areas of discourse. I do not experience the "dilemma" found by Margaret Higonnet: "Hardy specifically encodes Tess's voice as feminine...Yet Hardy's effort to singularize his heroine also leads him to differentiate her voice from stereotypes of the feminine"[17].

Soon, Tess falls asleep and the horse is killed. Just prior to drifting off, she thinks carefully and critically about what her parents have dreamed up for her life:

> Then examining the mesh of events in her own life, she seemed to see the vanity of her father's pride; the gentlemanly suitor awaiting herself in her mother's fancy; to see him as a grimacing personage, laughing at her poverty, and her shrouded knightly ancestry. (36)

She does not simply fall asleep at this point; Hardy shows her falling into sleep within a process of an increasing sense of unreality, compounded of the fantastic night shapes passing her as she guides the horse and cart, and of the fantastic and degrading life her parents have imagined for her. She understands that she lives in poverty, and that a rich suitor might well laugh at her for this. Here her mind is operating at several levels. She is experiencing a sense of despair over her future, a sense that may contribute to her relinquishing of control over her horse at this point.

Tess thus is not just a young woman who has gone through the Sixth Standard of school. Her separation from her uneducated parents on this score is important; but beyond this bare fact, I can sense that she has also learned a lot, probably more through teaching herself than from the "Standards." She not only knows things that her parents do not, but she thinks for herself.

When I observe that Tess has a good, perceptive, critical mind, I imagine that I will immediately be misunderstood as claiming some form of outstanding intellect or even genius for her. But that is a mistake that anyone steeped in Deweyan thought is not likely to make. From Dewey's democratic understanding of human capabilities, we can say that there are a great many potentially fine minds in this world. It is possible to notice and honor an individual's mind without getting into a dualistic split, in which some people have most of the intelligence and others are mainly only bodies. I imagine that the unconscious prevalence of this dualistic assumption is partially the cause of there having been virtually no attention paid to Tess's excellence of mind in 110 years of comment on the novel, while there has been immense attention paid to her body. We do not need to claim genius for anyone in order to see that they think. Moreover, in a Deweyan perspective, each mind has its individual traits, as Tess has hers. For Dewey, intelligence is not merely qualities of ratiocination possessed by the few; the qualities of creative thinking are widely shared among virtually all people. One of the most moving statements Dewey ever made, it seems to me, is his two-page "Foreword," written late in his life, to a book entitled *The Unfolding of Artistic Activity: Its Basis, Processes and Implications*, by an art-teacher named Henry Schaefer-Simmern. In this Foreword, Dewey writes:

> The first of the principles [in this book] to which I would call attention is the emphasis upon individuality as the creative factor in life's experiences.... This creativity...is manifested not just in what are regarded as the fine arts, but in all forms of life that are not tied down to what is established by custom and convention.[18]

From this perspective, it still is amazing that Tess can think well despite the destructive family context which is her form of "custom and convention." But that can happen: anyone can recall similar examples from personal acquaintance. From a Deweyan perspective, it is not remarkable that Tess can think, and think well. Yet, coming from the family she does, her thinking is especially impressive.

3. Her Sexual Thinking and Awareness

But does she think about sex? Here I abandon the temporary attempt to understand Tess's mind without giving any attention to her body. The question I have asked will be unwelcome to any readers who take literally Hardy's early description of her as "a mere vessel of emotion untinctured by experience" (21). Reading this phrase in a Victorian manner, it can mean that sex never entered into her consciousness. And she does say to her mother, after returning home from her stay with Alec, that she should have been warned about the ways of men. But this speech is uttered in the context of getting her mother off of her back; "the agonised girl" says "How could I be expected to know? I was a child when I left this house four months ago. Why didn't you tell me there was danger in men-folk? Why didn't you warn me?" (87). Tess says she "never had the chance o' learning" how to guard against men by reading novels the way ladies do.

No doubt Tess has no sophisticated method for fending off the many advances of someone like Alec. She does have chances to state a firm "NO" to Alec, and on those occasions when she does so, he accedes. One of the most marked patterns throughout the novel's meetings of Tess and Alec is that such No-sayings by Tess are followed with her saying or acting as if she does not intend that NO to stand. With at least some of her body-mind, she does want to be involved with Alec, and, by the time Alec kneels down and places his cheek next to hers in the woods, Tess has thought about sex.

She could have been thinking of it not long before the sex-scene with Alec when she declined to take part in a hay-trusser's dance, a scene that Hardy vividly, unforgettably creates. Tess "did not abhor dancing, but she was not going to dance here" (67). Why not? In my more naïve readings of this novel, I had been taken with the imaginative, sensual quality of Hardy's prose as he depicts this dance.

> Through this floating, fusty *débris* of peat and hay, mixed with the perspirations and warmth of the dancers, and forming together a sort of vegeto-human pollen, the muted fiddles feebly pushed their notes, in marked contrast to the spirit in which the measure was trodden out. (66)

To even imagine "vegeto-human pollen" is something of an accomplishment. Or so I had thought. The passage offered a striking affirmation, somewhat qualified but very powerful, of primal sexuality. But what I was doing was limiting my own experience by responding to the language as if this were a set-piece by Hardy, only tangentially related to Tess. From that perspective, I could marvel at Hardy's ability to show, in these lowly farm-workers, a vital outpouring of mythic, Dionysian sexuality, of "a multiplicity of Pans whirling a multiplicity of Syrinxes; Lotis attempting to elude Priapus, and always failing" (67). But in the "perceptive series" of my re-readings, I have come to experience the passage differently. I began to credit the sour notes: that the dancers have been drinking not just a good deal of beer, but "the curious compounds sold to them as beer by the monopolizers of the once independent inns" (65); that the dance takes place in "a windowless erection used for storage" (66); that the dancers "coughed as they danced, and laughed as they coughed" (66); that Tess is approached by a young man who "expostulated between his coughs" (67), urging her not to hurry from this scene even though she would like to be on her way. And, most tellingly, just after the dancers have come into a state of "ecstasy, and the dream began, in which emotion was the matter of the universe, and matter but an adventitious intrusion likely to hinder you from spinning where you want to spin"—it is just then that these dancers fall all over each other, to become an indiscriminate "twitching entanglement of arms and legs..." (67-8).

Hardy next alludes to the waning of affection in the married couples who are dancing: the pile-up of bodies is not "unusual...as long as any affection remained between wedded couples..." (68), which is to suggest that not very much affection actually does remain, and that at some not very distant point, perhaps there will be none. Tess, who stands aside as she witnesses this scene, does not want to be a part of it. When I learned to ask myself, what would I wish for Tess, here?—Tess, whom I've already come to like and admire—I have to say that she is making the right choice by getting away from it. My feeling is: she does not belong here. The irrepressible force of mythic, joyous sexuality, even though it is present, is ridden over and devalued in this declining rural culture. Joyous sexuality has become a mess; this is a culture in which once-vital folk habits have deteriorated into routines that preserve insensitivity. The scene, as one critic who keenly appreciated its evocation of a myth of primal sexuality observed, has "a nightmare quality".[19] If Tess were to move in the direction of these drunken dancers, she would be wasting herself.

Tess may or may not realize this, but I think it fair to say that she intuits it, however imprecisely. It is a way of her thinking about mating, if not directly about sex. And the scene might bring to her mind disgusting echoes of her own parents' marital union, undermined and supported with booze.

A much more pointed example of her sexual thinking occurs soon after. This comes in the scene in which she is confronted by Car Darch, a woman who had been Alec's lover. Car Darch is jealous of Tess, because Alec is now known to be after her. Acting from "a long-smoldering sense of rivalry [which] enflamed her to madness," Car Darch taunts Tess, calling her "first favourite with He [Alec] just now!" Car Darch bares her "plump neck, shoulders and arms to the moonshine, under which they looked as luminous and beautiful as some Praxitelean creation, in their possession of the faultless rotundities of a lusty country girl." She is getting set for a physical fight with Tess, and is making a sexual display of physical superiority. Tess taunts back: "if I had known you was of that sort, I wouldn't have so let myself down as to come with such whorage as this is!" (70).

Whorage is a most sexual term. Is it uttered only in response to the prominently displayed upper torso with the woman's breasts? Or, can we suppose that Tess realizes Car Darch had been Alec's lover, and that this constitutes what is commonly called "whorage"? Most comment on this scene has ignored the word. There is a possibility that the term has no sexual meaning, according to an angry denial by Hardy's wife, written after the novel was published.[20] But the context, which is what I pay attention to when I want to experience any scene, is so loaded with sexual terms that it is impossible to read "whorage" with an a-sexual eye. Car Darch first calls Tess "hussy!," and taunts her with acting superior just because Tess is now Alec's favorite (70). The other women know what has been going on. And Tess, who is not a totally gentle person, bursts out with this word. The subject of sex is on her mind.

Tess uses this term just prior to her accepting Alec's rescue from the physically dangerous situation with Car Darch and the other working women. She thinks, by "the spring of a foot" she could "triumph over them..." She then "abandoned herself to her impulse, climbed the gate, put her toe on his instep, and scrambled into the saddle behind him" (71). The impulse does not strike me as simply a sexual one. There is something in the quality of the situation that marks her action as that of a girl enjoying a moment of triumph over the other girls. (The late Kristin Brady persuasively developed the logic of this girlish triumph, and of Alec's undermining of it.[21]) Hardy in this scene creates a memorable instance of young Tess being both girl and woman. But by now, Tess is too well aware of Alec to suppose that he represents a non-sexual rescuer. Earlier, she would have heard plenty of words like "whorage" directed at her from Alec himself, when he fulminates over her clever ruse in repulsing his advances on his gig: "Then d'Urberville cursed and swore at her, and called her everything he could think of for the trick" (59). Her abandoning "herself to impulse" can hardly be limited to triumphing over the other women: it is also an impulse toward Alec.

The same may be said of a passage occurring earlier, showing her climbing up onto Alec's "spick-and-span gig or dog-cart, highly varnished and equipped," when she could have taken the simpler cart that had been chosen for her moving to Trantridge. She shows "indecision," and "would have preferred the humble cart." But after taking a serious look at her family, who are watching her from a distance, she gets on Alec's cart. Why? Hardy suggests "possibly" it was out of guilt for having got the family's horse killed. But because Hardy himself does not claim to be sure of her motive, his statement suggests that we as his readers try to understand why she is doing this. So did she mount the gig in order to avoid displeasing her employer? At this point, she still is under the illusion that Alec is merely the son of the mistress of the estate, not the one in charge of it. She might assume that he has some authority, but he cannot be mistaken as her boss. Hardy's comment slightly buffers the fact of her impulse, but the impulse is rendered: "Something seemed to quicken her to a determination..." "She suddenly stepped up; he mounted beside her, and immediately whipped on the horse" (54-5). Tess chose to get on this cart with a man whom she knows has boldly flirted with her and touched her, in her prior visit to his estate. Can we say she does not know that he is after her? Given her serious look down the hill at the Durbeyfields, I get the impression that she is making a choice through this bold bodily act, to move toward him rather than reaffirming the bond with her family, which she could have chosen to do by taking the simpler, unaccompanied ride.

It is not a choice for being taken on a wild terrifying ride with Alec that follows immediately upon her stepping up, but it is a choice to move toward Alec.

Still, there was something about Alec, or rather about being sent to inveigle Alec, of which Tess seems not to have been aware. There are enough passages to show that she is told that her assignment is to use her sexual attractiveness to get Alec to marry her. But she acts as if this never occurred to her. My impression is that in her deepest feeling, she does not let herself know this. It is a degradation she will not even think about. But being drawn toward Alec, and intuiting the possible pleasure and freedom that this might bring, is something that is agreeable to her.

To experience Tess, I have to think about her motives. They are not transparent, but I have this hypothesis about her: maybe Tess wants to get away, and part of her inordinate guilt is a result of wanting to abandon her family. When Angel first appeared, in chapter 2, Tess had felt something indefinitely erotic. Hardy presents this most strongly as a contrast between that body-within-nature feeling of the introductory description of Tess, and the "unspeakable dreariness" of her family's life, rendered in its first impression as she enters the house. To move from "the holiday gaieties of the field--the white gowns, the nosegays, the willow-wands, *the whirling movements on the green, the flash of gentle sentiment towards the stranger*—to the yellow melancholy of this one-candled spectacle— what a step!" (25, my emphasis). Ostensibly, Tess feels guilty at having stayed out and enjoyed herself, but a wish is conveyed: that it would be *great* to get away from this family and out into a world of joyous life. Whose wish? I experience it as her wish, Hardy's wish, and my own wish for Tess.

Meeting Alec for the first time, and after he has called her "my beauty," "my pretty girl," and "my pretty Coz" (43-4), Tess is faced with the attempt by Alec to get her to open her mouth and accept a strawberry he has picked. I found this passage a shock, even after innumerable readings of the novel, when I came back to it after a lapse of time. It is a shock because it feels so sexual, something I still hadn't expected—or at least not immediately—happening almost upon Tess's arrival:

> ...presently, selecting a specially fine product of the 'British Queen' variety, he stood up and held it by the stem to her mouth.
>
> "No, no!" she said quickly, putting her fingers between his hand and her lips. "I would rather take it in my own hand."
>
> "Nonsense!" he insisted; and *in a slight distress she parted her lips and took it in*. (44, my emphasis)

She took it in; any doubt of her willingness is overshadowed by the fact that she did it, and/or she let him do it.

In a moment or two, Alec leads her into a tent, and begins smoking. As he sends up a "blue narcotic haze," he stares at her. Tess munches on the repast he has brought for her, and "innocently looked down at the roses in her bosom" (45). These are roses they both had picked, and he had put some of them on her hat. Alec, Hardy interposes, "stood fair to be the blood-red ray in the spectrum of her young life" (45). In itself, it is not a condemning comment, but a tribute to Alec's virility. Even Hardy's qualification of it: that Tess did not realize he was going to be the "'tragic mischief' of her drama" is less than condemning, with its choice of the light word, "mischief." I wonder momentarily why "tragic mischief" is in quotes; the Hardy editions do not explain, and I pass on. Her body has "a luxuriance of aspect, a fulness of growth, which made her appear more of a woman than she really was." Alec cannot help but stare at her breasts; his eyes "rivet themselves upon her" (45).[22] At this point, Hardy tells us that her fullness of sexual development had bothered her enough to have expressed her discomfort to her girlfriends: "her companions had said that it was a fault which time would cure" (45; what an uncomforting thought!). Hardy thus is letting me know that Tess is aware of her sexuality. It embarrasses her, but she knows she has it.

Returning from this early encounter with Alec to the Durbeyfield family home, Tess is greeted by even her mother's appreciation of her sexual appeal: "Her mother surveyed the girl up and down with arch approval" (47). For the mother, Tess would be "a fool" if she failed to follow up the impression she had made on the rich Alec. This is good thinking, if the mother is considering only what is habitually thought in her class, but in relation to Tess, it is cruel. Trying to shake off the family's romantic invasion of her life, Tess "coldly" denies that Alec is "a mighty handsome man!" Her father calls her "Tess, the little rogue!" (49). To her parents, she is a valuable sexual object.

Her mother soon tricks her out in an erotically appealing manner, to be sent to work at the d'Urberville estate. The outfit intensifies the effect already seen of Tess as a nubile girl with a highly developed sexual body: her mother

> put upon her the white frock that Tess had worn at the club-walking, the airy fullness of which, supplementing her enlarged *coiffure,* imparted to her developing figure an amplitude which belied her age, and might cause her to be estimated as a woman when she was not much more than a child. (52)

Tess sees that this dressing-up is wrong, and protests "But I am going to work!"—but then acquiesces "with calm abandonment." She is aware of what they are doing with her. Tess knows that she is being presented as a sexual attraction; that it is not just "work." Yet she does not seem to get the point of why she is being used. Then, when her mother insists that this mode of dress is best, Tess rather passively lets her mother go ahead and dress her this way—with the work frankly admitted as just a "a little pretence" that will be necessary at first. Clearly Tess is not responsible for inventing this scheme. I do experience contempt for Tess's mother, who is oblivious to the enormity of selling her daughter. Yes, *selling*, in the sense of making a very good deal, in peasant terms, and without the slightest concern for Tess's individual needs; this is selling. This anger is fueled in me partly by Joan's own realization that Tess "is such an odd maid" that she very well might not want to go at all (53). I find myself thinking: If she is so "odd," why not allow her some self-direction? And it is very sad that Tess as she leaves is silenced: her "eyes were too full and her voice too choked to utter the sentiments that were in her" (53). I am able to sort out two strands of my feeling: Tess is a young sexual woman whose character I find very precious—and Tess is being sold off, which is rotten. There is no diminution in my understanding of Tess as sexual from my empathic realization that she is being hurt. There is also a third strand: something of an identification with Tess as I come to believe that she is partly re-shaping the mission upon which her parents have sent her, bending it toward her own desires.

These feelings of mine seem to be called out by the text of the novel: my feelings are inextricably both subjective and objective. Other readers will not have just these feelings, but to experience the book even in its first "Phase," some feelings concerning sex and this young woman would have to be felt. To deny this requirement is to not experience this book.

Unless a reader is determined to resist, however, there is little chance of such a failure: there simply are too many ways into the sexual themes. Several basically sexual strands of the experience are interwoven in this part of the novel: Alec's manipulative moves to help him seduce Tess, her mother's selling her off, and her own intrinsic sexuality. Her ambivalence about wanting Alec is just that: a short while prior to their having sex, she is distressed to the point of tears by "The sudden vision of his passion for herself in this result," the "result" being, her obligation to him for gifts he has made to her family, and maybe also the couple's arrival at a spot in the forest where they are lost (75). But she has this upsetting vision at just the point where she does *not* reply in the negative to his question, "Tessy—don't you love me ever so little now?" She replies "...But I fear I do not—" (75-6). She fears she does not love him, and says no more, breaking off into tears—but the expression leaves open the possibility that she might believe that she loves him, even that she hopes she does. How could she even know, at this point?

Hardy is at pains to leave that possibility open; many readers however have closed it, perhaps because it is too painful or too confusing to contemplate. When Tess leaves Alec, she has one of her opportunities to tell him why she is rejecting him. She has stayed for several weeks since the night in the woods. That night according to Alec was nearly 3 months after her arrival, and her departure comes at four months, on a Sunday morning in late October (81). Here we can inquire into the quality of that un-rendered sex scene. If rape were any part of her reason for leaving, she would allude to it or mention it outright. Nothing of the sort is said. Instead *she refers to their relationship in terms that are situational—as she*

*continues to do on virtually every occasion when the topic of their relationship
returns in the rest of the novel.* And again, she implies that she had either loved
him or had thought that she did.

In their exchange, Alec challenges her to say why she came to Trantridge "if
you didn't wish to..." When she does not reply, he goes on, resentfully:

> "You didn't come for love of me, that I'll swear."
> "'Tis quite true, If I had gone for love o' you, *if I had ever sincerely
> loved you, if I loved you still*, I should not so loathe and hate myself for my
> weakness as I do now!...My eyes were dazed by you for a little, and that
> was all." (82-3, my emphasis, ellipsis is Hardy's)

I take seriously her distinction between loving a man and "sincerely" loving him.
Human beings can have such doubts in their sexual relations, and Tess is quite
young. She must have been going through a confusing but potentially clarifying
thought process to have been able to say these things. And she is not entirely
bewildered: after all, she has decided to leave. But her words insure the
impression that her weeks at Alec's place, following the night they first had sex,
were also weeks in which they had sex—or, should I say, they made love? I
would suppose that the process of understanding whether or not she loved him,
sincerely, was going on through this period of love-makings. This would also be a
form of inquiry, a most personal one. It would have been an inquiry infused with
the hope that the negative feelings involved in her sexual initiation with this man
could be overcome: that it was not her fate to have been just had, and to have
been had without any sense of clear choice on her own part. She must also have
thought in these weeks about her parents' assignment of marrying him, although
this is not as clear.[23]

Some of the time she must have got sexual pleasure, perhaps even great
pleasure. Hardy in his commentary is very reluctant to admit anything like this,
but he nonetheless does, when he states, (in a circuitous sentence that seems to
me to show the author's anxiety) that she was "stirred" to "surrender" (87).
Maybe Hardy is trying to hide something here.

> She had dreaded him, winced before him, succumbed to adroit advantages
> he took of her helplessness; then, temporarily blinded by his ardent
> manners, *had been stirred to confused surrender awhile*: had suddenly
> despised and disliked him, and had run away. (87, my emphasis)

I know of readers who become contemptuous or even outraged at Hardy's
inability to clearly admit Tess's sexual responsiveness, but I think they cheat
themselves—they construct an "experience blocker"—by staying within this kind
of response. For me, the troublesomeness of the sentence is more than worth the
effort, and I come away finally being grateful to Hardy for his courage in saying it

at all in 1892, in the first one-volume edition of *Tess*. In 1891, in the original serial printing, it was still unsaid. Certainly Hardy was not backing away at this juncture from the sexual implications of his novel, as has been alleged. Nor was he implying coercion: it would be absurd for him to suggest that a woman who had been raped or otherwise assaulted had been carried away with Alec's "ardent manners."

When Alec merely shrugs at her explanations of why she came and why she stayed, Tess adds, "I didn't understand your meaning till it was too late" (83). Tess flares into anger when Alec refuses to believe this. I sympathize with Tess here, but considering all that has been rendered and implied thus far, I cannot fully believe her statement. She must have understood that Alec was after her; indeed on their ride away from the hay-trussers' dance, and toward the woods, he has complained to her that she has eluded and "snubbed" him for nearly 3 months, and calls her a "mere chit" (74). She knew what he wanted. I rather doubt, though, that she took his meaning to be that he would come down upon her as she slept in the woods at night, and have sex with her, after he had promised to escort her directly home. My feelings are mixed about what Tess knew: yet I do feel glad that she is leaving him. The emotional quality of her statement about not knowing his meaning feels right. I can also imagine that she is not denying that she had known Alec was after her, but that she had not realized he would be content to go on with a sexual relationship in which her love for him does not develop. I also ask myself if I feel as I do because I have been too frightened or too moralistic to have accepted the value of her relation with Alec. But after as close a self-scrutiny as I can give this question, it does not feel that way. Feeling my way back over what I have experienced so far, I find that I have been uncomfortable with what has been going on. Something just "feels wrong" about the situation. And, I suggest that other readers who try to consider all the factors in the situation will have a similar feeling. What comes through strongly is my admiration for Tess's firm decision to leave. I want her to do what she needs to do.

For a moment it seems that the emotional core of this departure scene will be felt as Tess's outburst of anger at Alec. But the anger is followed by apparent affectlessness as she permits Alec to kiss her: "Her eyes rested vaguely upon the remotest trees in the lane while the kiss was given, as though she were nearly unconscious of what he did" (84). Her cheeks as he kissed them felt "damp and smoothly chill as the skin of the mushrooms in the fields around" (84). That is hardly a feeling of sensual pleasure. Moreover even in their lovemaking, there is reason to believe that she had held something back. Alec says: "You don't give me your mouth and kiss me back. *You never willingly do that—you'll never love me, I fear*" (84, my emphasis). He has not been fully satisfied. If she does not "give" him her mouth, that excludes a major erotic area of her body from their lovemaking. The complaint gains unusual force for the reader because of the emphasis on Tess's mouth that Hardy had created almost as soon as he had introduced her into the novel. And it does seem to matter to Alec whether or not Tess loves him. He obviously does not mean that she should leave because she does not love him, but neither does it suggest that he is unconcerned about it. Tess here begins her complex reply, which I have already considered, in part. She had "often" said that she did not love him—which tells me that they had discussed this matter on several occasions. Yet with all its ambivalences, her statement ends with a flat declaration of not loving him: "But I don't" (84).

The immediate sequel of Tess's parting is her encounter with the "tex'-painter" who is busy condemning sinners. Hardy, blending with Tess, calls such graffiti a "hideous defacement," a leftover from an outworn Christianity. Nonetheless: "But the words entered Tess with accusatory horror." In the next few paragraphs, Tess twice tries with her mind to fight off the accusations: "I think they are horrible!...Crushing, killing!" (85). And when the painter begins to inscribe (with each word emphasized by a comma) the 7th commandment, Thou Shalt Not Commit Adultery, she summons critical resistance: "'Pooh—I don't believe God said such things!' she murmured contemptuously, when her flush had died away" (85-86). She is thinking critically about God. (Yet she is flushed.) But this thinking she cannot hold on to: the self-loathing she had spoken of to Alec returns, now without any argument with anyone else to spur it on: "her present feeling for this man," for Alec, "was what made her detest herself" (87; does the word "de-test" suggest "de-Tess"? She would be taking away her self from her self). For her the present feeling is what is important. She does not trouble to deny her mother's complaint, that while living with Alec, Tess was "thinking only of yourself" (87). In a way this is not true, since Tess surely was thinking also of her family's welfare. But insofar as she had instinctively refused to touch the family's assignment of trying to get Alec to marry her, and insofar as she was exploring, for several weeks after the night in the Chase, the nature and value of her sexual relationship with him, Joan has a point.

For me, the reader, the point is not an accusation. I think Tess had every right to do what she did. It is her body, her life. My own values undeniably are at work in this thinking. But I believe that these are also what the novel itself values at this point. In a later "Phase" of the novel, I think Hardy waivers, as I shall try to explain in chapter 5. But here, there is only implied approval for Tess's failure to carry out the mission her parents had designed for her, and implied acceptance of her staying on with Alec in what must have been a period of experimentation in sexual love.

For Tess herself, though, the question of self-evaluation is acute. Tess's mind, to the large extent that she is subject to a feeling of sinfulness and unworthiness, is now in the process of being functionally split off from her body. Her mind often becomes an accuser, an outsider, rather than operating as her own organ of intelligence. The reasons for this appear to be strictly social: these are her Christian society's teachings about sex. But one strand of her feeling is so personal and integral that it cannot be ascribed simply to indoctrination. Tess has come to detest herself for having had, and continuing to have had for some weeks, a sexual relation with a man whom she now finds that she does not love. During these weeks, I infer that she had been exploring the meaning for her self of this relationship. And now she has found that she does not love him. I know that somewhere in the great historic cultural background of her decision to leave is the notion that sex without love, especially when it is sex between social unequals, is shameful. But that standard is a very remote aspect of the scene, so far as I can experience it. Her leaving does not feel to me as if it were merely a reflection of society's teachings. It is her own revulsion. I experience it as an expression of her integrity, as she herself defines it. She knows that if she stayed on any further, she would descend to being a possession, not a person, or rather, not a "creature" but *his* creature: "I *should* be your creature to go on doing that, and I won't!" (83, emphasis in the text). It would also be natural for her to have "suddenly despised and disliked" (87) Alec once she realizes that he wants her to continue having sex with him even after she has found that there is no love.

4. Struggling for Life

Tess's mind is still highly capable of perceptive thought. There is a striking scene in church, where she thinks on the power of music.

> She thought, without exactly wording the thought, how strange and godlike was a composer's power, who from the grave could lead through sequences of emotion, which he alone had felt at first, a girl like her who had never heard of his name, and never would have a clue to his personality. (90)

Hardy's thinking blends with Tess's, in this and many other points. But he is clear on why music could affect her so: the love of melody, inherited from her mother, gave even "the simplest music a power over her which could well-nigh drag her heart out of her bosom at times" (90). I take it that the thoughts she did "not exactly word" about music are made possible by this exceptional power to allow her positive emotions to happen, at a time of her life when she is feeling dismal. In experiencing music, her body-mind unity is temporarily restored. But the whispering gossips in the Church soon discourage her from going there.

Her mind is only swept into fierce perceptual action, capable of rejecting its use as an accuser against her self, when her baby dies and she has to arrange for his burial, in the face of opposition from the churchman who does not dare to insult convention by giving burial to a bastard. For many readings, I have enjoyed and even exulted in Tess's sharp retorts to the social-religious pathology which would deny this kid, whom she names Sorrow, a simple rite of burial. And I have been moved by her simple solemn rite of baptism of her dead infant, performed in the presence of her younger brothers and sisters.

On re-reading this time, I realize that anger and awe have never been the only emotions. Tess's appeal to the churchman strikes a note of her own ethical code—one that is Thomas Hardy's too, I should think. After threatening to "never come to your church no more!," Tess moves on to make a plea that he tell her that her baby will not be singled out for hurt in its after-life, just because of its lack of a proper burial. "Will it be just the same? *Don't for God's sake speak as saint to sinner, but as you yourself to me myself--poor me!"* (101, my emphasis). The principle she appeals to is the inalienable humanity of one person in relation to another.

Tess here is drawing on her own thought on the ethics of human relationship. No doubt this is Hardy's thought as well: to distinguish the two here is not worth doing. What she is offering is not simply a tearful plea, nor a self-explanatory general standard for relating person-to-person. It is a combination of her felt reference to the human social situation, in which she is a "poor me," with the basic principle of relating in compassion, and without the barrier of a moral code. The phrase "poor me" can be brushed aside as merely self-pity, but I feel no need to do that. In this context, it acquires meaning. Her statement includes a critical element as well: one cannot judge another under the accepted sacred categories of "saint and sinner." To do so would disallow the relation of "you yourself to me myself." The accepted ethic must be set aside.

I thus find a considerable ethical intelligence at work in her statement. And I feel prepared for her further exercise of this faculty later in the novel.

The sorrow felt in this section is part of a process of emotional recovery by Tess, but one with intellectual sparks. Mind works with body. Her body is integral to her feeling, throughout this section. Prior to her son Sorrow's illness and death, "Tess had drifted into a frame of mind which accepted passively the consideration that, if she should have to burn for what she had done, burn she must, and there was an end of it" (97) But when the little boy is dying, such passivity is gone: "In her misery, she rocked herself on the bed." She imagines, luridly, the torments of her child in hell. "The lurid presentment so forcefully affected her imagination in the silence of the sleeping house that her night-gown became damp with perspiration, and the bedstead shook with each throb of her heart" (98). She cries, and begs God to at least "pity the child!" Then, "She leant against the chest of drawers, and murmured incoherent supplications for a long while, till she suddenly started up. 'Ah, perhaps baby can be saved! Perhaps it will be just the same!'" (98). This sequence shows how her body feelings energize her mind, as her mind also affects her body. Because the situation is so deeply felt, so *bodily felt* and expressed, the ideas flow. It is a scene of emotional recovery even in acceptance of her child's death. There is emotional wholeness for Tess at this point, despite her deep personal wounds.

Hardy seems to go through an analogous experience in his commentary within this chapter. He seems to be giving his all, using much of his entire repertoire of aptitudes: verbal, perceptual, analytical, and mythic. At the beginning of the chapter, taking temporarily the role of impersonal author, he creates with great care and precision the scene of the August harvest, although he first infuses it with his fondest speculations on the benefits of ancient "heliolatries": "One could feel that a saner religion had never prevailed under the sky" (92). Then, immediately after his presenting the colloquial speech of Tess's fellow workers on the matter of Tess having been raped (95), Hardy (without commenting on that question) moves into his personal voice for three substantial paragraphs devoted to understanding Tess's existence at the deepest levels he can imagine.

This passage begins ostensibly with a naive rhetorical trope, saying that it "was impossible for even an enemy" not to feel "a thousand pities" for Tess as she sat nursing her infant. But the sentence then *segues* into a description of looking upon Tess that is much too verbally woven with love and admiration to be contained within the single emotion of pity:

> It was a thousand pities, indeed; it was impossible for even an enemy to feel
> otherwise on looking at Tess as she sat there, with her flower-like mouth
> and large tender eyes, neither black nor blue nor grey nor violet; rather all of
> those shades together, and a hundred others, which could be seen if one
> looked at their irises—shade behind shade—tint beyond tint— around pupils
> that had no bottom; an almost standard woman, but for the slight
> incautiousness of character inherited from her race. (95-6)

I sense that the calm simulation of wisdom toward the end of this sentence is one of Hardy's characteristic blurrings of an emotional revelation that he would not wish to allow to stand unprotected. What he seems to be stipulating in that concluding or occluding clause is that Tess is not very special, she is "almost standard" (not "almost typical" as he had written in the 1891 first edition—a less provocative word-choice, but also less interesting). But this is absurd: such an intimate close-up description of the bottomless irises of so many hues could hardly be imagined as typical of all women. And the uncertain reference to an "incautiousness of character inherited from her race" remains indefinite. It may be one of Hardy's mystifying references to the d'Urberville family, but I cannot be sure. In fact, I have not developed much care for that part of the sentence, simply because no context ever seems to be given for understanding what Hardy might be talking about when he refers to an "almost standard woman." He seems to forget about it. The term has called forth some understandably suspicious attention from feminist readers, and for some of them, it seems to become the most riveting part of the sentence. But not being pre-occupied with the term, I find that the intensity of the sentence—its emotional core—lies in the description of Tess's "large tender eyes." Hardy is expressing an insistence that Tess's nature is so varied, in its bodily presentation through the hues of her irises, that it can never be plumbed to its essence, its "bottom." He also seems to be expressing some of his own experience of being overwhelmed by Tess as a woman. At the level of his own psyche, this may be his response to his feelings about women in their free nature. Though he seems overwhelmed, he is not threatened; he sounds very nearly ecstatic.

This lovingly fashioned sentence occupies a paragraph in itself. I recall, as I do at several points in reading this novel freshly, Dewey's unparalleled statement on artistic skill: "Craftsmanship to be artistic in the final sense must be 'loving'; it must care deeply for the subject-matter upon which skill is excerized" (*AE* 54).

Hardy now moves to an imagined reconstruction of Tess's process of reasoning toward change, as she determines to stop hiding and get out into the fields "this week for the first time during many months." Although her decision to make that change had "surprised herself," there has been a great deal of felt thought behind it. Her wasting away of her "palpitating heart" had taken place under the aegis of "lonely inexperience" (96). Her guilt feelings have unopposed scope when she keeps herself cut off from fresh experience. But her move toward expanding her life comes thus: "common-sense had illumined her" (96). *Illumined* is a vivid word choice: what is common can sometimes do wonders for the mind. The conclusion of common sense occurs to her on two levels: "She felt that she would do well to be useful again—to taste anew sweet independence at any price." The first part of this sentence is readily understandable as something her social background would suggest; the second however is a generalization on human need that has an undeniable appeal for me, set as it is in the context of a phase of experience when that independence has been denied. It is a common appeal, nothing elaborate, but one that gives the passage a good chance of having emotional importance for its readers. Who in fact has not experienced setbacks in which one's independence is badly compromised?—and then tasted the joy of recovering it? This must be one of the most common experiences supporting Dewey's concept of a rhythm in which we continually lose and then regain a sense of "active equilibrium" (*EN* 194). This feeling of the regained sweetness of independence is at the same time specific to Tess, and I imagine to Hardy as well: the two seem to me inseparable at this juncture. Dwelling for a moment on Tess's wish for independence, I also recall my sense of her wanting to get away from her family, desiring to move toward Alec—even at "any price."

Tess realizes (and/or Hardy muses) that "whatever [the] consequences" of her past experience, they need be accorded no prohibitive respect, because in the longer view of time passing, all her experiences will be "grassed down and forgotten," just as she will be. Yet this is not a morbid thought, not in this context. The ability to think of her social condemnation as *just a part of her life*, and of her life as a temporary existence, insignificant in the implacable movement of time, helps to free her. Moreover, as Hardy goes on to say, she knows that the sensory delights of Nature are as vibrant as ever: time cannot erase them from consciousness. Her grief, her pain, had done nothing to diminish them. "[T]he trees were just as green as before; the birds sang and the sun shone as clearly now as ever" (96). They still beckon to be enjoyed. I find that through shifts in my own attitude, I can avoid or enhance the experience of these comments. If I detach myself from the woman's predicament, then Hardy is only uttering a few truisms. But when I let myself feel what is at stake for Tess, I can take pleasure in their pragmatic functions of survival and rebirth.

The longer third paragraph of this commentary to some extent repeats the main ideas; it seems to engrave them more securely in my perception. But it also takes new ground. This time, Hardy separates himself from Tess sufficiently to use the format of what "she might have seen," but without claiming that she literally had these new thoughts. The new phase of comment is an imaginary venture into an impossible condition: *if* Tess were to find herself alone, "just created," on a desert island, would she have been "as wretched," would her condition as "spouseless mother" really "have caused her to despair?" (96). The answer seems to be a set-up: of course not, these troubles are caused by a repressive society, not by her. But Hardy's language is carefully qualified: "Not greatly." "Most of the misery had been generated by her conventional aspect"-- most, but apparently not all of it. And "her conventional aspect" is part of herself, even if it originates in society's sexual norms rather than in "her innate sensations."

Yet that daring final term of the paragraph, "her innate sensations," focuses attention back on the experimental thinking that Hardy has undertaken. A few sentences earlier he has built the striking series: "She was not an existence, an experience, a passion, *a structure of sensations*, to anybody but herself" (96, my emphasis). He is asking an almost prohibited question: what is a person like, what is a woman's bodily self, considered without the occluding and superficial judgments of her society? This is a question worth asking, not because any definitive answer can be had, but because it serves to reduce drastically, in thought, the encrustations of social judgment in a field where society has no business: in dictating what a woman may be, namely in her sexual behavior. That is because fundamentally society has no sensitivity for seeing the individual person. It cannot consider the woman in anything like the complexity and vulnerability that she is. Tess, Hardy writes, "was just a passing thought" to "all humankind," and even to her friends, "she was no more than a frequently passing thought" (96). Here I recall her obtuse parents, who gave so little thought to her.

Hardy's extensive commentary may be skipped over lightly, but if it is allowed to provoke responses in the reader, I can testify that it is potent. This is partly due to the *obligato* of bodily experience that sounds through it: her mouth, her eyes, her grief, her pain; "what had bowed her head so profoundly"; "she had made herself miserable the livelong night and day." The "pleasures" she would have found in her lone existence on the desert island would have been the pleasures of her body-mind. The passage in its existential concern also seems undeniably excessive for purposes of the narrative. If it were removed, would anyone know that something is missing? The experience of these paragraphs, combined with the story of Tess's baby and its burial, tends to expand far beyond the boundaries of this chapter. What is its context? That is not an easy question, even though it is a needed one. Here I must revert to Pepper's theme that in "contextualism," (or pragmatism), there is always "the *spread* of an event," its felt temporal qualities which cannot be expressed in terms of "a linear scheme" of time.[24] For the most part, we have the "spread" of our events without considering that there is anything out of the ordinary going on. But in this long commentary by Hardy, the spread is extraordinary; we are invited to "*take* in" (*AE* 60, Dewey's emphasis) more than we can at the point of reading. Reverberations from this passage can be felt all through the situation of the novel, both in later passages and those already read. Beyond any of the pages of the novel, these passages of Hardy's thinking may suggest the challenge to any one of his readers of trying to imagine what they really would be like, if they could somehow throw off society's voices of convention which try to exert control over their sexual bodies. To think of your "innate sensations," to think of yourself as "a structure of sensations," is a way of trying to allow your own sense of bodily experience to define yourself. That would be part of the "art-centered experience."[25]

Three

TOWARD RECOVERY

Tess in the next chapter becomes ready to leave home again. Unfortunately, the recovery of self in the context of her baby's death is not quite the equivalent of a recovery of herself for herself. That will be tougher. In fact, Hardy's extended meditation on Tess's recovery, which I have found to be both intelligent and moving, is misleading in one major respect: Tess, as both she and Hardy well know, is not simply "a spouseless mother, with no experience of life except as the parent of a nameless child..." (96). She has had sexual experience. She will have to deal with that. She is not one who has been "just created." Nonetheless this chapter marks the beginning of a surge of hopeful feeling in the novel that is almost impossible not to experience.

First Tess does a lot of thinking. We are invited to delve more directly into Tess's mind than we had been in the earlier chapters. She is thinking "philosophically" (102) about the events of her life-experience: her "undoing" with Alec, the dates of her baby's birth and death, "also her own birthday; and every other day individualized by incidents in which she had taken some share." Her re-awakening to life begins with an insight about her body: "She suddenly thought one afternoon, when looking in the glass at her fairness, that there was yet another date, of greater importance to her than those, the date of her own death, when all of these charms would have disappeared..."(102). Read with an automatic deference to Hardy's pessimism, we may assume she is envisioning death as her own desire. But read responsively in its context in this chapter, the passage has her sharply realizing that she does not want to waste the rest of her life. She—or is it Hardy—is asking: "Why did she not feel the chill of each yearly encounter with such a cold relation?" (102). That is, why does she not feel the chill of her eventual death? She is becoming much more aware that her life will one day end, but does not seem to have any morbid feeling about this. She is still too healthy: her direction is toward life, not death.

Her growth, which is both intellectual and emotional, is described with pleasure by Hardy, and it is of a piece with her bodily fullness:

> Almost at a leap Tess thus changed from simple girl to complex woman. Symbols of reflectiveness passed into her face, and a note of tragedy at times into her voice. Her eyes grew larger and more eloquent. She became what would have been called a fine creature; her aspect was fair and

arresting; her soul that of a woman whom the turbulent experiences of the last year or two had quite failed to demoralize. (103)

Here I will pause to ask, what does Hardy suggest by referring to Tess's "soul"? Is it something aside from the "body-mind"? It sounds to me, as I re-read the passage that Hardy implies "the idiomatic, non-doctrinal use of the word soul" that Dewey endorses in *Experience and Nature*:

> To say emphatically of a particular person that he has soul or a great soul is not to utter a platitude....It expresses the conviction that the man or woman in question has in marked degree qualities of sensitive, rich and coordinated participation in all the situations of life. (*EN* 223)

To use "soul" in this way is not to suggest a contrast with "body." It is to draw attention to "properties of sensitivity and of a marvelously comprehensive and delicate participative response characterizing living bodies" (*EN* 223).

Hardy comments, just at this point: he shifts the focus away from Tess in a move to a daring generalization: "But for the world's opinion those experiences would have been simply a liberal education" (103). The tone of this at first feels comforting, but as the novel has already shown, and as it will continue to show, the force of "the world's opinion" is so overbearing on Tess's life that the notion of her experiences being taken as no more than benignly educational feels bitterly ironic. Yet there is not exactly an effect of intrusion here: as is so often the case in this narrative, Hardy is showing a personal need to respond to his character's life situation. This roughens the "texture" of the narrative, but it also gives it some of its special quality.

Tess's well-warranted conclusion is that she "could never be really comfortable again" in her home village, and must leave (103). Her thinking here is both probing and naïve. "Was once lost always lost really true of chastity? she would ask herself. She might prove it false if she could veil bygones" (103). She is searching for a new definition of chastity, one that is not dependent on virginity. To achieve that would be a creative act of imagination. But even at this point in the narrative, without our knowing how the story will develop, her notion of trying to "veil bygones" sounds like a method that can never work. The question of chastity being regained has to remain unanswered at this juncture. She does have to leave: not only has her mind arrived at the imperative reasons for doing so, but her body is enforcing the decision. The "germination" of a new springtime "was almost audible in the buds: it moved her as it moved the wild animals, and made her passionate to go" (103).

Here Hardy clearly places Tess's recovery in the context of animal life within Nature. This is an important placement, but critics of this novel seem to have over-reacted to this aspect of Tess's character. You would imagine from reading the extant criticism that there are dozens of such references in the text.

Nature, especially "wild" Nature, has an attraction for many readers, even though the response to it may be one of alarm or disapproval. Although interpretations differ and sometimes erupt in protest, the experience almost unavoidably is centered in Nature; Tess's passionate movement here is in the context of bud growth and animal excitation.

The second "Phase" of the narrative ends with Tess's mind actively pushing her toward a full recovery. Even her realization that the d'Urberville ancestors are irrelevant to her own life does not deter her: she still hopes that by heading in the direction of their "former estates," "any strange good thing might come of her being in her ancestral land..." (104). She feels her youth, "surging up anew," and "bringing with it hope, and the invincible instinct towards self-delight" (104). Hardy is now able to ground her motivation for starting out again, in *instinctive pleasure-seeking, in the extended emotional sense of hope for fulfillment of a person's life*. This is Dewey's notion of growth, or one of its forms. In context, it is clear that Hardy does not regard Tess as a mere female bearer of instinct: Tess's hope would not have been possible without her having thought her situation through, and that would not have been possible without her having fully experienced her baby's death and disputed burial. Yet the instinctive pull toward "self-delight" cannot be denied. The appeal I find here is not simply in its explanation of Tess, but in Hardy's ability to connect with my own instinctive need for an unthwarted life—which I still feel, no matter how thoroughly I have learned that obstacles will always exist. It is a most common need, and in Dewey's view, its commonness can well be a merit, not a slur. "The more deep-seated...in the doings and undergoing that form experience, the more general or common" are those "impulsions or needs" (*AE* 290-91). This need for free development is deep-seated. Hardy in *Tess* writes *of* it, and also *for* it.

1. Love, Sex, Nature

It is difficult at first to experience chapter 16, the opening of the third "Phase" of the novel. Only when I am 13 paragraphs into it, does the chapter revert to the common theme it had sounded earlier, and now it is stated strenuously, almost in conflict with its message: "The irresistible, universal, automatic tendency to find sweet pleasure somewhere, which pervades all of life, from the meanest to the highest, had at length mastered Tess" (109). Although phrased mostly in the abstract, this statement meets with my assent: I find that the phrase "to find sweet pleasure somewhere" is the one touch here that makes contact with a vulnerable feeling of common need.

The chapter itself starts with Hardy nearly overwhelming the text for 10 paragraphs with his sociology, geography, genealogy, and learned allusions (107-9). Eventually this overture merges into an extraordinary quality that this narrative will retain for some 18 chapters. This quality might be given the name: *sexual love within Nature*. In some respects, it is more a matter of sex than of love. It is true that Hardy's great novels (except for *The Mayor of Casterbridge*) are all love stories, but it is also evident in *Tess* that Hardy knew what he was saying when he declared publicly that some of his novels delve into "the immortal puzzle—given the man and the woman, how to find a basis for their sexual relation—" This he stated in the preface to *The Woodlanders*, a piece appearing 4 years after the publication of *Tess*.[1] Few thinkers would have thought to name this search for a basis to the sexual relation "the immortal puzzle." I find it a phrase that captures my imagination. But except for Wayne Burns, Hardy's critics seem not to have taken notice of it.

The love that is sexual is what develops between Tess and Angel; the "Nature" in which it occurs is the combined action of landscape, agriculture, and weather. It is a term that calls for some "un-blocking" if experience is to go forward. To help with this task, I will retain the capital N on Nature because it helps to evoke the emotional value of the concept. It is a concept that has been excessively deconstructed in recent decades. But as the French theorist Michel Serres has said, in a book entitled *The Natural Contract*, we earthlings had better learn quickly to appreciate our place in Nature; else we will destroy our living base. "In fact, the Earth speaks to us using terms of forces, bonds, and interactions, and that's enough to make a contract. Each of the partners in symbiosis thus owes, by rights, life to the other, on pain of death".[2] Hardy does not think the Earth owes us such a debt, but the ultimate dependence of human life on Nature cannot be denied, "on pain of death." This is not the universal dying that faces all living creatures but the dying out of all human life because of the civilized ruin of life's earthly environment.

To be able to have an experience of this part of the novel, I must reject efforts to play down Nature by such simplistic philosophical dodges as critics are prone to invent, such as asserting that since the valley of the Froom river has a human-given name, Froom, therefore it is not Nature but part of Language. Or, in a glib variant, that because the river is called both the Froom and the Frome, and thus has a slightly varying name, it is therefore not to be responded to as if it were a beautiful river. Even J. Hillis Miller, a critic and theorist not noted for his feeling for Nature, concedes that "Man can never escape the biological inheritance that makes him part of nature".[3]

Nature can be blocked from experience if we stick to the truism that everything we name from the computer to the tree is part of language. It can also be blocked by assuming that Hardy is creating a version of Nature that is totally exempt from its inter-relation with culture. But Hardy is not so simple as to depend on a notion that he is describing farmland, the cow-country of Talbothays, as if it were untouched by civilization. Nor is his vision of the countryside created out of a naive fantasy of Nature as the unchanging essence. While the workers milking the cows are "encompassed by the vast flat mead which extended to either slope of the valley," Hardy goes on to say this landscape is no simple presence; it is "—a level landscape composed of old landscapes long forgotten, and, no doubt, differing in character very greatly from the landscape they composed now" (114). But neither is Hardy describing skyscrapers or city traffic. As phrased by a recent American thinker on the erotic, Joanna Frueh, speaking in opposition to Jean Baudrillard's declaration that "the great referent, Nature, is dead": "I know that nature as a word and as many ideas, is a product of the human mind; I also know that mountains, cactuses, deserts, and sunset exist."[4] For readers who can be responsive to Nature, the feelings of cityscape and landscape do have some difference, and Hardy is calling out that difference in his writing. At a level of deepest response, he is calling on "resonances and dispositions" that we have inherited in our very organisms, and which Dewey accepts and prizes eloquently in *Art as Experience*. Dewey also links these capabilities to aesthetic experience. Referring to the profound experiences of Nature described by Ralph Waldo Emerson and W. H. Hudson, Dewey says:

> I do not see any way of accounting for the multiplicity of experiences of this kind (something of the same quality being found in every spontaneous and uncoerced esthetic response), except on the basis that there are stirred into activity resonances of dispositions acquired in primitive relationships of the living being to its surroundings, and irrecoverable in distinct or intellectual consciousness. (*AE* 35)

This passage suggests powerfully why the Talbothays section of *Tess* can be a gripping experience—an experience that would be entirely different if Tess and Angel were two people in love who lived in apartment houses in some city. If we were to inject into Dewey's statement the role of sexual love within this context of nature experience, we would have a still stronger and more accurate indication of what the novel offers in its imaginative vision, and of what we have to "*take in*" (*AE* 60) if we wish to experience it.

Not everything in these chapters is a function of Nature. If it were, all qualities of resistance would be lacking, and the experience would flatten out into a scene without a sense of dramatic issue. Hardy is acutely aware that the courtship of Angel and Tess is infused with, even undermined by, civilized customs of sexual control that have nothing to do with Nature. We see in the course of their courtship how Angel's idealizations of Tess, and hers of him, allow them to relate in ways that repair their injured sense of self, and yet tragically block them from relating in sexual love. This does not mean however that there is no feeling between them that breaks free of such constriction.

The experience has the quality of a tension felt against the Natural. In Dewey's terms, the *resistance* to Nature in the form of frustration is what gives this section its experiential depth. Tess's idealizing of Angel, her guilt over her past sexual life with Alec, Angel's doubts about marrying a woman who is beneath him in class, his fearful self-control—all these provide a feeling of resistance, but all except his self-control are swept away finally by the power of sex within Nature which dominates this whole section of the novel.

In *Tess of the d'Urbervilles*, there is in this matter of Nature a very large experiential challenge: we are called upon to respond over an extended time of reading experience, for the better part of chapters 16 through 34, to a feeling of love developing in Nature. Love is fused with sexual feeling even though that feeling is never consummated. I know of nothing like this long sequence anywhere else in literature. Sexual love within Nature: Hardy can really write this relationship. It goes beyond any talk of ours about concepts. Response, however, is called for. Somewhere in the critical literature (I have now forgotten the place) is a bit of advice that signals an ominous turning away. The critic first determined that Hardy is indebted to Wordsworth in his writing on Nature, then labeled Hardy a sentimentalist for incurring such a debt, and thus released the wise reader from having to respond to Nature in this book at all, except with smug knowingness. A more complete experience blockage could hardly be invented. I am afraid that it has proven to be typical for much of the reading done professionally and pedagogically for the past several decades.

My own attitude is one of receptivity to the experience. I feel first what it must feel like to Tess.

"Tess had never before visited this part of the country, and yet she felt akin to the landscape" (108). The dark patch of trees she can see, where the d'Urberville ancestresses are laid, helps her to incorporate the landscape into her feeling of kinship. This seems to allow her to feel good about her mother, for once, and about her own beauty: "All my prettiness came from her, and she was only a dairymaid" (108). Her self is re-forming, gathering unto itself a quality of healthy self-love. Soon the sense of freedom in this new place (both its fresh quality of air and its privacy from snooping eyes) "sent up her spirits wonderfully" (109). Her mind now becomes extremely active, as she sings a pagan hymn that I would not have supposed was to be found in the psalter of her Sunday morning church services (nor that it is excerpted from the Morning Prayer service of the Church of England, but the footnotes tell me that it is): "O ye Sun and Moon...O ye Stars...ye Green Things upon the Earth...Ye Fowls of the Air...Beasts and Cattle...Children of Men ...bless ye the Lord, praise Him and magnify Him for ever" (109; all ellipses are Hardy's...or Tess's). She is creatively adapting this hymn as an expression of her own sense of recovery within Nature. Tess finishes this and (like Hardy) immediately retracts some of the joyousness: "But perhaps I don't quite know the Lord as yet." In its context, I find this a striking indication of her thoughtfulness. I recall now a piece of her thinking that occurred during her period of self-enforced isolation, when she created for herself a state of "absolute mental liberty" (91). "A wet day was the expression of irremediable grief at her weakness in the mind of some vague ethical being whom she could not class definitely as the God of her childhood, and could not comprehend as any other" (91). This shows several things about

Tess's mind: a capacity to deal with the perplexing quality of her religious questioning without forcing it into a conclusion, an ability to frame the problem of her personal troubles within a larger question of existence, and a capacity—a rare one, I should think—of conceiving *both* a universal problem of God as a "vague ethical being" *and* having emotional quality blended into the thought process. To imagine "irremediable grief" in the mind of some undefinable God is no insignificant act of felt reflection.

Despite the rich Nature evocation in Hardy's narration of Tess's arrival at "the Valley of Great Dairies, the valley in which milk and butter grew to rankness" (108), the mood is less than exuberant, because Hardy splices into his evocative account of Tess's entry into her new countryside certain carefully placed deflating comments. Tess feels "high contentment" for her "having started towards a means of independent living." But Hardy lowers this height by saying that she is content with this "slight" thing because she is like her father, in being easily, even lazily, satisfied (109-10). While this sounds quite critical, and shows that Hardy does not always defend his character Tess, I find it problematic. Without that comment by Hardy, Tess's working toward "independent living" would otherwise shine forth as a real achievement. Then, soon after, there is the notorious instance of Hardy's deliberate deflating the value of her delight: his interposition that Tess is no more significant in this new landscape than "a fly on a billiard table of indefinite length, and of no more consequence to the surroundings than that fly" (110). Another instance is his realistic explanation, in the next paragraph, which Hardy provides after she suddenly hears "a prolonged and repeated call—'Waow! waow! waow!'" (110). Hardy follows this by stating that all we are hearing is the sound of cows wanting to be milked. But to my ear Hardy is practicing a degree of conscious inhibition. From what I know of his temperament, he would not want to ever allow himself to feel as great (or to admit that he feels as great) as his descriptions have suggested. These deflations feel as if he personally does not want to be seen too clearly by his readers as the Nature celebrant and philosopher that he knows he is. He might also be protecting himself from charges of idealization or romanticizing.

The chance of confusion is considerable. But keeping a focus on what is experienced, rather than on the statements as such, will help. For any reader who chooses to reflect upon the passage, the question would arise: do I really feel Tess has no more significance than a fly? In my own reading, I find that I repel the effort to suggest that Tess is insignificant, just as I find that the resonance of the triple "Waow!" cannot be denied its primitive quality even when it is explained. I find that Hardy's preferred defensive barrier against feeling this quality is ineffectual. It has too much of the flavor of a conscious, artificial denial to be able to overcome the force of what has already been created. But is it then a wash-out, a non-functioning element? No; it is too nettling: I feel it as some sort of challenge to keep my interest in Tess at a caring level, despite what Hardy may occasionally say.

My motives for saying this are of course rooted in my own temperament. They would have to be. As Dewey put it in "Context and Thought," an important essay of 1931, the year he gave the lecture series that was to become *Art as Experience*, there is a certain "bias" in any endeavor, even if it be a bias for impartiality. This bias, which in Dewey's choice of a formal term, is called "selected interest," can be used responsibly (or otherwise), but it would be absurd to pretend that it can or even should be eliminated.[5] My attitude toward Nature in *Tess* is mine, although I doubt that it is mine alone. It also reflects my long unsatisfying experience with professional readers who seize upon any apothegm such as "she was a fly upon a billiard table" to deflect from the felt experience. One aspect of reading this novel is a realization of how small and vulnerable Tess is—or anyone is—in the context of the whole world of Nature. But does Hardy really want us to think of her as insignificant? That would be taking him too literally. A bit of resistance to the temptation to encapsulate a whole life into one striking generalization will pay off in making for a richer response.

This complex chapter of Tess's journey to and arrival at the fertile dairy region where she will work, finally comes to a settling (not settled) feeling in its last paragraphs. These are devoted to what I am startled to realize is a kind of "cow-culture." As Hardy focuses on the cows, I get a feeling of animals with a social history, one whose quality is evocative of time within nature:

> Long thatched sheds stretched round the enclosure, their slopes encrusted with vivid green moss, and their eaves supported by wooden posts rubbed to glossy smoothness by the flanks of infinite cows and calves of bygone years, now passed to an oblivion almost inconceivable in its profundity. (111)

It is a magnificent sentence, a lavishing of imaginative energy on what would ordinarily be perceived as nothing special. Similarly, the final sentence of the chapter, still on cows:

> Their large-veined udders hung ponderous as sandbags, the teats sticking out like the legs of a gypsy's crock; and as each animal lingered for her turn to arrive the milk oozed forth and fell in drops to the ground. (111)

The landscape is one of fertility, of surplus, of promises of animal and human contentment, of unstinting gratification.

The next chapter moves into a fairly calm, realistic mood, as Tess learns the routines of work at this dairy, but this mood suddenly becomes emotionally powered when she sees Angel: "it flashed upon her" that she has seen this man before; she undergoes a "flood of memories" concerning that earlier meeting, along with an immediate fear that Angel will have heard about her time with Alec (116). From there to the chapter's end, she is emotionally played upon by erotic fantasies about Angel—not Alec—conveyed to her by the three dairymaids, Marian, Retty, and Izz, who will become Tess's friends. In my re-reading the novel a number of times, these three women characters take on individualized qualities that I had somehow not wanted to notice at first. It is one of these women, Marian, who now provides her with the information that Angel is the son of the Reverend Clare, whose strictness she has heard of before from the painter of Biblical texts. Marian also relates that unlike his brothers, Angel has decided not to become a clergyman. This might suggest subliminally to Tess that Angel might be free to choose a profession that might somehow include her as his mate. That is, he becomes more available as an object for her fantasizing. As Tess falls asleep, the mood of the novel becomes reminiscent of the previous chapter's end, where fecund cows were dripping their milk. But now the Nature context is more personal and more erotic. Her mind suffused with thoughts about Angel, she "gradually fell asleep again, the words of her informant coming to her along with the smell of the cheeses in the adjoining cheese-loft, and the measured dripping of the whey from the wrings downstairs" (118). The passage is richly suggestive of her "body-mind" (to use Dewey's term once more) at this point undergoing an organic, sensuous, pleasurable, irresistible, and portentous change.

Everything in the relationship of Angel and Tess will depend on their capacities for perceiving each as part of the natural surrounding they are living in. They cannot always do this, and indeed they often try, by means of idealizing strategies, not to. Clare is at the very first able to perceive her sensuously, without idealizing, as he relaxes, and lets his mind wander without purpose.

> One day...when he had been conning one of his music scores, and by force of imagination was hearing the tune in his head, he lapsed into listlessness, and the music-sheet rolled to the hearth. He looked at the fire of logs, with its one flame pirouetting on the top in a dying dance after the breakfast cooking and boiling; and it seemed to jig to his inward tune; also at the two chimney crooks dangling down from the cotterel or cross-bar, plumed with soot which quivered to the same melody; also at the half-empty kettle whining an accompaniment. The conversation at the table mixed in with his phantasmal orchestra, till he thought: "What a flutey voice one of those milkmaids has. I suppose it is the new one." (123-4)

In this mood of unreflective listening, of indefinable energy movements within and outside of him, fused with homely details and the quivering plumes of soot, it is the sheer sound quality of Tess's voice that he perceives.

Tess is not just vocalizing; the next passage shows her speculative mind at work, imagining how a person—she herself—can induce an out-of-body feeling. You just lie on the grass at night (thus within the context of Nature) and look up at one of the stars, "and, by fixing your mind upon it, you will soon find that you are hundreds and hundreds o' miles away from your body, which you don't seem to want at all" (124). She is using her mind in a way that Hardy himself probably did; as a biographer, Paul Turner, shows, Hardy had recently had several non-threatening impressions of the soul outside of the body. But these were far from spectral: in a Botticelli painting, Hardy thought that the "soul is outside the body, premeating the spectator with its emotions."[6] Tess enjoys thinking of such things, and sharing her thoughts with her new friends. There is a feeling here of her increasingly healthy recovery from her isolation. But her thinking is not comprehensible to Richard Crick, the "Dairyman," as he feels obliged to announce to her in a disbelieving manner, just after giving Tess a "hard gaze" (124). With this response of the dairyman, Hardy could be providing a counter-weight to Tess's train of thought, warning the reader that it is unrealistic. But it does not feel that way: it is a fresh indication that Tess simply has more imagination than anyone in her social environment can appreciate.

Discordantly, Clare, who has "continued to observe her," now remarks to himself, "What a fresh and virginal daughter of Nature that milkmaid is" (124). His perception, his thinking of "Nature" in his own abstract sense of the term, is instantly linked with the ideal of virginity. This is perhaps a normal error for a male with his background to make, but an error that I imagine many readers at this point in the novel will experience with apprehension. Besides this, Angel's perception ignores what she has just been saying, her articulate speculation. In other words he does not notice her mind, and he mistakes her body. The overall effect upon him, however, is warmly pleasurable; he is able to "discern something which carried him back into a joyous and unforeseeing past, before the necessity of taking thought had made the Heavens gray" (124). Such wording suggests to my mind a state of infancy, but for Clare, it allows him to imagine a past that he may never have actually had. I say this because I recall Hardy's introductory excursus at the opening of this chapter, where Clare is described as habitually having "something nebulous, preocupied, vague, in his bearing and regard..." (119). There is a missing quality of unproblematic joyousness that he wishes to have with Tess. Obviously he is attracted to her; and from this point on, he has male fantasies about Tess, and not about the other milkmaids, whenever "he wished to contemplate contiguous womankind" (125). Hardy's preposterously rigid wording here (wording with which he ends the chapter and thus displays prominently) suggests Clare's inhibitions in sexual thinking, but also state that the woman is nonetheless thought about.

Angel immediately begins courting her by arranging the cows in a favorable milking pattern for her, which she duly notices and blushes over in his presence. She gives what easily could be taken as an involuntary sexual-love signal: "symptoms of a smile gently lifted her upper lip in spite of her, so as to show the tips of her teeth, the lower lip remaining severely still" (126). Angel is bound to notice this subliminally, even if he thinks abstractly.

Soon after, their attraction acquires depth; they meet outdoors, in Nature, in a fateful and amazing passage that only Hardy could write. The June night is full of mystery: "the atmosphere being in such delicate equilibrium and so transmissive that inanimate objects seemed endowed with two or three senses, if not five." Clare's simple musical expression on his harp produces notes that "wandered in the still air with a stark quality like that of nudity," and Tess makes her way through "juicy grass which sent up mists of pollen at a touch; and with tall blooming weeds emitting offensive smells—weeds whose red and yellow and purple hues formed a polychrome as dazzling as that of cultivated flowers" (127). This is Nature, and it has some of the rank quality of sex. Tess is part of an erotic context. One critic has intuited that Tess emanates an "intensity of female sensation," and undergoes waves of "orgasmic dilation."[7] Hardy's writing here is almost sure to produce intense interest and affect, and many have written about it. Explicating the details of this scene would occupy many pages, so rich is it in potential meanings. But that is not my project. The mood, the underlying quality of the scene, is not difficult to discern. It is one of intimacy and privacy, a merging with Nature that disarms all defenses, thus encouraging self-revelation on both Tess's and Angel's parts. In terms of the quality of the writing as it feels in reading this passage, Gillian Beer's comment seems right: "Here, hyperfecundity, the activity of growth, permeates language, even transgresses language. *Resistance to such fullness is felt in the writing, but also calm.*"[8] Dewey's characteristic denial of any compartmentalized separation between inner and outer experience would apply easily here, fully crediting the strong sense in the passage of inner feeling as well as outward relating to the environment and to another person.

My experiencing of this passage, unless I fight against the text, will draw on its connections with some personal moments in my own life: these are moments in which there is intense inner feeling connected with perception of a place—and yet part of an erotic relationship. What seems to be expressed here, for me, is what Dewey terms "an intimate union of the features of present existence [that is, of having this passage in *Tess*] with the values that past experience have incorporated into personality" (*AE* 78). My reading draws energy from such moments, while maintaining focus on the striking "[I]mmediacy and individuality" that "come from the present occasion" (*AE* 78) of encountering Hardy's writing. This is not very difficult to do; it happens for the most part automatically, and as Stephen Pepper pointed out, the human mind can do such connecting and accurate re-focusing almost effortlessly as it carries on the act of reading.[9] This psychological assumption may not be dealt with specifically by Dewey, but it would be easily accommodated in his thinking. It is at least very William Jamesian. It is part of any contextualistic psychology that grants human beings the ability to relate to new situations.

The talk between Angel and Tess in this scene is about their personal outlook on their whole lives. Responding to what he intuits as Tess's attitude of fear, Angel spills out an astonishing disclosure of his general view of life: "This hobble of being alive is rather serious, don't you think so?" (128). Tess speaks a beautifully articulate, foreboding prose-poem on "the aspects of things to her":

> The trees have inquisitive eyes, haven't they?—that is, seem as if they had. And the river says,—"Why do ye trouble me with your looks?" And you seem to see numbers of to-morrows just all in a line, the first of them the biggest and clearest, the others getting smaller and smaller as they stand farther away, but they all seem very fierce and cruel and as if they said "I'm coming! Beware of me! Beware of me!..." (128).

Hardy can dare to offer a unified body-mind experience, in which the caliber of thought is high, and the felt contact with Nature—felt by Tess, Angel and me the reader—is continuous. That there are cognitive misunderstandings between the pair in this scene is also important, but less so than the fact of its taking place, and the miracle of creative prose that Hardy makes it take place in. Dewey's celebratory thought on communication is especially appropriate:

> Communication is the process of creating participation, of making common what has been isolated and singular; and part of the miracle it achieves is that, in being communicated, the conveyance of meaning gives body and definiteness to the experience of the one who utters as well as to that of those who listen. (*AE* 248-49)

In this interchange, Tess is challenging Angel not to let her life play out to nothingness: from her imagination of "the river" that speaks to her of its indifference to her life (and to her looks), she has created a vivid fable of the "to-morrows": "they all seem very fierce and cruel and as if they said, 'I'm coming! Beware of me!'" But this dark thought leads at once to an openly-voiced human appeal: "But *you*, sir, can raise up dreams with your music and drive all such horrid fancies away!" (128, emphasis in text). In the ensuing days, this appeal to Angel is made even clearer: "My life looks as if it had been wasted for want of chances!" (130), she exclaims to him. She also compares herself to "the poor Queen of Sheba who lived in the Bible," thus incidentally showing her learning while telling Angel that she feels impoverished next to his own wealth of reading (130). This appeal is followed by a broad hint, taken from her folk psychology, that there are never enough good men to match the number of women: "there are always more ladies than lords..." (130). She also hints that an injustice has been done to her: "I shouldn't mind learning why—why the sun do shine on the just and the unjust alike" (130). It is a question he himself has asked. And she does not want to think that her "nature" and "past doings" are just like those of "thousands and thousands" of other people whose life stories are indistinct and unremarkable (130). Hardy, with an encompassing comment on her life, offers his own notation of the potential relation between unfortunate bodily experiences and the development of intelligence: "...experience is as to intensity, and not as to duration. *Tess's passing corporeal blight had been her mental harvest*"(129, my emphasis). She has a more developed mind by now, capable of historic speculation that is more personalized and more complex than her earlier fantasy concerning blighted planets. Hardy expands the context of her thought through his own defining terms: Tess, he comments, is expressing in her own way "the ache of modernism" (129). In this famous metaphor, he thus combines a sharp bodily feeling with a broad cultural meaning; and as I mull over his comment, I feel that there has been some quality all along in Tess's life that reaches beyond any local meaning within her immediate surroundings. But I begin to fear that Clare will not appreciate her thinking: he cannot even believe that "such a daughter of the soil" could be serious about injustice: she must have "caught up the sentiment by rote" (130-31).

If the force of these passages is real to the reader, then the experience may take on a personal meaning: for me it is a strong wish that I do not *want* Tess's life to be wasted. I want her to be fulfilled. I hope—against hope—that Angel can help her. I cannot allow the fact that I "know" the story is going to turn out tragically to block this wish at this point in my experience. Such knowing may further the sense of poignancy and include a feeling of loss, but it does not cancel what I feel of hope.

After the long chapter on their deepening relationship, the narrative of their attraction-within-nature cumulates rapidly and forcefully through four shorter chapters (20 through 23), to the end of this "Phase," where Angel embraces Tess, tells her how much he loves her, and where Hardy comments on the seriousness of such a juncture in the lives of two people: "something had occurred which changed the pivot of the universe for their two natures...[something] based upon a more stubborn and resistless tendency than a whole heap of so-called practicalities" (154). The "resistless tendency" is toward sexual union within Nature.

That emotional climax of this part of the novel comes at the end of a long augmentation of energy in the novel's prose, beginning with chapter 20. The process begins in Nature: "Rays from the sunrise drew forth the buds and stretched them into long stalks, lifted up sap in noiseless streams, opened petals, and sucked out scents in invisible jets and breathings" (133). Tess, still on the verge of conscious realization of her love for Angel, and untroubled by "reflections...awkwardly inquiring" of where the new current is going to carry her, is extremely happy (133). Hardy, writing in terms of a metaphor of natural growth, says she is getting away from her toxic family: "The sapling, which had rooted down to a poisonous stratum on the spot of its sowing had been transplanted to a deeper soil" (133). Angel, telling himself that he is just having "a philosopher's regard," "allowed his mind to be occupied with her..." (133). The two meet alone, ostensibly for work, each day at early dawn: "The spectral, half-compounded, aqueous light which pervaded the open mead impressed them with a feeling of isolation, as if they were Adam and Eve" (134). They are having an unsophisticated, non-ironic experience of themselves as the primal Biblical couple. This is what they experience even though "spectral, half-compounded, aqueous light" could have been experienced in a distrustful manner if this couple were not in love. The challenge for my own experience is to allow myself—my educated self—to respond to this, to feel something of the beauty of this woman and man in their relationship. I find some semblance in myself of their feeling of freedom in "isolation," and do not just let it pass, by making the habitual assumption that it is only a cliché. In this context it is not trite: the energy movement of the writing and of the couple's relationship has built an individualized context for it. At such time, Clare's regard for her is unified: she is a fine person, and is also a bodily and erotic one:

> ...Tess seemed to Clare to exhibit a dignified largeness both of disposition and physique, an almost regnant power—possibly because he knew at that preternatural time hardly any woman so well endowed in person as she was likely to be walking in the open air within the boundaries of his horizon; very few in all England. (134)

She is most beautiful to him—more perfectly beautiful than Hardy himself thinks her to be. Clare is in love, and from all we know of that state, some idealization of the loved one is normal. His "philosopher's regard" is tacitly forgotten. What Angel now feels about her is not be confounded with his culturally standardized idealization of her as purely virginal in all her thoughts and experience. And here there may be a blockage of the reader's experience that cannot be overcome: as Dorothy Tennov has found in her research, not everyone has ever fallen in love, nor can everyone feelingly imagine that such a thing ever really happens.[10] This is an obstacle to experiencing *Tess* so elementary that I must pass over it, except to say that it may help to explain why some readers cannot relate to this novel.

Though Clare is in love, he remains in character: his perceptions are quickly imbued with the tincture of his religious training. "The mixed, singular, luminous gloom in which they walked along together to the spot where the cows lay, often made him think of the Resurrection-hour." Hardy hypothetically extends this feeling, for the moment, with an ominous allusion to the Fallen Woman which would have occurred to Angel had he known Tess's life story: "He little thought that the Magdalen might be at his side" (134). In this mood, in this light, Tess appears to Angel "to have a sort of phosphorescence...She looked ghostly, as if she were merely a soul at large" (134). In other words, under the spell of his religious habit of mind, she loses her bodily dimension. The technical term "phosphorescence" might indicate the emission of light without heat, and/or of light caused by the decay of organic matter. But Hardy is far from endorsing his illusion: "In reality her face, without appearing to do so, had caught the cold gleam of day from the north-east; his own face, though he did not think of it, wore the same aspect to her" (134).

During such mistakenly spiritualized encounters, Clare would try to name her with chaste feminine titles of Greek mythology, thus showing how easily he confounds his Hellenism with his ascetic Christianity. But the quality, the feeling of this passage, then turns decisively; she easily stops him. "'Call me Tess,' she would say askance, *and he did*" (135, my emphasis). Immediately she becomes erotic and creaturely rather than spiritual, and he knows what she craves: "Then it would grow lighter, and her features would become simply feminine. They had changed from those of a divinity who could confer bliss to those of a being who craved it" (135). The passage immediately continues in its context of Nature:

> At these non-human hours they could get quite close to the waterfowl. Herons came, with a great bold noise as of opening doors and shutters, out of the boughs of a plantation which they frequented at the side of the mead; or, if already on the spot, hardily maintained their standing in the water as the pair walked by, watching them by moving their heads round in a slow, horizontal, passionless wheel ... (135)

—and now Hardy quirkily shifts to a decrescendo: "like the turn of puppets by clockwork" (135).

This downplaying of the lyrical feeling (a mood that seems even to include the "passionless wheel") that is naturally, non-humanly, unconcerned, now passes, and the next two full paragraphs return to a rich quality of Nature description. I find that the only way to experience this is to allow myself to surrender to it. To convey the quality involved, let me quote fairly extensively:

> They could then see the faint summer fogs in layers, woolly, level, and apparently no thicker than counterpanes, spread about the meadows in detached remnants of small extent. On the gray moisture of the grass were marks where the cows had lain through the night—dark-green islands of dry herbage the size of their carcasses in the general sea of dew. From each island proceeded a serpentine trail...at the end of which trail they found [the cow]; the snoring puff from her nostrils when she recognized them, making an intenser little fog of her own amid the prevailing one. (135)

Angel and Tess would either drive these cows back to the barton, or they "sat down to milk them on the spot..." I can sense here a fusion of the lovers, in their lovingly-described Nature surrounding, with the culture of the cows. Again, contrary to the conventional association, the fog, in its "detached remnants of small extent," feels in this context gentle and protective, not confusing. It is even individualized to the level of each cow, with its "intenser little fog of her own..."

Nor is this all:

Or perhaps the summer fog was more general, and the meadows lay like a white sea, out of which the scattered trees rose like dangerous rocks. Birds would soar through it into the upper radiance, and hang on the wing sunning themselves, or alight on the wet rails subdividing the mead, which now shone like glass rods. Minute diamonds of moisture from the mist hung, too, upon Tess's eyelashes, and drops upon her hair, like seed pearls. When the day grew quite strong and commonplace... (135)

—and here I expect a characteristic Hardyan gesture toward emotional let-down. Indeed it is supplied, but this time functionally, in the relevant sense of reiterating Tess's womanliness and the realistic place of womanhood in her culture: "...Tess then lost her strange and ethereal beauty; her teeth, lips, and eyes scintillated in the sunbeams, and she was again the dazzlingly fair dairymaid only, who had to hold her own against the other women of the world" (135). Hardy ostensibly is trying to be exact about calling what has just been described of Tess as "strange and ethereal." But there is too much that is not ethereal (if the word is meant to signify not-earthly) already lodged within the passage, and contributing to its palpable quality:

> trees rose like dangerous rocks...a great bold noise as of opening doors and shutters...the turn of puppets like clockwork...no thicker than counterpanes...the size of their carcasses...to feed after getting up...the snoring puff from her nostrils...to milk them on the spot...the wet rails subdividing the mead... (136)

Only when the scene is moved out of Nature, to the kitchen of the farmer's respectable wife, Mrs. Crick, do we get a real deflation of the mood, with the sound of a heavy table being moved with a "horrible scrape" (136).

2. Organisms Called Sex

Sex as subject-matter is rendered unmistakably in the augmented fantasizing of Tess's three women companions, who live in frustrated romantic love over Angel. One of them, Izz Huett, while "standing over the whey-tub to let off the whey...put her mouth against the wall and kissed the shade of his mouth" (140). Far from observing the standard Victorian prohibitions, at least two of these women hint that they might have gone to bed with Clare without benefit of marriage. Marian: "I would just marry'n tomorrow!" Izz: "So would I—*and more*" Retty: "*and I too*" (140, my emphasis). Later in the novel, Izz later actually agrees to be Angel's mistress until he can re-unite with Tess. But at this point, all three realize that they cannot have him: "One sighed, and another sighed, and Marian's plump figure sighed biggest of all. Somebody in bed hard by sighed too" (140-41). That "somebody" is Tess, who wonders why she must not "draw off Mr. Clare's attention from other women, for the brief happiness of sunning herself in his eyes while he remained at Talbothays" (141). But drawing his attention is what she is already doing and will continue to do. Tess as a woman knows that Angel could have seduced any of the other three: he "had the honour of all the dairymaids in his keeping," and is even more enamored of him because she believes he is a male who controls his sexual urge, so that working women, who live within a culture that devalues any woman who has sex without being married, do not get hurt; otherwise "more than one of the simple hearts who were his housemates might have gone weeping on her pilgrimage" (145). Tess can believe in him because, unlike Alec, Angel does not follow a program of seducing the working women. But this also suggests that he could do so, if he had wanted to, and the thought is suggested that he could seduce Tess as well. All these surmises are superseded, I find, by the further and more radical, felt thought that seduction is unnecessary: both Tess and Angel want to have sex, and in the context of Nature, they ought to consummate. I only realize this imperative sentiment when I put aside my knowledge of the fact that obeying their conscious, sexually negative restrictions, they did not.

The sexual aura gets denser, more intense. The "hot steaming rains" of July soon cause a flood, blocking the women's way to church on a primal "Sun's-day," a day "when flesh went forth to coquette with flesh while hypocritically affecting business with spiritual things" (144). If I pause to better take in this statement, I soon realize that it is neither the sun nor the flesh that are hypocritical, but the church culture. Both Tess and Angel are aroused sexually and are at the same time thinking of love when he carries her across the stream. Angel: "I did not expect such an event today." Tess: "Nor I...The water came up so sudden." Hardy: "That the rise in the water was what she understood him to refer to, the state of her breathing belied. Clare stood still and inclined his face toward hers" (148). In the context of the situation and the language used, this "rise" could be an erection. It is certainly a rise in sexual feeling. Angel: "O Tessy!" Hardy's description: "The girl's cheeks burned to the breeze, and she could not look into his eyes for her emotion" (148). A few paragraphs further: "Tess's heart ached. There was no concealing from herself the fact that she loved Angel Clare, perhaps all the more passionately from knowing that the others had also lost their hearts to him" (148).

For the three other women, who now are simply part of "one organism called sex," intensity rises to the level of "ectasizing them to a killing joy" (149). Judging from this passage, I suspect that Hardy as a male in his own culture must have felt that the sexual impulse is overpowering and humiliating: he calls it "cruel Nature's law" (149). It is a feeling I think far from uncommon. His gender bias allows him to say it about women, but not about men. For this he can be faulted. But is there a serious flaw, such as would interfere with experiencing this novel? Any reader with a minimum of sexual awareness will know that if the sex drive is universal, it is everyone's. The great effect of the passage for me, in the context of the energy movement within these chapters, is neither a lament for the "cruel" powers of sex over the human organism, nor a lesson in women's sexual psychology, but an intensification of the mounting sexual/love/Nature pressure in this part of the novel.

The next chapter, 24, is free, perhaps for the only extended time in the novel, of any suggestion of idealizing these sexual love feelings away from their natural, physical base. Nature is sexual, and human beings are part of it: "Amid the oozing fatness and warm ferments of the Var Vale, at a season when the rush of juices could almost be heard below the hiss of fertilization, it was impossible that the most fanciful love should not grow passionate" (151). Clare, the self-controlled male, now is "oppressed by the outward heats" of the weather just as he is "burdened inwardly by a waxing fervour of passion for the soft and silent Tess" (151). Tess here is sexy, and she is still a person with consciousness: as she milks her cow, her eyes are "fixed on the far end of the meadow with the quiet of one lost in meditation" (152). Clare feels the force of her "pink hands," as she grasps the cow's teats "so gently as to be a rhythmic pulsation only, as if they were obeying a reflex stimulus, like a beating heart" (152). "How very lovable her face was to him. Yet *there was nothing ethereal about it; all was real vitality, real warmth, real incarnation*" (152, my emphasis). The sexual significance of her "red top lip was distracting, infatuating, maddening" (152). By now he had "studied the curves of those lips so many times that he could produce them mentally with ease" (152). When he pushes all hesitation aside,

> He jumped up from his seat, and, leaving the pail to be kicked over…went quickly toward the desire of his eyes, and kneeling down beside her, clasped her in his arms. [Tess]…yielded to his embrace with unreflecting inevitableness. Having seen that it was really her lover who had advanced, and no one else, her lips parted and she sank upon him in her momentary joy, with something very like an ecstatic cry. (153)

At which point Clare pulls back, "for tender conscience' sake" (153). How cruel and unnatural that feels! The tenderness ought not to be one of conscience but of love. I interject, almost achingly, into my reading of the narrative, *why don't they go ahead?* I find that this is a question that is intrinsic to the experience, in the context of the story thus far. After allowing us to feel once again that natural sexuality cannot be blocked, Hardy is about to show that it can be. The tension is enormous.

The quality of the next "Phase," chapters 25-34, consists of continued wave-like surges of erotic-natural longing, alternating with counter-waves of frustration, anxiety, and fear. The wave pattern is important as experience: it is a different quality from undergoing ironic or ambivalent passages describing eroticism and its denial. I feel something of both the couple's—and Hardy's—

yearnings for gratification and, on the down-surge, the increasing anxiety of its denial. The scene Hardy has created of human erotic energy within the context of Nature allows him to build the narrative energy with increased complexity of motivation, and without having the reader lose contact with the pervasive quality: a sexually-toned feeling in contact with Nature.

But to this I would add one underlying trait of the experience that qualifies it and makes it richer: as Ian Gregor expressed it, there is a "pervasive sense of Tess's past" in all these Nature scenes, and that gives "poignancy and lyrical fragility to the emotions" that are evoked.[11]

Four

BEYOND FRUSTRATION TO EXPERIENTIAL DISASTER

Emotions, Dewey maintains, are significant qualities of "a complex experience that moves and changes" (*AE* 48). They are part of the human organism's bodily experience because emotion "is a mode of sense" (*AE* 36). Emotions are not simply bodily, however: they belong to the self—but "to the self that is concerned in the movement of events toward an issue that is desired or disliked" (*AE* 48-49). In any aesthetic experience there is subject-matter that is not simply emotion; there is "ideational matter." But such content does not stand apart from the experience in some impossibly managed purity of thought: emotion in aesthetic experience "subdues and digests all that is merely intellectual" (*AE* 36-7). In the section of the novel Hardy names "The Consequence," emotion is crucial. Dewey's statement, "All emotions are qualifications of a drama and they change as the drama develops" (*AE* 48), has never struck me as self-evident. But when I stop to consider what I am going through in the complex experiencing of this part of *Tess of the d'Urbervilles*, he seems to have phrased nothing less than a perfect insight.

In aesthetics, the problem of emotion hinges on one key question: Are emotions felt in the reading of literature of a completely different species than those felt in everyday life? Dewey would never say so. For Dewey, "esthetic emotion is native emotion transformed through the objective material to which it has committed its development and consummation..." (*AE* 85). And Pepper, in a short paper entitled "Emotional Distance in Art," argues that any emotions felt in literary experience are real emotions: they are not qualitatively different from ordinary emotions. To be sure, their intensity is usually reduced from that of a "real life" undergoing of an emotional event, and they are "not generated by source acts," that is, by actual events outside of the book, "nor by immediate apprehensions or anticipations of them..." Insofar as these qualifications apply, "psychical distance" is a valid concept regarding emotional factors in the literary experience—but only so far.[1]

I will try to trace the emotional process in this part of *Tess*.

1. Sins of the Father and of the Son

This "Phase" (Hardy's term) of the novel (chapters 25 to 34), with its integral connection to Nature, is also the place where Hardy modulates the quality by having a section in which there is no very strong movement of energy, when Angel spends time with his parents and brothers. The sustaining richness of Nature at the Talbothays dairy is suddenly suspended. But the suspension of something so powerful leaves an eerie feeling. It does not seem to be the common "foreshadowing" of Victorian fiction, but a way of building the experience. There are ideological conflicts between Angel and his parents hinted at in these chapters, but also a sense that something awful is brewing beneath their shallow emotional surface—something that will have an effect somehow later on in the novel. Angel, though he is sharply aware of the difference in quality between his parents' house and the dairy where Tess now lives, carries resonances of the aura of Nature with him. In this sense, there is no let-up of the sexual-love-Nature context, despite the lessening of intensity. His visit home is made under pressure of his sexual body, in the hope that he will receive permission to approach Tess by offering her marriage. Without getting clearance from his parents, however grudging it might be, he is blocked. "But it was not easy to carry out the resolution never to approach her. He was driven towards her by every heave of his pulse" (158). As he rides along the "narrow lane" toward his home, he is not even sure whether his attraction to Tess is capable of developing into "staunch comradeship"; all he really knows so far is that it may be "*a sensuous joy in her form only, with no substratum of everlastingness*" (159-60, my emphasis). In response to his father's need to be assured that Tess has "a Pauline view of humanity," Angel impulsively rattles off her supposed virtues ("regular church-goer, of simple faith; honest-hearted, receptive, intelligent, graceful to a degree, chaste as a vestal" (166))—but ends this recital with the prime characteristic which actually has occupied his thoughts: she is "in personal appearance, exceptionally beautiful" (166). That is not a point likely to win the approval of his father, who would have had Angel married to the ridiculously plain, Bible-toting Mercy Chant.

His parents cannot help but notice that Angel has undergone some de-repressing bodily change, some shedding of his "armor"[2]: "he flung his legs about; the muscles of his face had grown more expressive; his eyes looked as much information as his tongue spoke, and more" (162). He has been not only smitten by Tess, but has become immersed in Nature: he had begun "to like the outdoor life for its own sake and for what it brought…" (123). He had thrown off some of the "chronic melancholy" that Hardy asserts has been afflicting civilized people since their loss of faith in "a beneficient power," and had "made close acquaintance" with "the seasons in their moods, morning and evening, night and noon, winds in their different tempers, trees, water and mists, shades and silences, and the voices of inanimate things" (123). Yet while I am taken with how open Angel has become, I also feel troubled by his affinity with his rigid life-hating father. Although he has rejected the career path toward the Church, and has been acutely aware that his "squareness would not fit the round hole" that his parents had "prepared for him" (168), it is disconcerting and ominous to learn that he is "the most ideal religionist, even the best-versed Christologist" of the three sons (168).

Angel has ridden straight into the location where he must encounter his father's strict Evangelical beliefs. In his version of Christian theology, his father "loved Paul of Tarsus, liked St. John, [and] hated St. James as much as he dared..." (161). If I want to understand this, I realize that I have to look up some of the information. Just continuing to read—as I often have done—is not a satisfying way of having this part of the experience. There is a good scholarly note explaining the references in the Oxford World Classics edition.[3] But a more illuminating comment is to be found in a Bible edited by Ernest Sutherland Bates. Bates writes about the "Letter of St. James":

> [I]ts passionate protest against social injustice, together with its stout affirmation of the doctrine of salvation by works, seems to represent a conscious reaction against the subjective tendency of Paul's teaching. Almost rejected from the Canon because of its anti-Pauline character and denounced by Martin Luther for the same reason, it is yet the most modern work in the Bible, in its impassioned social-mindedness and in its style of mingled tenderness and satire.[4]

With this in mind, it now seems clear why Parson Clare could not bear this part of his religion.

For the Reverend Clare, "The New Testament was less a Christiad than a Pauliad," an uncritical emotional bonding to a creed of bodily denial: it "amounted, on its negative side, to a renunciative philosophy which had cousinship with that of Schopenhauer and Leopardi" (161). It is Hardy who is intimating some larger view here, since Mr. Clare is not one to have acquaintance with such heterodox texts as those of Schopenhauer or Leopardi. Why mention such "cousinship" at all? At this point, I can simply move on and ignore this learned allusion, or I can take my stance as a scholarly reader, which I am, and see how it affects my experience. I know that Hardy *personally* was attracted to the thought of Schopenhauer and to the poetry of Leopardi. But here in the context of Hardy's creative experiment as a novelist, he is risking some devaluation of his own pessimism by aligning it with the humanly destructive theology of the Reverend Clare. Nor did Hardy value either of these authors in simplistic terms for their "renunciative philosophy." His own note-taking on Leopardi indicates that he thought of him as one of the "impassioned revolutionaries" of poetry.[5] The effect I eventually derive from the inclusion of Leopardi and Schopenhauer in the passage from *Tess* is not one that adds stature to the Reverend Clare's intellect. It functions as a way for Hardy to suggest a broader scope for the novel's critical force. The novel is not aimed solely against Christian sexual repression, but shows an underlying awareness of other cultural sources of the renunciation of pleasure as well. Which suggests the question: how large is Hardy's intended scope here? It might be hinted at later in this novel where Hardy refers, as a condition of Angel's thinking, to "western civilization" (263). The context is Angel's warning to Izz, who is willing to run off with him: "But I ought to remind you that it will be wrong-doing in the eyes of civilization—western civilization, that is to say" (263). Clearly, Angel is making a distinction here between western and other civilizations; and, once again in *Tess*, the implicit context is not the totality of western civilization, but that civilization in its relation to codes of sexual behavior.

Angel has been through something that would not even be thinkable in his father's world: "To *the aesthetic, sensuous, Pagan pleasure in natural life and lush womanhood* which his son *Angel had lately been experiencing* in Var Vale, his temper would have been antipathetic in a high degree, had he either by inquiry or imagination been able to apprehend it" (161, my emphasis). At this point Hardy tells us that in the past, Angel had impulsively said to his father that "it might have resulted far better for mankind *if Greece had been the source of the religion in modern civilization*, and not Palestine" (161, my emphasis). These words had thrown his father into a state of dumb grief. As the philologist Lennart Björk has shown in his study of Hardy's thought, what Greece symbolizes at this time in Hardy's mind is a civilization that was closely aligned with Nature.[6] As Björk shows, it is not simply a matter of Matthew Arnold's concept of Hellenism. Angel's favoring of Greece is implicit with Hardy's own cultural-historical critique of the modern, Western world. Hardy associates ancient Greece and paganism with "native joyousness and exultation in life" (Hardy quoted by Björk, 133). The Greeks seemed to have been free of sexually repressive thinking even when they acted cruelly. In a Notebook entry on Greek sexual morality and the problem of women being forced into sexual relationships, Hardy wrote: "When a town was captured, the noblest & fairest ladies became concubines of the victors; such a fate was in no sense a dishonor of which they would be afterwards be ashamed–merely a misfortune".[7]

Amusingly, Hardy follows the account of the Reverend Clare's upset at his son's slipping into praise for the religious potential of ancient Greece by damning with repulsive praise: despite Angel's heretical remark, Rev. Clare "welcomed his son today with a smile which was as candidly sweet as a child's" (161). I cannot resist associating that "candidly" with a candied one. (Do I hear echoes of a Dickensian rendition of smugness?). I can feel here a kind of ghastly innocence in this father, one in which his doctrinal commitments are disguised to himself as obvious facts never to be questioned. But the smile, however it is felt, is obviously not going to suffice, in light of Angel's recent experience: "Latterly he had seen only Life, felt only the great passionate pulse of existence, *unwarped, uncontorted, untrammelled by those creeds which futilely attempt to check what wisdom would be content to regulate*" (161, my emphasis). This latter part of the sentence, after the word "untrammeled," seems to be part of Hardy's own thinking, his intimation of how things might be managed in a better society. It does not quite blend with Angel. But that part of the sentence has a slow-down in energy: the emphasis is on Angel having experienced "the great passionate pulse of existence" with no interference from Christian teachings.

As the remaining carefully rendered scenes of Angel and his father show, Angel is closer in his character structure to that of his father than their doctrinal differences would lead one to suspect. Earlier in the narrative, Hardy has specified that it was Article 4 of the Church of England's 39 Articles which Angel felt he had to reject, and thus break with the church. Article 39 proclaims that Jesus was Resurrected physically, literally, in the flesh (120). Mr. Clare to be sure does accept this doctrine, no doubt uncritically, but his attitude toward the human body does not sit well with the text of the Article: "Christ did truly rise again from death, and took again his body, with flesh, bones, and all things appertaining to the perfection of man's nature."[8] It now begins to feel ominous that Angel found unbearable this concept of the human body as perfection. Angel, like his father, also has a kind of innocence that connotes un-reflective belief in his own version of the truth. When the Rev. Clare quotes to Angel the passage from I Corinthians, "we are made as the filth of the world," Angel does not protest his father's designation of these as "ancient and noble words" (169). And "though the younger could not accept his parent's narrow dogma, he revered his practice and recognized the hero under the pietist" (169). But no one can so easily separate theory and practice as this division would demand. To his son, Mr. Clare is a hero, this passage explains, for allowing himself to be abused and beaten by the drunken men he attempts to "save." I get an uncanny feeling here that Angel is not actually rejecting the narrow dogma behind such an evaluation of heroism. Chapter 26 ends on a note of son-father affinity: "Angel often felt that he was nearer to his father on the human side than was either of his brethren" (170). By the "human side," Hardy explains, Angel refers to his father's "unworldliness," his freedom from material concerns. But unworldliness is a weird virtue for a man smitten with Tess's physical beauty.

2. The Wedding Goal: An End Fixed Upon

In chapters 27-29, after Angel's return from his parents' household, Tess and Angel's relationship leads to a resurgence of the feeling I have already noticed: there is a powerful suggestion called for by Hardy's writing in this section of the novel, that what they need, above anything else, is to consummate. Sexually. *Tess* is a late Victorian novel by a novelist who was born in 1840, but the effect is the opposite of what might be expected if a stereotypical notion of the literary period were to be allowed to control the experience.

That Angel, on returning from the repressive atmosphere of a visit back to his family, perceives subliminally a sign of the treacherous female in Tess is not surprising, given his confused attitudes toward sex, but there is no hint here that such a feminine aura is a condemnation:

> She was yawning, and he saw the red interior of her mouth as if it had been a snake's. She had stretched one arm so high above her coiled-up cable of hair that he could see its satin delicacy above the sunburn; her face was flushed with sleep, and her eyelids hung heavy over their pupils. The brim-fullness of her nature breathed from her. It was a moment when a woman's soul is more incarnate than at any other time; when the most spiritual beauty bespeaks itself flesh; and sex takes the outside place in the presentation. (172)

Given Angel's character structure and his movement toward change, this combination of the sensual and the soulful is just what would draw him on.

The language of this passage would seem to call for response in depth. In this context, I find that Tess's snake-like mouth is actually sexy, and not an automatic indicator of hidden misogyny. Snakes can be quite beautiful. But am I, or is anyone, capable of sustaining such response, in the present context of cultural history? To put the question differently, can readers of our own time enter into Angel's felt experience here, or must they pass it over, or simply condemn it? There would seem to be immense barriers, or experience blockers, in the way.

As an example, consider the feminist reading by Patricia Ingham. Ingham finds that in this passage, the narrator "construes [Tess] as all sex, reaching a description of generic 'woman' which is highly reductive."[9] Or so Ingham experiences it. Yet it is clear that while Hardy may believe in the concept of generic woman, it is Angel who is having this experience of Tess. This therefore is not simply the narrator's "generic" definition of woman, or Hardy's either, especially since nothing like the snake image occurs in Hardy's other descriptions of Tess's beauty, anywhere in the novel. It could hardly be a matter of "all sex" either, since it includes her incarnated "soul" and her "most spiritual beauty," unless Ingham assumes that soul and spirit are not only being expressed as flesh at this "moment" in Angel's experience, but are being equated with flesh in some permanent, reductive way.

The passage is undoubtedly erotic in nature. In Ingham's somewhat elliptical choice of quotation, it does treat Tess as "woman" rather than someone with individual qualities (those are described at many other points), but I do not see why that should be castigated in the present context. If we are not to create a new era of sexual repression, let us admit that there are times when anyone—woman or man—appears to a lover as completely sexual.

The moment soon passes, and Hardy goes on to particularize the description in a delicate way, one that demands a complex perception: "Then those eyes flashed brightly through their filmy heaviness, before the remainder of her face was well awake. With an oddly compounded look of gladness, shyness and surprise, she exclaimed, 'O, Mr. Clare—how you frightened me—I—'" (172).

When he embraces Tess, and puts "his face to her flushed cheek," she responds sexually, and her whole body is suffused with natural light:

> Tess's excitable heart beat against his by way of reply; and there they stood upon the red-brick floor of the entry, the sun slanting in by the window upon his back, as he held her tightly to his breast; upon her inclining face, upon the blue veins of her temple, upon her naked arm, and her neck, and into the depths of her hair. (172)

This is the sun that Hardy has said earlier was once and may still be a fitting object for humans to worship. "One could feel that a saner religion had never prevailed under the sky" (92). This mythic sun is male, but contrary to my critical expectations concerning patriarchal religion, he is also benevolently mild while having irresistible strength. His beams "broke through chinks of cottage shutters, throwing stripes like red-hot pokers upon cupboards, chests of drawers, and other furniture within; *and awakening harvesters who were not already astir*" (92, my emphasis). Notwithstanding the irresistible force of this sun upon material objects, its wakening of humans hardly suggests rapacious "penetration," as some critics of the novel have found. In fact, Hardy writes that this "luminary was a golden-haired, beaming, mild-eyed, godlike creature, gazing down in the vigour and intentness of youth upon an earth that was brimming with interest for him." (92)[10] Nature as a crucial, even sacred value is thus thoroughly mixed into the couple's loving. Angel "plumbed the deepness of her ever-varying pupils, with their radiating fibrils of blue, and black, and gray, and violet, while she regarded him as Eve at her second waking might have regarded Adam" (172). The chromatic change in her eyes suggests her ever-changing and yet same nature, which Angel here does not pull away from. (I have considered but have found unbelievable a feminist reading which holds that the narrator, assumed to be identical with Angel, is trying to "enter," that is, to penetrate Tess, "through her eyes".[11]) I recall here that in Diane Ackerman's *A Natural History of the Senses*, the iris is credited with immense individuality:

> Though on casual inspection, irises may look pretty much the same, the pattern of color, starbursts, spots and other features is so highly individual that law-enforcement people have considered using iris patterns in addition to fingerprints.[12]

Hardy, with his own profound understanding of the human body, could well have intuited something of this kind. As for the "second waking" of Eve, does this allude to the mythic moment when Adam is awakened by the now highly erotic woman with whom he has made love?[13]

Tess makes a verbal plea to get on with the skimming of milk, but as she works, "her hand trembled, the ardour of his affection being so palpable that she seemed to flinch under it like a plant in too burning a sun." And he licks the cream off of her finger; "he cleaned it," Hardy says, "in nature's way..." (173). Once I have allowed myself to feel that the urge to consummate the sexual impulse is part of Hardy's writing of this female and male, I can feel the emotional down-surge in this scene as Angel instead lapses into talking to her of "something of a very practical nature..."(173). It is a marriage proposal, but one that is worded in such a way as to swiftly de-eroticize the mood that has been built up: "I shall soon want to marry, and, being a farmer, you see I shall require for my wife a woman who knows all about the management of farms. Will you be that woman Tessy?" Tess of course knows that the purpose of this question is not to supply her with a job-description. She blurts several confusing negatives, unable to tell him that she has experienced sex. But among these negatives is also an ambiguous positive "I don't want to marry! I have not thought o' doing it. I cannot. I only want to love you" (173). The chapter ends with Tess feeling "turmoil" as soon as Angel inadvertanty alludes to Alec and "her own past" (175). Then, just as the sexual energy of the scene is thoroughly doused and dimmed, we are presented with a picture of women in Nature—the three milkmaids amongst their cows—that is the opposite of civilization's repressive Christian femininity:

> All the girls drew onward to the spot where the cows were grazing in the farther mead, the bevy advancing with the bold grace of wild animals—the reckless unchastened motion of women accustomed to unlimited space—in which they abandoned themselves to the air as a swimmer to the wave. It seemed natural enough to [Angel] now that Tess was again in sight, to choose a mate from unconstrained Nature, and not from the abodes of Art. (175)

This is primarily Angel's perception, and not Hardy's: Tess could hardly be denominated at this point as "unconstrained Nature" by Hardy. But Angel is feeling a lot, and he seems to have forgotten for this moment his requirement that his choice of a mate be "virginal."

Indeed there are little hints scattered around that in this culture, it is not always necessary to have a marriage license in order to make love. One of them occurs just after mention of the "bevy" of unconstrained females. To be sure, "love-making" in Hardy's vocabulary, does not mean having sex, but neither does it mean sexlessness:

> love-making being here more often accepted inconsiderately and for its own sweet sake than in the carking anxious homes of the ambitious, where a girl's craving for an establishment paralyzes *her healthy thought of a passion as an end.* (176, my emphasis)

Hardy can indeed think of this non-marital eroticism. In Deweyan terms, the "end-in-view" intimated here would be quite different from the fixed end, the marriage that Angel and Tess are now inexorably moving toward. That end-in-view would and should actually change, but given their moral code, it remains frozen.

Angel has proposed marriage. Could Tess accept this offer? By this time in the felt development of their relationship, her resolve to "never conscientiously allow any man to marry her" (141) seems to have been bypassed and rendered null, simply through the force of their attraction. When Tess puts Angel off, his reaction is not so much marital as sexual. He asks her, in fact, if she loves "any other man" (176). During their shared work of "breaking up the masses of curd before putting them into the vats," Angel suddenly bent lower and "kissed the inside vein of her soft arm" (177-8). Despite the fact that her arm, "from dabbling in curds, was as cold and damp to his mouth as a new gathered mushroom," she is instantly aroused: "But she was such a sheaf of susceptibilities that her pulse was accelerated by the touch, her blood driven to her finger-ends and the cool arms flushed hot" (149). Hardy then writes within an ethic of sexuality rather than of marriage: "Then, as though her heart had said, '*Is coyness longer necessary? Truth is truth between man and woman, as between man and man*,' she lifted her eyes, and they beamed devotedly into his as her lip rose in a tender half-smile" (178, my emphasis).

Angel soon bursts out with an expression of sheer frustration: "O, Tessy!...I *cannot* think why you are so tantalizing. Why do you disappoint me so? You seem almost like a coquette, upon my life you do—a coquette of the first urban water!" (178) Because he knows her as "the most honest, spotless creature that ever lived," he cannot understand how he can suppose her "a flirt" (178). Of course she is not a flirt, but as these passages say, she herself has some intimation that her actions are those of someone playing coy, and he is having a correct intimation that she is *not* the perfect, conventionally spotless creature. Clare becomes so "pained and perplexed" at her demurral that he runs after her, catches her, then blurts helplessly: "'Tell me, tell me!'...passionately clasping her, in forgetfulness of his curdy hands; 'do tell me that you won't belong to anybody but me!'" Tess however can still hold back, though not because of any denial of sexuality. Yes, she will say yes, she says—but first "I will tell you my experience—all about myself—all!" (178).This sounds to me like something other than a mere blurting of an excuse. I hear something more in this declaration than a simple need to confess: her sense that her actual life, not only her image, must be allowed to register in their loving embrace. She is still thinking; her "body-mind" is still connected, however much she is stressed. She has a painful analytic insight even in her most helpless bodily cry, at the end of this chapter:

"I shall give way—I shall say yes—I shall let myself marry him—I cannot help it!" she jealously panted, with her hot face to the pillow that night, on hearing one of the other girls sigh his name in her sleep. "I can't bear to let anybody have him but me! *Yet it is wrong to him, and may kill him when he knows!* O my heart—O—O—O!" (179-80, my emphasis)

This cry of sexual longing and terrible conflict I find deeply affecting—but only when I relinquish any image of myself as a superior, controlled professorial person. This is certainly a place for Dewey's notion of "a cultivated naiveté" (*EN* 40), if there is to be an experience here. In common human nature, I know that my body is not any more sophisticated than hers. This is a sexual body cry—a "body's cry of Where?" as Hardy has phrased it earlier, if there ever was one. And yet, with my re-readings, I have come to take seriously Tess's intimation that Angel when he finds out what her sexual experiences have been—could die. It is not only an expression of conflict over whether to marry or not marry; it is not in other words only an expression of female desire. It is a concern for this particular man. I do not know how literally I should read the word "kill," but I know that the blow will be a bodily one. Angel, as many passages already have shown, is not just a male "mind." He is also a sexual human body. And Tess is not completely wrong to be concerned about him later on, when he reacts so miserably.

As the pressure for release increases to a climax, Tess is overcome: here the emotion is one that fuses frustration with the hope for cónsummation: she "flung herself down upon the rustling under-growth of spear-grass as upon a bed, and remained crouching in palpitating misery broken by momentary shoots of joy, which her fears about the ending could not altogether suppress" (179).

Immediately, "In reality..."—and here Hardy begins a five-paragraph openly omniscient comment on her situation, blending this almost imperceptibly with her responses and with the Nature context: "every wave of her blood, every pulse singing in her ears, was a voice that joined with Nature in revolt against her scrupulousness" (179). She remained among the willows where she had flung herself down for the remainder of the afternoon. There she hears the "waow-waow!" of the cows. This is the only the second time that evocative call is mimed by Hardy's writing, since its introduction upon Tess's momentous entry into the rich dairyland countryside. After "the sun settled down upon the levels, with the aspect of a great forge in the heavens," she still has not given in to her desire, and very soon the natural context shifts to one of cruel frustration: a "monstrous pumpkin-like moon" arises, and the willows, "tortured out of their natural shape by incessant choppings, became spiny-haired monsters..." (179).

Finally, Tess gives in to her sexual self: "I can't bear to let anybody have him, but me!" (179-80). The chapter thus ends with a fusion of Hardy and Tess in emotional consort. The felt quality is that of frustration in motion, painfully and pleasurably reaching a peak and beginning to crumble. These paragraphs, nominally concerned with the answer to a marriage proposal, have barely alluded to it, and instead are rendered in a language of love: "to snatch ripe pleasure before the iron teeth of pain" could "shut upon her"—"that was what love counselled," and Tess, "in almost a terror of ecstasy" realizes that "despite her many months of lonely self-chastisement, wrestlings, communings, schemes to lead a future of austere isolation, love's counsel would prevail" (179).[14]

3. Body-Mind in Distortion

This new level of pressure and longing is probably even more intense than the first peak, and is all the more damaging when it too is thwarted. The characters feel all this, Hardy himself seems to be feeling it, and as a reader undergoing the experience, I feel what it must be like for them.

With the new complexity, there are painful indications of sexual love being not only frustrated or delayed, but of the severity of this feeling leading to a deformation of the love impulse. The point of change in quality seems to begin when the pressure of the marriage proposal is felt. It puts Tess into complete emotional self-conflict. "Tess had never before known a time in which the thread of her life was so distinctly twisted of two strands, positive pleasure and positive pain" (177). Before long, a more disturbing quality seems to invade her consciousness of Clare: "She loved him so passionately, and *he was so godlike in her eyes...*" (183). Godlike? This is strange! Hardy certainly has not presented Angel as having any godlike qualities. Hardy has characterized him as having "something nebulous, preoccupied, vague, in his bearing and regard," and as a man who had lost the qualities of mind-body vitality he had had as a child: "as a lad people had said of him that he was one who might do anything if he tried" (119). Yet for "years and years," until deciding to train himself for farming, he had been lost in "desultory studies, undertakings, and meditations..." (121)

After receiving her mother's letter urging her not to tell her now-exalted Angel anything about her sexual history, Tess tries to believe that "silence it should be" (192). But with this pseudo-solution, her emotional state immediately becomes so extraordinary that it must demand attention from anyone experiencing this part of the novel:

> ...she lived in spiritual altitudes more nearly approaching ecstasy than any other period of her life.
>
> There was hardly a touch of earth in her love for Clare. To her sublime trustfulness he was all that goodness could be—knew all that a guide, philosopher, and friend should know. She thought every line in the contour of his person the perfection of masculine beauty; his soul the soul of a saint; his intellect that of a seer. The wisdom of her love for him, as love, sustained her dignity; she seemed to be wearing a crown. The compassion of his love for her, as she saw it, made her lift up her heart to him in devotion....
>
> She dismissed the past; trod upon it and put it out, as one treads on a coal that is smouldering and dangerous. (193)

I have caught myself in earlier readings trying to skim over this passage. It makes me very uncomfortable. I was much like the critic Kathleen Blake, who claims that Tess's idealizing of Angel is not a very serious matter.[15] It took the prodding of my reader's responsibility by a psychological critic, Bernard Paris, to force me to face the fact: this whole description of Tess's condition feels pathological. In fact, if I could read the novel as the story of Tess's neurosis, Paris's expertly performed (and almost never cited) analysis in the light of the theories of Karen Horney would be definitive.[16] What has to be felt and admitted, I think, is that Tess's idealization of Angel now far exceeds the illusions of love. It is not a response to Nature or to Talbothays, nor to her pantheistic sense of religion, nor to Angel as he really is, nor to her own sexual self; any sources of energy from those parts of her situation are active only in some distorted form. There is an inflated quality that is all too clear. "Angel Clare was far from what she thought him in this respect; absurdly far, indeed" (193). Angel has a great deal of self-control, but this is due to his temperament, not to any supreme goodness or wisdom: "he was in truth more spiritual than animal" (193). Hardy's explanation of why Tess so badly mistakes Angel feels somewhat understated and abstract: Tess is "amazed and enraptured" and "in her reaction from indignation against the male sex she swerved to excess of honour for Clare" (193). I would say more: she is desperately creating a sense of certainty and safety in her attempt to deny any "touch of earth in her love for Clare,"[17] her seeing him as "the perfection of masculine beauty," as saint and seer. Her need for dignity is over-fulfilled by her imaginary "crown." This is not honor. The earlier directly felt "terror of ecstasy" is now simplified dangerously to nothing but ecstasy. And her belief that she is successfully stamping out her past experiences rings hollow. In the world of her actual Body-Mind, things just cannot be this "good." Nor can she.

Thus, toward the end of the "Phase," Tess makes a suggestion which I can only regard as sadistic. After her marriage ceremony, which is so formal that in it "the ordinary sensibilities of sex seemed a flippancy" (211), and just prior to her riding off triumphantly with Angel on what is supposed to be their honeymoon, she impulsively urges Angel to kiss each of the three women who have been desperately in love with him. She does this in spite of her intuitive understanding, expressed a few chapters earlier to Angel, that the lives of these three women are "Not so very different" from their own, and that contrary to what he has suggested, there are "very few women's lives that are not—tremulous" (184). These are the women who have openly, pantingly, pined for Angel. They have done their utmost to renounce Clare. In a body-to-body ritual of their own devising, they acted out this renunciation, literally in touch with Tess:

> And by a sort of fascination the three girls, one after another crept out of their beds, and came and stood barefooted around Tess. Retty put her hands upon Tess's shoulders, as if to realize her friend's corporeality after such a

miracle [of the milkmaid winning the hand of a gentleman], and the other two laid their arms around her waist, all looking into her face. (198)

They admit that they would like to hate Tess, but they cannot. Tess cannot accept this admiration, and insists that they are better than she: "And suddenly tearing away from their clinging arms she burst into a hysterical fit of tears, *bowing herself on the chest of drawers* and repeating incessantly, 'O yes, yes, yes!' "(198, my emphasis) The repeated Yes here is technically to say that she does indeed think Retty, Izz and Marian are better women than she, but in context, the Yes seems a helpless assent to accepting her good fortune and becoming Angel's wife. The three women, aware that Angel has never shown any interest in any of them, try not to allow her to think that they believe she is worse, and once again enact a bodily solidarity: "They went up to her and clasped her round, but still her sobs tore her...They gently led her back to the side of her bed, where they kissed her warmly" (198-9). Tess calms down and even admits that she is proud to be chosen by Angel. Secretly, however, she transforms this act of support by her roommates into a resolution to tell all to Angel (199).

But now, weeks later, just after her marriage ceremony, Tess does not let these three women have what little peace they have made; she gives her sadistic suggestion to Angel: "She impulsively whispered to him—'Will you kiss 'em all, once, poor things, for the first and last time?'" (213). He does so, without any conscious awareness of what his male body means to them. In the following chapter Tess learns that the women have been so upset by this "kindness" that one has tried to drown herself, a second has "been found dead drunk by the withy-bed," and the third, Izz Huett, is visibly depressed (218-19). For me, well inculcated by now into the series of perceptions that make up my reading of the novel, the pain that these women must feel is palpable, something I can more than infer. Hardy, who is often said by his critics to go out of his way to defend Tess's every action, does nothing to shield his readers from the brutality of Tess's kindness. He does not comment.

Then instead of realizing what she has done, Tess uses this episode to finally convince herself that she must tell Angel of her past with Alec. She imagines that this is only fair to the three women, an irrational equation made absurd by the fact of her having just been married to Angel. It is too late to be fair; he has been taken from them. Nor is there any indication at this point to show that Angel is attracted to these women.

But by this point, Tess's thinking about her relationship to Clare has become grotesque in its distortion. At a peak moment just prior to going to church for the ceremony, Tess manages to feel reassured that Angel will not reject her for her past, but Hardy describes not so much her relief at this but what I feel as sickening euphoria: "Her one desire, so long resisted, to make herself his, to call him her lord, her own—then, if necessary, to die—had at last lifted her up from her plodding reflective pathway" (210). This unnatural thinking is new for Tess, at least in such a degree. The long unsatisfied sexual desire, and her conflicted feelings concerning her own sexual past, are at this point confounded with concepts of secure ownership and of being owned, of triumph and of voluntary death. That this is disturbed thinking is made even clearer in the next sentence: "...she moved about in a mental cloud of many-coloured idealities, which eclipsed all sinister contingencies by its brightness" (210).

Is Hardy the commentator fully in synchrony here with his character, Tess? Not quite. As I read through the intense complexities of the marriage day, I at first find him eloquent on the topic of Tess's utter devotion: Angel, I am told, knew through bodily perception that Tess loved him: "every curve of her form showed that—" but what he did not know as yet—what Hardy knows—is "the full depth of her devotion, its single-mindedness, its meekness; what long-suffering it guaranteed, what honesty, what endurance, what good-faith" (211). This cast of virtues I find uncomfortably predictive of how Hardy will want to develop her in the aftermath, the "Phase" he entitles "The Woman Pays." The notion of a "guaranteed" suffering is of a piece with Tess's own reaching out for the security of being owned and owning. But Tess herself has glimpses of the dangers and delusory quality of such guarantees:

> Her idolatry of this man was such that she herself almost feared it to be ill-omened. She was conscious of the notion expressed by Friar Laurence: "These violent delights have violent ends." It might be too desperate for human conditions—too rank, too wild, too deadly. (212)

Despite her conscious awareness, her intermixture of erotic qualities, rank and wild, with violence and deadliness, feels as if it is becoming terribly entangled and confused. This is, as Hardy writes, "the highly-charged mental atmosphere in which she was living" (211). The mental is now split off; Nature is out of the picture. It is a crucial change of quality. In contrast to the natural context of the past 13 chapters, the church wedding bells offer only a "limited amount of expression," and while Tess "could feel the vibrant air humming round them," her self-image is utterly artificial. In this "condition of mind," she "felt glorified by an irradiation not her own, like the angel whom St. John saw in the sun" (211). Indeed this is not her own; it substitutes a mystical irradiation for her own sense of her body, with the suggestion of a sun that is part of a super-natural event. "By the time they reached home, she was contrite and spiritless" (212). When she does have a few moments alone and can focus her thoughts, she formulates the perfectly accurate objection to her marriage: "O my love, my love, why do I love you so!...for she you love is not my real self, but one in my own image: the one I might have been" (212). This objection she does not attempt to answer. The blockage in her thinking is blatantly noticeable. But deeper than whatever irony it may arouse is the meaning that emerges from a consideration of context. Once the context has been changed from the natural impulses of the two lovers to the controlled, conventionalized expectations of a formal marriage in the church, the powerful ideal of Tess as a virgin takes over and blots out any perception Angel has had of Tess as a real woman. Despite what her body is telling him—despite his knowing that "every curve of her form" showed that she loved him—he can only think of her as an ideal of womanhood rather than this particular, humanly vulnerable woman. That is what Tess is intuiting. Shortly after, she has Angel kiss her three women friends. This gesture can be felt as her self-punitive response, but she hurts more than herself.

Soon after, looking at her fingers mingling in a washbasin with those of Angel, Tess tries "to be gayer than she was," and tells him that all the fingers, hers and his, are "all yours." He of course does not mind this offering, but inwardly she cringes: "Tess knew that she had been thoughtful to excess and struggled against it" (215). I feel her attempt to maintain some sanity in an impossible situation. The next detail is about the sun, once more, but coming after the irradiation of St. John a few pages earlier, it cannot be felt as simply the natural sun. Instead it is a morally condemning pointer, and can be taken as Tess's own projected feeling, rather than simply an idea imposed by Hardy: "The sun was so low...that it shone in through a small opening and formed a golden staff which stretched across to her skirt, where it made a spot like a paint-mark set upon her" (215). This figure of the paint-mark must recall the painter of sexual, sin-condemning texts, earlier in the novel. But it is not Nature—any more than was that painter. The words of Revelations 19:17, to which Hardy has referred, are quite hideous:

> Then I saw an angel standing in the sun, and he cried aloud to all the birds flying in mid-heaven: "Come and gather for God's great supper, to eat the flesh of kings and commanders and fighting men, the flesh of horses and their riders, the flesh of all men, slave and free, great and small!"

This is not an image of undistorted nature, as has sometimes been assumed.[18]

4. Omens in Experience

The account of the wedding day and its immediate aftermath is suffused with omens. Hardy is enamored of omens—that is part of his own folk background—but in this sequence he gathers more of them than he does anywhere else in his fiction, so far as I can recall.

They are of a wide variety. The effect is one of corroboration: the mood feels ominous from every aspect. One of the first omens takes the form of Tess using some of her learning: she fancies that the wedding robe Angel has bought for her might change color and betray her, as did the robe of Queen Guénever in one of the Arthurian legend ballads her mother had once taught her (205). Hardy emphasizes this fear of Tess's by making it the end of a chapter (chapter 32). For the reader, it seems to bring back the feeling that Tess's family is only able to provide her with harmful stuff. And there are many more bad signs. The carriage Angel obtains for their ride to and from the church is a "cumbrous and creaking structure," redolent with the malign aura of the d'Urberville ancestors. The man who drives it is a grotesque presence, his body literally rotting: "He had a permanent running wound on the outside of his right leg, originated by the constant bruisings of aristocratic carriage poles during the many years he had been in regular employ at the King's Arms, Casterbridge" (210). In this context, the name Casterbridge might suggest castration. Tess believes she has seen this carriage before, but only in a dream, as if by unfavorable affinity with the d'Urberville blood. There is a local "superstition," Angel begins to tell her, about this carriage and some terrible past event that will cause harm to any member of the family, such as Tess, who happens to encounter it. But realizing that Tess is becoming upset, Angel then awkwardly declines to say just what all this is about (211-12). This increases the sense of anxiety. As Tess and Angel leave the dairy for the farmhouse where they expect to have their honeymoon, a cock crows loudly in the afternoon, which is considered very bad luck (213). The farmhouse itself is one that formerly was a part of the d'Urberville mansion, and when they enter it, Tess is overcome with the ghastly-looking portraits, "suggestive of merciless treachery," of two d'Urberville women of centuries past, in paintings that are irremovable: they are fixed into the wall (214). Worse still, Angel can see that "her fine features were unquestionably traceable in these exaggerated forms" (215).

The de-natured sun, as I have described, is now matched by de-natured stars: Tess receives a gift of expensive old jewelry from her in-laws; Angel perceives that they "gleamed somewhat ironically" in the firelight, but cannot believe his own mind: "'Yet why?' he asked himself" (217). He nervously decides that Tess, being a d'Urberville, can be suitably attired in these items of mere vanity. As the couple finish their supper, "there was a jerk in the fire-smoke, the rising skein of which bulged out into the room, as if some giant had laid his hand on the chimney-top for a moment" (218). This premonition is triggered by the otherwise humdrum fact of a servant bringing their luggage—unremarkable except that he also brings the news that her 3 chamber-mates have all suffered miserably in the few hours since Tess had left them and driven off with her husband. Soon, in the glare of the "now flameless embers" of the fireplace (with its "old brass tongs that would not meet"), Tess's "face and neck reflected the same warmth, and each gem turned into an Aldebaran or a Sirius—a constellation of white, red, and green flashes, that interchanged their hues with her every pulsation" (220). These are weird unnatural stars, with a quality of frantic exaggeration of what might be seen outdoors in the sky on a fine night, such as Tess had told of doing when she was first seen by Angel at the dairy (124).

How can these omens be experienced? I find them to cause an overall darkening and rotting of quality; a form of contagion of the human context.

Nature glowers not as a repetitive warning—if it is read this way, it leads to a habitual and ultimately boring response—but as a contagion of Nature taken from the way people act. *Of course* on Tess and Angel's wedding day, the omens are all awful, and no one will need a critic to give pointers on this, but the way nature is off-key and ugly is part of the feeling of how humans, acting on values that are counter to nature, spoil the celebratory consummation of a sexual-love relationship. This impression suggests that Clare's "hard logical" center of self, mentioned in the text only a chapter later, is active on this day *even though he feels just fine*; the marriage legality may be emboldening his expectations even beyond those he must have held back until this day, of a perfect virginal woman who will guarantee his happiness. The premonitions of evil, which is one way all of these things can be read, seem to me to be experienced as the emotional quality surrounding and permeating the crucial confession scene. It is felt as sickening before the actual occurrence of Tess telling Angel of her past. *The feeling moves retroactively; it is a dense, fluid movement of emotional energy occurring throughout the sequence.* But it is the event of her confession, in all its individualized intensity, that provides the quality to the whole set of omens.

This is emotion functioning as Dewey would expect (*AE* 48-50). In response, I have a feeling of horror mixed with lamentation for these lovers, whose most intimate desires are now being destroyed by forces within and around themselves. This feeling depends on my having identified with their desires. One may object (as usual) that such is merely my own manner of reading. But unless a reader were strenuously resisting the novel, I do not see how some such identification with what the characters are going through could be avoided.

The full quality of the portentous scenes leading up to and past the confession involves more than just Tess's need to follow her conscience and tell Angel the truth about her past. After the wedding ceremony, she thinks that she may not have "any moral right" to the name, Mrs Angel Clare. "Was she not more truly Mrs Alexander d'Urberville?" (212). This is a disturbing thought, and also an irrational one: she imagines that a woman becomes a man's wife simply by having had sex with him. I intuit here that Tess on her wedding day is disturbed by the intrusion into her mind of images of her love-making with Alec. Memories of Alec's lovemaking, of his thrusting penis, in other words, may be threatening to intrude upon her mind. She would also have memory traces of her own participation in that lovemaking. Angel, who experiences a euphoric feeling of Tess's sexual purity, is also in some doubt. I believe Hardy insinuates that Angel has more knowledge than he himself knows of, when Angel elaborately tells himself that she is on no account to be hurt:

> Looking at her silently for a long time: "She is a dear, dear Tess," he thought to himself, *as one deciding on the true construction of a difficult passage*. "Do I realize solemnly enough how utterly and irretrievably this little womanly thing is the creature of my good or bad faith and fortune? I

think not. I think I could not, unless I were a woman myself ...And shall I ever neglect her, or hurt her, or even forget to consider her? God forbid such a crime!" (215, my emphasis)

Why think of a crime that has to be forbidden by God, unless he is tempted to commit it? He is having some feelings of self-doubt and hostility here, along with an impressive realization that he cannot understand what it is like to be a woman—and perhaps an intimation that in fact he can. I find also a heart-rending combination in these thoughts of his demeaning but naive sympathy for her, "this little womanly thing," and his un-realized insight that she is "the creature" of his own good or bad faith. I recall now his nightmare a few chapters earlier, in which he fights against the man who has voiced the insult that Tess is not a "maid," that is, not a virgin (206). To be sure, a character had indeed said such a thing, and Angel had punched him, but when Angel repeats the struggle in a violent dream, Hardy has indicated Angel's unconscious knowledge that Tess cannot be defended on this score. "I am so sorry I disturbed you!" he had exclaimed then to Tess. "I fell asleep and dreamt that I was fighting that fellow again who insulted you, and the noise you heard was *my pummeling away with my fists* at my portmanteau..." (207, my emphasis). Tess had heard "a sound of thumping and struggling" (207). I realize now with whom Angel was struggling in this dream of his. It was himself.

5. Intimate Conflicts

Angel, the bridegroom who is about to consummate his marriage, now touches Tess in an unprecedented way: "coming in to where she sat over the hearth, [Angel] pressed her cheeks between his hands from behind. He expected her to jump up gaily and unpack the toilet-gear that she had been so anxious about..." (219). Instead Tess thinks of the "simple and innocent girls upon whom the unhappiness of unrequited love had fallen," and decides that now she must confess. Her thought processes are invaded with self-sacrificing reparation: "*It was wicked of her to take all without paying.* She would pay to the utmost farthing; she would tell, there and then" (220, my emphasis). Remembering Alec's seductive moves, I suspect that Angel's surprising little game of touch from behind also set off her memories of Alec. I recall at this point how she had earlier said to herself, on the good fortune of being about to be wed: "I don't quite feel easy...All this good fortune may be *scourged out of me* afterwards by a lot of ill. That's how heaven mostly does" (204, my emphasis.). After her confession, she asks, "Angel, am I too wicked for you and me to live together?" (227). It is an appalling question: her self is sheared down from its fullness to this medieval moral scourging. But Tess has not invented the concept of the wicked. Beyond the force of her personal conscience, there is in Tess some accumulation of the destructive sexual ethics of her culture. The feeling may not be too difficult to experience: I would say that even in our own culture, concepts of sexual wickedness and being scourged for it are still around, however much we have progressed. We need to avoid taking a smugly superior attitude that places the experience in an entirely outmoded past. (I will return to this problem in the concluding chapter.)

When Tess finishes her confession, the grotesque mood is continued and intensified: "The fire in the grate looked impish, demoniacally funny, as if it did not care in the least about her strait. The fender grinned idly, as if it, too, did not care. The light from the water-bottle was merely engaged in a chromatic problem." (225). One perceptive critic reads such details as evidence of Tess becoming an object: her self is being displaced on to the fire, the fender, and the water-bottle.[19] Her feelings are taken from her and dispersed into objects. But this could not be entirely so: in my construction of this part of the experience, Tess must be feeling a great deal in this scene. She is feeling the down-surge of her courage to confess, she is feeling love, she surely is feeling anxious, she is feeling completely vulnerable and at the same time hopeful, and she is crossing the threshold into feeling rejection. If there were a total displacement of her own feelings on to the objects, none of that could have happened. Angel as he becomes suffused with shock undoubtedly would be feeling the demoniacal glare of the objects, and Hardy himself may be undergoing the feelings he is creating. The tone of maddening indifference resembles the tone of his comment much earlier in miming the voice of the prophet Elijah, who had described a God who was too busy, talking or taking a journey or sleeping, to be bothered with protecting Tess. But as the critic just mentioned realizes, "it is difficult to ascribe the point of view consistently to one character or even the narrator alone" in this scene.[20] As it is experienced, I find that the glare is first of all felt as horrible, and then, before very much further in the continuation of this scene, it can be felt as the rotting and destruction brought into two human lives by the cultural ideal of virginity as these two people attempt to live by it, and through it. Tess herself could be partially aware of the atmosphere, as she speaks; the fact that she has her forehead pressed against Angel's temple, "with her eyelids drooping down" (222), would not prevent her from perceiving the field of glaring "irresponsibility" (225) into which she is offering her life.

Angel's "face had withered," as he absorbs the shock of what Tess tells him of her self and the abyss of clashing values opens before him (225). The feeling of an enforced smothering of energy is finally broken with Angel's "horrible laughter—as unnatural and ghastly as a laugh in hell." This is followed by Tess's shriek as she begs for his mercy. He sees Tess with a strained look on her face, with eyes that "make his flesh creep" (227).

The confession scene and its reverberations call out complex responses. Experienced at a cognitive level, it provides some of the vital information that had been missing from the scene of Tess and Alec's first sexual act: Tess here by uttering "no exculpatory phrase of any kind" is not claiming any mercy for herself as a victim of rape. Her confession is quite complete; it involves "re-assertions and secondary explanations" (225). This is an important specification, one that has been overlooked by critical readers who assume that Hardy is telling nothing of the content of Tess's speech.[21] Had Tess told Angel that she had been raped, I will credit Angel with enough human responsiveness to have expressed at least some hostility toward Alec—but he does not. He had been furious a few chapters back when he had heard a man insult Tess's sexual reputation. I now recall that there was no outraged reaction either, earlier in the narrative, when Tess told her mother what had happened between her and Alec (87). We are not given her words on that occasion, but Joan would have had to be completely anesthetized not to have reacted with shock and anger at her daughter's report of having been raped. These considerations are not final; even in the present context, one can continue to suppose that Tess had been raped, and that she manages to tell Angel of this in a non-evaluative, declarative tone. But we must wonder how credible such a supposition could be.

The quality of what happened sexually on that night with Alec remains far from clear. This is an "inquiry" or "search" (Dewey's terms) whose resolution, if it is ever to come, must still be kept suspended. We may learn more about it later—if we manage to keep it in mind. As E. M. Forster said in *Aspects of the Novel*, it takes a lot of memory functioning to really read a novel. Moreover, the quality of memory needed makes a special experiential demand: part of the reader's attention remains attached to a particular event, granting it a sense of mystery or of a yet-to-be-determined quality, while the reader continues on his or her way, further into the text and into the further accrual of memory. "To appreciate a mystery, part of the mind must be left behind, brooding, while the other part goes marching on."[22]

But all this about the question of rape at this point in the novel is not foremost in the experience. I am asking myself what it was that agonized Angel. It could not have been Tess's loss of virginity alone, although that undoubtedly shocked him, but what Tess must have acknowledged or intimated in her confession, since she was being determinedly forthright: that she had not disliked the sex she had experienced with Alec.

In a larger context, what Tess and Angel go through in the situation of her confession of her "bygones" is an ethical issue. In my own repeated encounters with this scene, it feels so rotten that Angel will not "forgive" Tess for having allowed the misleading perception that she is still a virgin, when in fact she has had a sexual life with Alec and has even borne a child. Or rather, that he will not somehow come to terms with the fact that she is sexually experienced, regardless of her failure to have told him about it. In earlier readings, I have hoped that Angel will agree when Tess says that her past is of exactly the same calibre as his. Angel, who has just finished declaiming on "the sinner that I was!"—but ominously quoting his father's favorite saint, Paul, on the virtues of purity—tells how he has always "hated impurity." He introduces into his already abstract speech a quotation from one of the odes of Horace, noting without comprehension that this makes "strange company for St. Paul" (221). For Angel, telling of his own sexual experience calls for as much verbal buffer and remoteness as he can manage. His choice of vocabulary for saying what he has to say to Tess becomes another layer of ominous quality in the scene, when Tess confesses to him without any sort of circumlocution. But after Angel's stylized preamble, he does confess that once in London he had "plunged into" 48 hours of "dissipation" with a woman (221). True to his method, Hardy provides no details of this event, of which he had already given a very brief account, many chapters earlier (121). It is not a surprise for the reader. But now, at the last second, Hardy switches from Angel's first person account of it to his own third person re-telling for Angel. This at first feels confusing, but I ask the relevant question concerning aesthetic quality: is there any significant loss in continuity for having the experience? That will depend on how the situation develops. Unlike Tess, Angel (or Hardy) partially exculpates himself by qualifying this experience as one in which he had been "tossed about by doubts and difficulties... like a cork on the waves...." (221). The phrase rings false, since he probably enjoyed having sex with the woman, whoever she might have been. It could not have been completely involuntary. Tess hears him out, and then "jumped up joyfully" and declares that her own past "cannot be more serious, certainly...because it is just the same!" (221-2) But is she right? Tess's thinking here takes the same form as it did when she hoped that her dying son would be spared in the afterlife: "Perhaps it will be just the same," she had thought, even if he is not given a Christian burial. But here in this new situation, such a plea is repelled by the man.

Weighing this event more carefully in my own mind—no doubt in a mind affected by my own cultural assumptions—I no longer think that Tess's and Angel's pasts were "just the same." I cannot imagine any man who would accept this equation, unless it were a man who was so far liberated that he did not care about such sexual matters in his wife's life. Living with someone in a sexual relation for several weeks and having a baby would not be felt as *just* the same as a two day episode of intense sensual-sexual indulgence. It is "the same" in the sense of being a sexual experience undergone in violation of the culture's norms, but it is different. It is a deeper level of involvement.

When Tess realizes that Angel has frozen, that he is not responding to her words, her first effort to persuade him is in body-language uncannily suggestive of an instinctual gesture of submission: Tess "stood there staring at him with eyes that did not weep. Presently she slid down upon her knees beside his foot, and from this position she crouched in a heap" (226). Her verbal plea for forgiveness is made from this position. Angel ignores this profoundly moving, virtually primordial gesture. How can he? He can hardly be unaware that Tess is crouched at his feet. Does he read it as mere feminine befogging of the issue? Or has he some vague inner awareness of the meaning of her gesture and therefore instantly closes himself from it as something from the "inferior" world of animal life?

Angel does not merely remain frozen here: he not only rejects her reasoning at just this point but breaks into his "horrible laughter." Nothing could hurt more than this, a potentially lethal blow to her self. She shrieks, crying "Don't—don't! It kills me quite, that!" She then overtly begs for mercy, which does not even draw an answer, and "sickly white, she jumped up" (226).

But beyond her naïve hope for forgiveness, beyond her unthinking reflex of showing submission, Tess has the power to think deeply about the problem at hand. For my past several readings of this novel, I have repeatedly found my interest condensing around a single one of her statements. She is saying this standing up, no longer in a begging position. She states the only principle that could save their relationship:

> I thought, Angel, that *you loved me—me, my very self!* If it is I you do love, O how can it be that you look and speak so? It frightens me! *Having begun to love you, I love you for ever—in all changes, in all disgraces, because you are yourself.* I ask no more. (226, my emphasis)

This is a simple human principle of continuing to love the other as a distinct self, continuing, that is, because of love for that self, that other person. I have to take Tess's statement here very seriously if I am experiencing this novel. It is not simply a statement about forgiving a woman for her concealing her loss of virginity. Something of greater scope seems to be at stake.

Personally, I always cringe at the proviso of "for ever"—but then I also realize that it finally is not essential to what Tess is conveying. Love, I have learned, is not for ever, even though it is felt to be that. It does have to go through "all changes and disgraces." The combination of these two terms is not a conventional mixture. Very few marriage ceremonies are ever going to include such a pledge. Nor would the more advanced thinkers, Sue Bridehead and Jude Fawley, in *Jude the Obscure*, speak in these terms. The burden of Hardy's ethical claim in this novel is located here. This ethical principle which is relatively easy to accept within a generalized notion of love, must be applied in an area of human life where it seems hardest: to the sexual life of each to the other, in a culture where both changes and disgraces are all too possible. Changes must be included because they are essential to growth, as Dewey clearly understands, and these changes are frequently painful. Disgraces are part of the equation because Tess and Angel (and we today) still live in a culture that easily generates disapproval in matters of sexuality. In our case, it might be a matter of peer-driven disgrace among the young for *not* having sex, followed by having it under that kind of pressure. That is also an experience that would do something to a person; those too are disgraces, or potentially felt as disgraces.

Tess speaks an ethic that Angel truly cannot understand. This feels both sad and infuriating. Tess is no longer his Tess in her changes and disgraces, as far as his mind can know. To him she is an "imposter," a "guilty woman in the guise of an innocent one." The enormity of his refusal is immediately evident in its deteriorating physical effect on Tess, a deterioration she is all too aware that Angel can see: "Terror was upon her white face as she [realized how he was seeing her]; her cheek was flaccid, and her mouth had almost the aspect of a round little hole" (227). Hardy's writing here maintains an immediacy through its grounding in the bodily life of his character. The experience continues to feel intimate to the reader partly because of the inherent tacit relation to the reader's own body.

The ethical chasm between the two is developed in such painful depth over the next several scenes and pages that it seems to me that Angel and Tess have been in their honeymoon farmhouse for a very long time; later in the narrative I am stunned when Hardy indicates that the torment went on for only three days (261). It may have been somewhat longer than that, if my checking back into the text is correct—but in experienced duration for me as reader, it is a long trial. Only a careless reader would say that Angel "deserts her on their wedding night."[23] If only the break had been so clean! It is in the drawn-out quality of the experience that the difference between them is brought to some conclusion. It is something in Angel's character structure, the "hard, logical deposit, like a vein of metal in a soft loam, that turned the edge of everything that attempted to traverse it" (237), that finally makes him odious. How can this man stay for days and nights in such proximity to Tess, squelching her attempts to speak with him, forbidding her to argue, seeing her misery, noting how dearly she loves him, hearing her offer to commit suicide for the sake of his reputation, then put her through the agony of watching him construct a plan to leave her, instruct her not even to get in touch with him—and not come around to the forgiveness, or rather the sheer human acceptance that she has asked for? What is this "hard, logical deposit" he lives by? There is a traditional masculine tone to it, with his insistence that the "facts" cannot be changed: Tess is not the woman (he had thought) she should be. Of course she never will be. Integrated with this impeccable logic of the facts is the ideology of sexual control: sex has to fit a formula of female virtue proclaimed by Angel's culture—indeed by many cultures—as unalterable truth.

Hardy had tentatively tried to explain Angel by recourse to a generalization: "The cruelty of fooled honesty is often great after enlightenment, and it was mighty in Clare now" (228). But Clare's was a peculiar kind of honesty, like that of his father, an unreflecting faith in sexual dogma that now provides his feeling of injured innocence. That explanation falls short of feeling what the experience leads to: Clare is monstrous. Yet he may not be entirely to blame: disturbing my impulse to affix blame and be done with the matter, is the possibility that Angel is not monstrous out of any character flaw alone, but as a function of a cultural "deposit"—Hardy's chosen term—within his self. D. H. Lawrence says it:

It is not Angel Clare's fault that he cannot come to Tess when he finds that she has, in his words, been defiled. It is the result of generations of ultra-

Christian training, which had left in him an inherent aversion to the female, and to all in himself which pertained to the female.[24]

But that attribution of cause, though it seems precisely accurate to me, neglects the quality of Angel's thought processes. Lawrence underestimates the power of the guise of "logic" in which Angel's rejection of the woman takes place. If logic can be taken as a synonym for "reason," then it is especially painful to read of Angel's point of decision for leaving Tess: he wakes up after his night of sleepwalking and tries to find some sort of "mental pointing" in his own mind. He "knew" that if his intention "did not vanish in the light of morning, it stood on *a basis approximating to one of pure reason*, even if initiated by impulse of feeling; that it was so far, therefore, to be trusted." He can thus feel he is not leaving her because of "hot and indignant instinct..." (245, my emphasis). I can hardly make it past this juncture in the complex, almost Kantian reasoning. The enormity of looking for a justifying basis in "pure reason" to leave Tess, the delusive self-reassurance that heated emotion, here confused with "instinct," is not involved, has a choking feeling for me as I read. But then the Kantian tapeworm sentence-construction goes on further, and changes in quality: the resolve to separate from her is "denuded of the passionateness which had made it scorch and burn; standing in its bones, nothing but a skeleton, but none the less there" (245). This affect, with its bodily image, is simply appalling.

Tess, in telling about her intimate life, has also been telling him too much about himself. Beneath his disgusting complaint that by marrying below his class, he has failed to "secure rustic innocence" (234), lies another level of miserable realization of how false with his own self he has been. He cannot admit that he knows this now. Instead he creates new barriers between himself and her.

Years into re-reading the novel, I recall at this point Hardy's initial characterization of Angel as having "a long regard of fixed, abstracted eyes" (119). I can see and feel those eyes now, as he convinces himself he is dealing with "pure reason." The "long regard" is now intensified to an utterly "fixed" and frightening level.

Long after this, Tess will write to him, "O why have you treated me so monstrously, Angel!" (343). But I, like most readers, will not need her letter to have the realization. In a portrait of a d'Urberville dame hanging "immediately over the entrance to Tess's bed-chamber," Angel Clare thinks he sees "*a concentrated purpose of revenge on the other sex*" (231, my emphasis). He does not enter the bed-chamber, as he had wanted to do, perhaps to consummate their marriage; instead he projects on to Tess his own need for revenge. It is revenge of the kind Lawrence had articulated: not against her as her self, but on the whole "other sex."

This is a horrible revenge. She is there with him, she is there in the living flesh eager to be made love to, but Angel does not break down. Hardy ventures one of his most disturbing assertions, but makes it feel weird: "Some might risk the odd paradox that with more animalism he would have been the nobler man. We do not say it" (240). But Hardy, as "we," *has* said it. Like many readers, I have tripped over this passage many times, unable to digest it. Why the denial, the feeling of not wishing to be responsible for the comment? I can try to pass by, and simply read on to find Hardy immediately saying that "Clare's love was doubtless ethereal to a fault, imaginative to impracticability" (240). That at least seems to make the point without retraction. But passing over the prior declaration does feels as if something important is being missed. As Dewey would ask, What is this passage doing with and in the experience of this novel? As my re-readings continued, I finally thought to ask myself what it must have been like to write this passage in 1892. Neither this passage nor the "ethereal to a fault" were in the manuscript or in the 1891 version. Could it be one of Hardy's blunders?

A suggestion by Rosemary Sumner helped me to overcome my blocked response. "This evasiveness," she wrote, "shows Hardy's awareness of being too far ahead of his time in suggesting such a view."[25] Yes: it took a lot of courage to say that a man needs to have more "animalism." To say that he is ethereal and impractical sounds more palatable, because more literary. But it is not the same thing, not quite. To call for more *animalism* must have been a jarring new thought to put into an English novel. D.H. Lawrence might have suggested something of this kind in his own novels, but it was too early for Lawrence. Anyhow, Lawrence has been dead for over 70 years: today I can think of few if any authors who would say that a male character needs more animalism. (To specify "more" also avoids the reductively medical implication that Angel was without any of the animal in his nature at all.) Weirdly buffered as the term is in Hardy's presentation, it packs a punch. Angel needs more animalism if he is to overcome his fear and make love to Tess, all right, and Hardy's narrative needs the term.

The mood of increasingly irreversible disaster for Tess and Angel is broken only in the extraordinary episode of Angel's sleep-walking. There Hardy for the first time since the ominous marriage ceremony allows the beauty of Nature to permeate the quality. Nature is beautiful in this context for its very lack of any attachment to a moral code, and for its fusion of peaceful and violent energies that allows the feelings of Tess and Angel to gain expression. Angel

at length stood still on the brink of the river.

Its waters, in creeping down these miles of meadow-land, frequently divided, serpentining in purposeless curves, looping themselves around little islands that had no name, returning, and re-embodying themselves as a broad main stream further on. ....The swift stream raced and gyrated under them, tossing, distorting, and splitting the moon's reflected face. Spots of froth travelled past, and intercepted weeds waved behind the piles. (243-4)

And Tess, though she is regarded by Angel's sleep-speaking self as "dead," can feel and can trust his bodily tenderness as he carries her, while he walks asleep.

He loves her. This gives her, and me, some hope. She resists the impulse to end both of their lives by propelling them both into the river (in what would have been a fine Victorian climax), and then dying together:

> their arms would be so tightly clasped together that they could not be saved; they would go out of the world almost painlessly, and there would be no more reproach to her, or to him for marrying her. His last half-hour with her would have been a loving one...(244).

This feeling I can imagine: the writing is powerful enough. But Tess can hope for more now, "for the revelation of his tenderness ...raised dreams of a possible future with him" (246).

The sleepwalking is about as bizarre a scene as anyone could imagine, yet it is not hard to relate to because the novel calls for and makes possible a sense of contact with Tess and Angel that can weather this drastic shift in narrative content. My literary training tells me to place this sleepwalking within the genre of the Gothic novel, but actually I do not read Gothic novels, nor do I believe it would be useful to introduce this category into my experience. I also hear over my shoulder the inhibiting label, "melodramatic." But in this instance, I must agree with the critic Michael Irwin, who found that "the extremity of stylization...does not exceed the extremity of feeling ...that the situation embodies".[26] Sensational in its framework, the scene proves lovingly subtle in its portrayal of Angel's unconscious in two different modes and Tess's ability to discriminate between them.

There is much in these otherwise thoroughly painful scenes that is part of the not uncommon experience of marital fights: Angel's use of controlled sarcasm to express his immense anger (227); her realization that "anger ruled" in this situation, combined with her abruptly shutting off her anger (227-8); his denial, as they part, that there is any "anger between us" (247); his outrageous withdrawal by taking refuge among his papers (237); the denial by both of them that deceit is an issue between them, when obviously it is (229); his throwing at her of the old charge that she is cursed because she is a descendant of an old "decrepit" family—something he would never have thought to say earlier (229); his contradictory insult to her status: "you almost make me say you are an unapprehending peasant woman" (229); her swift and brilliant protective self-definition: "I am only a peasant by position, not by nature!"; Tess violating her own dignity which had not allowed her any "exculpatory phrase of any kind" by her pleading: "Angel! Angel!...I was a child—a child when it happened! I knew nothing of men"(229). She "burst into a flood of self-sympathetic tears"—this coming after she had not cried at all when telling him of her past (227). More: Clare's genuine relief at seeing Tess safely asleep, combined with an immature resentful thought of how *she* can sleep while he must carry "the burden of her life" (231); Tess making extravagant, self-demeaning promises, as if to shame him into acquiescence: "I will obey you, like your wretched slave, even if it is to lie down and die" (227). I believe that anyone who has been in tense and extended marital fights will recognize that these are types of hurting and being hurt that can be inflicted with astonishing ease, so well do our egos cooperate with our aggression and/or our self-image in such times. And on the opposite side of the psyche, there are the moments, sharable because also common enough, when the love between them almost but not quite breaks through the cycle of accusations. Thus Angel turning back after being nearly drawn into entering Tess's bedroom (231); his sarcastic but firm and effectively prohibitive response to her plan to commit suicide, (235); his wish that he had "kissed her once at least" just after he had cruelly turned away from her "inclining her mouth in the way of his" (238); his moment of "unpremeditated hope" that she would look back as she leaves him (248). A few moments later, he "hardly knew that he loved her still."

Hardy's profoundly realized vision in these chapters of a long-drawn-out conflict between a man and a woman over their married, sexual relationship is probably unmatched by anything in earlier novels by any author. It unforgettably explores a new intimacy in the world of fiction.

In my work on the theory of the novel as a literary genre, I have maintained that intimacy is inherent to it in two great senses. One: novelists can deal with the bodily and mental life of characters, and have unlimited scope in imagining their private acts and thoughts. This inevitably will form connections with the reader's own intimate life. Two: the act of reading a novel is almost always done over an extended period of time (greater than it would be for seeing a play or reading a poem or listening to a musical composition) with only the individual reader, and no other people, taking part in the process. In this sense, it is a very private thing.[27]

As Dewey recognized, the "modern discovery of inner experience, of a realm of purely personal events that are always at the individual's command," has become part of our sense of being human. "It implies a new worth and sense of dignity in human individuality," through which the individual "adds something" to the context that nature and culture have provided (*EN* 136). Dewey is always at pains to remind us that "this world of inner experience is dependent upon an extension of language which is a social product and operation" (*EN* 137), but he knows and values what inner, subjective life is all about. As I read and re-read Hardy's chapters on the terribly destructive encounter between Angel and his new bride, Tess, my experience is emotional and personal throughout. So it will be, I suspect, for all of Hardy's readers who manage to "summon energy and pitch it at a responsive key in order to *take* in" (*AE* 61).

For me as the one experiencing, the whole sequence is strongly emotional in quality.

6. Problems of Aesthetic Quality

It is not done perfectly. Along with the minor flaws that always seem to crop up in a Hardy novel, there is one strained passage that stands out for me, now that I have had years to perceive and feel these chapters. It is the passage where Angel gives the final, killing argument to their marriage. Angel's final reason, the one that totally subdues Tess, is that he dare not stay married to her because some day, after their children are born, some person might taunt these hypothetical kids with the information that their mother once had a pre-marital sexual relationship. After speaking in character, of these "wretches of our flesh and blood," that is, their children, Angel lapses into unusually high-flown vocabulary, and Hardy soon follows with his own mannered support. Angel asks his wife if she can still honestly ask him to stay with her "after *contemplating this contingency*" (239; my emphasis here and in the next several quotations). Tess, Hardy confides, "had been so obstinately recuperative as to revive in her *surreptitious visions of domiciliary intimacy*" (239). But now her "honest heart which was *humanitarian to its center*" (239) gave in. She knows that "in some circumstances," it is better "*to be saved* from leading any life whatever." This is followed by an oracular, fateful quotation from "M. Sully-Prudhomme" (239)—a snobbish sort of name to invoke, I should think[28]—which Hardy awkwardly suggests Tess could actually hear. Hardy is writing as if Tess can hear what he says—another indication of his closeness to her as a character who is virtually a real person. But the explanation by Hardy goes on: Tess up to now had been tricked by "*the vulpine slyness of Dame Nature*"—a patently stilted expression— but now she realizes that her love for Clare "*might result in vitalizations*" (239), or in common language, children, who would be made to suffer as she had. Not content yet, Hardy now descends to gender bias for further support: ...*like the majority of women, she accepted the momentary presentment as if it were the inevitable.* ...And she may have been right. *The intuitive heart of woman knoweth not only its own bitterness but its husband's...*" (240). All I can think here is, How very consciously Biblical Hardy is being! He is distracting from the scene at hand. Finally, in a return to the reality of the situation, her husband's "*fastidious brain*" might eventually think these reproaches even if no one else said anything (239-40, my emphases). Almost all of this reasoning rings false. In fact, at the end of the novel, Hardy forgets about it: when Tess decides that she cannot be sure that her marriage with Angel ever will be free of his moralizing condemnation, there is no mention of the poor pitiful children who might hear society's gossip about their mother. But his own "fastidious brain" does continue to worry her.

In the context of this section on their long face-to-face domestic conflict, my affective interest centers not on this string of reasonings-with-adornments, but on the vivid description of Clare, a page earlier. Clare had been "meditating, verily...he was becoming ill with thinking; eaten out with thinking; *scourged out of all his former pulsating, flexuous domesticity*" (238, my emphasis). With this context in mind, I realize that his display of reasoning about their hypothetical children is the product of his sick mind now disconnected from his sexual body. This however does not account for Hardy's reinforcement of that thinking, which serves to make the feeling of this passage still more disturbing. As for Angel's fastidious brain, Hardy effectively rephrases it, a few pages later: "*the fury of fastidiousness with which he was possessed*" (248, my emphasis). Despite the tyranny he is enforcing, it is no fun being Angel. I can share some of Angel's anguish when he ruefully misquotes Robert Browning: "God's *not* in his heaven: all's *wrong* with the world!" (248). It is a feeling of bitterness that goes beyond referring to Angel himself; it does extend into the state of the world. He has made a miserable world for Tess and himself, and he suffers in it.

There is a further dimension of the experience at this point, one that is hardly mentioned by the novel's critics. It is "there" for me because I have already accepted Angel sympathetically as a character who has male qualities. Hardy's qualifying of Angel's masculinity as Shelleyan, of his having insufficient animality, and of his passion as being more "bright" than "hot" (193), does not lead me to dismiss Angel as a non-sexual person. Brightness, as a quality, is not simply an absence of sexuality, and Shelley, whatever his pretensions toward being an ethereal spirit might have been, had his own "hot" sexuality, such that he fathered five children. Angel is obviously miserable at this point, and I intuit that within his emotional state, there is a gut-level disappointment that he feels as he realizes he will not be consummating his love for Tess in a sexual embrace. If Angel were to be read as sexless or sexually disabled, in need of testosterone injections, the problem facing Tess would be reduced to a medical error of the human body, and the novel would lose meaning. For some male readers I have encountered, condemnation of Angel is little more than an indulgence in masculine boasting over a weak, supposedly impotent man. I also detect in readers who are prone to a reductive interpretation of Angel, a confusion of response, by which anger at Angel Clare's horrible treatment of Tess is unconsciously translated into a refusal to believe that he is a human being of the same species as that of the reader. Here again, Dewey's aesthetic argues for the advantages for experience of a difficult nearness rather than the comforts of protective distancing. It is difficult to grasp sympathetically the unstable psychological blending within Angel of temperament, constitution, conscious and unconscious belief systems, and sexual male. But it is worth doing. It is even necessary if the experience is to be had.

Five

FROM CONFUSING MOVEMENT TO INTEGRAL RESTORATION

After the break-up of Tess and Angel, the next several chapters (38 through 44) are of shifting, indeterminate quality. Despite an abundance of potentially or actually powerful episodes, such as Angel lying to his parents about Tess's "virtue"; Tess going home and being ill-received by both of her parents; Angel suddenly deciding to run off with and then immediately declining to run off with Izz Huett, in an alliance that is plainly intended as sexual and non-marital; Tess mercifully strangling some wounded pheasants and commenting on her own fate; Tess failing because of exceptionally (or incredibly) bad luck to reach Angel's parents, for help that she desperately needs; Tess shockingly defacing herself—even cutting off her eyebrows—so that she will not be sexually attractive to men she will meet; and Tess working with Marian in back-breaking labor outdoors in harshest winter—despite all these I have felt through many readings that something is going wrong with the novel as an experience. The episodes are not badly rendered, although I sense that there is a somewhat larger proportion of false notes. But these scenes, considered singly, can be very moving. They are all made real and capable of being experienced, but the cumulative drift of the story here gives me mainly a feeling of doubt. In fact, the only clear experience I have with this section is one of anger at Hardy for his manipulative ways of subjecting Tess to suffering upon suffering. On some readings, I even want to scream at him, *stop doing that to her!* Which is to say, I lose confidence in the integrity of this part of the novel. And I ask, why does Hardy have to do it? There are "plot" answers to this question, such as the need to motivate Tess for giving in to Alec once more, and the need to have her become so unfairly persecuted that her eventual movement into violence will be credible. But plot can be managed in many ways, and not necessarily by means of maximum suffering. And Angel too is made to suffer a disfiguring bodily illness; later in the story; he looks like a "Mere yellow skeleton" to Tess (365). That extreme state does not feel necessary to the development of the plot either.

I feel some sort of interference in the relationship between Hardy and his character, Tess. In this part of the novel, I have the feeling that he can only accept her sexuality, which he himself has created, if he subjects her to extraordinary punishment. He seems to be having a temporary failure of nerve after having created and developed Tess in the contexts of her life, with her relationships to the two men, for 37 chapters.

1. Energy Divided and Rediscovered

Why would this have occurred? In most of the novel, Hardy's loving but complicated relation with his Tess is held in an uneven but highly effective context of perception and event; in this section, the effects seems to be considerably out of control. To get anything for my own experience out of this situation, I seem to need to identify as best I can with what Hardy is experiencing as he writes this novel. What could he have been undergoing? I should think that some semblance of an explanation might lie within the cumulative effect upon Hardy of his own text, in which he had built up the sense of Tess's sexual body over a space of over two hundred pages, and had provided an extensive sensual context during the Talbothays dairy chapters. That might have been more than, or rather other than, what he had imagined himself doing when he began the process of writing. In his essay, "The Profitable Reading of Fiction," published in March, 1888, Hardy had declared: "The higher passions must ever rank above the inferior—intellectual tendencies above animal, and moral above intellectual— whatever the treatment, realistic or ideal".[1] Published at about the same time that Hardy would begin writing Tess, this stern warning might have anticipated a conflict soon to occur within himself in his work as a novelist. There seem to be no other statements resembling this one in any of Hardy's notes or essays. Now, midway through the novel, he might have been asking himself if he was still within those bounds, given what he had created. Was there any other novelist in Victorian England who had ever risked doing such a thing? And his process of writing still had far to go before the novel could be called completed. That would have felt more than normally anxious for the writer in mid-stream; it could have been fearful.

   This loss of the sureness of Hardy's art is not a matter of his making inappropriate comments; it is a problem with the integral quality of this part of the novel. It is only due to my feeling of a diversion from artistic form that some of the authorial comments start to seem false. Where did this begin? I seem to hear the beginning of Hardy's anxiety over how this novel might be received in one of his commentaries a little earlier on Tess's behavior during that most difficult period with Angel, following her confession (in chapter 36). One thing she could do to persuade him to stay and to consummate their marriage, rather than leave her, is to use her body to attract him. This she hoped to do not overtly, but simply by living in close quarters with him. This idea might have been felt as outrageously daring for a culture in which the fact of women's sexual desire was still subject to denial. A male novelist who did assert this fact would become open not merely to strong negative criticism as a novelist, but to moral stigmatization as a human being. Indeed, when reviewers began to cross the line from literary to personal criticism, as they did with *Tess* and then with *Jude*, Hardy came to his decision to cease writing novels entirely. Yet Hardy does want to write this sexual thought.

Hardy's description of Tess's hope of getting Angel to come to her by using her body is given in a tone of self-consciousness and is at first stated most awkwardly. It has attracted much puzzlement and complaint. It is Hardy's anxious prose trying to cover up his anxiety. Yet it can render something more for experience than the neutralizing of effect that at least one critic seems to derive from it.[2] Here is the text:

> Tess's feminine hope—shall we confess it?—had been so obstinately recuperative as to revive in her surreptitious visions of a domiciliary intimacy continued long enough to break down his coldness even against his judgment. Though unsophisticated in the usual sense she was not incomplete; and it would have denoted deficiency of womanhood if she had not instinctively known what an argument lies in propinquity. (239)

Having written these two cumbersome sentences, which seem to repel the reader's effort to feel what they are trying to achieve, Hardy is then able to allow himself to shift into one clear, forceful statement: "Nothing else would serve her, she knew, if this failed" (239). That can be felt, experienced.

As if to blur the effect of this statement, however, the paragraph goes on immediately to say that Tess realizes that all hope of winning Angel over has already been lost (239). Nonetheless, despite all his anxiety, Hardy had said it: Tess was a woman who did indeed think of letting her beautiful female body persuade Angel to make love to her rather than abandon her. She knew that this would be her last resort, that is, the strongest argument she could make, and she knew too that it had not worked. This is no small breach within the pervasive cultural denial of the existence of women's sexual desire.[3]

The incident several chapters later of Tess's mercy killing of the wounded pheasants includes both her own and Hardy's philosophical comment on the meaning of suffering. Tess realizes that compared to these birds, she is not "the most miserable being on earth," and Hardy tells of her shame for having been so gloomy: her sense of extreme misery was "based on nothing more tangible than a sense of condemnation under an arbitrary law of society which had no foundation in Nature" (271). Here again, I think it useless to try to fully separate Tess from Hardy. But I resist simply discounting the whole passage, as I have sometimes done, as a contrivance or set-piece inserted by Hardy just to score a rhetorical point. What I sense occurring in this passage is a mis-matching of Tess's "body-mind." Her attempt to diminish the import of her own suffering, and Hardy's sounding of his theme of Nature versus the arbitrary laws of society, both feel inexplicably unconvincing. From what I can experience, Tess's suffering has been real. She cannot even go back to Talbothays and apply for a job, because she cannot face all the pity and the "whispered remarks" about her that would be sure to occur (268). And at this point, she has just been baited by the "boor" who recognizes her as the woman who once was Alec's: "Why, surely, it is the young wench who was at Tantridge awhile—young Squire d'Urberville's friend?...Be honest enough to own it...hey, my sly one?" (269-70). Faced with this taunt, she cannot answer, and literally runs away. This feels very bad, to her and to me. But her denial of her suffering will only set her up for more suffering. Is that what Hardy needs?

Similarly, Hardy's philosophizing will allow him to go on punishing her. I imagine that his close identification with her will allow him to feel that suffering in himself as he writes. Hardy seems to be dividing his energy between writing the novel as a creative artist and using his energy to re-balance some troubling discomfort in himself. Eventually he will have had enough of this to forgive himself for writing a much more openly sexual book than he felt (or some part of his psyche felt) that he ever should have done, especially in the Talbothays section, and to allow himself to go on with the sexual-love plot. If such an intra-psychic bargain has been struck, it is a good one: the book might not have been write-able otherwise. But as a convincing portrait of and comment upon Tess at this point, the passage on killing the pheasants seems dumb. To use Dewey's term, Tess's Mind-, her intelligence, is working against her -Body, when she produces this discounting of her misery. Hardy's purpose of showing how arbitrary social law is, when it produces false guilt over sexuality, is put to the unlikely use of supporting Tess in not crediting the reality of her own suffering. Hardy himself must have an awareness that Tess really suffers, and he might also have been aware that his denial would only reinforce that impression.

If I de-emphasize the cognitive value of Hardy's statement, however, and respond to him as a person who is the author, then it feels all right: it feels, it is palpable, as his care and concern for the woman and her emotional state. It is part of a continuing context of his care for her.

This emotion-laden passage, nonetheless, is difficult to experience. Even though in Dewey's aesthetics, emotion is crucial for the formation of experience, its presence cannot produce coherence where there is some integral failure of imagination. The passage about the pheasants tends to distract from, rather than augment, Tess's interesting critical thinking. Just prior to this episode of the dying pheasants, she dwells upon the maxim of Ecclesiastes, "all is vanity." "She repeated the words mechanically, til she reflected that this was a most inadequate thought for modern days" (270). Thinking of her "wasted life," she goes beyond Solomon's wisdom: "If all were only vanity, who would mind it? All was, alas, worse than vanity—injustice, punishment, exaction, death" (270). Once again, the thought is Hardy's as well as Tess's; but I can imagine her capable of thinking this. She has enough independence of mind, especially when she is alone, as in this scene. She also has enough learning: I recall here Hardy's statement earlier that Tess, like all village girls, "was well-grounded in the Holy Scriptures" (97). That would make her more culturally learned in this respect than most literate people today. Hardy seems to be enjoying imagining the qualities of her mind at this point. But without warning, the tone shifts; it is as if Hardy had caught himself being rather playful. Suddenly Tess can wish for death: "I wish it were now." Despite this declaration, I soon wonder if she is really focused upon dying. Hardy calls her wish one of her "whimsical fancies" (270), and *segues* into her discovery of the fatally injured birds.

The Nature descriptions in this part of the novel, designed to show the horrible conditions under which Tess has to work outdoors, sometimes feel forced to the point of disbelief. There is an effort to reach for a vast cosmic significance. This bears upon the question of whether Hardy effectively contradicts himself in his portrayal of Nature. I am thinking here of Hardy's description of certain mysterious arctic birds:

> gaunt spectral creatures with tragical eyes—eyes which had witnessed scenes of cataclysmal horror in inaccessible polar regions, of a magnitude such as no human being ever conceived, [presumably not even Hardy?] in curdling temperatures that no man could endure...half blinded by the whirl of colossal storms and terraqueous distortions...of all they had seen which humanity would never see, they brought no account. (279-80)

One critic claims that Tess had now become like one of these birds,[4] but I do not see how anyone could experience her in this inconceivable and indeed preposterous mode. If I did not know better, I would call the passage a narrative conundrum in the manner of Jorge Luis Borges. Hardy may be trying to write a symmetrically reversed image of the benign and luscious Nature he had created in the Talbothays section, but he cannot do it. When I read this passage now, it slips past without moving me. Hardy's creative imagination could not carry out his programmatic wish to supply a thoroughly terrifying image of Nature, such that might have been a counter-weight to his favorable portrayal of Nature at Talbothays. His words come across as mere vocalizing.

Although this passage leads to a temporary interference with my experience of the novel, I do not permit it to expunge my strong overall impression that indeed the women working the fields in mid-winter are living in miserable conditions. My sentiment is something like this: the way they have to work is not a fitting way for anyone to earn an existence. I do not want Tess or her women friends or any other laborers out there in the harsh climate. The absence of an effective cosmic dimension to this section of the novel is no hindrance to experiencing what is movingly created in it.

One fairly clear sign of Hardy's faltering, and a more consequential one than that of the instance of the never-conceived, never-seen arctic landscape, is in his handling of Tess's motivation for suddenly abandoning her effort to seek help from Angel's parents. In this scenario, Tess overhears Angel's "clerical brothers," and Mercy Chant, the stick-figure caricature of a woman that Angel had been supposed to marry, discussing the pair of walking boots that Tess has hidden under a bush. They do not know whose boots these are, but they are eager to think that the boots must belong to some faking beggar who has come to the village to deceive them. This is the last straw: at this point, Tess gives up and walks away, as "[t]ears, blinding tears, were running down her face" (291). Hardy explains her conflicted state of mind:

> She knew that it was all sentiment, all baseless impressibility, which had caused her to read the scene as her own condemnation; nevertheless she could not get over it; she could not contravene in her own defenceless person all those untoward omens. It was impossible to think of returning to the vicarage. (291)

Yes, this is realism, this is Tess as a human being who cannot overcome the cumulative condemnations of her society even as she knows they are baseless. She cannot be blamed. But a few lines later, Hardy re-explains in other terms: "...she went her way without knowing that the greatest misfortune of her life was this feminine loss of courage at the last and critical moment, through her estimating her father-in-law by his sons" (291). This confuses matters: for one thing, the inability to approach her in-laws is hardly "the greatest misfortune of her life"; for another, Hardy is unconvincingly lording it over her mind, saying that she did not know of her own loss of courage; third, he is taking back the impression he has just given of a woman overwhelmed and defenseless by imputing this loss of courage; and finally he is saying that her loss of courage is "feminine." It is one of the few places in the novel where Hardy's gender bias actually damages its quality. The word "feminine" is not in the manuscript of *Tess*. Perhaps Hardy put it in, finally, because he himself was not sure why Tess turns back.

Whether he knows consciously or not, Hardy as creative novelist, one who is not merely an author functioning as narrator, does know why. And I hope I also "know," that is, intuit why, based on my feeling concerning not only this portion of the novel, but of the experience of reading all of it many times. I see three valid reasons why Tess turns back. The most important, felt, one, is that she just does not belong with the family of the good Reverend Clare. Do we not, as readers, instinctively feel that? To be sure, the text tells us that Rev. Clare would have been glad to help Tess. But his pity for her would have been hard to bear, and if the help were to extend beyond a mere hand-out, and go on over a period of time, Tess would more and more be forced to practice a concealment that has agonized her earlier: she would have had to keep silent on the cause of her husband leaving her. While the Clares would no doubt be more than willing to relieve their daughter-in-law's material suffering, they could not have avoided feelings of condescension and contempt for this violator of the biblical ideal of the "virtuous woman," the "virtuous wife" described in the Book of Proverbs. Reverend Clare earlier had pointedly read this out from the lectern in the family home, in Angel's presence, as the choice prayer to frame the discussion of why Tess has not come home with their son, following his marriage (257-8). Now Hardy's language betrays their condescension: Tess, their daughter-in-law, "might" turn out to be "a fairly choice sort of lost person for their love" (291). That declaration is preceded by a convoluted Biblical gloss on Publicans and Sinners, Scribes and Pharisees, which sounds utterly foreign to any simple human impulse toward sympathy. Later in the story, when the elder Clares do finally figure out what Tess's problem has been, they immediately turn on the sympathy that they give to "reprobates," and their tenderness is "instantly excited by her sin" (358). "Excited" is a lurid term, here. Pointedly, their sympathy is *not* aroused by "her blood, her simplicity, even her poverty..." (358). Even before this, when Angel's mother sees how distressed he is upon reading a letter from Tess, she condescends insufferably: "Don't, Angel, be so anxious about a mere child of the soil!" (356). This is much like Angel's earlier stereotyping of Tess as "a daughter of the soil" (131).

Considered in this light, Tess's un-resolve in reaching Angel's family is as little a matter of pure bad luck as was the mis-directing of her letter of confession to Angel prior to their wedding: in neither case does Tess, in her deepest wish, want to do the thing she is forcing herself to do. It is not for nothing that Tess's self-confidence decreases as she approaches the Emminster vicarage, and it is a sure intuition that tells her, as she stands outside of it, that she does not belong: "she could not feel by any stretch of imagination, dressed to her highest as she was, that the house was the residence of near relations..." (288-9).

Secondly, by leading from this incident to Tess's meeting, for the first time in years, with Alec, Hardy is able to sharply convey the feeling that Tess has actually been going toward Alec all along in this journey; it is her fate to get back to Alec. But, third, it is her self that makes this fate, that wants to get back to him. She may not know why. But her sharp rebuff as a sexual woman, suffered at the hands of Angel, may lead her toward the one man who has found her sexually acceptable and wholesome, even if her relationship with that man had failed. The reader who protests at her meeting Alec at this juncture is certainly fighting off the emotional core of this novel. Despite Hardy's notorious penchant for making coincidences occur in his plots, I cannot think of many readers who complain specifically about this meeting. Only a critic with contempt for Hardy and inclined to blame Tess could write that "Hardy himself seems blind" to the consequences of Tess's turning back, and even more smugly, that Hardy "does nothing to rationalize [Tess's] responsibility for this particular chain of events".[5] In terms of a Deweyan reading, with its emphasis on what is experienced, Hardy "does" something, a good deal, in fact, in this part of the experience, even if he does not do it in so many words.

2. Changing Toward Alec

Appropriately—and perhaps just in time—the rather ragged quality of the novel for the past 10 chapters changes, when, on her way back from her trip, Tess encounters Alec d'Urberville. Suddenly this feels "right." Hardy of course has plotted this, but I believe it works: it feels right for the life of Tess. Immediately the narrative regains shape, with Hardy's extended rendering of their "rencounter." That is a peculiar word I believe only Hardy uses; it means an unexpected and hostile meeting, not just a re-encounter, as I formerly assumed. Once again this novel becomes one of sex, love and Nature, although the process of experiencing these factors undergoes transformation as the characters' lives change.

Tess immediately suspects that Alec's new life as a fire-and-brimstone preacher is false, false to his own body: his facial lines have been "diverted from their hereditary connotation to signify impressions for which nature did not intend them" (298). Although she conscientiously puts this thought out of her head, the "rencounter" itself, in which he narrates his Christian conversion, leads her to exclaim, sadly, "...I cannot believe in your conversion to a new spirit. Such flashes as you feel, Alec, I fear don't last" (301). She says this while giving him "the large dark gaze of her eyes"—which begins at once to melt his new-found defenses against sexual feeling. Her thought at realizing this effect is an intense self-reflection on her sexual body: "there was revived in her the wretched sentiment which had often come to her before, that in inhabiting the fleshly tabernacle with which Nature had endowed her she was somehow doing wrong" (301). The words "wretched sentiment" are possibly the key to a feeling I find I often have in experiencing this passage: disgust. Tess then allows Alec to accompany her further down the road, "inwardly wondering how far he was going with her, and not liking to send him back by positive mandate" (301). Walking through the "bleached and desolate upland," they reach a ruined monument, "a strange rude monolith..." where, according to local legend, "a devotional cross had once formed the complete erection thereon" (302). Here I must assert that the word "erection" in my reading of Hardy often fails to have an innocent connotation. That may be the result of my prior experience in reading of a lot of Hardy, especially the minor novel, *Two on a Tower*, where the phallic puns near the beginning seem to me to be so marked that I finally do not care where they are intentional or not.[6] Here the suggestion of "a complete erection" suggests that their meeting takes place under the aegis of a phallic sexuality that has become ruined. Parting, he calls her "Tessy," and then perhaps in response to this endearment, she tells him that she had borne him a son who had died. Only then, when he is drawn to her afresh with this emotionally potent news, does she tell him clearly to stay away from her. But after being "struck mute" by her gratuitous announcement, he is not likely to obey: "I will think" (302) is all the promise he can make.

There follows an episode I find more disgusting: Alec makes her swear upon the monumental stone hand "that you will never tempt me—by your charms or ways" (302) The very idea feels wrong: she should not *have* to swear any such thing, not only because Alec should realize that she has no choice in having a sexually attractive body, but also because it feels like a perverse denial of natural sexuality. But maybe that is exactly what is being suggested.

The parting into separate pathways sounds in a new way the theme of sex versus its unnatural control. Alec tries to overcome his excitement by re-reading a pious letter from the Reverend Clare, but seems "to quiz himself cynically" while doing so. By reading other bits of "memoranda" he has with him, he is eventually able to douse the flame: "apparently the image of Tess no longer troubled his mind" (303). Clearly this is a struggle. As for Tess, she has a feeling of *petite mort* shortly after leaving Alec, brought on, Hardy says, by the sudden gruesome information that the monument upon which she has sworn had been set up to commemorate a "malefactor" who had been tortured, hanged, and buried there (303). The sexual meaning of *petite mort* as orgasm will not be silenced. But if an orgasm is intimated here, it has a perverse connotation: it is sex as punishment and mutilation.

In contrast to this feeling, and one sentence later, Tess sees a pair of lovers who have a kind of beauty within nature, even though nature is presented in a shadowy mood: "It was dusk...she approached a girl and her lover without their observing her." The next sentence modulates into a prose poem:

> They were talking no secrets, and the clear unconcerned voice of the young woman, in response to the warmer accents of the man, spread into the chilly air as the one soothing thing within the dusky horizon, full of a stagnant obscurity upon which nothing else obtruded. (303-4)

It is her old friend Izz, and a lover. Typically, Hardy pretends to over-ride the romantic impression he has just created by having Izz declare her indifference to "Amby Seedling" (the man's caricature of a name), but this encounter of Tess with the image of a woman and man in the dusk and alone, must suggest some re-awakening of her own need for love.

The quality of that need would be understood better if we could decide by now whether she is returning to a man who had once raped her. If he had not raped her, then her character, his own, and their relation will be imagined differently.

3. The Novel's Rape Inquiry Once More

Alec, still trying to live the life of an Evangelist preacher rather than a lover, observes in the next chapter Tess's grueling work situation and exclaims "Perhaps a good deal of it is owing to me!" This leads to his opening the topic of his own responsibility for what happened between them earlier. Here I know I must listen once more for anything that will throw light upon that night in the Chase when they first had sex: "Scamp that I was to *foul that innocent life*. The whole blame was mine—the whole unconventional business of our time at

Trantridge" (306, my emphasis). This speech once more leaves open the possibility of there having been a rape. Yet more emphatically Alec defines the problem as a whole situation rather than a specific act. His assumption of the entire responsibility is tempting to accept, but it is not trustworthy. For one thing, he is speaking as a preacher who is immersed in the glory of his guilt, and, more important, the earlier narrative of "that whole unconventional time" cannot be read as if only Alec were responsible for all of it. At the same time, his exclamation "What a blind young thing you were as to possibilities!" (306) corroborates the strong impression I have, earlier in the novel, that Tess really did not realize what she was getting into, despite her own attraction to Alec. And Alec does refer to "the trick" he "played" upon her (306), suggesting that Hardy's earlier characterization of him taking "adroit advantages" of her was accurate. There were tricks: after all, he did deceive her into thinking she was coming to work for his mother, when he himself had forged the letter offering her the job. His mother was a blind woman who had far less control of Tess's work situation than Alec himself did. And he did deliberately get her and himself lost deep in the woods on the night that he had picked up Tess and offered to take her home. But Tess herself does not seize on his statements to bring up any accusation. In fact, although for several pages the two are having a serious and sometimes heated conversation about their relationship (306-9), a relationship which Tess at this point regards as long finished, she does not say or hint that he ever physically violated her. If she felt that he had done so, or if Hardy himself had intended that meaning, she could hardly have regarded Alec simply as "her seducer" (293), as she does (or as Hardy describes her as doing) when she rencounters him.

Nor does she make any reference in any of their later exchanges to her having been physically violated. Neither does Alec, after he de-converts from Christianity to nihilism, and is quite frank about his failings with Tess, ever indicate that he has assaulted her. Given their opportunities in the novel to bring this matter up, their failure to do so finally argues strongly against the occurrence of rape. But, to repeat: rape remains a possibility. The Deweyan inquiry must draw to a close with this sense of a "warranted assertion," which is not expected to stand for all time or eliminate all doubt. But we are not left in the position of being "hopelessly dependent" on Hardy's "own desire" for our understanding of the event.[7]

To the question asked in a factual mode, namely, did Alec rape Tess? my Deweyan answer is that we can make a warranted assertion with the end-in-view of having the fullest and least hampered experience of this novel. The assertion is that, considering all the available evidence in the context presented by the novel, he did not. But this does not mean that the discomfort experienced, the sense of doom, that comes from reading with our own feelings of the fateful night in the woods, is therefore lifted from the book. The feeling of something going badly wrong in Tess's life at that point will not go away, unless we take the experience-cheapening way of simply crossing out from our experience those pages in which the scene is dealt with. I see no reason to do such a thing. The result of the inquiry for experience will lead to our own dealing with the problem in a different context.

The purpose of my caution is not to clear Alec's fine male name. It is to help focus on the problematic question of the quality of the sexual relation between Tess and Alec, which cannot be grasped by applying the word "rape" to it. We have to *imagine the quality of the specific relationship between this man and this woman,* rather than take refuge in the definitively bad word we can use. In this context, it is important for understanding that quality of a relation to focus our attention (to take a telling example) on Tess's declaration to Alec, made in the course of their conversation about their relationship, as it had been "in the old times," namely that "...there was never warmth with me" (320). Her "never" refers to the entire duration of those old times back at Alec's place, not to one violent event, if such ever occurred. The point is not simply to avoid all possible stereotypical categories of thought, but to be freed from some of the worst of these in order to think qualitatively about sexual relations. The reader can "*take in*" (*AE* 60). Hardy's use of "aesthetic distance," his refusal to describe directly what went on between Tess and Alec on that fateful night in the woods, eventually becomes a deepening of the experience. It is an achievement of the sexual thinking in this novel to have created such an opening for new perception.[8]

As their rencounter develops, we can feel Tess turning again toward Alec. Tess begs Alec not to ask who her husband is, but with body language that she might be aware is seductive: "she flashed her appeal to him from her upturned face and lash shadowed eyes" (308). (In fact, if by this point Tess were unaware of her sexual body language, she would be a mysterious fool, something like Remedios-the-Beauty in *One Hundred Years of Solitude*). Alec, even after learning that Tess is already married, now gives his attraction for her the name of *love*: "I own that the sight of you has waked up my love for you, which, I believed, was extinguished with all such feelings." (308). Tess then increases the level of intimacy by unnecessarily disclosing that her husband had left her because of Alec: "It was through you. He found out—"(308). Obviously this only makes Alec more fascinated. A page later, she tells Alec that he need not protect her from the attentions of her boss: "*He's* not in love with me" (309) —which is to acknowledge that Alec *is* in love with her and that she knows it. That night, Tess tries but is unable to write to Angel, to tell him of "some monstrous fear," the fear of giving in to Alec (310). She also has "a vaguely-shaped hope that something would happen to render another outdoor engagement [as farm laborer] unnecessary" (310). She is not seeking more suffering, nor expressing indifference toward having been raped. I can feel that she is being drawn toward Alec.

4. Work and Experience

The conversations and interactions of Tess and Alec continue in their intimacy and their increasingly bodily closeness all through the remaining half of this chapter (46); they continue to develop as a stunning climax is reached in the end of the next chapter. The texture of the novel during this increase of erotic energy is enriched and made ominous by the inter-spliced strands evoking the hard work of the farm laborers, especially of the women, and especially in relation to the Moloch-like farm machinery. These scenes never feel to me as if they are simply portraits of exploitation. I develop a feeling of frustration in reading of this hard work being done, and also come to question why Hardy is rendering it just here. If he simply wanted to show the misery of the agrarian working class, he would not have inserted a piece of historical information that marks this work-scene as a-typical. Alec says: "I have told the farmer that he has no right to employ women at steam-threshing. It is not proper work for them, and on all the better class of farms it has been given up, as he knows very well" (324). Hardy thus seems to be evoking a slightly different feeling than one of laborers being abused as a class. Partly by word choices used sparingly—"aborigines," "autochthonous"—Hardy tinctures this depiction of work with suggestions of primitive existence (315-16). But can they be felt as such? If they can, then Nature, in the primal sense of people laboring with their muscles out in the open sun, harvesting plants grown to meet the basic human need for food, must evoke a jarring conflict with civilization in the plight of these workers, who labor under such poor conditions. Such work is structured according to the man-made division of owners and virtual peons.

The scenes of enforced agricultural labor, so different in quality from those at Talbothays, are the primary mode in which Nature appears in this portion of the novel. At the Talbothays dairy, the workers' relations with their employer, Mr. Richard Crick, or "Dairyman Dick," had been significantly personal: they encounter him frequently in daily life, as if he is part of the community they live in, rather than simply the boss. Crick, moreover, is a decent man and not a bully—unlike farmer Groby, Tess's later employer. Crick's "household of maids and men lived on comfortably, placidly, even merrily." *They can still have "natural feeling,"* as long as their basic "neediness" is satisfied, and their susceptibility to seek after conveniences which they cannot afford has not taken hold of them (133, my emphasis). There are however enough touches in the portrait of life at Talbothays to indicate that it is not simply blissful. The workers, after all, work, and they work very hard. They have to get up each day at about 3 or 4 in the morning (139). And although the milkers sing along while working, their tone of voice is far from joyous (114). Crick, however decent he may be, has no more sensitivity than any of the other people present in the matter of sexual mores that most concerns Tess. In a delicate sociological shading, Hardy can evoke *a feeling of uncoerced work within Nature* at the dairy, while creating an opposing feeling, still under the open air, at Flintcomb Ash and the later farm on which Tess has now come to work.

The suffering of the ordinary farm-workers at the behest of merciless machines and bosses creates an unsteady fusion of Nature and the love/sex story line. The misery of soul-destroying agricultural work is intense, as is Tess's suffering, but the felt qualities are different. The workers have no hope for any alteration of their condition, nor does the developing history of the countryside promise them any; Tess still does have hope, despite herself, and I as a reader feel that hope against hope. The only hope for the other women workers evokes, is the hopeless romantic one of Tess's friends Izz and Marian in the novel. What they hope for, despite their knowing that it is impossible, is for a marriage to a highly attractive man who will allow them to satisfy their erotic longings, and in that new life, remove them from their toil. By evoking this fantasy of the women at several points in the narrative, Hardy gives up any simple effect he might have achieved in portraying the women solely as downtrodden workers. He instead creates a memorable scene of agricultural exploitation fused with a romantic dream of liberation through sexual love. This hybrid concoction is in a sense quite silly, but in a deeper sense, in a mode of response that I think is right for experiencing this novel, it is not so wrong-headed as it seems. To suggest that the women friends of Tess consider themselves not only as workers but as women who can desire sexual fulfillment under conditions that would free them of lifelong drudgery, is a way of honoring them.

Nature in its distorted form of oppressed human bodies getting food from the soil to satisfy the profit motive as well as the appetites of other people, is a tragic quality that is well suited for its role as complementing Tess's struggle in love. But as I will discuss later on, Nature in this book is not simple. Tess's tragedy and the tragedy of a dying agricultural folk community overlap in the experience of this novel, and share in the qualities of defeat, but Tess surely is not the community, as some critics have claimed. At some level of Hardy's artistry, there has to be some history, some historical context, for the action. I suspect that Hardy would have agreed with the view of Jean-Luc Godard, that "fiction is interesting only if it is validated by a documentary context,"[9] although he would not have been interested, any more than Godard, in attempting the false realism of pretending to copy, in the medium of the written word, some existing reality.

5. Now Always Victim

The quality now becomes one of felt disjunction: the sexual love story between Tess and Alec now has erotic quality without much sense of a complement in Nature.

The work scenes, presented in tandem with the Tess-Alec scenes, make for an intense exposure of vulnerability, almost as if my muscles and tendons have been extended to the point of feeling pain, thus miming my own physical participation. I do not quite absorb the work/nature/love sequence in its literal page order, however. This section has a climax that seems to draw its energies toward a single vivid instant: Tess, still at her work-scene, slaps Alec with a heavy work-glove, drawing blood. This she does as he reaches toward her to touch her, and as he simultaneously insults Angel. She then immediately utters an astonishing plea:

> "Now, punish me!" she said, turning up her eyes to him with the hopeless defiance of the sparrow's gaze before its captor twists its neck. "Whip me, crush me; you need not mind those people under the rick. I shall not cry out. Once victim, always victim: that's the law." (321)

No matter how many times I have encountered this passage on re-reading *Tess*, I am stunned and appalled. I do not want "my" Tess—the Tess I have formed in my imagination and taken into my self by this time—looking like this: like a sparrow about to have its neck twisted by its captor; nor do I want her speaking as she does. Am I alone? Does any reader welcome this cry? It is an ugly surprise, drawing suddenly on a "law" that Tess nowhere else mentions, and denying voluntary control over her life even in the act of striking Alec for his insulting reference to "that mule you call husband" (320). But of course striking him cannot really help her, in her situation. Among the mixed messages of this impassioned speech and angry gesture by Tess is a plea for mercy, inasmuch as the defiance Tess expresses admits that there is no hope that Alec will simply leave her alone. She is also allowing Alec to retaliate immediately with his own violence in return for hers; the lowly farm-worker woman has struck the gentleman, and she promises not to cry out. The most disturbing aspect is her identifying herself as a victim, her taking that name as her fate.[10] She might well do so, given her deteriorating situation. This is a large decline for a woman who had told Angel, even in her most agonizing time, that she is a peasant only by accident of birth, not by nature.

Much later in the novel, Tess tells Angel that she actually felt she might some day kill Alec, even as she strikes him (372). I find I do not think about this while reading the passage; things are not so neat. But the writing does convey a less defined quality of dangerous aggression that feels as if it is still there, unspoken, once Tess calms down. Then I forget about it, but I imagine it is still having an effect on me as I read the remainder of the novel. The sheer speed with which the event changes quality from defiance to submission is part of what gives it its sense of fearfulness. Hardy emphasized this through Tess's body-language when he wrote a sentence that was not in the manuscript: as Alec stretches his arm toward her waist, "She too had sprung up, but she sank down again".[11] And now she asks for punishment. There is a felt realization for me, and I think for many readers, that has never been so strong before this in the novel: Tess is not going to get clear of Alec. That this is a good intuition is confirmed in the next few pages, when she drops nearly all of her hostility to him, and makes no clear demand that he leave her. But this does not feel as if she is simply being drawn back to him as his lover; if it were only that I might feel some relief. The impact of this scene strongly suggests to me that Tess now is a person in disruption, one whose body and mind may not come into alignment, regardless of what choices she makes. To be drawn back to Alec, she must feel not only sexual attraction but a sense of worthlessness, based on all that she has gone through. This is not the way I would ever have expected the young woman I first read of in chapter 2 to have developed. The difference, which has been building up for a long time, suddenly feels shocking.

The physical act of striking Alec is not going to deter him; if he still has his appetite for aggressive courtship, such as he displayed after he picked up the young Tess in his dog-cart, it will stir him to new efforts. Alec, unlike myself as reader, has no inkling that what she says and does in her outburst on being a victim could have any quality of warning for him, or for their relationship: "I should indeed be foolish," he says, "to feel offended at anything you say or do" (324). Tess is going to still try, half-heartedly, to get clear of him, but she will not succeed. This is because, with Angel's absence becoming more and more evident, the desire in her that draws her to Alec becomes dominant. (And something in her does *not* want to go to her Clare in-laws for help). This desire is sexual, but I do not think it can be called simply sex or "sexual passion." The Deweyan awareness of a continually changing and developing context is especially important here: Tess's sexuality is not a fixed entity, immune from her own events. *It is her sexuality as it is now*, after undergoing the distortions practiced upon her by Angel and by her own sufferings, whether these are inevitable within her situation, self-generated, or to some indeterminate extent contrived by Hardy. This quality of sex would never have developed if Angel had not abused her and then left her to exacerbate her despair, but it is powerfully and disturbingly there. It is there in the language: "the sparrow's gaze before its captor twists its neck." This quality of sexuality had been suggested in the image of torture and mutilation two chapters back (303). The bird with twisted neck now implies the destruction of her body, not the captor's mastery of her sexual life. Why that image for Tess? The question keeps occurring; the passage remains disturbing.

Her long letter to Angel following this event conveys her inner state at this point. It is the longest passage in the novel where we have a fictional rendering of Tess's "voice" without the interruption of Hardy as narrator.[12] In it, she tries both to ward off Alec's impending sexual mastering of her, and her own realization that she does not belong solely to her husband. But she may realize that it could take much too long for this letter to reach her husband to do any good; since as she points out, she is "worried, pressed to do what I will not" (326). She is "sick at heart, not only for old times, but for the present" (325).

"MY OWN HUSBAND," the letter asserts at its opening. In much of it Tess takes the role of abjection in the hope of drawing Angel to her, but also, I intuit, of putting forth on the sheet of paper before her the words that will show how hopeless it now is to resist Alec. "If you would come, I could die in your arms! I would be well content to do that if so be you had forgiven me!" Further: "...I do not value my good looks; I only like to have them because they belong to you, my dear, and that there may be at least one thing about me worth your having" (325). More: "I would be content, ay glad, to live with you as your servant, if I may not as your wife..." (326) But she knows that Angel, even in the midst of his cruelty, had told her plainly: "You must not work like this...You are not my servant; you are my wife" (237).

The verbal pattern of this letter, with its simultaneous motives of remaining out of Alec's arms and of showing how useless it is to resist him, contains within it one passage that must challenge the sympathetic understanding of any reader of this novel who takes its subject-matter seriously. Tess pleads:

> I am the same woman, Angel, as you fell in love with: yes, the very same!—not the one you disliked, but never saw. What was the past to me as soon as I met you? It was a dead thing altogether. I became another woman, filled full of new life from you. How could I be the early one? Why do you not see this? (325)

This is an assertion that is full of problems, but it expresses something essential. To accept literally her claim that she had erased her prior experience with Alec upon meeting and falling in love with Angel is tempting; and there is a perceptive critic who accepts the claim as an instance of Hardy's own valuing of personal "growth."[13] But in Dewey's view (and mine), it would be naive to think such a thing. Growth, in Dewey's sense, cannot be had by denying what one has gone through. Yet somehow, Tess *is* the same woman. True, contrary to what she says, she has changed with her experiences and is not literally "the same," but her identity as a human being, as a woman, is the same.

A seeming paradox of experience is that there can be great change in a person's life, but no obliteration of a basic sense of identity. I realize that Tess is retracting her earlier recognition that Angel had been in love not with herself but with an idealized woman in her image. Here she is telling him that this was his error. He "never saw," never perceived, the woman he had disliked for her sexual past; she herself is the woman he desired. Despite her abject tone, she is demanding that he acknowledge her as herself. For herself, she is asserting her identity, and since identity is a concept that may be especially susceptible to a person's own attitude, she is helping herself to restore or retain that identity at a time in her life when she realizes it is in danger of dissolving. I find merit here in the position of the philosopher Peter McInerney, whose view is that the value of a concept of personal identity is the pragmatic one of increasing the sense of the connectedness among the stages of a person's life.[14] Tess's assertion thus clashes with the naming of herself as a helpless victim, a few pages earlier, and suggests that despite the "law" of being the victim, her fate as a woman is still undecided, even this late in the novel. Experience is not over. In understanding Dewey's philosophy, we assume that there is a "dynamic continuum of organic life" within any person's experience, and, as a recent commentator on Dewey explains, the habits that we acquire are processes that "enhance the continuity of this life."[15] Tess's identity is a central "habit," in Dewey's sense; she has not allowed it to be taken from her, whether by Angel or by the distorted working of her own mind against herself.

Aside from the contents of this letter, Tess's composing of it feels like an act of attempted recuperation of her mind. A few chapters earlier Hardy had shown his own realization that Tess had handed over far too much of her mind to Angel: when Alec accuses her of allowing her mind to be "enslaved" to Angel, Hardy comments that she has a "simplicity of faith" in Angel "that the most perfect man could hardly have deserved, much less her husband" (311). Her letter, even with its assurances of abject love, is a reassertion of the worth of her own mind.

The following chapters (49-52) end with Tess going to live again with Alec, but the sexual quality in these chapters is somehow dissolved. It can be assumed to be there, but it simply does not feel as strong as it had during the intensity of their "rencounter." Tess has not only lost hope for her husband's return; she also believes that even if he did return he would not forgive her. Or rather, this belief comes into consciousness with the act of writing, at last, an angry letter, telling him that he has been utterly cruel and that *she* can never forgive *him* (343). This is one of the few clearly assertive emotional acts by Tess in a very long time; it feels overdue and welcome. Immediately follows Tess's conclusion that "It was just as well to write like that as to write tenderly. How could he give way to entreaty? *The facts had not changed*; there was no new event to alter his opinion"(296). In locating the trouble in Angel's hard, logical deposit, where if "the facts had not changed," nothing in his attitude will change, she reasons well. But the inner thinking as Hardy presents it is also a justification for her own change: there is now no use in being faithful to Angel, since he is not coming back and is not going to change. Given these assumptions, the "new event" she is contemplating, namely living with Alec, will certainly give Angel a taste of the suffering he has inflicted. How else can he feel when he receives this letter?: "I will try to forget you. It is all injustice I have received at your hands!" (343)

To say only this much about her letter of dismissal to her husband, however, is to stay too close to the comforting thought that Tess now has freed herself from Angel. The term "injustice" has a stereotypical effect that can over-simplify her state of consciousness at this time. The fact that it feels to me that it took her much too long to recognize the injustice and to fling it in the face of Angel is a meaningful part of my experience of her life. At some point in my "perceptive series" of re-readings, I have felt that this letter is more desperate than self-assertive; that Tess is not rejecting Angel even if she writes as if she is doing that.

What she is doing is something dangerous for her self: she is directing anger at herself in an effort to jettison a love that is too much a part of her to be discarded. Even after sending this seemingly decisive letter, Tess rebuffs Alec—although with a weakening will—on two more occasions (345, 351). She is still hoping that she will not have to give up on Angel.

Tess's angry letter also occurs during a sequence in which Alec's character is developing favorable qualities. He need not be thought of in Tess's mind as a man of sexual energy only. He not only consistently offers life sustenance for Tess's family (which it would be reductive to assume is entirely a form of bribery to induce Tess back into his bed); he articulates some of the animus of the novel itself, when Tess's family is evicted from its life-long lodgings. Tess tells him that except for her not being "a proper woman," her family would have been allowed to stay in its house after the death of her father, even though they had lost their legal rights to do so (341). His response is vivid—but becomes so only in its context.

The eviction itself, with the kids and their recently widowed mother, can be emotionally wrenching, needless to say. What impresses me most deeply, however, is Hardy's delicate sense of sociological-historical-sexological understanding. He of course is not aiming at a precise historical report, but at an imagined virtual presentation of a historic situation. In that project, Hardy adds to the depth of the novel's potential for experience.

Earlier, the people in Tess's village had offered a mixed range of responses to the fact that Tess had had sex with Alec and had come back home to have his baby. These responses had ranged from a palpable condemnation in church to simple acceptance of her as a farm-worker among themselves, baby and all, to a certain romantic envy of her experience, and even a sympathetic sentiment based on the belief that she had been raped. " 'A little more than persuading had to do wi' the coming o't, I reckon. There were they that heard a sobbing one night last year in The Chase; and it mid ha' gone hard wi' a certain party if folks had come along' " (95).

The reported sobbing itself can be taken as evidence that Tess had been raped; certainly that is what the speaker means to say, and some critics tend to take this as conclusive testimony on a key issue. But there are many reasons why a woman could sob, and the speaker himself did not actually hear her. Tess, Hardy wrote, had tears on her face when Alec came back from his lone walk and had not yet touched her (77). The rejoinder by another member of the community shows that the account is not necessarily believed: "'Well, *a little more, a little less*,' 'twas a thousand pities that it should have happened to she, of all others. But 'tis always the comeliest!'" (95, my emphasis). Folk fatalism seems to inform this comment. The second speaker is taking the view that rape is not the most important fact about Tess's history, and is suggesting that it cannot be established as a fact of this case. The gist of her (?) comment is: It is the pretty women who get victimized. But there is no blame for Tess in this attitude, and the victimization refers to her having been made pregnant. If this passage tells us anything about rape in this novel, it is not about what actually happened but about the attitudes of the villagers. It shows that the topic of rape is at least mentionable, and if Tess were to have been raped by Alec, the men her village would not have thought of this as an event they could simply ignore. There is no assumption here that it is a shameful thing for the victim, only that she is due "a thousand pities."

On the surface, the inhabitants of Marlott village were tolerant; they had accepted Tess and did not ostracize her, even though their silent disapproval of her sexuality was important in her development into what she felt in her own mind was "a figure of Guilt" (91). But now, a few years later, they turn against the Durbeyfields and help to drive them all away, Tess included. Hardy as sociologist and historian describes sexual intolerance in this event as a function of several factors. For one thing, local tolerance might be worn thin by the thought that Tess is now a woman who has come home apparently rejected and possibly unmarried (they might think) from her affairs with two men. A crucial contributing factor, however, is economic chaos in the village. Most generally, "A depopulation was also going on" (339). Hardy bitterly cites the affectless words of unnamed "statisticians" who think that this movement of human beings is impersonal and voluntary: "the tendency of the rural population towards the large towns" (339). What actually happens in the village is that the "life-holders," a non-agricultural class that included "the carpenter, the smith, the shoemaker, the huckster, together with nondescript workers other than farm-labourers," had held their homes under lifelong leases. But as these leases expired with the death of the life-holder—and Tess's father was one of these—the landlords now refused to continue such arrangements. Instead the homes were "mostly pulled down, if not absolutely needed by the farmer for his hands" (339). The process is deadly for the community:

> Cottagers who were not directly employed on the land were looked upon with disfavour, and the banishment of some starved the trade of the others, who were thus obliged to follow. These families, who had formed the backbone of the village life in the past, who were the depositories of the village traditions, had to seek refuge in the large centres... (339)

Hardy here is writing about the class he himself came from, as Merryn and Raymond Williams pointed out;[16] this, then, is further evidence of Hardy's personal involvement in *Tess*. He is performing a compassionate, human identification with a defeated and virtually destroyed family that would have little in common with his own. I feel especially the body references here: banishment, starved, backbone. These combined with the typical understatement, "disfavour," make the passage hard-hitting, and with its analytical force it becomes totally convincing. The whole passage is an example of what Dewey means by the dependence of the imagination "upon the embodiment of ideas in emotionally charged sense" (*AE* 40). But the additional point is one concerning sexual mores: only now, only in this historic trend toward destruction of the village community, do the neighbors as well as the landlord regard the Durbeyfields as "expellable," soon after the father dies. Were it not for the family's bad reputation, with both parents drinking too much, and Tess's "queer unions," the family could have stayed on (if it could have paid a weekly rental). The process of eviction had begun much earlier, with Tess:

> Ever since the occurrence of the event which had cast such a shadow over Tess's life, the Durbeyfield family...*had been tacitly looked on* as one which would have to go, when their lease ended, *if only in the interests of morality*" (340, my emphasis).

So the villagers thought. But we might ask ourselves, by way of deepening our experience of this passage, how our own neighbors or we ourselves would react if there were a chance to be rid of a family that included drinkers and a transgressive woman. (And even if there were no economic crisis).

Tess then is not quite accurate when she tells Alec that the eviction is due to her not being "a proper woman." She is informing him, however, of a key factor, the coercion of sexual bigotry. Alec reacts at once: "D'Urberville's face flushed. 'What a blasted shame! Miserable snobs! May their dirty souls be burnt to cinders!'" (341). I find that I share vicariously in this vulgar outburst. Two significant things follow from it immediately: Alec offers to take care of "your mother's family" *even if he should grow tired of Tess*: to her expressed fear (and bargaining step) that he might tire of her and then leave her family in the lurch, he says: "O no—no. I would guarantee you against such as that in writing, if necessary" (342). He is clearly moving well beyond his former manipulative acts with Tess's family: this word of a commitment toward them is not simply a gift of a moment, to be paid for with Tess's sexual body.

Given the way her situation is developing, the rightness of returning to Alec at this point in her life is becoming clear to Tess: "...a consciousness that *in a physical sense* this man alone was her husband seemed to weigh on her more and more" (345, my emphasis). In the assumptions of her women friends, it is clear that her prior relation with Alec is going to have a strong pull on her once she has lost the hope of Angel's return: Marian declares: "'Tisn't as though she had never known him afore...His having won her once makes all the difference in the world'" (351). From their common sense perspective, this is a kind of deferred sexual bond, which asserts its force once there is no better sexual love choice. But they do not imagine Alec as Tess's "husband." That confusion is part of the individualized story of Tess's life. As the situation develops, the concept of "husband" is being reduced to that of sexual partner—partly a result, I imagine, of Angel's own earlier fantastic insistence that Alec, because he had had sex with her, was really her "husband in Nature, and not I" (239).

But is Alec really her husband, in Tess's mind? The limiting phrase "in a physical sense" qualifies or haunts this passage. It makes me ask: how is Tess thinking? And I sense a confusion in her body-mind. The very concept of a husband "within Nature," or one "in a physical sense" only, is so confusing in its mix of the natural and the cultural, as to guarantee trouble for her. I do not know of a single other instance in which a writer of the Victorian era used the concept "husband in Nature." It sounds crazy. It took me many readings to connect this notion of the nature-husband with Hardy's insight: Tess, when being wooed by Angel, has "*a religious sense of a certain moral validity* in the previous union" with Alec (183, my emphasis).

Other than the relationship between Alec and Tess, the quality of the novel now seems to become strangely sluggish, as Tess delays her acceptance of Alec. To be sure, there is movement in a literal sense: Tess's mother and siblings are forced to move from their home, and are even kept out in the rain as they hunt for lodging in Kingsbere, the "half-dead townlet" (348) where the once grand d'Urbervilles are buried. But there is little energy in the narrative. The suffering of Tess's family hardly arouses her. Her father's death a few chapters earlier has passed without any word of her grief (338).

Hardy deflects emotional quality at this juncture, first by explaining that the demise of Tess's father will mean the closure of the family's leasehold on their house. He follows this with a comment from afar, a paragraph on the theme of eternal change in which the Durbeyfields somehow were destined to be caught. Once their ancestors had held power as d'Urbervilles, but now they are only an impoverished family. "So do flux and reflux—the rhythm of change—alternate and persist in everything under the sky" (338). This ends chapter 50. I have learned after several re-readings of the novel to ignore this passage; it does not seem to lead to any enhancement of my experience. But ignoring it has an effect: it shifts my focus to the strange absence of any response by Tess to the death of her father. It becomes less strange when, at length, I recall how her father had doubted her report that she had married Angel. "The perception that her word could be doubted even here, in her own parental house, set her mind against the spot as nothing else could have done" (252). In his final speech in the novel, made when Tess comes home to help care for him, he rattles on about his noble descent and what ought to be done for him (334). For Tess, her father had always been a loss.

True, she is doing all she can to get her family re-settled. The younger siblings sing a pathetic hymn in tones of "phlegmatic passivity" (344). Hardy's tone becomes grotesque as the penultimate "Phase" of the novel ends. Marian and Izz, Tess's two surviving dairy-maid friends of old, write a quaint warning letter to Angel telling him that he is about to lose his wife to "an Enemy in the shape of a Friend," but then lapse into "a mood of emotional exaltation at their own generosity, which made them sing in hysterical snatches and weep at the same time" (351-2). My own emotions are also confused and difficult to identify clearly, as I enter what Hardy designates the final "Phase" of this novel, a phase to which he gives the name "Fulfillment."

6. "Ah-It Is My Fault!"

Feelings of doubtfulness and uncertainty predominate in the early part of this Phase, as I follow Angel's searching for his lost wife. His search, carried out while he is recovering from a severe illness—his mother almost fails to recognize him, so gaunt is he (356)—is fused in my experience of this section with the problem or question of whether he has changed, or is at least in the process of changing. Is he still the man of "a hard, logical deposit" that will stop him from loving Tess? By this time, Hardy has shown that Angel has at least the beginnings of insights which would allow him to change. Thus, after parting from Tess:

> ...he became weary and anxious; and his anxiety increased. He wondered if he had treated her unfairly....as the motive of each act in the long series of bygone days presented itself to his view, he perceived how intimately the notion of having Tess as a dear possession was mixed up with all his schemes and words and ways. (254-5)

Such is his self-critical thinking. To perceive that his notion of possessing Tess has been "intimately...mixed up with" all the elements of his personality, including his "schemes," has the potential for a central breakthrough, and it would be one if it were followed out with care. There is also a passage with far less abstraction, and a quality of vivid experience: One night

> He almost talked to her in his anger, as if she had been in the room. And then her cooing voice, plaintive in expostulation, disturbed the darkness, the velvet touch of her lips passed over his brow, and he could distinguish in the air the warmth of her breath. (258)

But Hardy makes clear that Angel still has a long way to go: Angel has not perceived the "deeper shade" hanging over him, "namely, the shade of his own limitations" (258).

Here I think is a juncture that marks a major difference between a strictly analytical *versus* a Deweyan approach to human change. The logic of Angel's thinking may not be very important, considered from a Deweyan perspective. The key factor is that Angel's process of change is at least under way. Its outcome will be shown in how he acts in the future, not in whether he fully realizes the flaws in his moralizing logic.

The reasoning that immediately follows, in fact, in which Hardy imagines what Angel might better have said to his parents in lieu of desperately exclaiming "She is spotless!" (258), is still within the logical framework of Angel's "hard logical deposit": Tess is "stained" and perceived as being in a "sorry" state, but "he forgot" that "the defective can be more than the entire" (259). Logically, then, according to Angel's sexual-moral code, she is still "defective." But as the word resonates, it seems to me to become enveloped in the more central sexual-love interest of the novel. Could Hardy be suggesting that a woman who is "defective" in the sense of not being a virgin but sexually experienced, is actually more valuable as a mate than one who is still technically "entire"? The thought at first seems downright weird, but then seems to lodge in my consciousness. Again, as I have said, in a pragmatist understanding of the passage, its discrete logic at this point does not matter; what matters is how this thinking could serve Angel's impulsion toward change.

Hardy returns to this theme many chapters later, as if to allow that the process had been going on in Angel's self for a long while. In one longer segment in chapter 49, Hardy, writing in synchrony with Angel's consciousness, portrays the man going through a mix of considerations on Tess. The passage is compromised artistically by Hardy's efforts to occlude the degree of Angel's monstrous action, but I now realize that it is not thereby ruined. In a way, the pleading not to judge Angel too harshly functions as Hardy's warning to himself and to his readers that the concern of this passage is the process of change rather than the evaluation of Angel's behavior to Tess. It is a directive to help us focus, and not simply an apology for Angel's treatment of Tess. The method is also indirect: if we make the hasty assumption that Angel (and Hardy) should be dealing explicitly and only with the issue of Angel seeing the guilt for his mistreatment of Tess, we will insure our disappointment.

Some parts in fact do not seem to bear directly on the problem of change: the fact that Angel witnessed the suffering and pathetic deaths of some English settlers who had come to Brazil (328), seems at first to be irrelevant—except that his experiencing this would have attuned him to the primary vulnerability of life, and helped to move him off of his logical fixation with the morality of any sexual code. He *begins* now "to discredit the old appraisements of morality" (328). A "regret for his hasty judgment began to oppress him" (329). Before long, he is told "plainly," by an Englishman he happens to travel with, and one who has shared in witnessing this suffering, "that he was wrong in coming away from her" (329). I imagine that this sort of direct statement, coming from the one person to whom he has divulged his experiences, is needed to cut through Angel's impasse; it may have real value for the process of change. But it is not decisive, it is not a magical conversion experience, nor does Hardy present it as such; as Hardy immediately makes clear, there is a crude sexual detail Angel still has to wrestle with, namely "that abhorrence of the un-intact state, which he had inherited with the creed of mysticism" (330), in other words, from his immersion in Christianity.

This sexual-body image obviously still weighs heavily upon him, even as he thinks of lessening his condemnation. He brings in to his internal rehearsal of his return to Tess a series of factors, not logically related, but which have led him to his present situation: the "inconsistencies" of his "Hellenic Paganism"; Izz Huett's telling him how extremely much Tess loves him; Tess's appearance on their wedding day: "How her eyes lingered upon him; how she had hung upon his words as if they were a god's" (329-30). He also realizes only now, as he allows into his mind the perception that he should have had during his crisis with Tess, "how pitiful her face had looked by the rays of the fire," when she could not yet even take in the fact that he was rejecting her (330). That is a powerful thought, both for Angel and for me, the reader, because it is fueled by the emotional intensity of their unconsummated honeymoon: it takes energy from those scenes, which continue their "spread" through the novel. And finally, in a reversal of his earlier disdain for her descent from the d'Urbervilles, he thinks now of how this could be something good. Hardy makes no suggestion that this line of reasoning is realistic: it is "a most useful ingredient to the dreamer, to the moralizer on declines and falls." Angel thinks of Tess's ancient Norman family not in the abstract but as a way of re-envisioning her face: "In *recalling her face again and again*, he thought now that he could see therein a flash of the dignity which must have graced her grand-dames..."(330, my emphasis). This last, cumulative detail permits him to repair his ability to honor Tess, which is something he needs to do, and without lapsing into his previous trap of totally idealizing her. This thinking leads Angel to have a bodily response: "The vision sent that *aura* through his veins which he had formerly felt, and *which left behind it a sense of sickness*" (330-1, my emphasis). Hardy is not saying that all this felt great. There is change going on, but not a simple turn-around.

The next two small paragraphs, which end this passage, allow Hardy to name the process as love: "So spoke love renascent," but what this phrase refers to specifically is an obscure Biblical reference, formed appropriately as a question: "Was not the gleaning of the grapes of Ephraim better than the vintage of Abi-ezer?" This appears to be a baffling reference, since even if I look it up in Judges, chapter 8, I find that it refers to a battle led by Gideon against the Midianites. It seems hopelessly irrelevant—but this never is the case when Hardy cites the Bible. With my patience for absorbing Hardy's method of writing, this allusion eventually acquires a dual rationale. My initial impression is that here Hardy as narrator simply joins Angel in his moralizing reflections. In its context, however, the concern of this passage is not with a woman's absolute value, but with what an enlightened Angel might have told his parents when they demand of him that his Tess be worthy of the praise of the Biblical King Lemuel, who is quoted (from Proverbs 31) on the nature of the virtuous woman and ideal wife. "Many daughters have done virtuously," Angel's father quotes as he prays aloud, "but thou excellest them all" (257).

Angel can change only if he incorporates into his process some of the culture of his father, the Reverend Clare, for whom this kind of Biblical allusion would have an immediate appeal. In this guise, the passage is important for its style of thought, not for its content. Also, the story of Gideon provides an analogue for the radical thought suggested earlier: Gideon's question, in the context of Angel's thinking, is a suggestion of the greater value of Tess for himself, with her sexual experience, than Tess would have had for Alec as a virgin. In the Biblical analogy, Angel is asking whether it might be better to have "the gleaning of her grapes" than to have been the first to have taken her "vintage."[17] Hardy's word-choice of "vintage" can easily suggest "virginity" in the present context. This goes beyond the weak abstract statement just preceding, which says that Tess "outvalued the freshness of her fellows" *"[d]espite her not inviolate past..."* (331, my emphasis). This is not despite, but because. I can imagine that Hardy would have had great reticence in making a comment on the value of a woman's sexual experience with a man other than the husband, but nonetheless he has said it. I can imagine that Angel could only allow such a thought to enter his conscious mind if it were buffered in an analogy from a Biblical source having nothing to do with sex. But he does let it enter. I realize that is a radical notion to have in a Victorian novel—but there it is. I do not pretend to know what degree of deliberate intention Hardy put into this thought, but he did write it.

Thinking of whether any context has been created for such a concept of a Biblical passage being used in an erotic mode, I now recall another statement, one that I have always ignored, which I have read two chapters earlier. It comes in a plea by Alec for Tess to return to him.

> The words of the stern prophet Hosea...come back to me. Don't you know them, Tess? "And she shall follow after her lover but she shall not overtake him, and she shall seek him; but shall not find him: then shall she say, I will go and return to my first husband; for then it was better with me than now." (320)

As one annotation points out, Hardy makes Alec slightly mis-quote the passage, and ignores its context, rendering it as a personal and sympathetic love-plea, which it is not what it is in the passage from Hosea 2:7.[18] Alec follows up immediately with his invitation to Tess to hop aboard his "trap," saying "you know the rest." The stern Hosea thus becomes an erotic helper. Similarly, not many pages further on, the phrase "her not inviolate past" (like the term "defective" earlier) not only refers to the state of non-virginity, but suggests that it might be superior to that of virginity. If Angel can really think this, even half-consciously, then he is changing.

Anyone attempting to experience this novel must take into account the historic context of the conditions Hardy faced in writing *Tess*, particularly regarding the subject of sexuality. Such is a truism. What might be more valuable is a recognition of the generalized inhibition in English culture concerning sexual expression in literature or any of the arts. This is not simply a problem for Hardy, nor is it strictly Victorian, nor even solely English. Edward Bullough, in his 1913 essay on "psychical distance" in art, wrote that anything sexual would normally interfere with the limits that a reader or viewer could tolerate; hence an extra degree of distance is needed in dealing with any such subject matter:

> ...it is safe to infer that, in art practice, explicit references to organic affections, to the material existence of the body, especially to sexual matters, lies normally below the [spectator's] Distance-limit, and can be touched upon by Art only with special precautions.[19]

For readers in a less inhibited age, this note concerning historical context is best employed as a signal to be responsive to the sexual meanings that might be expressed with "special precautions," such as in Hardy's apparent honoring of the "defective," that is, non-virginal, Tess. It would be counter-experiential to use the information in the manner of traditional historical criticism, as a signal to limit our responses to what contemporaries of Hardy might have been willing to see.

Hardy may be charged with overloading the entire series concerning Angel's struggles with too many factors, and lapsing into obscurantism in his effort to contrive a change in Angel's psyche. But that depends on my trust and patience as a reader, on my willingness to meet the passage with the understanding it calls for, and for my continuing to care about the issue it deals with, Angel's process of change. I would say that the obscurity is functional. The impression of overloading is mistaken; the passage on the "gleaning of the grapes of Ephraim" is better thought of as one of several instances of necessarily self-perplexed reasoning, drawing on sources at several levels in Angel's personality. That is a process Angel is undergoing.

The outcome of his self-questioning remains in doubt. During his separation from Tess, Angel has a thought which shows him to be unaware of the great harm he has done her: "it had seemed the easiest thing in the world to rush back into her arms, the moment he chose to forgive her" (357). But having arrived at his parents' home "it was not so easy as it had seemed" (357). After having been home for a few days, he "hunted up" Tess's long letter, and re-read it. Hardy now re-quotes a sizable portion of this letter, not because readers might have forgotten it (it had been rendered in full only a few chapters back), but because this time it is bound to have a new effect on Angel. "I must cry to you in my trouble—I have no one else," this excerpt begins (358). It is the third sentence in the letter, and it seems to define the focus of Angel's attention. I imagine that Angel is hearing her "cry" now, hearing her voice, in an emotionally receptive way. The letter had moved him when he had first read it, but now he reverts to it in the context of his deepening process of change. What will be the result? In a Deweyan answer to this question, Angel's change cannot be regarded as real until it is proven pragmatically in the event itself, his re-finding of Tess. I can imagine at this point that an additional factor is operating: Angel's illness at such a vulnerable juncture in his life may help to break down his defenses, and that this will make change more possible.

Angel's search for Tess spreads through two and a half chapters, and involves many variations. One of the most vivid, energy-laden moments occurs in his conversation with Tess's mother, Joan, who would have sent him on his way with her judgment that Tess would not even want him to get in touch with her. Angel momentarily accepts this, but then bursts out: "I am sure she would!...I know her better than you do." The mother replies, "That's very likely, sir, for I have never really known her" (361-2). This exchange makes the quality of Angel's love for Tess feel real. At the same time it reconfirms Tess's individuality: however much she is a woman of her culture, she cannot be understood according to conventional values, and her mother has come to realize this.

Standing before Tess, and not yet realizing that she is living with Alec, Angel, looking like a "[m]ere yellow skeleton," speaks decisive words that allay some of my doubt: "I did not think rightly of you—I did not see you as you were....I have learnt to since, dearest Tessy mine!" (365). I have found in repeated readings that even the last three words can be experienced sympathetically, when, that is, I do not allow my culturally-learned embarrassment of "sentimental" language to block me. When a given expression is regarded as sentimental, the problem all too often is a fear of experiencing emotional involvement.[19] The words "dearest Tessy mine!" are simply the ones that Clare is speaking, with feeling, and they are right ones, within the situation at hand. That is how he would speak.

Their meeting is dramatic in the serious sense of involving the drama of their entire emotional lives. In my reading experiences of the novel, I can feel this scene to the extent that I have felt the meanings of their lives all through the novel. They can barely get through it. Tess "seemed to feel like a fugitive in a dream, who tries to move away, but cannot" (365). Partly, she is trying to move away from Angel himself; if he should embrace her or touch her, the effect might be to overwhelm her and draw her back to him. "Don't come close to me, Angel! No—you must not. Keep away." (365). But this is followed by his plea to still love him and to return to him, assuring her that his parents now will welcome her. To this, she is not only unable to say a flat No, but actually agrees—for a moment: "Yes—O yes, yes! But I say, I say it is too late" (365). She is finally able to say, in language that reaches for a final term Angel cannot argue with, "He has won me back to him" (366). She then adds stinging remarks, which assert her right to be with Alec and convey her anger at Angel for leaving her. "The step back to him was not so great as it seems. He had been as husband to me: you never had!" (366). Plainly, Angel is to understand that her sexual relation to Alec is like that of a wife to a husband, and not that of a slave to the man who has bought her. Tess then sends Angel away: "will you go away Angel, please, and never come any more?" (366). He is overcome, of course, but he has heard her every statement, and is certainly being hurt. His one verbal response to her is unequivocal, making no excuses, and accepting his responsibility for what has happened: "Ah—it is my fault!" (366). That is all he can say: "Speech was as inexpressive as silence."

At this point in the text, a year after publication of the first edition, Hardy added in 1892 a sentence that has attracted disbelieving comment:

> But [Angel] had a vague consciousness of one thing, though it was not clear to him until later: that his original Tess had spiritually ceased to regard the body before him as hers—allowing it to drift, like a corpse upon the current, in a direction dissociated from its living will. (366)

Possibly Hardy was nervous about readers who would assume that Tess has been sexually responsive with Alec. At least one critic is sure that Hardy himself could not bear to think such a thing of the character he had created.[20] Perhaps this is so, but as is so often the case with the problem of the quality of sexual contact in this novel, we are told nothing directly. I think we have to admit that we cannot be all that knowing about their intimate situation.

For me the problem is not that of dis-allowing Hardy's comment, but of following the difficult shift in the image of Tess, who is first presented as looking quite breathtaking in the fine cashmere dressing gown and slippers that Alec has provided for her: "Her great natural beauty was, if not heightened, rendered more obvious by her attire" (365). There is no question that Tess *looks* like the sexual woman we have long known her to be. In her appearance there is an immediate feeling that she is living contentedly with Alec. Now, a few paragraphs later, I am trying to absorb the notion that she regarded her bodily self as a corpse! There seems to be a deliberate effect of disjunction here. I find that there can be no full reconciliation of the two disparate views of the quality of Tess's life at this point. But that may be the point of the experience here. Had Hardy merely wanted to cover up the fact that she seems to be in her full female beauty, I suppose he would have altered the first impression, letting her appearance have some mark of ambivalence, rather than clumsily tagging on a new idea at the end of the chapter. But upon reading more responsively, I begin to credit the sentence in its context: it is an impression had by Angel, and it occurs to him long afterward. It may have occurred to Hardy himself in the aftermath of the first edition of *Tess*, but there is no reason why he could not have had a valid further perception. And, most importantly, Angel only has this impression *after* the agonizing exchange of words between him and Tess: at that point in her misery, she could well have looked as if she were giving up on her body and regarding it as dead. His perception thus alters with the emotional movement of the situation itself.

I cannot see her in her life with Alec as a "corpse," if that is taken to imply that she has been frigid, or totally disconnected from her own bodily experience. Nor do I suppose that Hardy was trying to say such a thing. Yet all cannot have been well between her and Alec. Even if she is sexually responsive with Alec, there would be much to continue to trouble Tess in a relationship with a man who is not the one she believes in as her own choice. This would be the case even if Alec is, in her guilty fantasy, her husband in "a physical sense." I think it likely that while making love with Alec at this stage, Tess's mind is troubled with fantasies of Angel, the would-be lover toward whom she had developed and maintained an intense, loving, erotic, and idealized relation, and for whom she had felt an immense longing for his return. As she says to Angel, after she kills Alec: "I could not bear the loss of you any longer—you don't know how entirely I was unable to bear your not loving me" (372). Alec, she later says, "nagged me about you [that is, about Angel]," which indicates that he was not sure of his "mastery" even though he had got her back to live with him. I think too, when I connect this situation with Tess's earlier, exceptionally vivid taking of the role of the victim who is to be whipped, crushed and (in Hardy's comment) fatally throttled, that the quality of her life in bed with Alec might have been more like acting out in sex of her belief in punishment than a pleasurable embrace.

Alec himself may have become more fascinated with making moral reparations to Tess and with having the fantasy of "mastering" her than with sexual pleasure. He seems more weird than he intends to be, the last time he is seen in the text, just before Tess goes back to live with him. He lies silently on one of the d'Urberville tombs, and frightens Tess badly, but then jumps up and supports her before she falls over, following with a strangely pleasant tone of apology: "'I saw you come in,' he said smiling, 'and got up there not to interrupt your meditations.'" Not surprisingly she soon tells him to just "Go away." The episode ends with him whispering to her, not of love or sex but of coercion: "Mind this; you'll be civil yet!" (350-51). Was he trying to frighten her or not, when he was lying there? Or was he acting out some unconscious need of his own?

The next thing we know about him in the novel is that she has gone to live with him.

As Dewey remarks in his *Ethics* (in 1932, or one year after delivering the lectures that became *Art as Experience*), "not every satisfaction of appetite and craving turns out to be a good."[21] After having for years resisted Hardy's suggestion, through Angel, of Tess regarding her own body as a corpse, I have come to think that it belongs in the experience of the novel. It belongs there for its quality of difficult questioning. It makes me ask myself, what sort of fulfillment could Tess actually have had with Alec? For readers who have constructed for themselves a simple character, such inquiry is unnecessary: she has agreed to live with Alec, she is a sexual woman, and they make love. But considering the body-mind of Tess as she lives with Alec and looks forward to a future with him, I think of some of Dewey's statements on fulfillment in *Art as Experience*: "Pleasures may come about through chance contact and stimulation; such pleasures are not to be despised in a world full of pain" (*AE* 23). Now between

Tess and Alec, there is more going on than chance contact, and whatever their pleasures may have been, they cannot have been negligible or worthless. Dewey goes further than this, however:

> But happiness and delight are a different sort of thing [than pleasures]. They come to be through a fulfillment that reaches to the depth of our being—one that is an adjustment of our whole being with the conditions of existence. (*AE* 23)

I find it hard to believe that Tess could have found such fulfillment in a life with Alec. She could have lived with him, made love with him, settled down with him, and more or less accepted him. She would have given up any hope for deeper emotional fulfillment. But I recall now Hardy's wording, from the extraordinary passage of his comment on Tess's initiation into sex, that Alec is "the wrong man" for this woman (77). Taking in this comment once more, after having seen how things have turned out, I know that *if* he is the wrong man, it is not in the sense of committing some terrible crime against her. It is in an overall sense of his qualities: despite his sexual attractiveness, he finally seems to have nothing in qualities that would lead to further development, such as would be fitting in a mate for a woman like Tess. Alec has become a more sympathetic character in the latter portions of then novel—and certainly a responsible one. I have felt that change in him, but even though I have experimented in some of my readings of the novel with perceiving him as just the right mate for Tess, I cannot get over the feeling that there seems to be something lacking in him. (I will say more about this in the last chapter.)

Being the "wrong man" would not be simply a matter of Alec's own qualities as a human being. There is also the sense that Tess, by having started her sexual-love life with him, has loaded into herself a set of unfinished satisfactions and dissatisfactions that would be difficult to resolve. To say this is to allow that her early experience with a man leaves a deep mark upon her, on her "body-mind." partly because that man was the first she had made love with, and over a time of several weeks. To this extent, her loss of virginity combined with the ensuing weeks with Alec, becomes a concern for Hardy, the novel, and her—and for me, the reader, quite aside from the ideology of masculine control over women. Her chances of recovering her self by living with Alec, after all that she has gone through at the hands of Angel, seem extremely dim. After all, she has only recently given up her hope of having Angel, and must be mourning for him in the month (approximately) that she lives with Alec. If I recall now that Hardy had written earlier in the novel, that but for the force of public opinion, she would "simply" have gone through a process in "liberal education" (103), I now realize that I must recall also Dewey's sense that education, if it means emotional reconstruction of the self, is not an easy process. Maybe Hardy, despite his use of the modifier "simply," had never meant that it would be. There cannot be easy learning in the kind of life situation he is dealing with.

Possibly, life with Alec would be the best Tess could hope for, given what her experience has been and what her mind has made out of it. Maybe experience itself intrinsically has nothing better to offer. Such is reality, or so we might think. At times, I can think that life does not even have any great potential for fulfillment. So we must all think at those times when we feel how often experience disappoints. Tess, however, soon finds that she has not given up. Nor has the novel.

Six

CONSUMMATIONS

Tess kills Alec. This is a narrative event so burnt into my consciousness after many readings that I nearly forget to ask what I experience. Do I feel relieved that Alec is dead? Is he such a bad person that Tess must kill him? Upon re-reading this part of the novel several more times, I think not, but this is because given Hardy's oblique description, I can barely feel anything as Alec's blood forms a "gigantic ace of hearts" on the ceiling of the landlady's parlor just below Tess and Alec's bedroom. Nor do I have any feeling for the

> dead silence...broken only by a regular beat.
> Drip, drip, drip. (369)

Or on Alec's final "appearance" in the novel: "The wound was small, but the point of the blade had touched the heart of the victim, who lay on his back, pale, fixed, dead, as if he had scarcely moved after the infliction of the blow" (370). Hardy discourages a response to this killing, except as it can be felt in Tess's terms. The melodramatic possibilities of having a woman slash up a man in a murderous rage seem to be flatly rejected by Hardy's stipulation that Alec had just a single small wound that "touched the heart…" As if to further steer the reader away from a sensational response to this killing, Hardy ends the chapter by reporting without comment the gossipy quality that the news of the murder soon acquired: "In a quarter of an hour the news that a gentleman who was a temporary visitor to the town had been stabbed in his bed, spread through every street and villa of the popular watering-place" (370). Clearly, there is no pathway toward an experience in such an external approach to this event.

Hardy, notoriously criticized for entering the narrative to defend Tess, says not a word in her favor on the matter of her murdering her lover. But he is not interested in the problem of the murder itself. Although I know that ethically, there is no excuse for this murder, I find that I feel only faint sympathy for Alec at this point. This is due neither to my acceptance of the idea (discussed in Chapter One) that Tess is taking a grand revenge upon all the injustices done to her, nor that Alec is a mere cardboard villain unworthy of my sympathy. The controlling context remains sexual. Insofar as ethics are concerned, we may discern a suggestion that adult sexual love is so essential a need, within the cultural context of "the ache of modernism," that it can lead a kind, compassionate, and passionate person to commit murder, when that need is subjected to outrage. As

Tess puts it, in one of her last statements in the novel: "How wickedly mad I was! Yet formerly I could not bear to hurt a fly or a worm, and the sight of a bird in a cage used often to make me cry" (377). Tess's situation does not justify killing anyone, as she herself recognizes at this point. But if her situation were grasped in its larger social and psychological implications, it might help to make for a society in which sexual love is at last supported with all the intelligence it would take for making fulfillment possible.

Hardy could have chosen to focus sympathetically upon Alec's murder. And I can only have what I can have with and in this novel's experience. I can always attempt to deliberately de-value the experience, in whole or in part. As Dewey recognizes, we do have to evaluate where an experience, once it is had, might be leading us. We cannot prolong an experience beyond its range of felt immediacy, and it is valuable to have "intervening periods of discrimination" in which we can consider the possibility that the experience has been constructed with "cheap means employed upon meretricious stuff" (*AE* 150). If Hardy is determined to condone the murder of Alec, then I might discriminate and de-value this aspect of the novel. But when I consider what the novel actually "does...with and in experience" (*AE* 9), I find that I must reaffirm my confidence in Hardy's choices: *Tess* would not be a better book if Hardy had made a distinctly ethical issue out of the murder of Alec. It is a novel about sexual love and Nature, and that is the subject-matter to which it devotes its energies. Hardy discourages a response to the killing of Alec, except as it can be felt in terms of what Tess is feeling.

1. Motives in Context

In those terms, there is ample explanatory motive. Overtly, consciously, she realizes the unbearable loss now for the second time of her "true husband" (not "her husband in Nature," whatever that might mean) who might very well die of the illness from which he is suffering and who would die as a result of Tess's "sin." His yellow skeleton appearance standing before her would likely shock her into responding guiltily. The sin would be that of becoming Alec's sexual lover once more, although now Angel has cleared his mind of his fascination with her "un-intact state." Alec, even if she did finally chose to stay with him, would be felt as responsible for leading her to this loss. This is not a denial by Tess of her own responsibility for being with Alec. Her agony over that choice can be felt throughout the situation; it needs no overt statement.

But Alec's "cruel persuasion" is of more than a single dimension. It had taken the form of playing upon her pity for her helpless family: "My little sisters and brother and my mother's needs...they were things you moved me by..." (368). Less overtly, but implied overwhelmingly, is the factor of what Tess sees as his "cruel persuasion," reinforced by his assurance that Angel would never return (368). "Now look here, Tess," he had said, "I know what men are, and bearing in mind the *grounds* of your separation, I am quite positive he will never make it up with you" (342, emphasis Alec's). Was that really a lie? Or was it merely masculine over-confidence? It is offered as knowledge guaranteed by the authority of a man who knows men. That is not a form of knowledge Tess could gain on her own, especially if the man is of the professional class rather than working class, and is a man who has been acting in a most unforeseen way. Now Alec may know "men," but he does not know Angel. I imagine that her outrage as she suddenly realizes this deep sexual-body deception is the most decisive force that impels her to the act of killing him. To say so will not violate with absurd rationality a context in which she is extremely upset and disturbed.[1] Hardy, as usual, did not directly say it in his text. That may be one reason he conspicuously invites further attention to Tess's distraught speech as she quarrels with Alec in their last conversation. Not only could the landlady, Mrs. Brooks, "only catch a portion" of what was being said; the sizable portion of the speech by Tess that she does "catch" is punctured by seven separate ellipses. As for Alec, we are not told that he said a thing during this fragmented speech, only that he had asked her, when he heard her moaning, "What's the matter?" (368). But, significantly, we know what his last statements must have been about, for as Tess soon tells Angel: "he [Alec] bitterly taunted me, and *called you by a foul name. And then I did it: my heart could not bear it*: he had nagged me about you before" (372, my emphasis). In other words, she stabbed him exactly at the juncture of his insulting Angel, much as she had violently slapped Alec with the heavy glove when he had told her she "should be willing...to leave *that mule you call husband for ever*" (320, my emphasis). Her final burst of aggression, enabling her to wield the knife, thus sounds as if she had become incensed not only at the sexual deception she feels he has practiced on her, but at his failure to take seriously what she is thinking and saying.

2. Hearing Tess: Voice and Words

But before any of these motives are introduced, Tess gives way to an emotional expression with her voice that is deeply affecting. As a quotation in print, it is this: "Oh-oh-oh!" The landlady hears Tess repeat the single syllable in this form, followed by a silence, and followed by a repetition: "Oh-oh-oh!" The tone is one of "a low note of moaning, as if it came from a soul bound to some Ixonian wheel—" (367). This repeated cry feels as if it is linked to the vivid triple repetition she had uttered at the point of her giving in, long before, to her desire for Angel: "O my heart-O-O-O!"(180). I continue to pay special attention to Tess's voice, having learned that I must do that almost from the moment she had been introduced into the novel. Here in this scene, before going on to her fateful last quarrel with Alec, she is again in agony over love, not with a quality of ecstasy this time but with misery over what she has just done: sent Angel away, for good. What her moan of "oh" seems to do, with its bodily source that is deeper than any mere vocalization—what it does, and not simply what it means—is to express her transformation of Body-Mind, coming out of a love for Angel that she cannot deny. It is a huge emotional change from the opening of the sequence in which she "rencounters" Angel.

Exploring another approach to understanding her murderous act, or considering a different strand of its experiential texture, I remember that Tess had long intuited that she might kill Alec, ever since that day when she slapped him with her work-glove. And, as she says, she has killed him to make herself acceptable in the eyes of Angel. It is a futile homicidal act of erasing her relationship to Alec:

> He has come between us and ruined us, and now he can never do it any more. I never loved him at all, Angel, as I loved you. You know it, don't you? You believe it? You didn't come back to me, and I was obliged to go back to him. Why did you go away—*why* did you—when I loved you so? I can't think why you did it. You didn't come back to me and I was obliged to go back to him. But I don't blame you; only, Angel, will you forgive me my sin against you, now I have killed him? *I thought as I ran along* that you would be sure to forgive me now I have done that. It came to me as a shining light that I should get you back that way. (372, my emphasis)

This emotional speech has something of a stream-of-consciousness quality. The explanation she gives makes some sense, emotionally, but it also feels as if her mind, as she ran along following her act of murder, has supplied her with a reason that she may not have had at the time. It is as if one hemisphere of her brain has done something grossly irrational and contrary to all her own values, and then the other half has quickly made something reasonable out of it. A sequence of this kind is frequently encountered in experiments with "split brain" patients, and that may be the way the human mind works when it encounters seemingly impossible contradictions in its own acts.[2] As a line of reasoning that claims she killed Alec in order to assure her acceptance by Angel, the speech soon loses any validity it might have had for Tess. Tess herself does not seem to believe the explanation she has given: within a few pages we find her declaring that Angel will never accept her as the woman she is, and when she tells him this, she makes no further mention of having killed Alec as a way of assuring her marriage to Angel.

In one aspect of her speech, Tess is allowing that in a lesser but real way, she did love Alec. She is acknowledging something important for me as the reader of this novel to hear—and important for herself: that her love for Alec, while it was not as central for her self as what she feels for Angel, was love. It is only a glancing reference, to be sure, but if the purpose of her speech is only to assure Angel that she loves only him, there would be every reason not to mention that she had ever loved Alec in any way at all. She was living with a man for whom she had some love, and she is sure that she loves another man much more than that, and with a different form of attachment. That is impossible for me to understand, as long as I stick to the habitual cultural assumption of love being a state of commitment to one person, or of one single quality. Even when this unwarranted notion is put aside, her relationship to Alec remains too complex to be classified as either love or not-love. This causes difficulty for me (or for us) in experiencing this novel, but that is a trouble that cannot be avoided. Nor, as I must have made clear by now, can I simply dispose of the problem by saying that her love for Alec was sexual while that for Angel is a-sexual.

Angel does not seem to be upset by Tess's admission; it is one made so incidentally and with such excitement that it most probably passes him by. Nor does he appear to be impressed with Tess's sacrificial logic, or her "shining light," although he is its beneficiary. Is he even considering what her words mean? It is hard to believe that he does not hear her, or at least that he does not recall these words of Tess having loved Alec, during the next several days of their being alone together. But he only knows that at this juncture, he will try with all his ability to protect Tess; he does not flinch from doing so when he suspects that her wild story of having killed Alec is true. For once, he not only marvels at the strength of her affection for him, but is amazed "at the strangeness of its quality" (372). In contrast to his earlier mistaken self-control, Angel now "kissed her endlessly with his white lips, and held her hand," and swears he will not desert her, but will protect her no matter what she has done to Alec (373).

3. Experiencing a Lovers' Union

What happens next implies, I believe, that Angel does realize two things: first, that because they cannot simply continue running without rest, they will find a place to stop for a time; and second—and here I am allowing my intuitive sense to make a sympathetic leap—that this place of rest is also a place where they can make love. She must realize this as well. There is no statement of it, but (in a manner that Dewey would understand) the emotional quality of the love scene that soon follows filters back into this one, where the two lovers are walking along and half-consciously considering where they will stay for the night. Emotion, as Dewey maintained, "selects what is congruous and dyes what is selected with its color, thereby giving qualitative unity to materials externally disparate and dissimilar" (*AE* 49). It is because of some effect of emotional energy in the ensuing scene that I feel the likelihood of Angel and Tess desiring and anticipating that they now can make love.

Nature is again part of the context for their love, this time for their sexual consummation. They are first engaged in simple primal acts like walking through the countryside and getting something to eat, and then finding a place to sleep. Tess resurrects her idealization of Angel: "To her he was, as of old, all that was perfection, personally and mentally. He was still her Antinous, her Apollo even..." (373). Earlier in the novel, such perceptions seemed simply to be distortions, but there is no repetition here of her earlier irrational ecstasy. She does not feel she is wearing a crown. The context has changed. In effect, she is using the idealized image to deny the reality of his "[w]orn and unhandsome" appearance, in which "she did not discern the least fault..." (373). Her image of him is completely at odds with how he looks to an ordinary eye, but she is on her way to bed with him. That is rather different. For her, "his sickly face" is just as "beautiful" to her as when she had first beheld him (373), and there is no further mention of his illness.

> *With an instinct as to possibilities* [Angel] did not...as he had intended, make for the first station beyond the town, but *plunged still further under the firs, which here abounded for miles. Each clasping the other round the waist they promenaded over the dry bed of fir-needles, thrown into a vague intoxicating atmosphere of being together at last,* with no living soul between them; ignoring that there was a corpse. (373, my emphasis)

The image of their clasping suggests their improvised and effortless personal ritual of consummation. Hardy reminds us of Alec's corpse, thus maintaining a tenuous hold on a real fact of the situation, but lets them forget about it—as they would have to do if they are to sustain any mood for their own love-making. Hardy had introduced the idea a few pages earlier: "Both seemed to implore something to shelter them from reality" (366). Now their imploring is satisfied. Nature as context continues to be felt even as their walk takes them into "an old brick building" in which they are to spend several days: "Through the latter miles of their walk their footpath had taken them into *the depths of the New Forest,* and towards evening, turning the corner of a lane, they perceived behind a brook and bridge" a signboard advertising the vacant mansion (374, my emphasis). The "New" Forest, an allusion not annotated in any of the editions, is actually quite old: it was set aside as a hunting ground by William the Conqueror in the year 1089. They walk along in it, clasping, until their route takes them to the house near these woods.

Tess thinks that they might just sleep outdoors, but he believes it will be too cold during this English May. Even indoors, they are in a temporarily unoccupied house, where by daylight "A shaft of dazzling sunlight glanced into the room..."(375). The mood of the passage for me the reader is not quite as sunny as they seem to find it, since the sunbeam throws light on the wooden headboard of the bed, which has a carving of what is "apparently Atalanta's race." That is a bit of Hellenism that may go by unnoticed, but it does tell of an ancient myth in which the consummation of love occurs. In the myth, this is followed by rather dire consequences, but Hardy does not allude to the aftermath, only to the joyous consummation. Atalanta "loses" her footrace, which obliges her to marry her pursuer and consummate their sexual-love desire. As for Tess and Angel, "by and by they were enveloped in the shades of night, which they had no candle to disperse" (375).

At night their room is "strangely solemn and still..." (376). They spend five days and nights *"in absolute seclusion*, not a sight or sound of a human being disturbing their peacefulness—such as it was. *The changes of the weather were their only events, the birds of the New Forest their only company*" (376, my emphasis). Hardy specifies their large bed, in which they sleep, and he details Tess's clothing draped near that bed on the morning when a housekeeper happens to peer into their room: she notices "the elegance of Tess's gown hanging across the chair, her silk stockings beside it, the pretty parasol, and the other habits in which she arrived, because she had none else" (377). The clothes are off. As if to emphasize this, Hardy added in a slight revision of 1919, that when they decide to leave this room, Tess "arose, [and] clothed herself..."(378).[3] These have been nights and days of love, sexual love, in the natural, loving context that Tess has always wanted: she calls it "all that's sweet and lovely!" and "inside" this place, she says, there is "content."

I recall Hardy's earlier comment that Angel might do with more "animalism" in his character, which might suggest that the man cannot fully enjoy sex with Tess even now. But this would amount to taking the earlier comment as equivalent to a denial of his having any capacity for sexual response, even in this situation where he is no longer obeying his viciously destructive ideal of virginity. Angel, however, has had sexual experience, and in this new context, I can imagine that Angel can love Tess and make love with her. He has changed enough for that

In imagining the quality of this love, I recall as well Hardy's notion that "the defective can be more than the entire," the phrase that is left in an emphatic position as the final one in chapter 39, and is later alluded to in the obscure Biblical reference that Hardy applies to the process of Angel's changing. If these highly idiosyncratic but striking phrases are called back into experiencing this section, we now can think that Tess's sexual experience with Alec proved valuable in her lovemaking. I do not claim that there is strong warrant for imagining the love-situation in this way, but the text at least suggests it.

Angel also knows that "within" this place of their love-making, "was affection, union, error forgiven; outside was the inexorable" (376). The error forgiven may be his own, not hers. We have a significant word-choice: error, not sin. And should an "error" even be "forgiven"? Does not that terminology still reek of the notion of sin? But no, "forgiven" is the word that each of them would have thought. The feeling of this idyll for the novel's readers can be great, providing that the experience is not blocked by an inhibition against imagining love-making, or by an incurable contempt for Angel as love-maker, or by a failure to connect the heavily sensual-sexual Nature of their meetings at Talbothays, where their relationship was formed, with their consummation of it in this duration of several days and nights. It is not a great deal of time for the two to be together, considering what they mean to each other, but is much more than a mere moment. It is long enough for a lot of experiencing to take place. The body-mind unity that Tess has sought—and which she believes she can obtain only with Angel, not with Alec—is possible during this limited time.

I find that fulfillment palpable and therefore credible; others do not. I feel invited to imagine that Tess can throw off her feelings of being a victim, crushed and beaten and strangled, when with Angel at this point. I do not assume that Hardy is trying to give me a medically exact estimate of Angel's capabilities, nor do I take the opposite line that he is creating an empty fantasy of love-making that could never have occurred in non-fictional reality. I suppose that Angel would have an access of energy from the new erotic love-situation, and can respond without being hampered seriously by his physical illness. If anything, his physical weakness might bring an increase to his level of intensity. Experience for the reader can be blocked in many ways here, and it has been. There may even be a tacit prohibition in professional critical practice against allowing oneself to imagine qualities of love scenes for which there is little or no objective, textual evidence. But this would be purchasing safety at too great a price: much of the experiential challenge of *Tess* is for the very kind of imagining that this critical "law" would prevent. As long as my fallibility is admitted, and no claims for certainty are made, imagining the qualities of sexual love here and in the other key scenes of this novel is valid and necessary for the experience to occur.

As a gesture toward un-blocking experience in this mode, let me suggest that not all imagined perceptions of sexual-love in the reading of fiction are automatically to be categorized as "voyeurism," despite the glib assumptions encountered in academia. Some critics (such as Peter Widdowson) go so far as to duplicate an earlier period's moralistic concern with lewdness every time Hardy writes a visual and erotic description.[4] They foster an attitude that destroys any ability to respond with empathy to this—or any—fictional lovemaking.

The term *voyeurism*, and its implied role of the reader as *voyeur*, is a perfect "experience blocker" for descriptions of lovemaking. In current practice, this role is often invoked uncritically.[5] Although nothing prevents any reader from taking the role, nothing in *Tess* demands that it be taken. The notion that we must peep at Tess and Angel from a secret vantage point constricts and dilutes the potential for having a perception.

Here perhaps is a test case: late in the novel, when the landlady, Mrs. Brooks, looks through the keyhole and sees Tess agonizing over the return of Angel, I perhaps should be having the experience of the *voyeur*, but in fact I do not. After all, this is the arch-voyeuristic act, keyhole peeping! Although Tess is kneeling as she moans and speaks before the seat of a chair, with "her hands clasped over her head," Alec is off in the next room. Tess's bare feet, it is true, "protruded upon the carpet." And "the skirts of her dressing-gown and the embroidery of her night-gown flowed upon the floor behind her..." Despite the keyhole, her bare feet and the details of her clothing, I do not find this sexy. Perhaps others do, but my impression is that they only assume they do because any keyhole scene has been stereotyped in popular culture. I find that I must concentrate my attention on the quality of the "unspeakable despair," and on Tess's words concerning her situation. The special problem for experiencing this speech is in its brokenness: the landlady cannot "catch" all of it (367-8). Nonetheless it is some 200 words in all, and thus a considerable declaration. (It is once again revealing of current attitudes toward experience that those who complain of the masculine Hardy not allowing Tess to speak at the major moments of her life generally ignore so much of what she says.) The speech is accompanied near its end by some specific body details: "her lips were bleeding from the clench of her teeth upon them," and her long lashes over her closed eyes "stuck in wet tags to her cheeks." In their context, and over the course of a series of perceptions in re-reading, how are these experienced? "Voyeurism" seems not a good instrumental "naming" (Dewey's term) for what might be going on.

This is not to deny the possibility of experiencing several kinds of erotic qualities in the reading of love scenes. In a Deweyan account of *Tess*, I would not attempt to compartmentalize erotic responses into the sexual versus the sensual or the sensuous (*AE* 26-7). For my part, I agree with Joanna Frueh, in her book *Erotic Faculties*, that there is no way to firmly separate erotic quality from pornography.[6] I am not about to discard erotic quality because of this problem.

I do not ignore the several descriptive terms in this idyllic part of the novel which evoke a childish escape from reality on the part of the lovers. But to emphasize that factor seems needlessly destructive of the experience here. Perhaps other readers need to apply their own standards of harsh reality.[7] I must have the opposite need; I want to be sheltered and indulged. Yet beyond these biases is a psychological truism: in view of their dangerous situation, these lovers need to create a defensive shield around themselves. I feel: *Let them do it!* And if they are acting in some sense as children, I can imagine that they have a level of immaturity they can fall back upon without damaging— indeed making feasible—their union in sexual love. The quality of childish immaturity does not cancel the perception that they have such a union. And, to the extent that they do remember that Tess is being hunted by the police—that outside lies "the inexorable"—that may give their love-making a quality of forbidden and dangerous pleasure.

Despite its quality of completeness, their union is not one that matches the promise of the Talbothays scenes. The fact that they have to hide away from every other person, for fear of the law, makes their lovemaking essentially different from what the novel dreams of earlier. Nature and sex and love had been imagined as integrally related, and the meaning of Nature had included not only a pair of lovers but a surrounding society, a social context, with a love of life. Even the cows, with Hardy's suggestion of their ethological culture, would have been somewhere in the vicinity of the love scene, as it was first imagined in this novel. That scene never takes place. And in Hardy's next novel, *Jude the Obscure*, the human couple is reduced down to itself alone: Nature is virtually erased by civilization, and the civilization in which the lovers must live is a hostile one. For a moment in *Tess*, though, there can be a sense of the consummation of sexual love, within an attenuated but nonetheless still existing context of Nature. I find that such a meaning can be felt by letting the force of the erotic that seems to permeate this section be admitted as part of the tragedy. Its very diminution is part of my experience.

Limited as this episode is in time, it still has its own quality of fulfillment. I find as well that the conventional "tragic romance" element, in which the sexual love is affirmed for the reader only because it is soon to be "paid for" in death (the *Liebestod* of romance literature) is less affecting than the hunger or longing or wish that this love could go on, even though I know that it cannot. As Tess exclaims, "Why should we put an end to all that is sweet and lovely!" (376).

4. How Angelic Now?

We still would want to ask, how deeply has Angel changed? He is not portrayed as having any of his old idealizing thoughts about Tess as Hellenic goddess. To be sure, Angel cannot be supposed to have totally overcome all traces of the ideas about women that he has built up throughout his life. If Hardy had chosen to write a thorough psychological exploration of Angel's transformation, he would have had to include years of struggle to overcome his ingrained habits of thought. Yet, granting that Hardy is using a focus that tacitly implies fictional condensation of what would have been only the breakthrough into a new quality of loving, I might not have thought to radically doubt Angel's change, at this point in the novel, had Tess herself not raised the doubt. She asserts that some day he would despise her, that indeed "considering what my life has been, I cannot see why any man should, sooner or later, be able to help despising me" (377). This is a projection of self-worthlessness that goes beyond Angel. It is an estimate of what all the men in her culture will think of her. Is she wrong? Maybe not. After all, even Alec, who had assured her that he never despised her despite her having had sex with him (312), could accept her while being pretty certain that she had had no other lovers. But Tess is generalizing beyond what anyone could know; and she is generalizing in a way that projects a uniform image of what all the men in her world would do in their emotional response to her life. Angel himself flatly denies that he could ever despise her. Why is that not reassuring to her? Angel's judgment of her is terribly important to Tess. Indeed she has come to Angel as "the one man on earth who had loved her purely, and who had believed in her as pure" (373).

The word "pure" by this time in the novel has become saturated with many meanings. Hardy had even shown it in a sardonic sense when he tells why Tess and her family were kicked out of their village: "By some means the village had to be kept pure" (340). In my own experience of re-reading, I know that the simple connection of "pure" with "virginal" no longer means anything. I also know that I cannot securely define the term, as if it were of one fixed meaning. Yet some interpretation is called for at this point, even if it is tentative: this again is not the occasion for utter caution and safety. By "pure" and "purely," then, I think Tess and Hardy at this point might mean—at the least—a love that is genuine enough to promise emotional wholeness and growth, both in sexual and mental life, or in Body-Mind, to use Dewey's term once more. Angel, despite his misperception of her sexual history, had thought that he wanted to love her entirely, for herself—and in that sense, purely. In the intensities of the Talbothays section of the novel, he had perceived her during some of his experiences as a bodily, sexual woman; that is pure enough. When, early one morning, she runs up to his room to wake him, "in her bed gown," he as much as tells her that he is getting sexually aroused (183). (Tess, for her part, had perceived some of the individual man that is Angel, prior to losing touch with him in her pathological idealization of Angel as a god.) The "pure" aspect in this formulation is that it requires the assumption of each, by each, that the other is worthy of such a relation. To say this much does not tell me what the novel could be leading to, for my experience of the term, "Pure Woman," as it is inscribed prominently in Hardy's sub-title. To that difficult problem I will have to come back. Here I am mainly exploring Angel's change, or his inability to change.

In her last statement before telling the police, quietly, that she is "ready" to be taken in and undoubtedly executed, Tess offers a parting accusation that could have left Angel feeling unforgiven: "...and now I shall not live for you to despise me" (382).

It sounds like the ultimate statement of no confidence in him. But there is a context: when resistance to the many armed police surrounding her is clearly useless, Tess says it. But would she not have been willing to try to live with Angel? And can we be sure that he would have come to despise her? How can she be so sure? The novel is asking this: it is an analytic quality that feels as if it is intrinsic to this ending, one that may be as important as the highly charged emotional events themselves. More accurately, it is an integral part of experiencing those events.[8] I think it is important to keep this question in its unanswerable state. Tess might be mistaken: her thinking, fine as it had been at earlier points in the novel, has shown any number of distortions by now. The idyllic love-making with Angel has surely provided a union of Body-Mind. There is no further mention of Angel as the perfect man or as Apollo. But perhaps there now is a relapse.

My inability to decide on this matter of Angel's disposition to someday despise her threatens to wreak havoc with Hardy's plot. For *if* Angel has really changed, then Tess may be making an almost inconceivable error: she has killed Alec and set in motion the forces of law that will kill her, when all she would have had to do would have been to take her leave of Alec and go to live with her chosen lover, Angel. I do not feel any anger in Angel when Tess tells him that she has returned to Alec: there is only deep sadness and his responsive statement that it is all his fault. Still, Tess unavoidably feels some uncertainty regarding Angel, regardless of how thoroughly he had changed: their marital trauma cannot simply be erased from her mind. And the tragedy would be all the greater if he has changed and she cannot realize the fact.

I realize that Hardy himself pronounced judgment on this question, after the novel's publication: Angel could not really have changed, and would have reverted to blaming Tess for her past sexual life with Alec. Angel and Tess "would never have lived happily. Angel was far too fastidious and particular. He would inevitably have thrown her fall in her face."[9] But apparently Hardy had to say this to readers who had had some experience of the novel and did not think the matter so obvious. In fact, the early reviewers were quite puzzled about why Tess murders Alec. Hardy in any case was over-simplifying: it is not a certainty that *if* Angel were to come to think of Tess again as a fallen woman, that he would be unable to critically reject this thought, nor that their marriage would collapse. I will suggest—and not altogether in jest—that she might have got mad enough to "brain" him with a milk-pail.

Hardy made the statement I have quoted in an interview published in April, 1892. He was speaking in the context of explaining why he could not oblige the many readers who had written to him while *Tess* was still coming out in serial, "begging me to end it well."[10] Such an ending would have badly hampered any sense of the experience continuing on problematically in the reader's mind after the final page, and would have destroyed its tragic seriousness. Hardy took care of that danger quite effectively

When I think too insistently on these possibilities, I find myself losing contact with the experience the novel is making possible, and yet these thoughts will not be silenced. They are at the indeterminate edge of the situation, and as Pepper realized, there is no good method for drawing a firm boundary around a situation. And yet you do have the situation, which does not extend infinitely into time and space. That is a basic feature of Contextualism.[11] But if you are feeling that you are getting too far away from the immediacy that is there, then you may always have recourse to returning your attention to the affective core of the event and regaining contact with where the people (the characters) are. In this spirit, I put aside but I cannot forget the question of what they might have done if only they had done otherwise. The doubt, the perplexity, is real. Perplexity is a normal fact of life, as I said much earlier. That is one of the strong points of Dewey's *Experience and Nature*. But here, with this problem in *Tess*, I see no way to resolve it through inquiry.

Angel, for his part, has been working under the assumption that it is best for Tess and him to escape; he has no objection to their living together, even if it should turn out that she really has committed murder (something he does not yet know for sure). Nor does the thought of turning her in to the forces of the law seem to occur to him. I imagine that this thought hardly occurs to readers of *Tess* at all, so thoroughly is the novel able to secure our identification with Tess and preserve our imaginary loyalty to her.

When I ask, what am I feeling about Tess (and Angel) being pursued and captured by the police, the fact that she has committed a murder—which is the reason they are being sought—does not come to the foreground. It is a true fictional "fact," but it seems not to be what is being experienced. It feels much more as if the pursuit to the death of Tess is a function of the murderous disapproval by a repressive society of the sexually fulfilled love of this couple.

5. Endings

Hardy's bold artifice of having Tess arrested while waking from a sleep of exhaustion in the ruins of Stonehenge is one of the "endings" he constructs. The lovers approach Stonehenge as simply a place for their rest and refuge; they have walked about 30 miles since early morning.[12] It feels as if they are really trying to get away; if they were not, they could just as well have stayed where they had been and wait for Tess to be arrested. But the quality of the narrative changes as they realize where they are: Stonehenge. For Hardy, this is the place where he knows Tess will die. In my earlier attempts at experiencing *Tess*, I had imagined that Hardy had known this all along. But that assumption does not allow for his own ability to work his way through the integral fictional development of her fate within the context of her life. In an interview published in April, 1892, Hardy said about Stonehenge: "...I describe [it] exactly as I saw it on *that sad day when I decided Tess must die*—can I ever forget the misery of that day?"[13] This does not sound like a plan held firmly in mind; it does sound like an author undergoing the emotional conflicts brought about by the artistic requirements of his fictional character, Tess. Although no specific visit to Stonehenge at this time has been recorded, Hardy lived within biking distance of the site, as he pointed out in 1899.[14]

The overt symbolism of Tess as a sacrificial victim is moving; it seems "right." Simply put, I am saddened, and I feel more or less intensely grieved, according to the varying responses I have to this capture, on my different readings of the novel. This feeling is in some readings mixed with relief; I have felt for some time now that Tess is doomed and that she need suffer no further. At the same time my mind keeps asking the questions the novel has lodged so thoroughly in my experience: why *is* Tess being sacrificed? Is it really necessary for her fate to be what it is? What if she *had* escaped and had lived with Angel? Who or what is causing her life to be sacrificed, that is, to be ravaged and cut short and thus mostly wasted? This last question is the problem of the whole novel: she, one of the most memorable and cherishable woman characters in fiction, has been squandered on a social world that cannot find a way to accept her and let her live. Possibly, as her final comments on being despised seem to hint, she believes that a woman with her sexual experience can never be accepted by any man. Why?

In this section, I have conflated her being captured with her actual death by hanging. Of that scene, Hardy keeps us at a distance, even emotionally. He could have milked the situation for intense pathos, but he must have realized that this would be a cheap effect, or one that would become uncontrollable. Possibly, too, if he had rendered the scene of the hanging directly, the result would have been nearly unbearable. I know of no complaints by critics, even those who have an interest (or who maintain a grudge) in the scenes in which Tess's inner life is not written by Hardy, of not being given her thoughts and responses while approaching the scaffold. Why not? Needless to say, it is an important event in her life. It seems that Hardy again does what the novel most calls for at this point: he leads me into a somewhat analytic (but not affectless) state at the point of Tess's death.

Hardy's second ending I find difficult to relate to. Perhaps that is how it is meant to be taken: as too difficult to absorb. I think I know what the critic John Goode means when he writes: "I have read and re-read *Tess of the d'Urbervilles* many times during twenty years, and I still find the end impossible to read."[15] In my own re-readings of the novel, I know that for a long time, I unconsciously elided any "having" of this part of the novel, and was only alerted to this omission by an article by my mentor, Wayne Burns, published in 1972.[16] Up until then, it was as if this part of the experience of *Tess* did not even exist. I had been avoiding the whole question: Why does Hardy make the last episode that of Angel with Liza-Lu, Tess's younger sister, silently witnessing from a distance the flag that signals Tess's execution, and then walking on, away from the town, possibly to eventually make a marriage of their own? They do not even claim Tess's body for burial—contrary to all folk custom. Tess's assurance to Angel that her young sister "has all the best of me without the bad of me," and her urging that he "train her and teach her...and bring her up for your own self!" (380), might play into a still unextinguished wish for a restoration of her virginity, impossible to fantasize in her own body but transferable to Liza-Lu. The word "train" blends with further ugliness into Hardy's description of the police officer, who walks "as if trained" and leads the arrest party (381). The very notion of the man training the woman for his own self points to an uncanny understanding on Hardy's part of what Freud said decades later in his essay entitled "The Taboo of Virginity"[17]: that it is an effort by the man to extend sexual ownership of his spouse back to the date of her birth, thus thoroughly denying any sexual development apart from her submissive giving over to him. Within Angel's ideal of female purity, Liza-Lu is a fulfillment--one of the ironic "fulfillments" of this last Phase.

Wayne Burns (as early as 1972) has suggested that Hardy may have had the Victorian Deceased Wife's Sister Acts rebelliously in mind.[18] I had given little attention to this possibility, until I happened to hear an audio version of *Tess,* read by the actress Eleanor Bron.[19] When she pronounced the name of the city where Tess is executed, I seemed to hear "incest" and "sister" in the sound: Wintoncester. What does Angel "win" there? Does he really "win" Liza-Lu, or is the tone suggesting that he must take her as a kind of punishment, as another reader of the novel believes?[20]

It is an unnerving ending rather than a purely tragic one. Wintoncester, one of only two cities in the novel,[21] is marked with the unnatural: despite the "landscape beyond landscape, till the horizon was lost in the radiance of the sun *hanging* above it" (384, my emphasis), there is no feeling of Nature developed in the chapter, and *hanging* is the city's event. Liza-Lu and Angel have ascended "a long and regular incline of the exact length of a measured mile" (383), after which they look back. The "fine old city" shows its "quaint irregularities of the Gothic erections", but what really sticks up is a shape unknown to Nature: "a flat-topped octagonal tower" (384) of the building in which Tess is legally killed.

If only Hardy had been content to omit this one last suggestion of a sexual alliance and simply have uttered his oracular sardonic judgment: "'Justice' was done, and the President of the Immortals, in Aeschylean phrase, had ended his sport with Tess" (384). This seems to be Hardy striking his own final blow as commentator in his own text, and must have been a personally satisfying utterance. He might have been aware that it would both distress his readers and challenge them to find a way to read around his excessive pronouncement. Hardy's tone here encourages me to feel what is already prevalent: that the world has been terribly and senselessly unfair to Tess. And when I think for a moment about Hardy's "Aeschylean phrase," I notice that it comes from the tragedy of maximum defiance, *Prometheus Bound*; it is taken from one of the hero's defiant speeches against Zeus, the "president."[22] But no: Thomas Hardy's story of a "Pure Woman," ending as Angel seems to be following Tess's advice to choose Liza-Lu (326), resonates with sexual *im*purity, that is, tyranny, at the very moment when it offers its defiant tribute to a woman whose destruction shames the very gods. Rendering the end even less digestible, Hardy inscribes the last line in a mode of opaque peacefulness: "As soon as they had strength, they arose, joined hands again, and went on" (384). The feeling is bafflement. In re-reading this sentence countless times, in the context of the end paragraph, I find that I do *not* think of *Paradise Lost* here, despite the allusion,[23] nor would it do me any good if I were to do so. Liza-Lu and Angel are not "wandring," as Milton's pair are, and the black flag signaling Tess's death, which "continued to wave silently," is devoid of any suggestion of a lost paradise.

But Hardy once again knew what he was doing—"knew," that is, in the sense of what was most valid creatively, for his novel, even if he may not have thought the issue through, consciously. By ending on Angel and Liza-Lu, he is destroying the overly symmetrical shaping of his novel that he (or his readers) might wish to have. The notorious patterning of red-blood-sexuality-fate in such instances of Tess's red ribbon, the horse's fatal bleeding, and the stabbing of

Alec, now thoroughly loses any capacity it might have had to contain or frame the novel. Liza-Lu and Angel do not fit within it. Nor is any simple fatalistic repetition possible, since young Liza-Lu's sexual body is not sensual and attractive, as Tess's has been. She has "the same beautiful eyes" but is "slighter," and is a "spiritualized image of Tess" (383). The thought at last occurs to me that Hardy may not be so benighted as to be blessing, recommending, or approving of the union of Liza-Lu and Angel. On further thought, I realize he has undermined an unworthy feeling of my own, which his plot would otherwise have suggested: as in many narratives, Tess is "paying' for her sexual sins by dying. I would not like to recognize that trite thought, but it has no doubt percolated through my consciousness. But now with Liza-Lu and Angel going off into the distance, there is an element of grotesque, even of ridiculous, exaggeration. The heroine is saying not only the formulaic *Now I die tragically for my sins*, but that *Now I make overpayment for my sins by handing my sister to the man who caused me so much of my trouble and who basically despises me.*

Hardy makes no overt statement on this matter, nor does he stylistically ironize his description of Liza-Lu and Angel. But after I register the shock of the execution, and after I admit the confusion brought by the seemingly unnecessary additional romantic union, I intuit that there is a further implication. I am not sure just what it should be called, but I think it could be formulated something like this: the tragedy of Tess is not self-contained and self-concluding, as might be assumed if the narrative really ended with her execution. In its core form of "sexual chaos"—a term invented by Wilhelm Reich[24] and quite applicable here— the tragedy lingers on and spreads. The final union of Angel and Liza-Lu destroys any suggestion of appeasement for the reader. It is as if the novel is saying to us: Just because you have sympathized with Tess's victimization and undergone with her a sense of her suffering, do not for one instant assume that this novel's problem in sexual love-relations has been solved. I also feel something like: *and this failing is intolerable.*[25]

As Dewey would recognize, these endings are not the summation of the experience. In the form that a work of art takes, the final end "is final only in an external way" (*AE* 142). The "consummatory phase" of a complex work, the phase in which the work is absorbed in its experienced meaning, is not just a matter of the ending; it is "recurrent throughout a work," and in experiencing a great work, "its incidence" can "shift in successive observations of it" (*AE* 144). Dewey is right: Hardy's plot endings furnish no more than nominal closure to the powerful sequence of experience that makes up the novel. The novel's completeness as an experience can only come out of the relation of all the emotional history of Tess, of her two unfit lovers, of their life in the context of the novel's vision of Nature, and of what all this may imply for the life of the reader.

Seven

EXPERIENCE GOES FURTHER

There is a factor in all this that is so essential and so simple, that theory and criticism now seem embarrassed to say it: Tess is a woman. And as Kathleen Blake has argued, it is now almost impossible to use the word "woman" without blundering into some sort of derogatory generalization embedded in the language.[1] Yet I would not therefore banish the word: the risks will have to be taken. Like any woman Tess is more than just a type of the female, but with all her unique qualities, her womanliness is undeniable. From a Deweyan perspective, it is a fallacy to suppose that womanliness and individuality are not to be assumed in the same person. Exactly the opposite is the case. Depth-psychological approaches which would designate Tess as "the female subject," must blunder into the destructive type-casting that we would all hope to avoid. The novel is "about" Tess as woman, or as Dewey would say, that is the heart of its "subject-matter." Whence then even my own sense of embarrassment? From what I can discern of critical history, a moment came in 1969, prior to the major wave of feminist criticism which has its own genuine but conflicted relation to the fact of Tess being a woman, a moment when Tess could no longer be a woman for the most advanced, theoretical critics. And this would badly mis-direct any further critical understanding of how this novel is experienced. Of course, like any seemingly momentary event, it would have had a temporal context; it would have been a flashpoint for a process that had been building up fuel for a long time. To my mind, such a moment might be marked by the publication of J. Hillis Miller's review of Irving Howe's book, *Thomas Hardy*.[2] Howe had written a perceptive, admiring chapter on *Tess*. He had idealized Tess, but he had also arrived at a guiding generalization for experiencing her: "And what must never be forgotten in thinking about her, as in reading the book it never can be, she is a woman."[3] Miller is one of the most distinguished American literary critics. He has written several influential critical works on Hardy, beginning notably with his book, *Thomas Hardy: Distance and Desire*, published in 1970. In this review, which came out a year earlier than that book, he had been praising Howe for several pages, but at this point Miller executes a sudden shift in tone, and treats Howe's remark about Tess as a woman to be a prime error, a mistake so serious that it sounds like an insult to literature itself: "One might wish that a novel would be identical with life, or an exact mirroring of it, but *literature constitutes a realm apart*. Tess can be met nowhere but in the novel, and no strategy can close the gap between literature and life."[4]

Could Miller perhaps have been so disturbed by Howe's statement as to think that someone would imagine Tess Durbeyfield so real that he might meet up with her in person? From a Deweyan perspective, anyone who would lay down as a law the dualism of literature being "a realm apart" forms an insurmountable barrier against experience. Tess is not a real person, but in the experience of reading this novel, there is reason to respect almost any reader's impulse to take her *as if* she were one. I have written in two earlier essays on the art of the novel that such is the most likely way to have any experience regarding most fictional characters.[5] Most people—even most critics who deny that they read in this manner—appear to make exactly that assumption. It is even, at times, that of J. Hillis Miller, who writes: "I for one find the description of Angel Clare's failure to consummate his marriage to Tess almost unbearably painful."[6] It is the common assumption, but as Dewey maintains in his discussion of the term "common," that is nothing against it. The sharable quality of that which is common can be valued for its function in drawing people together in a fractured and fractious world where their differences already have plenty of room for expression, and are the dominant factors in their social relations to one another. Literary criticism, such as the present book, can become instrumental in accordance with Dewey's basic model of what thinking critically is ultimately for: to enhance and deepen the common shared meanings, and thus to improve the quality of experiencing this novel. If it fails to do this last, it fails.

Tess is a woman. To have the experience, we can only accept her as such. In some ways that is hard to do, since Tess is not nearly as ideal as Howe made her out to be. I have pointed to her sadism and to her increasingly irrational thinking. Nor, though she is a woman, is she entirely a fitting subject for feminist criticism: no matter how much her being a victim of the men is brought out, no matter how terribly Hardy is convicted of chauvinist manipulation and omission of Tess's inner thoughts, the fact remains that she is a woman whose life is centered around men. This is not a feminist way for a woman to be. Tess's strong independence of mind on matters of religion and sin occurs mainly when she is not engaged in a relationship with any man; once she is involved, her critical thought declines, and she puts all her self into the relationship. It is easy to see (and easy to say) that this is exactly what traps her, but it is more valuable I think for experiencing this novel to approach it as Hardy's way of exploring the troubles that a heterosexual, trusting, highly individualized woman has when she encounters masculinity as it exists in one not atypical kind of modern culture.

Tess as woman is endowed with great capacities for not only centering her life on men, but in the case of Angel of devoting her self to a man. This today is hard to admit: it is difficult to admit that such a quality even could exist—except as a kind of pathology—nor that it has human value. But once the inhibition against saying these things is lifted, it may be possible to affirm that in the relations of women and men, a woman's loyalty to her man (man—not "husband" I believe, for that is one of the confusions in Tess) is one of the greatest gifts of life. Never mind that a great many men in our own era appear to have abused this gift to the point of having lost it. *Tess* as a novel is powerfully suggesting that such a capacity does exist, and even that it is a primal value in womanhood. It no doubt can make for uncomfortable sexual politics to say this, but that does not eliminate the fact. Nor is it insulting to women who share such a capacity with Tess. In the novel, Tess's loyalty to Angel is carried to such an extent that it indeed becomes self-destructive, pathological, sickening—what have you. That is very frightening.

But when the action of the novel is considered as a whole plot or story, her troubles happen because Tess meets two men, two basic types of men who still exist, surely, within the male psyches of our own day, even if not necessarily as distinct individuals. If we can have a level of meaning that is not necessarily limited to always regarding Alec and Angel as two separate beings, they may suggest a dangerous oscillation regarding women within the cultural norms of masculinity. In one of the last times I taught *Tess* to undergraduates, one young man quit reading it half-way through; this was not entirely because he was a poor student unused to reading long books, but also (as became clear when I persuaded him to take up the book again) because he was angry and upset at Hardy for creating two such un-lovely men. Both of these male persons can inhabit one mind: in fact, in every one of my teaching and writing experiences of *Tess*, I have found myself making the Freudian slip of referring to Angel as Alec, or Alec as Angel. I recall the strange feeling of the passage at the end of chapter 46, in which Alec laughs gloatingly as he credits Angel with providing the theological ground, transmitted through the woman, for his own slide back into his role of sexual male. Angel, he exclaims, "was paving my way back to her!" (314). Again, Hardy emphasizes the remark by making it the final one in a chapter. Michael Millgate has suggested that Hardy might have been developing in his two male characters the two conflicting sides of his suicidal friend, Horace Moule, a combination in one man "of extreme refinement with a capacity for sensual self-abandonment."[7] There is much of Angel in Hardy himself; this may account for Hardy's futile efforts to defend him at several points in the novel. But he did not neglect the other side of his psyche: just after publication of the novel, Hardy cut off his beard and grew his mustache so that he looked quite a lot like an older Alec.[8] And, in a letter written just after the first, serial version of *Tess* had come out, I think Hardy uses the name "Angel" where he meant to say "Alec."[9]

Alec and Angel are men who do not know how to treat Tess. Both are men who have a limited notion of what their own selves may be. Angel, portrayed as caught between a Hellenism he cannot make his own, and a viciously anti-sexual Christianity that he needs to overcome, becomes part of Hardy's broader social criticism in this novel, in which secular liberation is undermined by a long tradition of sexual repression based in religion. Alec grows considerably from the rather unsympathetic figure he is at the beginning, but there still is an indefinable sense of narrowness about him; possibly this is an effect of his never becoming connected with the context of Nature that Hardy writes for Tess and Angel. Alec seems to have no vision of life beyond living idly with Tess, whether she really wants to do that or not. He would have set up a little poultry farm at his cottage, where Tess's mother could work, and her siblings could be sent to school. He and Tess would live there (342). It is a generous offer, but is it a plan that Tess would have wanted for her own development? That Alec does not consider. As he has indicated, he would think it foolish to take seriously anything she says or does (324). To use one of the most central of the Deweyan terms, there would be little prospect for Tess's *growth* in such a life.

Tess's wasting of her loyalty to men also happens because the repressive gender ideal of her culture disables her enough to make her almost completely dependent on these men for any sense of a self. She suffers from this dependency, which could have been a disposition already given within her temperament, but need never have reached the extremity it does in the course of her life. She is compelled by her own deep wishes to enforce her dependency—but these wishes are themselves distortions of a capacity for relationship. When she leaves Alec at the end of their first phase, she is asserting her need for a free autonomous life (though she is not renouncing all future chances of a relationship with a man); when she returns to him she has given up that hope for freedom and autonomy— only to destructively re-assert it when Angel shows up again. Her dependence (which is a human need denied in current ideologies of gender) and her desire for freedom could have combined to have become the core of a healthy female psyche. As it is, as it has to be in the context of this novel's realistic situation, her deep need for a life with a man is what ultimately leads her to tragedy. In fact, Hardy's own (and apparently unique) definition of tragedy, written into his notebook a decade before *Tess*, seems to hold good here:

> Tragedy. It may be put thus in brief: a tragedy exhibits a state of things in the life of an individual which unavoidably causes some natural aim or desire of his to end in a catastrophe when carried out.[10]

This fits: Tess's "natural aim or desire" leads her into catastrophe. But there is a whole context—"a state of things in life"—that goes into making this an experience.

To say simply that Tess is a woman still leaves something important out of this account: she is beautiful. Her beauty is of a somewhat unconventional kind, but it is there. Her beauty (a physical beauty that is inseparable from her self) gives special value to her character. In sheer human worth, she is no more valuable than any other person, as Dewey would confirm. Yet in her beauty, she is naturally gifted: she is a gift of Nature. The Bible has a passage in praise of a virtuous woman, a good part of which is quoted in Angel's face by the Reverend Clare when the son arrives home without Tess after their wedding (257). It proclaims a strategic denial of beauty's value: "Favor is deceitful, and beauty is vain."[11] But beauty is an unavoidable signal, experientially considered, perhaps one that is even anchored in our evolutionary natures, telling us that it is destructive *for our worth to our selves* to waste this kind of person. It is tragic in the deepest way. It seems even to speak of our human extinction. As a man I feel this, but can it be that women readers would not share in their own way in such a thought? If her beauty can also be imagined as dangerous, I would think this is not due simply to the myth of feminine evil, but because, as Joanna Frueh has said: feminine beauty "is a departure from the ordinary, provoking and luring the viewer into uncommon thoughts and feelings."[12] This happened not only to Tess's two male lovers, but also to the women who got to know Tess: witness the extraordinary supportive behavior of Izz, Marian, and Retty.

1. In What Senses Pure?

I do not believe it worthwhile to consider Tess as a woman who sins; the novel has created a rich context for undermining the very category of sexual sin. She is "pure," to use Hardy's deliberately problematic word in his sub-title, in that Tess is purely herself, beyond the reach of the concept of sin. As Hardy wrote in the 1892 Preface to *Tess*, "pure" is not meant to take "the artificial and derivative meaning which has resulted to it from the ordinances of civilization." There is to be considered "the meaning of the word in Nature, together with all aesthetic claims upon it..." (4-5). But by 1912, in his additional Preface, he both defends "pure" as what he himself felt on completing the writing of *Tess*, "as being the estimate left in the candid mind of the heroine's character"—and expresses his resignation by saying that it would have been better not to have written that word (7). It appears in fact that there is very strong resistance in culture (both in Hardy's and our own) to consider new meanings for this word.

The governing cultural assumption still seems to be this: if Tess actually wanted to have sex with Alec, she is not a pure woman. That is what a male critic, W. Eugene Davis, concluded, in what I believe is the first printed article to insist firmly upon the text's evidence that Tess herself allows she has had some sexual love attraction to Alec: "If I had gone for love o' you, if I had ever sincerely loved you, if I loved you still, I should not so loathe and hate myself for my weakness now!..My eyes were dazed by you for a little, and that was all" (82-3). By saying "that was all," Davis pointed out, Tess is allowing that "all" includes some affection.[13] Indeed *the whole sentence prior to this admission does everything except declare unambiguously that she has never loved Alec*. Thomas Hardy had never hidden this statement (nor the fact that Tess stayed on with Alec for weeks after the event in the Chase): it is there in plain view in the text. He may have tried to occlude it with his some of his commentary, as Davis recognized, but he did not erase it. Nothing prevented his readers from seeing it. Yet (except possibly for some of the earliest reviewers who hated the sexuality of the book), it took 76 years, until 1968, the date of Davis's short article, for any critic to take notice and connect this part of the novel with the term "pure woman."[14] The presumption was that if Hardy wrote "pure woman" as subtitle, he meant a woman not sexually drawn toward Alec, one purely coerced into having sex with him. In this sense Tess is impure. Davis (whose article now seems to have been forgotten) concludes that it might be best to throw away the adjective "pure": "Perhaps... 'a pure woman' is not the best description of a woman whose impurity makes her human and makes her actions in the novel credible."[15] A decade later, Laura Claridge (apparently not knowing about Davis's article), mounted an equally revealing attack on Tess's purity. Claridge gave her article a title that cleverly imitated Hardy's own subtitle for the novel: "Tess, A Less Than Pure Woman Ambivalently Presented." Claridge based her argument on the assumptions that Hardy intended Tess to not have been sexually drawn to Alec, and that he meant for Tess to be as virtuous as the ideal Christian who would forgive those who harm her. Claridge masks her moral condemnation of Tess under the guise of finding formal contradictions in Hardy's narrative. But when it comes to reading Tess's key sentence, about not having sincerely loved nor at present loving Alec, Claridge quotes selectively, trimming it down to a flat statement meaning that Tess "has *not* loved Alec."[16] She then blames Hardy for confusing this problem, and goes on to refute the notion that Tess could be regarded as pure.[17]

Hardy however did mean to apply the term. He even said, in a letter written in January 1892, that this "second title" of the novel "is absolutely necessary to show its meaning."[18] Despite his expression of regret, he did not expunge his attribution of a "pure woman" in the subtitle from the several later editions of *Tess* that he saw into print. The expunging has been done for him by later editors: the main editions now in print do not print the subtitle on the title page of the novel, although they refer to it within the front-matter. For the pragmatist critic, the question is, what can we do with it? I myself do not consider any human being pure, if by that is meant lacking aggression or having a mind that never has a sadistic or "abnormal" impulse. I am enough of a Freudian to have long ago ceased entertaining such expectations. From experiencing the novel, it is more than clear to me that "pure" cannot mean Tess behaves according to an ethic that would permit her to do no harm to anyone. Nor could it mean that she has no sexual pleasure with Alec. I am willing to think that with part of his mind, Hardy intended "pure" in a conventional anti-sexual sense. But I give him more credit as a thinker, and I know that in my own reading experiences, his novel has long impelled me to search for a non-conventional meaning of "pure." Why not accept this search, this Deweyan "inquiry," as part of the experience? Why not accept it in the experimental spirit of Dewey's belief that the reader of a work must go through a creative process that is comparable to that of the writer? (*AE* 58, 60.) Could Hardy not experiment with the use of the term "pure"? I imagine that he could look back upon completing the manuscript, and realize that he had been doing just that. It was at that point that he impulsively added the subtitle.

One commentator, Peter Widdowson, asserts that Hardy is talking "nonsense" and knows it, when he writes "faithfully presented."[19] Widdowson too easily assumes that Hardy's conscious awareness that a narrowly mimetic copy-ism—sometimes thought to be "realism"—is a dead end for fiction, is equivalent to Hardy renouncing any connection with realism whatever. This would entail that Hardy has no intention of creating credible portrayals of human beings within a credible social context. Dewey also saw no inherent value in narrowly mimetic artistry: "The mere act of transcription is esthetically irrelevant...", but he goes on to sound the issue as one of experience: "....save as it enters integrally into the formation of an experience moving to completion" (*AE* 57). That "save" makes all the difference. I will opt to "save" Hardy's term "pure" by taking his phrase "Faithfully Presented" as an invitation to risk embarrassment and to be faithful to my own sympathetic experience of *Tess*.

We now know that Hardy was almost certainly aware of at least one major feminist effort at the time of *Tess* to re-define "purity." It occurs in the essay by Mona Caird, published in March 1890, entitled "The Morality of Marriage."[20] In this essay, Caird is arguing for the marital freedom of men as well as women, and she expresses an instrumental motive that Dewey would have endorsed: "Experience tends to prove that freedom is the right and beneficent condition for all things human; ...it promotes growth and makes room for it."[21] Earlier that year, Hardy is said to have tried to help Caird publish another radical article, "The Evolution of Marriage." His effort in that instance failed, but it is reasonable to think that two months later, he read her related article on marital morality published in the *Fortnightly Review*, coming as it did during the composition of *Tess*.[22] As John Goode shows in a long quotation, Caird ended that article with a serious consideration of the question "What, after all, is 'purity'?"[23] Although conventional purity is a lie, Caird finds that "[t]here is another kind." It is a kind that originates in "the love of nature." It carries the "vivid modern sense of the splendor of life, 'the beauty of the world.'"[24]

There is also an implied negative of pure: those like Angel who try to build their lives around the attempt to suppress Nature, particularly sexual nature, are doing something impure. Alec, with his setting a "trap" (her words to Angel, 372) for the young Tess by sedulously taking advantage of his position in idle wealth, is hardly pure either: his art of manipulation and terrorizing is not simply healthy male desire.

I recall how it felt to read for the first time, of Alec's sudden and dangerous breakneck pace taken with his mare, when young Tess gets onto his gig (155). The text has a number of phrases to show that this ride could be regarded as sexual in nature, such as the "figure of the horse rising and falling in undulations before them" (57). But, I do not see this as arousing to Tess.[25] Thinking of how such a ride must have felt to a girl/woman on this first exposure to Alec's pre-planned wildness (his horse had been well-trained for it), her emotion must have been one of terror. The horse Alec says could easily get them killed. This is not foreplay, even if it does lead to the first "kiss of mastery" (58). Similarly, after Tess jumps down from the cart, and Alec tries to entrap her, her feeling must be one of terror: "Turning the horse suddenly he tried to drive back upon her, and so hem her in between the gig and the hedge." (46). As one woman graduate student wrote in a paper, this is much like those physically threatening encounters with men that women have good reason to fear. Alec's cussing her out in this episode, using every bad word he can think of (59), is also not erotic; it is an action that contributes to my sense of him as a person whose virility, genuine as it may be, is overlaid here with irate willfulness.

Nor are his self-dramatizations later on as Milton's Satan, or as a sepulchral effigy of one of the d'Urbervilles (336-7; 350-51), the actions of a man who is content with his natural sex appeal. These little scenes which he creates do not seem to me to carry erotic charge, nor to cause Tess to be drawn toward him. Of the simplistic allegory, Alec=Satan, I feel nothing. The scenes may help Alec to overcome some inner disgust of his own. Alec even recites aloud several lines about Satan and Eve from *Paradise Lost*; Tess seems to reassure him with "I never said you were Satan or thought it" (337). By this point in the novel, Alec has changed enough to speak of "all that's tender and strong between men and women" (324), by which he could be referring to a "pure" relationship between man and woman. Could it be that he himself does not feel ready for such a thing?

Tess is pure by struggling for fulfillment as a heterosexual woman, and doing so within the cultural context of "the ache of modernism," as Hardy famously phrased it (129). Angel, the man she chooses, is a modern man who tries to rebel against the religious life and the kind of marriage that has been marked out for him by his parents. He remarks "cynically" to Tess, during their conflict, that "perhaps we shall shake down together some day, for weariness." In other words, he understands that conventional marriages often lead to resigned acceptance: "thousands have done it!" (241). But he does not want that. Tess's life is placed in the period of our history where traditional patterns of choosing a mate are becoming unsatisfactory and less possible; to someone like Tess they seem to be value-less. She could not be very aware of the historic implications, but plainly she does work at the difficult task of finding a mate for herself according to her own choice, and without directing herself to the men of her own class. That search is central: the "body's cry of 'Where?'" might then find an answer. I cannot believe that her goal in life was simply to die, to have her "life unbe," as a few critics would have it.[26] Nor, at another extreme, would it have been to find the

> fulfillment of her natural sympathy for all creatures, and more important a comprehensive evolutionary awareness of her existence—a way of uniting

her natural qualities, her folk roots, and the d'Urberville inheritance in an intuitive sense of a large identity in "Nature's teeming family".[27]

That is much too grand, philosophical, impersonal and un-sexual. If she is seeking anything it is fulfillment in and through sexual love—which is not to say that sexual love is all she would ever want in life.

Hardy's imagination—his dream—of her being fulfilled in a social world that retains a prehistoric connection with the fecundity of nature, virtually drops out of the novel after the disaster of her encounter with Angel's "hard logical deposit." To notice this and to allow oneself to feel the difference is not to assume that the primitive-pagan aura of Talbothays has no importance, nor that its echoes in the quite old New Forest are unimportant to experiencing the novel.

Stonehenge, where Tess ends her brief sexual-love fulfillment, also is very old. But it is a precision-built artifice, and it offers no suggestion of human love within Nature. Its pre-historic connotations in *Tess* are of a life-sacrificing culture that preceded but was not necessarily more favorable toward love than is the repressive Christian culture that exists in the novel. In the context of this novel, Stonehenge has nothing of the qualities of the benign "heliolatries" that Hardy had wishfully evoked many chapters earlier (92), when the prospect for Tess's fulfillment had not been denied. In the last section of the novel, Tess can seek only personal fulfillment, but with no positive social context.

She does err: she makes terrible mistakes in her thinking, which had been very promising when the book begins. At first, she is perceptive and imaginative, and she continues intermittently to be so. In the midst of her conflict over whether to accept Angel's proposal, for example, she reflects aloud to Angel on the basic strangeness of the dairy farm's function. This occurs one rainy evening when the couple have to deliver a shipment of milk on to a train heading for London. "Strange people we have never seen" will be drinking the milk that Talbothays has produced; these are people "Who don't know anything of us, and where it comes from; or think how we drove miles across the moor to-night in the rain that it might reach 'em in time." Angel, unappreciative, shifts the topic back to the big question he has been popping (188), but a sense of Tess's thought does come through in this passage. The most interesting quality I find here is not her sociological realism in understanding the great gap between worker and consumer,[28] but the poetry of her selection of milk-drinkers in her imagined London: "Noble men and noble women—ambassadors and centurions, ladies and tradeswomen—and babies who have never seen a cow" (188). I find this language charming; it seems to be a moment of indulgence by Tess (and by Hardy) for her self, one that shows another, never to be developed, facet of her mind.

Inevitably her thinking becomes twisted by the effects of her misfortunes and by her own inability to resist the concept of sexual sin that the novel shows (and that she herself knows) to be deadly. She does harm in her sadistic treatment of her three women friends and co-workers. But could she have helped doing that? And she kills Alec, which might also be an effect of her twisted thinking, but that act actually feels less harmful in experiencing the novel than her injuring the three women. This is the novel's experiential emphasis: on sexual love and its fulfillment, not on the immorality of murder. I actually *feel* Tess does harm at the end in her promulgating of the taboo of virginity upon Angel and Liza-Lu. The former possibly does not even need to believe in virginity if he has learned anything, and even if he does still have such a belief, the practice of training up a woman to fill it is bound to be dehumanizing for the sister, as well as for himself.[29] What does Liza-Lu think of this plan for her life? And how could it be within Tess's rights to have regarded her younger sister as a female to be consigned to Angel?

These are real harms done to people, not "sins" from a repressive morality. In experiencing the novel, Tess nonetheless can be valued in her womanly individuality for all she is, and all that she might have been. This "all" is a great deal, evoking a sense of "the beauty of the world"—the phrase used by Mona Caird. I imagine that every reader will have some sense of that beauty; it is a necessarily vague "sense," not a precise property. "Pure" becomes an experienced quality only because I feel I can endow her with the term, following Hardy's suggestion, by accepting what his novel has wrought. Her eventually damaged thinking does not detract from my sense of her self. Her self I experience as pure: whole and undestroyed and priceless. That self is a woman's, is individualized, is sexual and instinctive, is relation-seeking, is integral with Nature, and is that of a thinking person.

These affirmations are admittedly unguarded. I do not claim that anyone else will necessarily share them, but I do think most readers who experience this novel will arrive eventually at some comparable, many-stranded admiration and affection for Tess, with each reader developing her or his own selection. Most readers have done so. Those who cannot, are shut out of this novel, I am afraid, and the exclusion is so basic that it would be futile to attempt to persuade them that there is an experience here to be had.

In retrospect I now see that Tess's action in telling Angel of her past sexual experience has become part of the feeling that has led to my admiration. Beyond all her confusion over whether or not to tell, I think there is a principle at stake whose value I would not wish to downplay. Tess refuses to live a lie. She refuses to enter into a sexual/marital life with someone who is not merely ignorant of, but is seriously deluded about her sexual self. That is a kind of purity. It may be scoffed at as a self-destructive sacrifice, as an action for an absurdly ideal good that could never have been implemented in the context of Angel's character. But when all concessions are made, there still seems to me to be something in Tess's act that has genuine value for the creation of a loving sexual relation. Even Angel finally seems to have realized this.

As the novel so beautifully suggests, there is no need for Tess's sexual experience to be held up to some moral bar of judgment. As a woman she is entitled to have that experience, to make mistakes in it, to make choices the conventional world does not understand, that her men do not like, or of which we—today's readers—disapprove. She was also entitled to a better beginning of her sexual experience than having a man descend upon her as she sleeps—even if she has been sexually drawn to that man, and even if he did not actually rape her.

2. Making Value

I know of a few male readers who think that Tess should have been content to stay with Alec, the sexual male, and that she had no reason to return to her anemic Angel. But that makes her out to be not just irrational but idiotic: a woman whose most personal judgment of her needs is worthless. I simply do not experience her that way. Undoubtedly, a failure on the part of the reader to develop any sympathy for Angel would lead to a lack of sympathy for her choice. That would be a very serious experience blockage. But as I hope I have shown, Hardy makes it possible to understand and even to sympathize with Angel as a confused, vulnerable, damage-dealing and sexual human being who finally goes through a process of change. Nor can I deny the strength of Tess's affection for Angel when he returns so unexpectedly. She unhesitatingly, and passionately, declares that she loves him: "Yes, O yes, yes!" (365). Her voice soon becomes that of an earlier time, with "her tones suddenly resuming their old flutey pathos" (365). The sound qualities imagined here are part of what makes her statement convincing.[30]

In accepting her choice, I am concurring with what I take to be her own ethic of sexual tolerance. The attachment to her that I feel, the powerful identification I have with her, is not merely in despite of her sexual misadventures; it necessarily is inclusive of them. In her own words, or Hardy's words—and I think the two are indistinguishable here—love continues through "all changes, in all disgraces, because you are yourself" (226). I take these words in their common usage to have some sort of common-sense context, in which an unspecified limit is implicit: despite the word "all," there is no suggestion of an ethical absolute requiring one to accept any action whatsoever of one's spouse or lover, no matter how unfair or outrageous it might be. To use Hardy's phrasing, this ethic could be "illumined" by common sense (96). But the words, as they occur in the emotional context of Tess's plea to Angel, imply going far beyond conventional attitudes toward sexual love.

In Dewey's philosophy, the necessity in some contexts for rejecting the rules of conventional morality is clearly stated. This need occurs regularly, because moral codes and practices as they usually exist are "saturated" with the irrelevant sanctions of "praise and blame, reward and punishment." To be sure, we cannot just jettison all sense of good and evil; Dewey is no Nietzschean. But while he recognizes that getting "beyond good and evil is an impossibility for man," there is still the obstacle of conventional morality that confuses virtue with conformity, and in that context, there is every need to rebel in the interests of a better, ideal, morality: "as long as the good signifies only that which is lauded and rewarded, and the evil that which is currently condemned or outlawed, the ideal factors of morality are always and everywhere beyond good and evil" (*AE* 351). In *Tess*, we have what conventionally could be called an evil story: a man is unjustly murdered and the author avoids focusing on that evil, while another man who has hurt Tess terribly is rewarded with her love, and possibly with her sister's love as well.

In re-reading and re-processing the many layers of experience in *Tess*, I believe we get down to the basic value of cherishing Tess for the womanly life itself that she is, both in her exceptional difference from other rural women of her time (which makes it possible to feel something of the great person she could have been if she had really been allowed to develop) and her ordinary vulnerability and commonness. What Dewey calls the "ideal factors of morality," which I take to mean here, the freer life that Tess seems to be calling into existence, do not achieve fulfillment beyond the brief time with Angel. In the tragic mode appropriate to the book, we can realize, or re-realize, how much wastage of the human capacity for sexual love and of the human relationships that could develop from it, still goes on in our own world. In *Tess*, it is a loss not only of personal fulfillment but in some imprecise way, a loss as well of the whole value of Nature.

But can I, or we, just acknowledge all this and then sadly nod the head? From a Deweyan perspective, we do not just "take" this; having *undergone* the novel there is also a phase of *doing*. It is a phase that could go on for a lifetime, of our own more intelligent struggling for Dewey's "growth," and for Hardy's sexual-love "fulfillment." In its longest reaches, the *doing* is ultimately a matter of working toward a society in which that fulfillment is made not only possible but is not blocked by other priorities, whether these be moral, religious, "pop"-cultural, or the behavioral "laws" of corporate business.

In using the term "fulfillment" in a positive, non-ironic sense here, I do not think I am violating Hardy's creative spirit. Hardy, it is true, inscribes in *Tess* the supremely pessimistic view that "such completeness [of sexual love] is not to be prophesied, or even conceived to be possible" (46). This hyperbolic denial he registers as far back as chapter 5. But with 54 chapters yet to be read, a reader cannot afford to take this declaration as a controlling limit on an experience still early in its development. Nor is this limit actually observed: by the end of the novel, such love certainly can at least be "conceived to be possible." Statements made in a novel about what can never be done in the entire human future must pose special difficulties for experiencing. They may best be taken as one of Hardy's "impressions," as his own responses to his fictional situations, and as making no pretense to greater truth. Taken literally, they would be overblown claims to knowledge of the future.

We do know that Hardy, however pessimistic he was, contributed in 1894 to a symposium on sexual relations. In it, he favored sex education—which is not the stand of a person who thinks the situation hopeless. He recommended giving both young women and young men "a plain handbook on natural processes, specially prepared." He ended by expressing regret that civilization thus far has never found "a satisfactory scheme for the conjunction of the sexes."[31] But that is a far cry from proclaiming that none could ever be found, or rather (to think in Deweyan terms) that no amelioration of this failing is possible. In reading *Tess*, is it even possible not to experience a sense of hope for a "natural" relation, meaning one that is undistorted by civilized sexual prohibition, between Tess and Angel during the Talbothays Dairy chapters? It is tragic that this fulfillment does not come, except briefly when it is truncated by Tess's death. But that is rather different than saying that the entire impact of the novel is purely pessimistic. If there had never been hope, the outcome would not have been felt as tragic. The Talbothays section is extremely evocative of hope; and, in a Deweyan sense, it is one of the major consummations in the experience of this novel.

Nor am I alone in holding that there are limits to the novel's pessimism. Arnold Kettle found that the relationship of Tess and Angel in the last phase of the novel, even though he thought it "in one sense unreal," is "in a more important sense...a fulfillment, a harmony, a completion, and a justification of what Tess has been seeking."[32] That is an unparalleled statement for so Marxist a critic to have made. It is also Deweyan in recognizing that there can be a sense of "completion" experienced at points other than the literal end of the work. Raymond Williams found that "a warmth, a seriousness, an endurance in love and work" are defeated at the end of *Tess*—but they are "not destroyed."[33] Gillian Beer concluded that "*Tess* is jubilant as well as terrible".[34] The critic John Paul Riquelme, whose method of deconstruction I cannot emulate, rightly sees in Tess's plea to Angel at the point of their crisis, "Forgive me as you are forgiven," a plea for freedom together. This "freedom of mutuality is not attainable," the critic knows, in the novel itself, but the novel is far from renouncing it.[35] Quite the contrary: *Tess* instead evokes such mutuality of the sexes as a profoundly desired possibility.

3. The Coherence of Hardy's Nature

I do not deny that there is deep pessimism in *Tess*; but what is it pessimistic about? Nature itself? As far back as 1947, Harvey Curtis Webster, in his careful study of Hardy's novels, had found them showing "the struggle for existence, directed by an indifferent nature." But he did not believe *Tess of the d'Urbervilles* fit into his overall pattern. Tess Durbeyfield, Webster thought, is more truly defeated by "society's cruel conventions."[36]

As Dewey would maintain, pessimism can hardly be an emotion without an issue or drama attached to it (*AE* 48). I notice looking back upon what I have written that nowhere do I take up explicitly the novel's pessimistic aspect. Although I did not consciously choose to avoid the topic, I might have made the right choice for allowing my experience of the novel to deepen, inasmuch as I did not have the temptation to fit my varied feelings and reflections into an over-arching cosmic speculation possibly held by the author. But pessimism does call for some attention in reading *Tess*. The most relevant pessimistic feature has to do with Hardy's pronouncements on sex itself as an unavoidable natural force affecting humans so powerfully that they do not have control over their lives. In the critical writings on *Tess*, these statements are regularly displayed with little attention to their contexts, as if to indicate what the critic or reader "knows" of Hardy's view of the world. But to my knowledge, no critic remarks actually feeling badly about sex because of this. There is pseudo-knowledge here, but little undergoing toward an experience. I certainly do not feel pessimistic about "the invincible instinct toward self-delight" (104), nor does Hardy's tone in the context of that declaration suggest anything of the sort. Self-delight is what this section is all about, the delight of the self in love. I find that Hardy is fully accurate in his creation of a lush and fertile landscape that causes self-control over sexual desire to be greatly diminished, melted down, in both Tess and Angel. As Dewey would always realize, the matter is not purely literary: this melting-down would be easy to imagine for most of Hardy's readers, assuming that they have some experience of fine hot weather in a beautiful place.

As for the three milkmaids who pant helplessly for the sexual-body love of Angel Clare, that is painful. I can say I know of similar feelings of sexual longing in my own experience, and I am sure countless people can testify to such feelings. It is far from uncommon. But is it a root cause for pessimism? After all, we must reflect that Hardy in this case is not simply making a claim for the cruelty of the great cosmic mis-match between the development of human emotional capabilities and the evolution of civilization. Izz, Marian, and Retty are longing for sexual release in a romantic context (and do not expect to get it with the farmhands they know), but that in itself is no sign that they wish for what can never occur in human life. The overwhelming impetus of the Talbothays Dairy sections is toward the positive expression of sexual desire as the natural and essential way of being human. I must agree here with Lennart Björk: the perceived cruelties of Nature, such as they are in regard to sexuality, undoubtedly are weighted by Hardy as less damaging to human fulfillment than those of sexually repressive civilization.

Looking back upon my many experiences of *Tess*, I find that Björk is quite right that no "simplistic naturalism" is implied. Björk chose a single sentence by Thomas Hardy (spoken to William Archer) as this novel's overall orientation insofar as it bears on pessimism toward life's possibilities: "Whatever may be the inherent good or evil in life, it is certain that men make it much worse than it need be."[37] The source is the forgotten book, *Real Conversations*, by Archer.[38] Hardy went on to make an eminently sane statement on the inherent defects of life: "When we have got rid of a thousand remediable ills, it will be time enough to determine whether the ill that is irremediable outweighs the good."[39] That, I think, would be very close to Dewey's view. Björk works out several economical and logical rebuttals to those who have claimed that Hardy's attitude toward Nature in *Tess* is seriously confused.[40]

Thinking back to Tess fantasizing that this earth is a "blighted" star, I wonder if Hardy chose the term "blight*ed*" to suggest that something had been done to human life on earth to spoil it. The other planets she imagines are "splendid and sound," but earth is not given parallel antonyms like ugly and unsound (35-6). Earth surely has not become blighted because of the "inherent will to enjoy" (to take up Hardy's formulation of the problem in chapter 43). If anything, such blight is a result of what Hardy calls "the circumstantial will against enjoyment" (278). Whatever is "inherent" in human nature cannot be done away with, but to designate a force as "circumstantial" means that it could be altered through intelligent effort: the circumstances can be made to change. And the "will against enjoyment," whatever self-defeating compulsion this may hint at in human life, need not always be allowed to triumph.

Considered in full, with context in mind, Hardy's valuing of Nature in this novel does make sense. He is not contradicting himself, for example, in having Nature be the source of the inherent human drive toward pleasure in the "Rally" and "Consequence" Phases, and later in the novel showing how miserable Nature can feel to Tess and Marian as they work in the harsh wintry fields. For one thing, women at work on utterly mind-numbing, physically exhausting tasks under a cold sky are not brought there by Nature but by employment conditions. These are conditions we can bitterly feel if we allow ourselves to respond to the description. But that does not give them metaphysical status. And second, it is too self-flattering to suppose that Hardy is so stupid as to be unaware of this. Rather than indulging the self-inflating assumption that Hardy is blindly contradicting himself, it would be better for taking the experience to a richer depth, to credit Hardy with allowing his highly positive evaluation of Nature to be challenged within the novel itself by the harshness of the outdoors that we all know is there. There is a risk that Hardy chose to take: Nature can be felt to be every bit as much evil as it is beneficial. To have this impression at some point is, I should think, almost inevitably part of the experience. But with enough attention to the contexts and individualized qualities in which these opposed perceptions take place, the reader, I believe, will not sustain that impression.

As for the objection that Nature in the form of sexuality is exactly what got Tess involved with Alec, and therefore could not be a positive value, this is answered concisely by Lennart Björk: "there is of course" nothing in Hardy's 'Nature as norm' position which postulated that sexual drives are indiscriminate."[41] Nature could not have been set up to be all that dumb, neither by evolution nor by Thomas Hardy. Tess was drawn toward Alec and toward Angel, not toward sex with anyone she happened to meet. The three dairymaids are subjected to a "killing joy," but they do not run out and fuck the first man in sight. They do not have to do any such thing because they themselves have found ways to deal with this not utterly overwhelming passion: knowing too well that they could not have Angel, they attained "a resignation, a dignity..." (150). As Hardy plainly notes, their passion lacked nothing in the eye of Nature, while it lacked "everything to justify its existence in the eye of civilization" (149). In context, the fault therefore is not in Nature. In fact, their "killing joy" is felt to have that quality not because of the sexual drive itself, but because of their own "full recognition of the futility of their infatuation, *from a social point of view*" (149, my emphasis). The milkmaids had not wanted or expected to be so struck by "cruel Nature's law" (149), but a contextual taking-in of the entire passage overcomes any first impression that the source of the cruelty is Nature in itself.

It is Tess herself, and no doubt Angel as well, who suffer so severely from the frustration of their sexual impulses as they try to obey cultural norms, that their lives become distorted to the point of being pathological. Dewey, despite his under-theorization of sex, would have understood and sympathized. Even as he protested in 1922 against the faddish psychoanalytic attribution of all psychological ailments to the single-factor of sexual repression, he recognized that "[t]he intensity of the sexual instinct and its organic ramifications" account for a great many of the mental illnesses that call for psychiatric care.[42] Furthermore, sex according to Dewey is not just one of the several human needs that undergo distortion; it has been hit especially hard by society's restrictions: "social taboos and the tradition of secrecy have put this impulse under greater strain than has been imposed upon others."[43] But nature itself is not what is evil.

We do not know if Hardy ever read Darwin's *The Descent of Man and Selection in Relation to Sex*, published 20 years before *Tess*. We do know that he proudly says he was one of the first "acclaimers" of *The Origin of Species* when it came out in 1859.[44] Had he read the second book, published in 1871, he could have seen much evidence for the position that in human sexual selection, there is scope for choice on the part of both men and women. The point would have been obscured by some of Darwin's formulations of masculine gender superiority,[45] but it is there. As Geoffrey F. Miller has pointed out, Darwin spent some 600 pages in this book on the topic of sexual selection, far more than he did on the nominal topic of human evolution in general.[46] For myself, and for anyone encountering Hardy's *Tess* today, there is no need to limit the connection with evolutionary theory to Darwin's biases. Rather than assuming that Hardy as author simply adopted Darwin's masculine gender bias on this subject, we may accept the problems of sexual choice as a way of letting the experience of this novel grow to its fullest dimensions. Hardy at his most creative level did that.[47]

Let me vent my reasons for rejecting three other arguments made for Hardy's supposedly incoherent view of Nature. Joan Durbeyfield readily will say, of her daughter's troubles with Alec, "Tis nater, after all, and what do please God" (88). Critics of Hardy's vision of Nature in *Tess* have sometimes seized upon this statement as evidence of his inconsistency. But Joan, pairing "nater" with God, is on a different tack—one that might suggest that there is something amiss with this folk psychology. Joan, who in any case is not Hardy, has some motive for excusing what has happened to Tess, since she herself has much of the responsibility for sending Tess off to Alec in the first place. Tess is placed in the power of the institution of the human family, where her mother had been planning matches for her since infancy, but her type of family is not a fact of nature. When Hardy, early in the novel, aggressively derides Wordsworth's phrase, "Nature's holy plan," the context clearly shows that he is referring to the Durbeyfield family, a very civilized construct, not to Nature in its larger sense (28). If this passage suggests that the reader has to think about what is Nature and what is unnatural, if it undermines the assumption that the family is always the best place for a child—so much the better. As for Angel's perception, the day after his wedding to Tess, that she looks "absolutely pure," that is his problem, and not a matter of Hardy undoing himself. "Nature, in her fantastic trickery, had set such a seal of maidenhood upon Tess's countenance that he gazed at her with a stupefied air" (234). He is indeed stupefied, confounding to the utmost Tess's natural beauty with his own cultural ideal of Maidenhood = Female virginity = Sole value of woman.

Even less impressive is the supposed contradiction between Tess's responses to Nature, and the notion that Nature is just something she makes up in her mind. When specific contexts are allowed to guide reading, no support for such a notion can be found. I have seen commentary that rips from its context Hardy's remark that to Tess, "natural processes...seemed a part of [Tess's] own story...for the world is only a psychological phenomenon..."(91)[48] The phrases are taken from a passage in which the guilt-stricken Tess would let her "whimsical fancy" roam freely: "the phantoms and voices antipathetic to her" which she heard in Nature were "a sorry and mistaken creation of Tess's fancy—a cloud of moral hobgoblins by which she was terrified without reason" (91). At a later point the text does say: "Upon her sensations the whole world depended to Tess; through her existence all her fellow creatures existed, to her" (158). I have found no feeling in reading the book that could support this idea, and by the time it occurs in chapter 25, Tess and the reader have already been undergoing the "Rally" phase of natural recuperation for 10 chapters. In context, there is no contradiction: the sentences are part of Angel's contorted thought processes as he tries to figure out what his conscience owes to Tess. He appears to be projecting his own feeling of being sensuously overwhelmed by Tess, who was to his perception a person "so far-reaching in her influence as to spread into and make the bricks, mortar and whole overhanging sky throb with a burning sensibility" (158).

Nor is there any contradiction involved in feeling that life, or "the world," is immensely unfair to Tess, this sexual, intelligent woman—and that her suffering (even her psychological "complex," whatever it may be) is only made possible by the action upon her of civilized sexual morality. Tess, as many readers have seen, has a temperamental disposition toward passivity, a quality that becomes a considerable factor in her misfortunes. Yet it is too easy to block the complexity and depth of the experience if we say only this much. Her decision to return to Alec, for example, is one made with much hesitation, and takes some period of time for her to reach. She is not allowing herself to be passively swept away by his entreaties. Rather than regard her as innately deficient because of her disposition, I find that her passivity would never have reached pathological levels without the events through which she lives her life, and the moral code of sexuality in which her culture judges them. Letting her mother dress her up in a sexy way for display to a man who has flirted with her is not in the same league, *qualitatively*, as letting a man reject her for day after painful day, following her wedding ceremony, and not turning toward him either with fierce aggression or with erotic persuasion.

Even if Tess hates some of her own sexual history at the end of the novel, the instigating sources for such hatred are clearly cultural. I do not suppose any reader would seriously claim that her qualities of self-destruction would have reached the level they do in this story if her society were to have been free from its phobia of sexual love.

It would take no effort to score a point against Hardy's vision of Nature by simply quoting the comment on "the hour for loving" which I find so heartbreakingly poignant early in the novel: "Nature does not often say 'See!' to her poor creature when seeing can lead to happy doing; or reply 'Here!' to a body's cry of 'Where?' till the hide-and-seek has become an irksome, outworn game" (46). The skeptical reader may choose here to point to Nature in the role of tormentor rather than norm. Yet there are few if any critics, so far as I am aware, who take this point in relation to this passage. It is logical enough; why not say it? Perhaps for several reasons: for one, the palpable absurdity of expecting Nature to deliver at just the right moment lovers individually suitable for each of us. Hardy is not being silly; that is not what he is suggesting. In fact he has just controlled the context to avoid such a meaning one paragraph earlier, where he carefully qualifies the complaint that Tess is getting involved with Alec instead of with the man who would be "the right and desired one in all respects" by adding: "—*as nearly as humanity can supply the right and desired* " (46, my emphasis). As soon as I consider the context of his remark about a body's unanswered cry of "Where?" (and I can do some of that simply by reading on into the next sentence) I realize that it is society ("humanity") not Nature, which has to be better attuned to the needs of the human lovers: we need something much better, Hardy writes, than "the social machinery...which now jolts us round and along..." (46). Nature has no "holy plan." Nor is sexual selection a function anyone could simply hand over to Nature when it comes to finding a mate. But this is not to say that Nature is therefore malevolent or irrelevant in human sexual life and love.

Hardy's vision of the place of sex within Nature is potently rendered in this novel. It raises huge basic questions of value. For readers who are disposed to answer positively to these questions, the novel is leading them to an inquiry on life at its source. The questions? For the sake of giving them the personal and yet common focus that the novel seems to me to call for, they might be phrased as follows: 1) does sex between adults have any basic, non-trivial, connection with Nature? 2) Does sexual love between adults have not only a connection with, but a *ground* or *basis* in Nature? A further question, one that is more difficult to formulate or to defend, might be: 3) Is the loss of countryside, or in today's language, of biodiversity, or "the wild," and of the forms of agriculture that do not depend on damaging the environment or its workers—a threat to the bodily, sexual health of each of us?

For anyone who might be inclined to think about these questions, it is important to recall that as far as Dewey is concerned, Nature is not some sort of foundational ultimate. It is thoroughly fused with the doings and undergoings of human experience. And it keeps changing: "[W]hy not accept, with Shakespeare," Dewey asks, "the free and varied system of nature itself as that works and moves in experience in many and diverse organizations of value?" (*AE* 325). Or, as Stephen C. Pepper put it, the Contextualist can counter the skeptic's assertion that Nature is being taken as having a determinate structure that belies the basic pragmatic position of the importance of ever-changing contexts, by asking the skeptic this question: "How can you be so sure that nature is not intrinsically changing and full of novelties?"[49]

4. Gender Issues and Experience

Gender too exists within Nature, but by this date, we now have a shared awareness that traits and qualities customarily attributed to gender may have little or nothing about them of the naturally given. The many comments on gender in *Tess* have been widely discussed, especially by feminist critics. I have not taken them up as a separate theme, because I see them functioning in different ways within their contexts. There is no doubt that Hardy is thinking of Tess as woman, Alec and Angel as men, and that the novel is inconceivable otherwise. This is not to say that Tess has no masculinity nor that the men have no femininity. It is not to deny even that there is an indefinable homo-erotic link that can sometimes be felt between Angel and Alec. Traces of a lesbian desire between Tess and her three female friends might also be intuited.

Despite these virtually undeveloped thematic openings, it is necessary for experiencing the novel to extend attention to the heterosexual relationships in it. One of the most prevalent "stencils" now in use by critics has the effect of avoiding this task, by shifting the focus of reading to the psycho-philosophical topic of what is termed "the gaze." In the case of *Tess*, with its authorship by a man who has a powerful visual imagination and a creative fascination with women, the "gaze" automatically becomes "the male gaze." It is undeniable that Tess, no matter how she is conceived, reaches a bad end. But with the use of the critics' privileged concept, Tess's life as a character is transformed; she changes from being a woman involved with men into an image of a male-constructed female figure whose function is to illustrate how she can fall victim to (or to partially escape the power of) the male gaze. Elaborations of the novel that employ this stencil come to a pre-conceived moralizing conclusion: the male gaze, always assumed to be inherently harmful and demeaning, ultimately controls or destroys Tess, unless she can be said to have fought her way partly free from it. To the extent that such a program of interpretation is followed, no experience of the novel in Dewey's sense (or mine) could occur.

At a more abstract level of interference with the possibility of experience, it is possible to argue that Tess is nothing more than the figment of a male voyeur's fantasy. This basically is what the critic Kaja Silverman is saying, in an article that has often been cited as extraordinarily insightful.[50] Silverman neatly sutures the novel into the compendious Lacanian world-view, where nothing has ever been known not to fit. She concludes that the all-important narrator-voyeur of *Tess* only serves to provide male readers with the illusion that they need not undergo castration (taking this term in Lacan's special sense), when according to Lacan, they most certainly have been. As for women readers, the novel has nothing much to offer since they undoubtedly are castrated already in the Lacanian sense, and should know it. Those who buy this argument are hardly likely to work very hard to get their own experience out of *Tess*. Tess, Silverman argues, has neither the stable exterior nor the integral interior of a character; in other words, she is a figure caught within the pincers of the male gaze, and cannot be regarded as an individualized woman.[51] Peter Widdowson, who endorses Silverman's view, similarly insists that Tess "has no character at all;" she is only everyone else's construct, and especially she is a construct of the novel's narrator.[52]

Another form of critical denial of a sense of contact between the reader and the central woman character of the novel has been developed by Penny Boumelha, who argues that there is so much narrative confusion in the presentation of Tess that her very coherence as a character disappears.[53] This disintegration is then valued as a blow on behalf of the liberation of femininity from its stereotypes. Boumelha herself badly simplifies the novel in order to find it rejectable as a story of life-like human beings: *Tess* "turns upon a...fixed polarity of gender. In this schema, sex and nature are assigned to the female, intellect and culture to the man."[54] Actually, Alec, a man, has plenty of sexuality, which must mark him as more "natural" in the sense of refusing repression than Angel, and Angel despite his "hard logical deposit" is also a sexual male. He knows what it means to offer to run off with Izz Huett. Tess, for her part, has her culture of knowing the Bible, as well as an "intellect" of her own that she mistakenly hands over to Angel for tutoring. She is certainly deeply connected with nature, but considering the complex development of Tess's character, it makes little sense to say that this is a role that is "assigned" to her schematically.

It is also plain to see that Hardy responds to his own emotionally powerful story of woman and man partly by allowing a great many of his thoughts on gender to enter into the texture of his writing. Undeniably, these are the thoughts of a man. But the question that counts is this: do his specific attributions on gender cause any dimming or dumbing of the experience? Rarely, such as when Hardy gives Tess a "feminine loss of courage" (291), I think they do. At other times their bearing is oblique. Thus the famous remark that a "field-woman," unlike her male counterpart, "is a portion of the field; she has somehow lost her own margin, imbibed the essence of her surrounding, and assimilated herself with it" (94). I think this in itself is an insupportable notion. (Or is it only an "impression," as Hardy would be likely to say?) Hardy in fact presents it in tandem with an explanation for the men not looking as blended-into the field as the women: the men wear clothing that is fairly awkward, not to say ridiculous. They wear "trousers supported round their waists by leather straps, rendering useless the two buttons behind, which twinkled and bristled with sunbeams at every movement of each wearer, as if they were a pair of eyes in the small of his back" (94). Compared to this, the women are "part and parcel of outdoor nature..." (94). But all of this seems to have no effect on Hardy's description of Tess, the woman this novel is actually about, and who continues to be individualized in this very scene. It may even contribute to her being set off as different: "This morning the eye returns involuntarily to the girl in the pink cotton jacket, she being the most flexuous and finely drawn figure of them all" (93). I never experience that Tess "melts into her environment", despite the statement in the text concerning the generic "field-woman." It is one of Hardy's ideas that does not acquire any energy in my reading. To write that "she felt akin to the landscape," as Hardy describes in her "Rally" or recovery phase (108), implies that she feels a close relation to this place, not that she merges into it. Even when Hardy writes that Tess's "quiet glide was of a piece with the element she moved in," the context shows that this is part of her intentional solitude, during which she sought and found "absolute mental liberty" (91). She could induce this mood by using her intelligence to locate the precise experiential entry point: "She knew how to hit to a hair's breadth that moment of evening when the light and the darkness are so evenly balanced that the constraint of day and the suspense of night neutralize each other..."(91).

5. The Doom of the D'Urbervilles

What about another theme I have neglected, the portentous d'Urberville family line that seems to hang over Tess and follow her in the details of Hardy's commentary, right through all of her events in the novel? Is that not a sign of a natural universe that is predisposed to destroy her? I admit that Hardy's periodic references to the old family line of the d'Urbervilles I find difficult to experience. I said almost nothing about the opening chapter of the novel, in which the d'Urberville theme is first introduced; that is because I find nothing in that chapter of a strong feeling quality. As I have said, the novel really starts, as far as experience is concerned, with chapter 2, when we meet Tess and Angel, after which the first chapter takes on some emotional force, retroactively. The d'Urbervilles are easily explained as embodying in one sweeping Hardyan invention, the effects of heredity, as that concept might have been understood by some thinkers in Hardy's time. But explaining is no guarantee of experiencing.

Through many of my early readings, I had kept expecting to feel something important about Tess's connection with her d'Urberville ancestors, but I have concluded that such an experience does not occur. There is no action of Tess, and no disaster that befalls her—no situation, in other words—for which the major motivation or cause is traceable to the past existence of the d'Urbervilles. I must agree with the critic Andrew Enstice: "The d'Urberville connection is never a strong influence on their [Tess and Angel's] affairs".[55] The quality of Hardy's writing can deteriorate when he writes of the d'Urberville heritage as if it were a cause of Tess's actions. When Tess slaps Alec with the heavy glove, Hardy writes: "Fancy might have regarded the act as the recrudescence of a trick in which her armed progenitors were not unpracticed" (321). I can understand why a sensitive critic could find this language "qualified, circumlocutory, and ponderously academic," in contrast to the vividness of the act itself: "The abiding impression is that she does it."[56] Another critic has proposed a linkage between Tess's personality and the d'Urberville heritage, but this requires seeing Tess as a "fierce" person, which I find I cannot feel, despite her few violent acts.[57] On the other hand, to literalize the d'Urberville influence leads to mystifying and over-simplifying results. Thus, J. Hillis Miller concludes that Tess's killing of Alec is not her own doing: "The murder is not her act, but is performed by her ancestors acting through her."[58] Possibly Miller is reflecting an experiential inhibition here, of not wanting to see Tess as a killer. Such reluctance seems to be evident in a number of other critics' commentary on this part of the novel, as John Sutherland has shown.[59]

Even the main spring of the plot, Tess's journey to "claim kin" with her newly discovered (pseudo-)relatives, the d'Urbervilles, is not simply a stroke of fate. Tess's parents were trying to take advantage of a fact of descent, by sending or selling their daughter to the young man they imagine will marry her, but that is quite different from saying that they did this just because they had chanced to discover John Durbeyfield's aristocratic ancestry. They were using a pattern of thought embedded in a culture long endured to the spell of riches. The situation is too complex to allow any direct attribution of cause.

As far as they may effect the experience of the novel, the d'Urbervilles are a dubious entity. We read that one factor in Tess's pride "perhaps was a symptom of that reckless acquiescence in chance too apparent in the whole d'Urberville family" (248). But since we have no scenes that recreate any of the d'Urbervilles as characters, that "too apparent" attribution is hard to trust as a factor in the reader's experience. For me, the most memorable impact of the d'Urbervilles into the experience of the novel occurs during the highly emotional and disturbing section on Tess's wedding day. Tess is quite taken aback at "Those horrid women!"—those portraits of d'Urberville women who had lived two hundred years earlier (214-15). They would be horrible to her even if they were not d'Urberville dames, and are even more so if she realizes that they are some of her ancestors. But it is Angel who falls into the assumption that since Tess has a facial resemblance to "those harridans," she must inherit their quality of evil (231). That is several removes from the assumption that the novel or Hardy are definitively endorsing the bloodline of these women as having a direct effect on Tess's character.

What the d'Urberville references "do" in the experience of the novel can either be misconceived simplistically as a determining curse upon Tess from the past, or felt as strands in the textural quality of the scenes. The simplistic interpretations, those which hold that Tess is doomed to repeat patterns that had been set long before her birth by the lives of her ancestors, the d'Urbervilles, would have to explain how it is that she does not become an aristocratic, vicious snob; and why, in the second to last sentence in the novel, her ancestors are depicted as sleeping on unknowingly in their elegant but worn sepulchers while she is not to be buried with them—or even, as far as we are informed, to be buried anywhere. It is interesting for the problem of experiencing the novel that few commentators claim her proud retort to Angel, that she is a peasant "only by position, not by nature" (229), as evidence of her own belief in her descent from the d'Urbervilles. Although the inference would be a logical one, I myself have never thought of it while reading that declaration of her difference from the cultural values of her family and village. In the process of experiencing the novel, it does not need a lineage to make it feel that her retort is warranted.

Yet the d'Urberville heritage has an effect within the experience of the novel. Literally taken, it is ineffectual, but as an underlying metaphor of ill-omen, it has its power. Like other aspects that might appear to be simply signs of inherent doom, it has a social, and therefore "circumstantial" aspect: the d'Urbervilles were rich and unjust, sometimes brutal. That a long history of injustices committed by one's family in the past may subtly undermine a life being lived in the present is not unthinkable. Perhaps the aggregate of injustice has a way of spreading over time into the life of a descendant. Hardy apparently felt so, and shaped the d'Urberville metaphor accordingly. We do not start off life with a clean slate: the past has been here. The thought that a descendant would be picked out mysteriously for punishment for actions by her ancestors feels to me, in reading this novel, as a clearly "fictive" or imaginary element of the whole. But this does not make it meaningless. As Dewey maintained, a problem of "validity of reference" regarding perceptions that are contrary to fact (such as the occurrence of the Ghost in "Hamlet") is created when we mistakenly assume that all perceptions have "the same kind of meaning." There is no blockage when we realize that "[e]xistential events that form a drama have their own characteristic meanings." Operating with that assumption, which we might do without any sense of strain as we experience a work of fiction, we get "an enhancement of the meaning of a moving state of affairs" (*EN* 242). If I try to read the d'Urberville heritage as *literally* accounting for Tess's fate, it becomes a limiting over-simplification for experience. But it actually is a special type of affective thread running through the overall fabric.

In Dewey's view, major human problems naturally occur to us in a basic sequence of, first, an unanalyzed awareness of something going wrong, followed by an effort at discrimination of just what factors are involved. There is at first, for both the artist and for the reader, "an inclusive qualitative whole not yet articulated, not distinguished into members." It can be felt so strongly that it may even be called "a total seizure" (*AE* 195). This mood does not simply deteriorate into analytical parts: "it persists as the substratum after distinctions emerge; in fact they emerge as *its* distinctions" (*AE* 196, Dewey's emphasis). In first experiencing *Tess*, an overwhelming, largely unanalyzed sense of injustice is probably felt before there is any precise analytical realization of its sources. Or, if not exactly unanalyzed, it is felt as coming from everywhere—from the d'Urbervilles, her self, her family, her culture, God, the universe, and from Thomas Hardy. Eventually, as the experience of the novel becomes more whole, the various senses of injustice become sorted out and woven together. Some prove to be of little consequence, others are immense. The experience becomes coherent without our having to deplete it of its emotional quality, and in the case of *Tess*, we can create two parallel but different major affirmations: *Yes*, we can realize afresh that human emotional life is much sadder and tragic than it should be; and *Yes*, we will always keep struggling to make it understandable, bearable, livable, and even pleasurable. To make that struggle a pragmatic one, we will need to use our whole human intelligence. For one thing, we will need to see where the pain is coming from, and where it is not. In Dewey's carefully phrased conclusion to *Experience and Nature*, intelligence, is

> a critical method applied to goods of belief, appreciation and conduct, turning assent and assertion into free communication of sharable meanings, turning feeling into ordered and liberal sense, turning reaction into response... (*EN* 325)

Is this view one that Hardy would find irrelevant, considering how frequently human struggles lead to defeat? Probably not: to say it, Dewey goes on, is "not to indulge in romantic idealization. It is not to assert that intelligence will ever dominate the course of events; it is *not even to imply that it will save us from ruin and destruction.*" (*EN* 325-26, my emphasis). Dewey is not entirely removed from the feeling of cosmic pessimism that Hardy often conveys. "The world is a scene of risk" Dewey writes; "it is uncertain, unstable, *uncannily unstable*" (*EN* 43, my emphasis). A person can recognize this, and feel it deeply, without giving up all effort to make experience more secure and satisfying. To fold up into passive resignation under the weight of the evils of human existence would be to ignore what Dewey calls "the precarious promises of good that haunt experienced things…" (*EN* 68). Neither Dewey's philosophy, Hardy's personal views, nor Hardy as the novelist of *Tess*, suggest that we do such a thing.

6. A Qualitative But Not Mono-Qualitative Whole

Tess of the d'Urbervilles is "an experience," in Dewey's sense. It is also an aesthetic experience, by virtue of meeting Dewey's formulation:

> An object is peculiarly and dominantly [NB: not totally] esthetic…when the factors that determine anything which can be called *an* experience are lifted high above the threshold of perception and are made manifest for their own sake. (*AE* 63)

I think however that it is not an experience totally unified around one pervasive quality, as Dewey was also disposed to demand of a great work of art. Were it that, I would not be re-experiencing strains of unevenness and discordance in the narrative as I have constructed my series of perceptions in reading the whole novel many times. I thus am not able to join fully in Dewey's idea that the beauty of a work of art is our response to "the consummated movement of matter integrated through its inner relations into a single qualitative whole" (*AE* 135). Just thinking back to the large problem near the opening of the novel, in which Hardy writes emphatically of the terrible fate that Tess has met when she first has sex with Alec, along with the sense he also conveys that it is not clear what the quality of this sexual event might have been, I realize that no amount of inquiry or explication or sensitive response is going to fully "clear up" that passage. It will always be felt as "sticking out," somehow, rather than being absorbed into a "single qualitative whole." The point for my Deweyan account is that this sticking out is a creative challenge for the experience, and not a defect. The "single qualitative whole" is an emphasis in aesthetic judgment that Stephen Pepper deliberately avoids in his delineation of Contextualism. That is one more reason, and possibly the best one, for my needing Pepper in this experiential commentary on *Tess*. I am much more attuned to Dewey's statement, also made in *Art as Experience*, that we must not assume that "there is just one unifying idea or form in a work of art. There are many, in proportion to the richness of the object in question" (*AE* 318).

But even beyond that admission of openness, I think that it is important to feel the jarring, disunifying effects of having the aura of a sensual world, reminiscent of what Hardy took to be Hellenic paganism, built up poignantly in the Talbothays section, then drained right out of the novel after the crashing failure of Angel's human acceptance of Tess as a sexual woman—to be partially restored and then destroyed again in the last phase. My method has been to follow the experience of *Tess* wherever it seems to lead, quite aside from any discussion of its singular unifying quality: that can hardly be discussed anyway, as Dewey remarks: "it can only be felt, that is, immediately experienced" (*AE* 196).

It is worth considering that the overall quality of *Tess* is the sense of care and concern we as readers feel for Tess. That can only come with immediacy from the way she is created and presented; it is a quality that is enhanced by Hardy's own enveloping caring, even of his loving her, both as expressed in his commentary, and in his continuous creating of her fictional life. But I would not wish to claim that this quality permeates every aspect of the novel, making it into "a single qualitative whole." I have been guided, I hope, by whatever qualities I have found. I have tried to lay out the novel's "matter" in such a way that its experience can be deepened and made richer, even if no one reads the novel as I have. I am sure that no one will—at least not exactly—and my own understanding of *Tess* will no doubt change further when I next read it. As the contemporary Deweyan philosopher Jim Garrison has remarked, "Because of the rhythm of loss and recovery of integration, we never conclusively complete the task of practical deliberation."[60]

It is possible, however, to sing the praises of inconclusiveness in too strident a voice. In today's critical climate, the critic tends to take pride and to seek safety by claiming no more than a tentative, contingent, and admittedly self-created interpretation. Dewey might be cited in support of such a stance. But it is also Dewey who argued, in *Experience and Nature*, that it is faddish and foolish to regard change or instability as the only conditions of life (*EN* 49-50). Sheer frictionless flux, after all, is not what serious change is all about: Change, Dewey writes, "as it is in experience," is "a call to effort, a challenge to investigation, a potential doom of disaster and death" (*EN* 49-50). And change is not the only essential trait of experience. There is also in this world of ours a certain amount of stability, or relative stability. A good experiential account of *Tess of the d'Urbervilles* might aspire to showing that there are certain unavoidable qualities to be experienced. If they are unavoidable, they are not going to vanish with the next reading. Within the limits of human fallibility, there is nothing wrong with *trying* to achieve some meaning that will stick; as Dewey said, "The striving to make stability of meaning prevail over the instability of events is the main task of intelligent human effort" (*EN* 49). The flaw is in denying that such stability arises from the striving and the human effort, and claiming that the object—in this case the novel *Tess*—is of some fixed pre-existing nature that is independent of anyone's personal reading. That, and the further fallacy of assuming that what is relatively stable for those who might experience the novel at this time in history, is going to stay stable for all time. With all due limitation recognized, however, some things are likely to stick, at least for a while.

7. An Extra-Aesthetic Factor in Experience

Before moving on to this book's conclusion, let me suggest at this point a maxim that may apply to any deep aesthetic experience, but is perhaps seldom recognized. In every such experience, there will be some extra-aesthetic factor involved, some unavoidable influence or theme of the reader's life that has no obvious link with the work of art itself. Yet without some such factor at work over the process of having the experience, there might not be much "there" to have. For every person, the un-obvious factor will be different. In my case, the extra-aesthetic factor is my long relationship with my mentor, Professor Wayne Burns. As I reach the end of this experiential account, I realize how far I am from Burns's way of reading this novel.

For example: for me, the words in which Tess expresses her love for Angel (when Angel at last locates her and finds that she is living with Alec), are virtually audible whenever I re-read the scene. I believe I can feel the sound of her voice. But for Burns, whose experience for Tess goes back through many decades, they seem not to be present.[61] My difference with Burns is worth exploring at some length. If Burns had not introduced me to the aesthetics of both Dewey and Pepper in the mid-1950s, my book on *Tess*—my whole life I think—would be different. I could even have diverted my Deweyan experiential account of Tess to a self-analytical study of my personal development. But I decided not to take that route in this book, valuable as it might be for myself. It is Burns's radically different approach to Tess, first published over thirty years ago, in an article now included in the select bibliography of the Oxford University Press's World's Classics edition, and revised in 2002, that is important for readers of this volume to consider.[62]

Burns constructs a distinctive reading of the sexual love issues in Tess. He argues that even though Tess hates and despises Alec, she has been sexually responsive with him; her killing of Alec in part expresses her guilt for this responsiveness. Alec, for Burns, is the destroyer of the ideal of womanhood. Alec represents no ideal; he is just there as a sexual male. But I find this claim more problematical than it first appears to be. The verbal interchanges between Tess and Alec show that their sex, such as it might have been, has not led them to the gratification such an appetite would suggest. Their talk implies that they have already differed over her refusal to kiss him "willingly," which he takes as a bodily proof of her lack of love for him and as a point of dissatisfaction with her response. Tess seems to accept this analysis. She comes across in the novel as a whole as a sexually passionate woman, but was this passion gratified with Alec? The fact that Tess and Alec are attracted to each other does not guarantee that they have passionate sex, and there are some signs in the text that it was not so good. "And there was never warmth with me" (320), Tess declares to Alec. He does not contradict her.

The problem from a Deweyan perspective is one of quality: if we cannot clearly intuit that Tess was sexually *passionate* with Alec, then we cannot attribute her move back to him in the last part of the novel as being motivated almost entirely by sexual attraction. We would then have to consider the confusing mixture of motives that Hardy creates. But it is the fact of her own passionate sexual response to Alec, Burns maintains, that Tess cannot accept, and it is also what is especially unpalatable to Thomas Hardy himself. This results in what Burns regards as inept and illogical narrative commentary on Hardy's part.[63]

In Burns's account of the novel, the relation of sexual mores to Tess's tragedy is denied: "the tragedy is not, as Hardy proclaims, that of a pure woman done in by the cruel application of a moral law".[64] He does not go into the problem of whether or not Tess was raped by Alec, nor consider in any way that she may have been violated by him.[65] Other major elements are shorn away. The Talbothays section draws minimal comment. Angel is treated as a man who is insufficiently male. This seems not enough to allow for an experience of what Angel is going through as a man. Burns also discounts much of the potential experience in the final sections: Alec's murder and Tess's capture at Stonehenge are mere Victorian melodrama to him, and the long-delayed lovemaking of Tess and Angel cannot be felt as credible. There is no basis for argument here: what one does not feel cannot be argued into experience.

Burns is primarily concerned to show that his "Panzaic principle," his original theory that the body is "always right" in novels, is effective in *Tess* through the presence of Alec. Burns makes this case, but with too high a cost to the experience. He tries to essentialize Tess's character by analyzing her responses in the earliest scene in which she appears, in chapter 2; but this is to assume that her character is complete at the start, and avoids fully considering the effects of experience in forming her character as it actually develops.[66] He sees that Tess is torn between Angel and Alec, but his experience of this tension appears to be compromised, since he can see no value for her passionate female nature in her final choice of Angel rather than Alec as her husband and mate. In other words, her choice between the two men, which is the most important choice she ever makes, is devalued. But if she is torn by her own sexual self in two directions, and chooses the way that is so etherealized as to deny sexual passion, this inevitably suggests that Tess is an emotional idiot. I would interpose here the words of Jack Johnson, the famous Black boxer, whose choices of lovers were contested by the media and by the law. "I have eyes and I have a heart," Johnson said, "and when they fail to tell me who I shall have for mine I want to be put away in a lunatic asylum."[67]

I say once more that part of the problem here is experience being cut short by the adoption of a rigidly negative evaluation of Angel. With Angel regarded as a sexually deficient male, Burns is led by the logic of his construction of the experience to regard Tess's choice of mate as contrary to her own sexual needs, and a capitulation to the demands of sexual repression. It would be impossible, on Burns's reading, to even begin to imagine Angel as a lover at all. When he does allow that in one of the Talbothays scenes, Angel is "on the verge of feeling unetherealized sexual passion" for Tess, Burns quickly reverts to his abstract level of analysis: Angel "manages to etherealize his passion."[68] As I experience this passage, Angel is not de-sexualizing his passion; he is controlling it in order to make what he believes is a necessary detour: his proposal of marriage (172-3). This is not to say that the sense of a denial of sexual consummation at this juncture is not a painful part of experiencing *Tess*.

A more serious problem in having the experience of Tess is created by Burns's refusal to identify with Tess's romantic aspirations. Her need to combine sexual gratification with love for a man whose character she admires and adores, a man she needs as a support in her recovery of her sense of integrity, is nothing more than a disastrous, sentimental delusion as far as Burns is concerned.[69] I find, on the contrary, that the concept of romantic love is too central for experiencing this novel to warrant such an approach. The novel shows that Tess's romantic love leads to a tragic outcome, but I do not think you can maintain a uniformly skeptical distance from Tess's deepest wish and still "have" the novel.

8. On a Kind of Self-Destruction of Experience

These reflections should not be taken as a denial that other readers' experiences of the novel differ radically from my own. They manifestly do: particularly, those approaches which emphasize Tess's pathological or self-destructive qualities, those that deny altogether that Tess is a valid portrayal of a woman, or those that fix upon Hardy's gender bias and his confusion of issues in his commentary. I know of two highly sensitive readers, both of them my friends, who have recently read *Tess* and have had genuine experiences of it, one by responding with a feeling of virtual "seizure" toward Hardy's stylistic creation of both character and scene; the other by feeling painfully caught up in the novel's sense of an implacable determinism over Tess's fate. Others I know of hold to strong inclinations to totally detest Angel and to see Alec mainly as a rapist and exploiter. These are serious readings, and I do not dismiss them. But I hope I have shown a more profitable reading of this fiction, if I may borrow Hardy's essay title, "The Profitable Reading of Fiction."[70] What I have said about *Tess* is not presented as some infallible guide, but on the other hand it may be that I have performed a "series of responsive acts that accumulate toward objective fulfillment" which Dewey specifies in his discussion of what the perceiver of a work of art can do (*AE* 58). The validation (or rejection) of such a hope can only come through the testing that would occur in the act of a reader going back to the novel and taking it in freshly, experiencing it anew.

In the recent critical literature on *Tess* there are also suggestions that Hardy is craftily reversing various conventional plots of the Victorian era, or is undermining even the basic conventions of the genre of the novel. These suggestions can be more or less supported, but when they are emphasized and made into the central feature of the novel, they quickly lose touch with the emotional qualities of *Tess*. They also serve to deny, and disastrously so for any sense of experience, that the novel's subject-matter is the sexual-love story of Tess. Most troubling to me are the highly competent readers who present detailed evidence of Hardy writing the novel in such a way that every one of his apparent moves toward warm sensual feeling is undermined by (often subtle) textual clues pointing to tragedy ahead. I think for example of Tony Tanner's much-praised article of 1968, "Colour and Movement in Hardy's *Tess of the d'Urbervilles*,"[71] or Margaret Higonnet's introduction to the most recent Penguin edition.[72] I have encountered such readings for years, but impressive as they seem to be when read, they are simply irreconcilable with what I feel when I go back and actually read the novel. I cannot believe, to take an absurd example, that when Hardy uses the term "Thermidorean" to describe the July heat at the Talbothays dairy, he means to allude to the execution of Robbespierre.[73] Hardy, says Dale Kramer, in many ways "simultaneously mocks and honors Tess's comprehension of values."[74] Mocks? I cannot believe this. Or, I am asked to believe that *Tess* shocks its readers by "reproducing" the "illogic and divorce between experience and value" in modern consciousness.[75] But that again is simply not the case at Talbothays, where experience and value—of the characters and of the reader, me—move toward a coherence within Nature that bears directly on emotion and sexual attraction. There is something more to be had within this experience than merely "reproducing" our confusions.

Nature is certainly not a simple one-dimensional force at Talbothays, nor anywhere else in Hardy. As I have suggested, however, some of his hyperbolic negative attributions toward Nature, especially those regarding Tess's hard labor in the fields under the wintry sky, are very poorly expressed: in terms of quality, they are no match for the Talbothays experience.

I wonder if those highly literate readers who sedulously gather all the negative instances regarding Nature, but who pay little attention to their affective qualities and their contexts, have considered what they are doing with their experience. In a word, they are flattening it out, canceling the feeling that a major section of the novel may arouse by positing a neatly opposite feeling. "If the imagery of a green world that suffuses the Talbothays romance is idyllic, it is also anti-romantic."[76] I can readily accept, following Dewey, that there has to be some tension or resistance in Hardy's lovingly written vision of Nature if the reader's experience is to amount to more than trite satisfaction (*AE* 65-6,159-66). But pushing her argument, Higonnet seems driven to a ridiculous conclusion. When the warm, sensuous aura of Talbothays is interrupted by a day of un-lovely work, in which the farmhands all have to search the fields for the source of some garlic that is tainting the cows' milk, Higonnet asserts that Angel and Clare are being given a "warning" which they fail to heed: "*Et in Arcadia ego*—I too am in Arcadia, says Death."[77] That this Day of the Garlic should be confounded with Death, and that the lovers should find some warning from Nature against their love in this quite surmountable problem, is an instance of the distortion of experience that comes from attempting to balance or to overpower the sensual impressions of Hardy's Nature with a negating force. To do this sort of thing makes for a diminished and ultimately affect-starved experience. In sheer force and bulk, I have no doubt that the evocation of the life-affirming aspects of Nature at Talbothays is far more potent than the contrary signals, several of which seem to me exaggerated by, or even invented by, some of *Tess*'s critics. Just recalling the force and beauty of the nature descriptions renders incredible the suggestion that Hardy did not intend for his readers to respond, except with equally strong negative feelings, to the evocation of Nature in that whole crucial section of the novel.

9. Hardy's Outlook on Human Emotion

What Hardy was most pessimistic about was not life in general, Angel's "hobble of being alive" (128), but its potential for emotional fulfillment. Hardy in his notebook made an oft-quoted pessimistic statement that he dates April 7, 1889—exactly while he was writing *Tess*:

> A woeful fact—that the human race is too extremely developed for its corporeal conditions, the nerves being evolved to an activity abnormal in such an environment. Even the higher animals are in excess in this respect. It may be questioned whether Nature, or what we call Nature, so far back as when she crossed the line from invertebrates to vertebrates, did not exceed her mission. This planet does not supply the materials for happiness to higher existences.[78]

The thought is a profound one, and resonates, sometimes very strongly, in *Tess*. Yet it is also a dubious one to apply *in toto* to the novel, because at Talbothays, Nature certainly did "supply the materials for happiness" to Tess and Angel. Because of the constrictions they felt they had to live within, they failed to take what Nature offered.

Unnoticed, I believe, in the attention that has been given to this striking cosmic speculation by Hardy, is the immediately following passage.

A day or two later brought [Hardy] a long and interesting letter from J. Addington Symonds...concerning *The Return of the Native*, which he had just met with and read, and dwelling enthusiastically on 'its vigour and its freshness and its charm.'[79]

Now Symonds was not just one more admirer of Hardy's work. From the research of Lennart Björk, it is now known that Symonds's writing on ancient Greece had by this date become a key influence upon Hardy's pagan interpretation of Hellenism.[80] This was an intellectual interest of Hardy's that ran directly counter to his pessimism, and as Björk argues, it was a strong force in *Tess*. I suggest that Hardy, in his autobiography, is making a qualifying connection when he recounts Symonds's encouraging comment as taking place only a "day or two" after the entry on cosmic pessimism.

Writing to Symonds a week after the pessimistic entry in his notebook, Hardy says that he had read the latter's essays "as correctives" to those of Matthew Arnold's. Hardy also discusses his own predilection for creating sad and tragic stories. It is something he cannot in conscience help but do, given his "own views." He might have added, I believe, that something in his own temperament drew him toward pessimism, but that this was a vital defense for him against the threats of existence. There is more than irony in the fact that Hardy complained about how bad life is and yet held himself together, created 14 novels and 950 poems, and lived to the age of 87 with scarcely more than one or two illnesses. Pessimism is in one sense a great defense for certain people. But Hardy's creative purpose is not the endorsement of pessimism; his purpose is cautiously reconstructive: as he tells Symonds,

the first step towards cure of, or even relief from, any disease being to understand it, the study of tragedy in fiction may possibly here & there be the means of showing how to escape the worst forms of it, at least, in life.[81]

9. Risking *Tess*

But such arguments, whether over Hardy's pessimism or over the kinds of experience *Tess* can be, are not made for the winning. From the standpoint of *Art as Experience*, the question is not whether one approach is objectively superior to any other. Pepper's idea of the text as a "control object" could hardly give us the confidence to claim that degree of truth (unless we are talking about patently inaccurate descriptions of the characters and actions). The only important question concerning these varying aesthetic experiences of different critics is this: granted that evidence has been presented accurately and with care, will the reader's experience of the novel be deepened and made more fruitful by what the critic has constructed from this novel? Or will it be blocked or diminished by allowing the potential experience to go to waste?

My work has been toward confronting all the major aspects of the novel, as these may be experienced, and as the whole of the novel becomes an experience. I have shown my belief in Pepper's conception of the aesthetic work of art "as a succession of cumulative perceptions leading up to a total funded perception which realizes the full appreciative capacities of the physical object," the text of the novel. But as Pepper also said, in the same passage from *The Basis of Criticism in the Arts*, such completeness of perception is rarely realized by the critic of the great work of art; in fact it is possibly reached "not even by the creating artist himself, [since] so many possibilities of realization may unconsciously enter in."[82] My aim has not been to seek an impossibly difficult totality of full perception, but to make the experience of the novel as rich and meaningful as I think it actually can be. To do that requires re-re-readings, a process that Pepper recognizes as centrally important in experiencing a complex aesthetic work of art. Dewey might agree; he would almost have to agree given his commitment to having an aesthetic experience as fully as possible, but he does not theorize on this issue, nor, I believe, do most other aestheticians.

Such experiencing should sound like an unobjectionable, harmless endeavor. Unfortunately, there is a strong resistance always to having a major experience in a culture that has little use for it: a great deal of our culture operates on a kind of experience-depleting automatism, and thus has much to fear from people going deeply into new experiences that might lead them to unforeseen personal and social ends. In professional criticism of *Tess*, in other words in exactly the institutional locale in which the experience ought to be enhanced, this fear, I believe, has become endemic. There is always the chance that people might experience *Tess* in their own way, rather than following the dictates of advanced critical theory. In an essay published in 1999, the late Kristin Brady notes rather uncomfortably that Hardy's fiction "still draws fascinated readers..." who might be in danger if they happen to be uninformed about such issues as "the position of women in nineteenth century England, Hardy's class status, or the Victorian literary marketplace."[83] But informing is not so much the aim in this statement as policing. As Peter Widdowson insists, elsewhere in the volume, *The Cambridge Companion to Thomas Hardy*, the "discourses" of *Tess*, "*have to be* accepted as unstable and contradictory."[84] Widdowson's italics leave us no choice: he agrees with those critics who regard Tess herself as composed merely of the "object-images" she is made to bear, and these are "primarily" those of the male "gaze." This is a theory, and there has been support for it--but why do we "*have to*" accept it? Kristin Brady completed her sentence on the new and fascinated readers of Hardy's fiction, not by urging that their experiences be respected and deepened, but that they should be studied: Hardy "still draws fascinated readers, and the dynamic of that fascination is an important topic for literary and cultural analysis."[85] There is even a chance that readers will revert to the condition of understanding Hardy's women characters as "bestial" and "instinct-led."[86] By flashing these terms in her concluding paragraph, Brady might have been hoping to discourage anyone from having an experience in which sexual instinct might very well be important. Had she chosen to, she could have re-quoted Havelock Ellis's less inflamed statement about Hardy's fictional women: "They have an instinctive self-respect, an instinctive purity."[87]

No feminist critic, I think, has quite matched the hostility combined with expertise of Garrett Stewart's "'Driven Well-Home to the Reader's Heart': *Tess*'s Implicated Audience."[88] Distributed widely in the St. Martin's Press "Bedford Books" series of Case Studies in Contemporary Criticism, this piece in effect attacks the novel in the apparently sincere guise of offering theoretical criticism. Stewart claims to show that Tess is "never more than, in the rhetorical sense, a fine figure of a woman," and that the plot of the novel is likewise nothing but rhetorical illusion, unworthy of our response. Stewart, who in other writings has sought to find sympathetic understanding for the "voice" of the fictional narrator, strongly (but perhaps inadvertently) implies that in this novel, the author, Hardy, merely has plugged himself into two prefabricated computer-like programs, one for Character and one for Plot, and thus has deceived all his readers into thinking that he had done something of a creative nature in writing *Tess*. I do not exaggerate: anyone reading this article will see that it is exactly what Stewart is doing, although it is not what he is saying. Stewart's discomfort shows through as he concludes:

> To understand the process as well as the product, there is no way for the implicated reader to stand outside [the text]. You stand, instead, sutured into and skewered by it--nailed by both the very fascination through which the novel's appeal to sympathy has both drawn you in and taken you in. Appearances to the contrary, it is not an altogether pretty picture.[89]

Once again, "fascination" is treated as a danger, as is sympathy. Stewart sounds frustrated and angry, gestures at a straw man (the "altogether pretty picture"), and reaches for sadistic terms. The fact that readers become involved is slightly criminalized in the phrase, "the implicated reader." Why? I suggest it is because theoretically-driven criticism that so often grabs for itself a role superior to that of the reader's experience of the literary work of art, has failed as yet to fully exert its dominion over many readers' experiences of *Tess*. Dewey's point, that critical reflection comes only later; that in aesthetic undergoing, "direct and unreasoned impression comes first" (*AE* 150), would be countermanded by the theorist saying, "Wait! Not until you've got the benefit of my enlightened guidance." In our time, Dewey's seemingly commonplace observation, "To steep ourselves in a subject-matter we have first to plunge into it" (*AE* 60), rings truer than ever.

In the course of my account of this novel, I have myself used many of the tools of literary criticism, of Dewey's philosophy (in other words, theory), and of my own intellectual and emotional development.

Every critic, like every artist, [Dewey wrote,] has a bias, a predilection, that is bound up with the very existence of individuality. It is his task to convert it into an organ of sensitive perception and of intelligent insight, and to do so without surrendering the instinctive preference from which are derived direction and sincerity. (*AE* 327)

My own long-held interests in the problems of sexual love and the work of Wilhelm Reich have undoubtedly played a great role in what I have written. So too has my virtually lifelong belief in the value of the genre of the novel, with its ability to create characters that are experienced "as if" they were real people with human sexual bodies, living in their social contexts. The fact that I got my education in a scholarly world where everyone learned how to do the extremely close reading that went under the name of the New Criticism has surely had a major effect upon my habits of interpretation. My intense study with Professor Wayne Burns at the University of Washington in Seattle, and my clash with him in the early 1970s over the interpretation of *Tess*, has fueled my motivation to deal with the novel repeatedly. My Jewish identity has had some effect on my perception—my claim—of an ethical core within the long marital argument between Angel and Tess. But these interests have provided me with no license to read just as I wish. The valuable critic, Dewey declares, must "seize upon some strain or strand" in the work of art "*that is actually there*, and bring it forth with such clearness that the reader has a new clue and guide in his own experience" (*AE* 318, my emphasis). In that light, I believe the strongest factor behind my attempt to probe the experience of *Tess* has been the novel itself, with the many unforeseen experiences it has called forth, in my years of teaching. That was my personal experience in dealing with this novel, but I imagine that many other teachers could provide similar testimony.

One strand has always been obvious. The issue that exercised readers at the outset, and has continued to do so at many junctures in the experiencing of *Tess*, is worth noticing once more: the crude issue of female virginity. Dewey in 1935 wrote that he considered *Tess* one of the twenty-five most influential books of the previous fifty years.[90] Although Dewey did not explain why he thought so, he might have been thinking of just this social issue, the novel's unmasking of the destructiveness of the taboo of virginity. If *Tess* has had some impact on Western civilization's partial renunciation of this taboo, that is surely a human tribute to the book's value. But for two major reasons, that does not mean it has become dated. For one, the irrational worship of female virginity has not vanished from human culture. Far from it; we have only to think of its functioning within many societies which have not given up this standard, or even within the fundamentalist populations of that supposedly most advanced nation, the U.S.A. In fact, the United States government now spends millions of dollars each year to promote pre-marital virginity for all, men and women, in the form of "abstinence only" sex-education programs. Although there is no reliable evidence, after years of promoting these programs, that they do anything to persuade adolescents not to have sex, and even in the face of the fact that such programs will leave millions of secondary school students without any substantive sex-education, the funding was increased substantially in 2002. Federal law in the U.S. *requires* that such programs must teach that "a mutually faithful monogamous relationship in the context of marriage is the expected standard of human sexual activity."[91] Recent research has even found that some young American women allow anal intercourse because of a fantasy that any form of sex other than vaginal penetration is a form of abstinence. Under the cultural pressure for abstinence, young women are being diagnosed with pharyngeal gonorrhea, a result of their determination to protect "technical virginity."[92] In the opinion of Dr. Lynn Ponton, a distinguished psychotherapist who deals with American adolescents, youth culture has reverted to the sexually repressive attitude on virginity that was held in earlier decades: "I believe that in response to the liberal period of the 1970's and 80's, we've returned to the double standard of the 1950's."[93]

The second reason that the issue of virginity does not cause *Tess* to be dated is that the novel never was locked into this one issue. As an experience, it has a much greater scope. If readers allow themselves to see only the theme of feminine pre-marital sex, then the experience of the novel will be cut short. In the interest of practicing a cultivated naiveté (a trait that Dewey thought was quite necessary to maintain), it might be good to look back at one of the first serious critical articles on Hardy's fiction, "The Novels of Thomas Hardy" by W. P. Trent. Trent, writing in November 1892, early in the history of the reception of *Tess*, wisely admitted that it might be too early to attempt to judge this novel; it

> is possibly too fresh in our minds and the verdicts of its various critics and readers are too jarring and confused to enable us to feel certain that we are criticizing it fairly, and not merely taking up the cudgels for or against certain very pronounced opinions of its author.[94]

Hardy's "opinions" on the injustice of the taboo of virginity were probably what Trent had in mind. But then he greatly qualifies the statement. While it *seems* at first that Hardy had succumbed to the tendency of writing a novel with a purpose, he really does not do that: "We confess that the power and the movement of the story are so great that it is only when we read a review of it that we are conscious that its author had any purpose save that which is common to every true writer of fiction--viz. to tell a story which shall please."[95] Trent, who was one of the founders of *The Sewanee Review*, was an astute reader of literature. As I would reconstruct his point, "the power and movement of the story" in its entirety are much more predominant in the experience than any pre-conceived purpose Hardy may have had.

While the scope of *Tess* is undoubtedly much greater than any isolated issue, there is still a need to focus on the struggles of sexuality within Nature and

Civilization, if *Tess* is to be experienced. But in criticism, has the ability to focus on that issue been lost? Surveying the current repertoire of interests favored in academia leads me to repeat my claim that a shift toward non-contextualized Theory or impersonal cultural examination makes an experience in Dewey's sense much more difficult to have. It is not a matter so much of literary texts being ignored, but of the application of highly developed "stencils" to these texts, so that a book like *Tess* is read for its ability to fit the stencils rather than for its potential for developing into an experience. This is a shift in the academy that has had vast consequences. Critical theory interests me deeply as an instrument for guiding and deepening my own critical efforts to experience literature. But insofar as Hardy is concerned, I admit that I do not care about Hardy's novels having become, since the late 1960s, "a fertile testing-ground for theoretical practice."[96] That is not what I take literature to be for. I suggest that it will become obvious to anyone reading the theory-driven criticism of our day, that the notion of a "testing-ground" has been in practice a situation more aptly described as Hardy's novels becoming passive recipients of triumphant theories that attempt to pre-occupy them.[97] Ironically, many of these writings complain about Hardy's need to control his women characters. He may have had such a need, although only in conjunction with another need to let them turn out as they must in terms of their own development. Hardy's control never approached the total grip that most of his present-day critics exert upon his fictions.

The critical and theoretical tools, as well as my self, are not the "end-in-view" of my work. As Dewey has said, in *Experience and Nature*, "Standardizations, formulae, generalizations, principles, universals, have their place, but their place is that of being instrumental to better approximation of what is unique and unrepeatable" (*EN* 97). I would apply that to experiencing Tess as well as *Tess*.

NOTES

Preface

1. Joseph Warren Beach, *The Technique of Thomas Hardy* (New York, 1962), p. 193.

Chapter One

1. All page references given without identification of author or source are to: Thomas Hardy, *Tess of the d'Urbervilles*, ed. Juliet Grindle and Simon Gatrell. Introduction by Simon Gatrell. Explanatory Notes by Nancy Barrineau. (Oxford, 1988).

2. John Dewey, and James Tufts, *Ethics* (Second Edition), in Dewey, *The Later Works (1932)*, vol. 7, ed. Jo Ann Boydston. (Carbondale IL, 1985), pp. 171-2. (Dewey's emphasis). Originally published in 1932. Tufts is co-author, but Dewey wrote this passage as well as the entire section entitled "Theory of the Moral Life."

3. Dewey, *Ethics*, p. 171.

4. Ian Gregor, *The Great Web: The Form of Hardy's Major Fiction* (London, 1974), p. 178.

5. J. Hillis Miller, *Thomas Hardy: Distance and Desire* (Cambridge MA, 1982).

6. See Hardy's "Thoughts of Phena, At News of Her Death," *Collected Poems*, 62. The composition of this poem, begun according to Hardy on 13 March 1890, and completed after the death on 19 March of Tryphena Sparks Gale, occurred during the process of writing *Tess*. Hardy delivered the first installment of the novel to his serial publisher in October 1890 (Michael Millgate, *Thomas Hardy: A Biography* (New York, 1982), p. 307). He would have been thinking of Tryphena at the time of working on *Tess*. In the manuscript of the novel, the page on which the name "Phena" would appear is missing; thus we do not know at what stage of composition the name became part of the text. See the heavily annotated edition, showing Hardy's numerous revisions, *Tess of the d'Urbervilles*. ed. Juliet Grindle and Simon Gatrell (Oxford, 1983), p. 77.

In the most authoritative biography of Hardy, Michael Millgate minimizes the importance of Tryphena in Hardy's life. This I believe over-corrects earlier efforts by other scholars who are thought to have made too much of her. See for example, F. R. Southerington, *Hardy's Vision of Man* (New York, 1971). For a useful exchange on the problem, see Southerington, "Young Thomas Hardy," *Paunch*, no. 51 (1978), pp. 29-42; Robert C. Schweik, "A Commentary on F. R. Southerington's Critique of Gittings' *Young Thomas Hardy*," *Paunch*, no. 51 (1978), pp. 42-8. In my own reading of the biographies, I find it undeniable that she was a crucial early love of Hardy's. Even Millgate concedes that they might have made love, but makes the deadpan claim that "it would not have been extraordinary" if they had. See Millgate, *Thomas Hardy*, p. 106. At the time, Tryphena would have been 16 or 17 years of age: rather Tess-like! Hardy was ten years older.

Hardy's painful personal sense of the wrong man taking the woman is probably at work in *Tess* as well, although there seem to be no explicit clues to this in the text. Helen Paterson, the woman who illustrated *Far From the Madding Crowd*, got married one month before Hardy himself married Emma Lavinia Gifford. In 1906, Hardy wrote to his friend Edmund Gosse that he would have married Paterson, "but for a stupid blunder of God Almighty." (*Ibid.*, p. 159). One must wonder what that "blunder" could have been.

7. Thomas Hardy, *The Life and Work of Thomas Hardy,* ed. Michael Millgate (London, 1984), pp. 9-10.

8. Millgate, *Thomas Hardy*, pp. 345-6.

9. Tim Dolin, "Notes," *Tess of the d'Urbervilles,* ed. Dolin (London, 1998), pp. 401-2.

10. Stephen C. Pepper, *The Basis of Criticism in the Arts* (Cambridge MA, 1963), pp. 66-7.

11. Freud, quoted by Clarence P. Oberndorf, *A History of Psychoanalysis in America* (New York, 1964), p. 182. My emphasis.

12. Paul Turner, *The Life of Thomas Hardy: A Critical Biography* (Oxford, 1998), p. 2.

13. Dale Kramer, *Thomas Hardy: Tess of the d'Urbervilles* (Cambridge UK, 1991), p. 78.

14. Hardy, *The Life and Work*, ed. Michael Millgate, pp. 225-6. See also Joan Grundy, *Hardy and the Sister Arts* (London, 1979), p. 64; J. B. Bullen, *The Expressive Eye: Fiction and Perception in the Fiction of Thomas Hardy* (Oxford, 1986); Leonée Ormond, "Painting and Sculpture," *Oxford Reader's Companion to Hardy,* ed. Norman Page (Oxford, 1999), p. 296.

15. See J.B. Bullen, *The Expressive Eye*, pp. 193-4.

16. Roberta Smith, "Conjurer of Ethereal Mysteries," *New York Times*, 1 March, 2002.

17. Margaret R. Higonnet, "A Woman's Story: Tess and the Problem of Voice," in *The Sense of Sex: Feminist Perspectives on Hardy*, ed. Margaret R. Higonnet (Urbana IL, 1993), p. 16.

18. Lionel Johnson, "The Argument," *Tess of the d'Urbervilles* , 3rd edn., ed.

Scott Elledge. (New York, 1991); reprint from Johnson, *The Art of Thomas Hardy* (London, 1894). Johnson's proposal for reading *Tess* with strict refusal to credit any of Hardy's commentary is carried out, in effect, by Juliet McLauchlan, *Tess of the d'Urbervilles (Thomas Hardy),* (Oxford, 1971). (Notes on English Literature). From a Deweyan perspective, this approach to the novel may be considered an experiment to determine if a richer experience will result. What seems to occur, however, is a split in continuity of attention, with some passages receiving sensitive treatment and others, judged to be "intrusions" on Hardy's part, being rejected without serious consideration.

19. John Dewey, "Context and Thought," *Later Works*, vol. 6, ed. Jo Ann Boydston (Carbondale IL, 1985), pp. 3-21.

20. Johnson, "The Argument," p. 241.

21. J. I. M. Stewart, *Thomas Hardy: A Critical Biography* (New York, 1971), p.180.

22. Richard Shusterman, *Pragmatist Aesthetics: Living Beauty, Re-thinking Art* (Oxford, 1992), pp. 84-114.

23. Wolfgang Iser, *The Act of Reading: A Theory of Aesthetic Response* (Baltimore, 1978), p. 29.

24. Philip Jackson, *John Dewey and the Lessons of Art* (New Haven CT, 1998), pp. 35-40.

25. Richard Shusterman, "Art as Dramatization," *Journal of Aesthetics and Art Criticism* 59 (2001), p. 372n.

26. The major exceptions might be Louise Rosenblatt, Stephen C. Pepper, and, much more recently, Richard Shusterman. See listings in Bibliography. Pepper in fact is necessary in some ways to my work. But Dewey's sense of social purpose integrated with his aesthetics of experience has meant more to me, over the years, than anyone else's approach.

Few pragmatist studies of experiencing novels have been done. A major exception is the chapter on Henry James's fiction, in Jonathan Levin's *The Poetics of Transition: Emerson, Pragmatism, and American Literary Modernism* (Durham NC, 1999), pp. 117-46. Rosenblatt, in *Literature as Exploration* (New York, 1995) briefly discusses some 70 novels. But most pragmatist literary criticism thus far has centered on poetry. Philip W. Jackson's *Dewey and the Lessons of Art,* pp. 96-108 offers a reading of a poem by Elizabeth Bishop as its examination of a literary work.

27. Pepper, *The Basis of Criticism in the Arts*, pp.142-71.

28. Stephen C. Pepper, *World Hypotheses: A Study in Evidence* (Berkeley, 1961), p. 249.

29. Bradley's "Poetry for Poetry's Sake," which dates from a lecture given in 1901, and from which this excerpt is taken by Dewey, runs counter to Dewey's aesthetics. Dewey would not have been drawn to Bradley's poetic ideal of "an all-embracing perfection." See A. C. Bradley, *Oxford Lectures on Poetry*, (London, 1965), p. 26. Dewey was reading with a selective sense of what could be valuable for a contextualistic aesthetic. Bradley himself throws away the great insight at the opening of his essay (from which Dewey quotes) by then saying: "But that insurmountable fact [of individual response moving through the succession of experiences] lies in the nature of things and does not concern us here" (*Ibid.*, p. 4).

30. Reader Response criticism in academia during the 1970s and '80s devolved into two models, both of which I find unsatisfactory for experiencing literature. In one, developed by Norman N. Holland, response was reduced to the reproduction of themes from a reader's "identity-theme," in other words to what the ego would habitually and inevitably find in every situation. See Norman N. Holland, "Unity Identity Text Self," *PMLA* 90 (1975), pp. 813-22. Personal change or transformation became theoretically inconceivable. This is an obvious denial of experience in Dewey's sense. The other mode, that of David Bleich, allowed for total subjectivity in response, to the extent that the text had no control over the experience at all. See David Bleich, *Subjective Criticism* (Baltimore, 1978). This made for a denial of experience, in Dewey's sense, since in a world where we could just think anything we pleased as we encountered a work of art, there would be no tension or resistance, and hence no learning or growth. (*AE* 22-3; 65-66).

A third model, however, that originated by Michael Steig, avoids both of these pitfalls. Steig's *Stories of Reading: Subjectivity and Literary Understanding* (Baltimore, 1989) seems not to have attracted any followers. This is undoubtedly because it would take great literary sensitivity, a courageous commitment to personal disclosure, along with an openness to change, to emulate. Although he works within the terms of theories of "interpretation," Steig often seems to me to be talking about experience rather than hermeneutics.

31. The text of the novel I regard as the "physical continuant" in the process of the reader's construction of the perceptual experience, as Pepper argued in *The Basis of Criticism in the Arts*, pp. 142-71. Pepper also developed the notion of the text as a control over response, in "The Control Object, A Vehicle of Aesthetic Communication," in Pepper's *The Work of Art* (Bloomington IN, 1955) pp. 90-121. Pepper overstates the degree of control an artist can have over a reader's response to a given passage, but his view that there is an undeniable connection between experiencing a work of art and what the text says through its use of culturally shared language, is one that I can endorse, based on my own observation of literary response.

32. The pragmatist literary theorist Louise M. Rosenblatt also recognizes that the literary work, as a text, signals to the reader that an "aesthetic" rather than "efferent" (factually concerned) response is called for. See Rosenblatt, *The Reader, the Text, the Poem: The Transactional Theory of Literature* (Carbondale IL, 1978). At the very time when non-Deweyan Reader Response theory was only being developed, Rosenblatt was

refining her own model, which she had begun much earlier in *Literature as Exploration* (originally published in 1938), to show that there can be full respect for individual response but that this will be meaningful only within the reader's "transaction" with a literary text. See also Rosenblatt's restatement of her position: "Readers, Texts, Authors," *Transactions of the Charles S. Peirce Society* 34 (1998), pp. 885-921.

33. Jacques Derrida, "Structure, Sign and Play in the Discourse of the Human Sciences." *The Structuralist Controvcersy*, ed. Richard Macksey and Eugenio Donato (Baltimore, 1972), p. 272.

34. Jay Martin, *The Education of John Dewey: A Biography* (New York, 2002), p. 405.

35. David A. Granger, "Expression, Imagination and Organic Unity: Remarks on Deciphering John Dewey's Relationship to Romanticism." *Proceedings of the Midwest Philosophy of Education Society, 1999-2000.* (Chicago, 2001), pp. 218-32.

36. Jackson, *John Dewey and the Lessons of Art*, p. 11.

37. Pepper, *World Hypotheses*, pp. 239-242.

38. Dewey, quoted in "Textual Commentary," *AE*, pp. 379-80.

39. Larry A. Hickman, *John Dewey's Pragmatic Technology* (Bloomington IN, 1990), pp. 181-2.

40. John Dewey, "From Absolutism to Experimentalism," *Later Works* vol. 5, ed. Jo Ann Boydston (Carbondale IL, 1984), pp. 147-8. My emphasis.

41. Richard Shusterman, *Pragmatist Aesthetics*, p. 37.

42. Thomas M. Alexander, *John Dewey's Theory of Art, Experience and Nature* (Albany NY, 1987), pp. 119-182.

43. Bernard Paris, in a probing interpretation of Tess as a neurotic woman (applying the theories of Karen Horney), pays almost no attention to her sexuality. See Bernard J. Paris, "Experiences of Thomas Hardy," in *The Victorian Experience*, ed. Richard A. Levine (Athens GA, 1976), pp. 203-37. Michael Ragussis, a fine critic of fiction, argues that the novel is about naming and identity. See Michael Ragussis, *Acts of Naming: The Family Plot in Fiction* (New York, 1986). Elisabeth Bronfen maintains that Tess's story "becomes an allegory of the process of dying..." It becomes so quite rapidly, since even in chapter 2, "she is always already distanced from life into an allegorical figure of fatality." See Elisabeth Bronfen, *Over Her Dead Body: Death, Femininity and the Aesthetic* (New York, 1992), pp. 233-4. J. Hillis Miller finds that sex is just one of a dozen elements that make up "a system of mutually defining motifs, each of which exists as its relation to the others." See J. Hillis Miller, *Fiction and Repetition: Seven English Novels* (Cambridge MA, 1982), pp. 126-7. In Miller's earlier book on Hardy, sex was subordinated to his all-

embracing theme of the Immanent Will. (Miller, *Distance,* passim). Peter J. Casagrande, in his book on *Tess,* subordinates the sexual to his own theory of Hardy's belief in the aesthetics of beauty combined with ugliness. (But Casagrande nonetheless offers perceptive comment on the rape/seduction problem.) See Peter J. Casagrande, *Tess of the d'Urbervilles: Unorthodox Beauty* (New York, 1982). John Goode asserts that it is useless to think of Tess's sexuality because she is "constructed by her gender and class," and anything natural about sex has been "appropriated" by the rule of the middle class. The novel, Goode believes, "is not about Tess's sexuality—it is about the articulation of sexual politics...and its incorporation into the social relations of production." When Tess is rejected by Angel, their entire problem lies in the linguistic exchange between them— which is to imply that the bodily fact of Tess having been in bed with Alec has nothing to do with it. See John Goode, *Thomas Hardy: The Offensive Truth* (Oxford, 1988), pp. 115, 123-4. Goode is among the few critics who do comment on how it feels to experience *Tess,* and he makes perceptive comments, but his allegiance to Marxism always comes first. More recently, Marjorie Garson treats the novel as a "tension between nature and aristocracy which I believe underlies the narrative." See Garson, *Hardy's Fables of Identity: Woman, Body, Text* (Oxford, 1991), p. 138. All these critics are capable readers who offer substantial support for their interpretations, but their efforts contain a massive denial of the sexual subject-matter of experiencing *Tess.*

A more complex instance in which such denial is at least partially overcome is to be found in the work of Dale Kramer. In his early book, *Thomas Hardy: The Forms of Tragedy* (London, 1975), Kramer gave almost no attention to sex in his chapter on *Tess.* But when he later wrote a short book on *Tess* only, he came to the conclusion that sex is indeed crucial: Tess's drive for self-identity and self-realization is "especially centered...in sexuality..." See Kramer, *Thomas Hardy: Tess of the d'Urbervilles* (Cambridge UK, 1991), p. 98. Very few of the novel's critics have said this. But the insight is not developed or elaborated upon by Kramer, nor is its significance explored.

The fact that there are numerous critical works on *Tess* dealing with the portrayal of gender, Hardy's masculine bias, the allegedly voyeurist quality of Hardy's "gaze," (etc.) does not mean that attention has often been directed to the quality of sex and of sexual love in the lives of the characters in the novel.

44. John Dewey, *Human Nature and Conduct. The Middle Works,* vol. 14, ed. Jo Ann Boydston (Carbondale, Il, 1988), p. 107.

45. *Ibid,* p. 105.

46. *Ibid,* p. 107.

47. Mary Jacobus "Tess: the Making of a Pure Woman," in *Thomas Hardy's Tess: Modern Critical Perspectives,* ed. Harold Bloom (New York, 1987), pp. 57-60.

48. As Juliet Grindle shows, Hardy made 3 small revisions for an edition of the novel in 1919. She has also determined that 15 very minor revisions which Hardy had made in paperback editions of *Tess,* but had forgotten when he revised the text in later years, should

be included in her definitive edition—definitive, that is, within human fallibility. All of these changes are listed in the excellent scholarly edition, *Tess of the d'Urbervilles*, ed. Juliet Grindle and Simon Gatrell (Oxford, 1983).

49. James Gibson, *Thomas Hardy: A Literary Life*, (New York, 1986), p. 119.

50. John Paul Riquelme, "Introduction," *Tess of the d'Urbervilles* (Boston, 1998), p. 12.

51. Jacobus, "Tess: The Making of a Pure Woman," p. 58.

52. Dolin, ed., *Tess of the d'Urbervilles*, p. 434.

53. Jacobus, "Tess: The Making of a Pure Woman," pp. 55-6.

54. Leonard J. Waks, "The Means-End Continuum and the Reconciliation of Science and Art in the Later Works of John Dewey," *Transactions of the Charles S. Peirce Society* 35 (1999), p. 606.

55. D. H. Lawrence, *Study of Thomas Hardy and Other Essays*, ed. Bruce Steele (Cambridge UK, 1985), p.100.

56. John Dewey and James Tufts, *Ethics*, p. 270.

57. William Watson, Review of *Tess*, in *Tess of the d'Urbervilles*, ed. Scott Elledge, pp. 386-7.

58. Rosemary Sumner, *Thomas Hardy: Psychological Novelist* (New York, 1981), p. 139.

59. Jacobus, "Tess: The Making of a Pure Woman," pp. 51-2.

60. Marjorie Garson, *Hardy's Fables of Integrity,* p. 149.

Chapter Two

1. T. R. Wright, *Hardy and the Erotic* (London, 1989), p. 108.

2. Contextualism, or pragmatism, is the only one of the major groupings of philosophical theories that attends sympathetically to *fusion*, according to Stephen C. Pepper. In fusion, the qualities of details are merged in the quality of the whole event. There can be degrees of fusion, ranging from instances where the merging is relatively complete, or fully "relaxed" fusion in which the details stand out on their own but are to some degree intermixed. In philosophies other than pragmatism, fusion "is interpreted away as vagueness, confusion, failure to discriminate, muddleheadedness." Pepper illustrates the concept with the deceptively simple example given by William James: lemonade. That drink can be thought of as consisting of its components of lemon, water

and sugar, but the taste of the drink is something different from its elements, of which it is a fusion. See Stephen C. Pepper, *World Hypotheses: A Study in Evidence* (Berkeley, 1963), pp. 243-6. That commentators on *Tess* have seldom noticed the fusion in Hardy's description of her mouth with the sound qualities of the UR in her local dialect is evidence enough of the way common sensibility has failed to take heed of the phenomenon of fusion. Higonnet, for example, who has written on the functions of Tess's voice, fails to take notice of this passage. See Margaret R. Higonnet, "A Woman's Story: Tess and the Problem of Voice," in *The Sense of Sex: Feminist Perspectives on Hardy*, ed. Margaret R. Higonnet (Urbana IL, 1993), pp. 14-31.

3. William A. Davis, Jr., "The Rape of Tess, English Law, and the Case of Sexual Assault," *Nineteenth Century Fiction* 22 (1997), pp. 397-401.

4. Pamela Haag, in her book *Consent: Sexual Rights and the Transformation of American Liberalism* (Ithaca NY, 1999) makes this clear. See also Melanie Williams, "'Sensitive as Gossamer'—Law and Sexual Encounter in *Tess of the d'Urbervilles*," *Thomas Hardy Journal* 17 (2001), pp. 54-60. Williams shows that the terms "rape" and "seduction" are both historically unstable. In her reading of the text, Tess was soundly asleep "for some time during the encounter." Williams, *Ibid.*, p. 37. This suggests that Tess could have taken no active part in the sexual act; she was raped. But Shirley A. Stave has argued that Hardy's specification that Tess was "sleeping soundly" will lead to the opposite conclusion: "Awake, the voices of her education would have prompted her to resist; asleep, it is her body that responds first, and responds willingly." Stave, *The Decline of the Goddess: Nature, Culture, and Women in Thomas Hardy's Fiction* (Westport CT, 1995), p. 103.

5. Jim Garrison, *Dewey and Eros: Wisdom and Desire in the Art of Teaching* (New York, 1997), p. 154.

6. Shusterman's and my point about the propensity among professional critics to create innovative interpretations at the cost of experiencing the work of literature is well illustrated by Catherine Gallagher's article, "*Tess of the d'Urbervilles*: Hardy's Anthropology of the Novel", in *Tess of the d'Urbervilles*, ed. John Paul Riquelme (Boston, 1998), pp. 422-40. Gallagher proposes that Hardy's use of the name "Tishbite" is the key to a secret, "encrypted" anthropological meaning of the entire scene of Tess and Alec having sex—and by extension of the entire novel. In an elegant and arcane argument, Gallagher removes the focus of discussion to (among other anthropological texts of the late 19th century) J. G. Frazer's *The Golden Bough*. There, she locates a pattern of sacrifice, applies it to the story of *Tess* (mostly confining her attention to references to sacrifice), finds that it cannot work in the modern context of *Tess*, assumes that it is intended to work in this novel, and concludes that the novel therefore scuttles itself. Clearly only an elite readership could relate to and critically evaluate Gallagher's interpretation. Gallagher asserts, over-confidently, that her understanding of the passage in Hardy would have been clear to a "dutiful" 19th century reader with a fair understanding of the Bible, but she offers no evidence that anyone did read the passage in the manner suggested (*Ibid.*, pp. 432-3). Gallagher, like most anti-experiential theorist-critics who dominate current practice, is particularly anxious to cast doubt on the emotional validity of the novel (*Ibid.*, p. 438). This

is a sickness of our time.

7. H. M. Daleski, *Thomas Hardy and the Paradoxes of Love* (Columbia MO, 1997), p. 159. Ellen Rooney more plausibly finds that this, like all the other signals in the text which might settle the issue by declaring there either had or had not been a rape, is inconclusive. See Ellen Rooney, "Tess and the Subject of Sexual Violence: Reading, Rape, Seduction" in *Tess of the d'Urbervilles*, ed. Riquelme, pp. 467-72. But she exaggerates the extent to which Hardy is even attempting to settle the question of seduction versus rape. The result is her appropriation as her own discovery of Hardy's creative refusal to allow these terms to govern the situation of the novel.

8. J. Hillis Miller, *Fiction and Repetition* (Cambridge MA, 1982), pp. 122-4.

9. Paul J. Green, "Tess, Memory, and Trauma. (unpublished manuscript). See also Jean Brooks, *Thomas Hardy: The Poetic Structure* (Ithaca NY, 1971), p. 239: "Tess's association with blood is often neutral, or at least ambivalent."

10. A far more sensitive account of the color red in *Tess* is given by Tony Tanner, "Colour and Movement in Hardy's *Tess of the d'Urbervilles*", in *Thomas Hardy's Tess of the d'Urbervilles: Modern Critical Interpretations*, ed. Harold Bloom (New York, 1987), pp. 9-23. But for reasons that I think will be evident, I do not find it very convincing.

11. Thomas M. Alexander, *John Dewey's Theory of Art, Experience and Nature: Horizons of Feeling* (Albany NY, 1987), pp. 68-118.

12. Bruce Wilshire, "Body-Mind and Subconsciousness: Tragedy in Dewey's Life and Work." In *Philosophy and the Reconstruction of Culture: Pragmatic Essays After Dewey*, ed. John J. Stuhr (Albany NY, 1993), pp. 257-72. Charlene Haddock Seigfried introduces the term and quotes its definition in her feminist reconstruction of Dewey's theory of experience, although she does not go on to make further use of it. See Seigfried, *Pragmatism and Feminism: Reweaving the Social Fabric* (Chicago, 1996), p. 162.

13. Elaine Scarry, "Work and Body in Hardy and Other Nineteenth Century Novelists," *Representations* 3 (1983), p. 90.

14. Peter Brooks, *Reading For The Plot: Design and Intention in Narrative* (Oxford, 1986), p. 144. See also Jules David Law, "Sleeping Figures: Hardy, History, and the Gendered Body," *ELH* 65 (1998), p. 250. "[W]ithin the terms established by the novel, Tess's body is genuinely regarded as a vehicle for historical meaning and a site for the expression of historical changes…" Also, *Ibid.*, p. 254: Hardy in his later novels "moves toward the figure of the individual human body proper as he struggles to represent social crises."

15. Elliot B. Gose, Jr., "Psychic Evolution: Darwinism and Initiation in *Tess of the d'Urbervilles*," in *Tess of the d'Urbervilles*, 3rd edition., ed. Scott Elledge (New York, 1991), p. 427.

16. John Bayley, *An Essay on Hardy,* (Cambridge, 1978), p. 190.

17. Margaret R. Higonnet, "A Woman's Story: Tess and the Problem of Voice," in *The Sense of Sex*, ed. Higonnet, p. 17.

18. John Dewey, "Foreword to Henry Schaefer-Simmern's *The Unfolding of Artistic Activity*" in *The Later Works,* vol. 15, ed. Jo Ann Boydston (Carbondale IL, 1989), p. 315.

19. Jean Brooks, *Thomas Hardy: the Poetic Structure*, p. 239.

20. Tim Dolin, "Notes," in *Tess of the d'Urbervilles*, ed. Dolin (London, 1998), p. 414.

21. Kristin Brady, "Tess and Alec: Rape or Seduction," *Thomas Hardy Annual* 4 (1986), 127-47.

22. James Kincaid, writing as late as 1992, discounts the specific sexual aspects of Tess, even her breasts, whether in this scene or anywhere else in the novel. He maintains that she is not a character at all, but only a "form," a phantasmal creation for the exercise of sadism by both Alec and Angel—who also are not characters. To his credit, however, Kincaid is unable to maintain this abstracting of character when he encounters the agony Tess goes through later on with Angel: "there is nothing imaginary about the pain Tess feels on her honeymoon..." See James Kincaid, *Child-Loving: The Erotic Child and Victorian Culture* (New York, 1992), pp. 327, 332. But in an endnote, Kincaid again asserts that Tess, Angel and Alec are not to be regarded as characters: they are instead "vehicles for setting up intricate and various structures of sexual expression and responsiveness" (*Ibid.*, p. 340). I wonder if Kincaid's need to fight against experiencing the novel as a story of human characters in their living experiences is what reduces the scope of his response to the single factor of sadism.

23. I find no warrant for saying that trying to get Alec to marry her was her only reason for staying on, as have Barnard J. Paris and Peter J. Casagrande. See Paris, "Experiences of Tess," in *The Victorian Experience*, ed. Richard A. Levine (Athens GA, 1976), p. 221; Casagrande, *Tess of the d'Urbervilles: Unorthodox Beauty* (New York, 1982), p. 29. Since neither of these critics deal seriously with the sexual aspects of the novel, it is understandable that they would see no other motive.

24. Stephen C. Pepper, *World Hypotheses: A Study in Evidence* (Berkeley, 1961), p. 240.

25. Philip Jackson, *John Dewey and the Lessons of Art* (New Haven CT, 1998),	p. 35.

Chapter Three

1. The significance of this extraordinary declaration by Hardy was first pointed out

by Wayne Burns, in *"The Woodlanders* As Love-Story," *Recovering Literature* 5:3 (1976), pp. 21-51.

The statement occurs in the context of the long opening sentence:

> In the present novel, as in one or two others of this series which involve the question of matrimonial divergence, the immortal puzzle—given the man and woman, how to find a basis for their sexual relation—is left where it stood; and it is tacitly assumed for the purposes of the story that no doubt of the depravity of the erratic heart who feels some second person to be better suited to his or her tastes than the one with whom he has contracted to love, enters the head of the reader or writer for a moment.

See Hardy, *The Woodlanders*, ed. Dale Kramer (Oxford, 1985), p. 25

Incredibly, Gail Cunningham considers the statement as a segment of Hardy's writing that "seems both inept and somewhat cowardly." Cunningham, *The New Woman and the Victorian Novel* (London, 1978), pp. 89-90.

2. Michel Serres, *The Natural Contract* (Ann Arbor MI, 1995), p. 39.

3. J. Hillis Miller, *Thomas Hardy: Distance and Desire* (Cambridge MA, 1970), p. 111.

4. Joanna Frueh, *Erotic Faculties* (Berkeley, 1996), p. 45.

5. John Dewey, "Context and Thought," *The Later Works*, vol. 6, ed. Jo Ann Boydston (Carbondale IL, 1985), pp. 3-21.

6. Paul Turner, *The Life of Thomas Hardy: A Critical Biography* (Oxford, 1998), pp. 124-5.

7. Rosemarie Morgan, *Women and Sexuality in the Novels of Thomas Hardy* (London, 1988), p. 88.

8. Gillian Beer, *Darwin's Plots: Evolutionary Narrative in Darwin, George Eliot and Nineteenth Century Fiction* (London, 1983), p. 489. See also John Hughes, *"Ecstatic Sound": Music and Individuality in the Works of Thomas Hardy* (Aldershot UK, 2001), p. 32: "The mixing of waves of colour and the waves of sound is merely one more example of how music for Hardy overcomes the distinctions of things, creating paradoxical effects of indetermination, in whose passages there is no diminishment of individuality, but on the contrary, a fuller expression of it."

9. Stephen C. Pepper, *Aesthetic Quality: A Contextualistic Theory of Beauty* (New York, 1937), pp. 236-37.

10. Dorothy Tennov, *Love and Limerance: The Experience of Being in Love* (New

York, 1979), pp. 13-15.

11. Ian Gregor, *The Great Web: The Form of Hardy's Major Fiction* (London, 1974), p. 199.

Chapter Four

1. See Stephen C. Pepper, "Emotional Distance in Art," *Journal of Aesthetics and Art Criticism* 4 (1946), pp. 235-9. For a comparable position by a recent aesthetician, see Jenefer Robinson's appreciative critique of Nelson Goodman's *The Languages of Art*. The grief and despair that are expressed in *Anna Karenina*, Robinson maintains, call for our understanding of the way such emotions can be "expressed in life as well as in literature." See Robinson, *"Languages of Art* at the Turn of the Century," *Journal of Aesthetics and Art Criticism* 58 (2000), p. 217. Goodman, like most analytic philosophers, does not meet this challenge.

2. Wilhelm Reich, *The Function of the Orgasm: Sex-Economic Problems of Biological Energy*, translated by Theodore P. Wolfe (Cleveland, 1971), pp. 114-30.

3. Nancy Barrineau, "Explanatory Notes," *Tess of the d'Urbervilles*, ed. Juliet Grindle and Simon Gattrell, (Oxford, 1983), p. 395.

4. Ernest Sutherland Bates, editor, *The Bible: Designed To Be Read as Living Literature* (New York, 1936), p. 1184.

5. Thomas Hardy, *The Literary Notes of Thomas Hardy*, vol. 1, ed. Lennart A. Björk (Goteborg, 1974), p.263.

6. Lennart Björk, *Psychological Vision and Social Criticism in the Novels of Thomas Hardy* (Stockholm, 1987), pp. 139-40.

7. Hardy, as quoted in Björk, *Psychological Vision*, p. 131.

8. Hardy, *Tess of the d'Urbervilles,* edited by Scott Elledge ((New York, 1991), p. 91n. (Editor's note).

9. Patricia Ingham, *Thomas Hardy: Feminist Readings* (Hemel Hempstead, 1989), p. 73.

10. The experience is occluded by Kaja Silverman, who, in her pursuit of a feminist-Lacanian reading, takes note only of the male identity of the god, and attributes to this figure an aspect of "superiority" over the "spectacle." See Silverman, "History, Figuration, and Female Subjectivity in *Tess of the d'Urbervilles,"* *Novel: A Forum on Fiction* 18 (1984), p. 24. Hardy's highly wrought and emotionally powerful description of Tess doing the work of binding (93-4) is tendentiously reduced by Silverman to "an exhaustive visual interrogation and a historical overview" (*Ibid.*). Nothing in the passage is quoted or discussed. In this complaint about Hardy's use of

the male gaze, Silverman seems unaware of her own exerting of total control over the text.

11. Penny Boumelha , *Thomas Hardy and Women: Sexual Ideology and Narrative Form* (Brighton UK, 1982), p. 120.

12. Diane Ackerman, *A Natural History of the Senses* (New York, 1990), pp. 232-3. In fact, this method now has come into wide use.

13. See Tim Dolin, "Notes," *Tess of the d'Urbervilles* (London, 1998), p. 432.

14. The power of this passage is evident in its ability to nearly overcome the critical framework or "stencil" (*AE* 59) of Ellen Rooney, a feminist critic whose compassion for Tess is never in doubt: Rooney admits that here "Hardy comes close to representing Tess as a desiring rather than only a desired/desirable subject." "Tess as the Subject of Sexual Violence: Reading, Rape, Seduction," in *Tess of the d'Urbervilles*, ed. John Paul Riquelme (Boston, 1998), p. 480. For Rooney, Tess's breakdown into "almost a terror of ecstasy" feels like "terrified subjection to external force" (*Ibid.*, p. 481). Rooney is assuming that anything Tess feels to be overwhelming is not her own feeling but a force located outside of her own Body-Mind.

15. Kathleen Blake, "Pure Tess: Hardy on Knowing a Woman," in *Critical Essays on Thomas Hardy*, ed. Dale Kramer (Boston, 1990), p. 95.

16. Bernard J. Paris, "Experiences of Thomas Hardy," in *The Victorian Experience*, ed. Richard A. Levine (Athens GA, 1976), pp. 203-37.

17. In my much earlier experiences of this novel, I was foolish enough to take this declaration, "There was hardly a touch of earth in her love for Clare" as Hardy's misunderstanding of his own character. I thought I was trusting "the tale not the teller," as D. H. Lawrence advised. Actually I was treating Hardy as if he lacked a basic understanding of his character, and I had been failing to realize how much the sentence captures Tess's own extremity of rationalization. See Efron, "The Tale, the Teller, and Sexuality in *Tess of the d'Urbervilles*," *Paunch* (Feb., 1967) no. 28, p. 63.

18. See Tony Tanner, "Colour and Movement in Hardy's *Tess of the d'Urbervilles*, in *Thomas Hardy's Tess of the d'Urbervilles: Modern Essays in Interpretation*, ed. Harold Bloom (New York, 1987), p. 10. By ignoring context, Tanner frequently forces the textual evidence to support his conclusion that Nature for Hardy provides nothing but a pessimistic outlook for human beings. Tanner plays down the societal origins of Tess's suffering to such an extent that he can regard her guilt for simply living in her own sexual body, her "fleshly tabernacle," as evidence that nature, in Hardy's novel, "turns against itself" (*Ibid.*, p. 20).

19. Susan David Bernstein, "Confessing and Editing: The Politics of Purity in Hardy's *Tess*," in *Virginity, Sexuality and Textuality in Victorian Literature*, ed. Lloyd Davis (Albany NY, 1993), pp. 176-77.

20. *Ibid.*, p. 176.

21. Ellen Rooney, who insists that Hardy is afraid to allow an account of Tess's own woman's desire concerning the initial sex between Alec and Tess, scoffs at the value of this information. Indeed she claims that Hardy is virtually laughing at how his readers are excluded from knowledge here. She does not report the important point that Tess's confession included "re-assertions and secondary explanations." See Rooney, "Tess as the Subject of Sexual Violence," pp. 472-3. To ignore this segment, however, seriously reduces the scope of Hardy's passage.

22. E. M. Forster, *Aspects of the Novel* (New York, 1927), p. 87.

23. Joseph Allen Boone, *Tradition Counter Tradition: Love and the Form of Fiction* (Chicago, 1987), p. 110.

24. D. H. Lawrence, *Study of Thomas Hardy and Other Essays*, ed. Bruce Steele (Cambridge UK, 1985), p. 97.

25. Rosemary Sumner, *Thomas Hardy: Psychological Novelist* (New York, 1981), p. 142. A similar point is made by Desmond Hawkins, *Thomas Hardy: Novelist and Poet* (Newton Abbot UK, 1976), p. 132.

26. Michael Irwin, "Readings of Melodrama" in *Reading the Victorian Novel: Detail Into Form* (New York, 1980), pp. 5-11. That Angel's love for Tess comes through in his sleepwalking was perceived by Richard Carpenter, *Thomas Hardy* (New York, 1964), p. 130. I am much in debt for my own understanding of the scene to John Herold, "'Winking Toads' and "Beatific Intervals': From Contextualism to a Pluralistic Reading of *Tess of the d'Urbervilles*" (unpublished paper, 1990). Joseph Warren Beach wrote in 1922 that "Angel's sleep-walking tenderness is a sign of [his] relenting." See Beach, *The Technique of Thomas Hardy* (New York, 1962), p. 191.

27. Arthur Efron, "Perspectivism and the Nature of Fiction: *Don Quixote* and Borges," *Thought* 50 (1975), pp. 148-75; "The Novel from the Western World: An Instrument for the Criticism of Civilizations," *Works & Days* 3 (1985), pp. 29-52.

28. Sully-Prudhomme won the Nobel Prize for Literature in 1900, but has been so forgotten that I doubt his name means a thing to readers of *Tess*. I have never run across any of his writings nor any other references to him. As Norman Page concludes, after long experience in reading Hardy, some of Hardy's allusions fail to function in their role of enriching the reading. See Norman Page, "Art and Aesthetics," in *The Cambridge Companion to Thomas Hardy*, ed. Dale Kramer (Cambridge, 1999), pp. 42-3. The reader who wants to understand the novels not only has to learn to respond to those allusions that are meaningful, but to strain out those that are not. Those allusions that do have a function can add a great deal to the experience.

Chapter Five

1. Harold Orel , ed. *Thomas Hardy's Personal Writings* (Lawrence KS, 1966), p. 114.

2. Penny Boumelha, *Thomas Hardy and Women: Sexual Ideology and Narrative Form* (Brighton, Sussex, 1982), pp. 124-25.

3. See A. D. Harvey's *Sex in Georgian England: Attitudes and Prejudices from the 1720s to 1820s* (New York, 1994), pp. 38-53, which provides an illuminating earlier historical background to this denial of feminine desire (*Ibid.*, pp. 38-53). Harvey also offers a theory for the increased emphasis on women's virginity that arose in tandem with such denial. He points out that in Shakespeare's *Measure for Measure*, Isabella, a celibate woman who is planning to become a nun, is threatened with sexual violation, but is never described as one whose virginity is endangered. It is her whole body that is at risk, but it is a body still implicitly capable of female desire. In later times in England, when women were not credited with more than a minute degree of sexual desire, the male act of taking a woman's virginity came to be regarded as the only point of erotic gratification. From a Deweyan perspective this problem is one of quality. A narrow assumption about female sexuality, like the one Harvey discusses, may help to explain why most critics have paid little attention to the qualitative aspect of Tess's sexual experiences. There are indications in the text of what those qualities might have been, and for a reader approaching the novel freshly today, there is every reason to take note.

4. Margaret R. Higonnet, "A Woman's Story: Tess and the Problem of Voice," in *The Sense of Sex: Feminist Perspectives on Hardy,* ed. Higonnet (Urbana IL, 1993), p. 22.

5. Marjorie Garson, *Hardy's Fables of Integrity: Woman, Body, Text* (Oxford, 1991), pp. 137-8.

6. Thomas Hardy, *Two on a Tower* (London, 1975), chapter 1. On Hardy's sexual writing, note as well the 14-page section of his early novel, *Desperate Remedies* (London, 1974; originally published 1871) where a lesbian attraction seems to be strongly denoted. It is impossible to say whether Hardy intended this effect, or if he was aware of it (*Ibid.*, pp. 56-70).

7. Ellen Rooney, "Tess as the Subject of Sexual Violence: Reading, Rape, Seduction," in *Tess of the d'Urbervilles*, ed. John Paul Riquelme (Boston, 1998), p. 475.

8. Despite the shifting quality of my "perceptive series" of readings of *Tess*, this perception of the relationship as the effective context of the rape issue has been reaffirmed steadily over four decades. I had a realization of it as early as my first (unpublished) paper on *Tess* in 1961, and wrote of it in my *Paunch* article. See Arthur Efron, "The Tale, the Teller and Sexuality in *Tess of the d'Urbervilles,*" *Paunch* (1967) no. 28, pp. 55-80. Many further readings and teachings of the novel have come back to this same conclusion. It is also the view of the late Kristin Brady in her fine but not often quoted article on this

problem: "Hardy de-emphasizes the actual loss of virginity and draws the reader's attention to the issue that most concerns Tess herself: not the manner of the initial penetration but the nature of the whole sexual relationship, from its beginning to its end." See Kristen Brady, "Tess and Alec: Rape or Seduction?" *Thomas Hardy Annual* 4 (1986), p. 133.

9. Jean-Luc Godard as quoted by Phillip Lopate, "'Breathless' Turns 40, Its Youthful Impudence Intact," *New York Times*, 16 Jan. 2000. See William Greenslade, "Rediscovering Thomas Hardy's 'Facts' Notebook," in *The Achievement of Thomas Hardy*, ed. Phillip Mallett (London, 2000), pp.174-5.

10. The passage is often passed by, but it has drawn at least two challenging interpretations that I find impossible to reconcile with the context. Rosemarie Morgan disposes of the discomfort that Tess's speech might bring by interpreting it as a deliberately staged parody on Tess's part of female submission, designed to confound Alec. See Morgan, *Women and Sexuality in the Novels of Thomas Hardy* (London, 1988), p. 97. This has never occurred to me in my own many readings. The reason undoubtedly is that the context of the passage shows that Tess's outburst does not ruffle Alec; indeed he soon comes back at her with a threat to once again be her "master." He accompanies this threat with physically shaking her, "so that she shook under his grasp" (321). This happens at a time when her limbs had already been trembling from the effects of her exhausting work. Her knees had been "trembling so wretchedly with the shaking of the machine that she could scarcely walk" (317). The unfortunate effect of Morgan's reading of Tess's character is her construction of a Tess so vibrantly sexual that she is nearly immune to weakness, conflict or doubt, let alone to irrational thinking. It makes for a total denial of the disturbing quality of the passage.

A more complex but also reductive effect is implicit in the reading by Wayne Burns, who takes the passage as evidence of Tess's shocking recognition of her inability to control her sexual passion in accordance with her moral beliefs. See Wayne Burns, *The Flesh and the Spirit in Seven Hardy Novels* (Alpine CA, 2002), p. 137. This hardly accords with the image of the bird about to have its neck twisted, and indeed Burns does not deal with that wording. If it were a matter of Tess realizing that she is trapped by her own conflicted sexuality, as Burns maintains, then she would not be referring to someone else, namely Alec, as the one who will "punish me!" If she were speaking in character at all, she would see herself as her own victim, and punish herself accordingly.

11. Hardy, *Tess of the d'Urbervilles*, ed. Juliet Grindle and Simon Gatrell (Oxford, 1983), p. 453.

12. I should think that those critical readers who are sure that Hardy has refused to allow Tess to express her own desire, or to tell her own story, would be most interested in this letter. Higonnet, who has made a special study of the problem of Tess's voice and the difficulty of telling her story, describes the letter as "passionate and eloquent," and as giving Tess's voice a "substantiality" that it could never have had when it was only presented as oral, but fails to quote or discuss any of the letter's contents. See Higonnet "A Woman's Story" p. 23. In her 1998 "Introduction" to *Tess*, however, Higonnet does quote and discuss one segment of the letter, but now emphasizes its value in understanding

Hardy's highly advanced sense of character, rather than its significance as Tess's voice. See Higonnet, "Introduction," *Tess of the d'Urbervilles* (London, 1998), p. xxiii. Boumelha claims that "Tess is most herself—and that is, most woman—at points where she is dumb and semi-conscious" See Penny Boumelha, *Thomas Hardy and Women*, p. 122. But Boumelha does not discuss the letter, which is patently neither. Rooney also says nothing about it, nor do either of them discuss Tess's other letters. The same over-looking occurs in Kaja Silverman's article, and may help her to support her belief that the masculine gaze "never" lets up. See Silverman, "History, Figuration and Female Subjectivity in *Tess of the d'Urbervilles*," *Novel* 18 (1984), pp. 7, 23. These unconscionable omissions seem to me evidence of the disastrous results for experiencing the novel that stem from the cultivation of distrust and contempt for Hardy as a masculine narrator. Even when he creates passages in which Tess's own voice is rendered, he is not considered worth taking seriously. John Goode, however, understands that Tess's letters to Angel are integral to the novel's development of her voice, and argues that in this part of the novel, her voice is not to be explained as simply a function of social determinism. See Goode, *Hardy: The Offensive Truth* (Oxford, 1988), pp. 130-31. Higonnet basically agrees with this analysis, but distances the experience; for her, the late location and the inclusion into the text of Tess's letters "supports the illusion that Tess has developed…into an articulate subject…" Higonnet, "A Woman's Story," p. 23.

13. Higonnet, "Introduction," p. xxiii.

14. Peter McInerney, "Conceptions of Persons and Persons Through Time," *American Philosophical Review* 37 (2000), pp. 121-33.

15. Vincent M. Colapietro, "Embodied, Encultured Agents," in *Dewey Reconfigured: Essays in Deweyan Pragmatism*, ed. Casey Haskins and David I. Seiple (Albany NY, 1999), p. 69.

16. Merryn Williams and Raymond Williams, "Hardy and Social Class," in *Tess of the d'Urbervilles,* ed. Peter Widdowson (New York, 1993), pp. 25-27.

17. Nancy Barrineau, "Explanatory Notes," *Tess of the d'Urbervilles* (Oxford, 1998), p. 406.

18. *Ibid.*, p. 453.

19. Edward Bullough, "'Psychical Distance' as a Factor in Art as an Esthetic Principle," in *A Modern Book of Aesthetics*, ed. Melvin M. Rader (New York, 1935), p. 325.

20. See Deborah Knight, "Why We Enjoy Condemning Sentimentality: A Meta-Aesthetic Perspective," *Journal of Aesthetics and Art Criticism* 57 (1999), pp. 411-20. I think once more of Dewey's great phrase, "fear of what life may bring forth" (*AE* 28).

21. Wayne Burns, *The Flesh and the Spirit in Seven Hardy Novels*, p. 125.

22. John Dewey and James H. Tufts, *Ethics. The Later* Works, vol. 7, ed. Jo Ann Boydston (Carbondale IL, 1985), p. 191.

Chapter Six

1. Robert C. Schweik has shown that some interpretations at this point presume a quality of rationality that is completely at odds with the emotional tone of Tess's utterance. See Schweik, "Less Than Faithfully Presented: Fictions in Modern Commentaries on Hardy's *Tess of the d'Urbervilles*," in *Reading Thomas Hardy*, ed. Charles P.C. Pettit (New York, 1998), pp. 49-52.

2. See Anna Fels, "Mind Fills the Need to Explain," *New York Times*, 17 Dec. 2002. As Fels shows, such "explanation" can occur without benefit of surgical intervention in the minds of people confronted with a perception of their own action that would otherwise be unaccountable.

3. See Hardy, *Tess of the d'Urbervilles*, ed. Juliet Grindle and Simon Gatrell (Oxford, 1983), p. 533.

4. See Peter Widdowson, editor, *Tess of the d'Urbervilles* (New York, 1993), pp. 2, 17-18. (New Casebooks)

5. See Widdowson, *Ibid*. In his large compilation of Hardy's poetry, Widdowson has grouped about 50 of Hardy's poems under the heading of "The Male Gaze." See his edition, *Thomas Hardy: Selected Poetry and Non-Fictional Prose* (New York, 1997), pp. 136-185. The effects of this gaze, Widdowson declares, are "prurient" or "pathetic." He insists that "scopophilia is a fundamental drive and discourse" in Hardy's work, *Ibid.*, p. xxix. Even if this is an accurate observation (I have reservations about it but cannot discuss them here), it can all too easily serve to place the reader in a position of diagnostic supremacy. Such a reader is far removed from actively risking the experience of the poems and novels. The fact that many Hardy poems "celebrate women's sexuality and strength," as Widdowson belatedly mentions (*Ibid.*, p. 372), would be lost under the critic's stencil.

6. Joanna Frueh, *Erotic Faculties* (Berkeley, 1996), pp. 7-8.

7. See Bernard J. Paris, "'A Confusion of Many Standards': Conflicting Value Systems in *Tess of the d'Urbervilles*," *Nineteenth Century Fiction* 24 (1969), pp. 70-1; Wayne Burns, *The Flesh and the Spirit in Seven Hardy Novels* (Alpine CA, 2002), p. 130.

8. My experience on this point differs from that of H. M. Daleski. Daleski is one of the few critics to discuss Angel's change, and one of the few who shows that he has thought seriously about the sexual quality of the relationships in the novel. But here I believe he allows metaphors of completion to direct his experience: "For Angel...the wheel has come full circle in the rhythm of change..." Angel now shows "a willingness and readiness to let go." H. M. Daleski, *Thomas Hardy and the Paradoxes of Love* (Columbia

MO, 1997), p. 178.

9. Thomas Hardy, as quoted in *Tess of the d'Urbervilles*, ed. Scott Elledge (New York, 1991), p. 388.

10. Hardy, *Ibid.*

11. Thomas M. Alexander locates the crucial passage in *Art as Experience* (*AE* 197) where this position is stated. See Alexander, *John Dewey's Theory of Art, Experience and Nature* (Albany NY, 1987), p 254.

12. See the map provided by Tim Dolin, "Notes," *Tess of the d'Urbervilles*, ed. Dolin (London, 1998), p. 471.

13. Thomas Hardy as quoted in *Tess of the d'Urbervilles*, ed. Elledge, p. 389, my emphasis.

14. Hardy, "Shall Stonehenge Go?" in *Thomas Hardy's Personal Writings,* ed. Harold Orel (Lawrence KS, 1966), p. 196.

15. John Goode, *Thomas Hardy: The Offensive Truth* (Oxford, 1988), p. 137.

16. Wayne Burns, "The Panzaic Principle in Hardy's *Tess of the d'Urbervilles*," *Recovering Literature* 1 (1972), p. 38-40.

17. Sigmund Freud, "The Taboo of Virginity," *Standard Edition of the Complete Psychological Works*, vol. 11 (London, 1953-74), pp. 181-208.

18. Burns, "The Panzaic Principle in Hardy's *Tess*," *Recovering Literature* 1 (1972), p. 39. John Goode is definite: the Deceased Wife's Sisters Act is exactly Hardy's target. See Goode, *Thomas Hardy: The Offensive Truth*, p. 137.

19. Eleanor Bron [Reading], *Tess of the d'Urbervilles*, abridged audio version (London, 1994).

20. See Lisa Sternlieb, "'Three Leahs to Get One Rachel': Redundant Women in *Tess of the d'Urbervilles*," *Dickens Studies Annual: Essays on Victorian Fiction* 29 (2000), p. 361.

21. The only other one, "the steepled city of Melchester," barely enters into the reading experience. (Sandbourne where Alec lodges with Tess is hardly a city.) When Angel and Tess are running from the law, they have to slink through Melchester at night, afraid to even step on the pavement where their tread might cause an echo. They are unable to take notice of its "graceful pile of cathedral architecture" (378).

22. Hardy's word-choice of "president" to stand for Zeus is also the choice followed by David Grene, in his distinguished translation of Aeschylus's tragedy. At this juncture in the play, Prometheus is speaking with bitter irony as he swears that he will give no help to "this president of the Blessed" when Zeus needs to fend off the plot by which he will finally be dethroned. Aeschylus, "Prometheus Bound," trans. David Grene, *Aeschylus II* (Chicago, 1956), p. 145.

23. Dolin, "Notes," p. 464. In contrast to my own experiencing, Ian Gregor found the allusion to Milton and every word of the final description of Angel and Liza-Lu replete with felt meaning. Gregor's involvement with the novel went far beyond his use of a limiting "stencil." I am by no means claiming that my experience of this passage is superior to his, only that it is different. The aim of pragmatist criticism is never the elimination of all differences among the readers of a literary work. See Gregor, *The Great Web: The Form of Hardy's Fiction* (London, 1974), p. 196.

24. Wilhelm Reich, *The Function of the Orgasm*, trans. Theodore P. Wolfe (Cleveland, 1971), p. xix.

25. Here we may recall the view of Lascelles Abercrombie, in one of the earliest critical studies of Hardy: *Tess* as well as *Jude* burn with so strong a spirit of revolt against the evils they depict that they cannot be considered pessimistic. See Abercrombie, *Thomas Hardy: A Critical Study* (London, 1912), p. 142.

Chapter Seven

1. Kathleen Blake, "Pure Tess: Hardy on Knowing a Woman,"in *Critical Essays on Thomas Hardy*, ed. by Dale Kramer (Boston, 1990), p. 216. See also Rebecca Stott, "'Something More to Be Said': Hardy's *Tess*," in *The Fabrication of the Late-Victorian Femme Fatal: The Kiss of Death* (Houndmills, 1992), p. 185: "...any representation of woman (no matter how well-intentioned) enacts a kind of textual exploitation by taking Woman as its text and by inscribing its 'coarse pattern' upon her, reducing her to a passive object denied subjectivity."

2. Irving Howe, *Thomas Hardy* (New York, 1967).

3. J. Hillis Miller, "Howe on Hardy's Art," *Novel: A Forum on Fiction* 2 (1969), pp. 272-7.

4. J. Hillis Miller, *Ibid.*

5. Arthur Efron, "Perspectivism and the Nature of Fiction: *Don Quixote* and Borges," *Thought* 50 (1975), pp. 148-75; Arthur Efron, " The Novel From the Western World: An Instrument for the Criticism of Civilizations," *Works and Days* 3 (1985), pp. 29-52.

6. J.Hillis Miller, *Fiction and Repetition: Seven English Novels*, (Cambridge MA, 1982), p. 119.

7. Michael Millgate, *Thomas Hardy: A Biography* (New York, 1982), pp. 294-5.

8. Paul Turner, *The Life of Thomas Hardy: A Critical Biography* (Oxford, 1998), Plate 16.

9. Thomas Hardy, *The Collected Letters*, vol. 1, ed. Richard Little Purdy and Michael Millgate (Oxford, 1978), pp. 245-6.

10. Thomas Hardy, *The Life and Work of Thomas Hardy,* ed. Michael Millgate (London, 1984), p. 182.

11. Prov. 31:30.

12. Joanna Frueh, *Erotic Faculties* (Berkeley, 1996), p. 152.

13. W. Eugene Davis, *"Tess of the d'Urbervilles*: Some Ambiguities About a Pure Woman," *Nineteenth Century Fiction* 2 (1968), p. 399.

14. I say 76 years, not 77, since the statement as we now have it appears in the 1892 *Tess*, not in 1891. In 1950, and thus well before Davis, Desmond Hawkins had also referred to Tess having been "stirred to a confused surrender." But Hawkins barely alluded to the issue. See Hawkins, *Hardy the Novelist* (Newman Abbot UK, 1950) p. 81. In an article preceding Davis's by a few years, Elliot B. Gose, Jr. referred to some of the same passages in this part of the novel, and also noted that Tess's involvement with Alec was not altogether involuntary. See Gose, "Psychic Evolution: Darwinism and Initiation in *Tess of the d'Urbervilles*," in *Tess of the d'Urbervilles* ed. Elledge, p. 426. A clear recognition that Tess could not have been completely unwilling in her sex with Alec during the weeks that she stayed on with him was published in 1971, in a small book on *Tess* designed for English high school students. See Juliet McLauchlan, *Tess of the d'Urbervilles (Thomas Hardy)* (Oxford, 1971), pp. 39-40. McLauchlan, however, does not try to connect this perception with the term "pure woman."

15. Davis, *"Tess...*Some Ambiguities," p. 401.

16. Laura Claridge, "Tess: A Less Than Pure Woman Ambivalently Presented," in *Tess of the d'Urbervilles*, ed. Peter Widdowson (New York, 1993), p. 67, emphasis Claridge's.

17. *Ibid.*, pp. 68-77.

18. Thomas Hardy, *Collected Letters*. Vol. 1. p. 254.

19. See Peter Widdowson's introduction to *Tess of the d'Urbervilles* (New York, 1993), p. 15. (New Casebook).

20. Mona Caird, "The Morality of Marriage," *Fortnightly Review* 53 (1890), pp. 310-30.

21. *Ibid.*, p. 329.

22. See Rosemarie Morgan, *Women and Sexuality in the Novels of Thomas Hardy* (London, 1988), p. 167.

23. John Goode, *Thomas Hardy: The Offensive Truth* (Oxford, 1988), p. 118.

24. Mona Caird, as quoted in John Goode, *Thomas Hardy: The Offensive Truth*, p. 118.

25. Compare H. M. Daleski, *Hardy and the Paradoxes of Love* (Columbia MO, 1997), pp. 156-57, who does regard this as erotically stimulating for Tess. Daleski seems to be considering the language without taking into account the context of her experience.

26. See J. Hillis Miller, *Thomas Hardy: Distance and Desire* (Cambridge MA, 1970); Frank R. Giordano, Jr., "'I'd Have My Life Unbe': Hardy's Self-Destructive Characters* (University AL, 1984).

27. Bruce Johnson, "The Perfection of Species and Hardy's *Tess*," in *Thomas Hardy's Tess: Modern Critical Perspectives*, ed. Harold Bloom (New York, 1987), p. 42.

28. John Goode, *Thomas Hardy: The Offensive Truth*, p. 126.

29. These issues are well brought out by Wayne Burns, *The Flesh and the Spirit in Seven Hardy Novels* (Alpine CA, 2002), pp. 131-3.

30. In a sensitive reading of how this scene may be experienced, John Goode comments on the expressive power of Tess's speaking voice, which he attributes not to what she says but to her having an impact that does not depend on language. Goode finds that here, for once, the male gaze which Angel directs upon Tess is fully "reciprocated" by her own, return gaze. Tess's "Yes, O yes, yes!" is ignored, however, apparently because Goode needs to warn sternly against any "privatized privileging of experience (by which we could possess 'Tess' by an act of love)." See Goode, *Thomas Hardy: The Offensive Truth*, pp. 132-33.

31. Thomas Hardy, "The Tree of Knowledge," in *Thomas Hardy's Personal Writings,* ed. Harold Orel (Lawrence KS, 1966), p. 249.

32. Arnold Kettle, "Introduction," Thomas Hardy, *Tess of the d'Urbervilles* (New York, 1966), p. xvii.

33. Raymond Williams, "Love and Work," in *Tess of the d'Urbervilles*, ed. Elledge , p. 471.

34. Gillian Beer, *Darwin's Plots: Evolutionary Narrative in Darwin, George Eliot and Nineteenth Century Fiction* (London, 1983), p. 258.

35. John Paul Riquelme, "Echoic Language, Uncertainty and Freedom in *Tess of the d'Urbervilles*," in *Tess of the d'Urbervilles*, ed. Riquelme (Boston, 1998), p. 520.

36. Harvey Curtis Webster, *On a Darkling Plain: The Art and Thought of Thomas Hardy* (Chicago, 1947), pp. 77, 178.

37. Hardy, as quoted by Lennart Björk, *Psychological Vision and Social Criticism in the Novels of Thomas Hardy* (Stockholm, 1986), p. 113.

38. William Archer, *Real Conversations* (London, 1904), p. 47.

39. Archer, *Ibid.*

40. See Björk, *Psychological Vision*, pp. 110-15.

41. Björk, *Ibid.*, p. 111.

42. John Dewey, *Human Nature and Conduct. The Middle Works*, vol. 14, ed. Jo Ann Boydston (Carbondale IL, 1981), p. 114.

43. *Ibid.*

44. Hardy, *The Life and Work,* ed. Michael Millage, p. 158.

45. Evidences of Darwin's gender bias are the focus of feminist interpretations of Darwin's influence on Victorian fiction. See for example Patricia Murphy, *Time is of the Essence: Temporality, Gender, and the New Woman* (Albany NY, 2000), pp. 25-6. But as Gillian Beer has recognized, in *The Descent of Man*, men and women became Darwin's "problem." Sexual choice is not understandable as a straightforward matter of natural selection. See Beer, *Darwin's Plots: Evolutionary Narrative in Darwin, George Eliot and Nineteenth Century Fiction* (London, 1983), p. 10.

46. Geoffrey F. Miller, *The Mating Mind: How Sexual Choice Shaped the Evolution of Human Nature* (New York, 2000), pp. 36-37. See also Natalie Angier, "Author Offers Theory on Gray Matter of Love," *New York Times*, 30 May 2000.

47. For Hardy's creative, and not simply pessimistic, use of Darwin in dealing with Tess, see Roger Robinson, "Hardy and Darwin," in *Thomas Hardy: The Writer and his Background*, ed. Norman Page (New York, 1980), pp. 128-50. See also Roger Ebbatson, *The Evolutionary Self: Hardy, Forster, Lawrence* (Brighton, 1982), p. 27; William Greenslade, *Degeneration, Culture and the Novel 1880-1940* (Cambridge UK, 1994), pp. 151-81; and Kevin Padian, "'A Daughter of the Soil': Themes of Deep Time and Evolution in Thomas Hardy's *Tess of the d'Urbervilles*," *Thomas Hardy Journal* 13 (1997), pp. 65-

81.

48. See Robert C. Schweik, "Moral Perspective in *Tess of the d'Urbervilles*," *College English* 24 (1962), pp. 14-28.

49. Stephen C. Pepper, *World Hypotheses: A Study in Evidence* (Berkeley, 1961), p. 279.

50. Kaja Silverman, "History, Figuration and Female Subjectivity in *Tess of the d'Urbervilles*," *Novel: A Forum on Fiction* 18 (1984), pp. 5-28.

51. Silverman, "History, Figuration and Female Subjectivity," pp. 15-22. See also Jules David Law, "Sleeping Figures: Hardy, History, and the Gendered Body," *ELH* 65 (1998), pp. 223-257, for a reconstruction of Silverman's view, in which Tess's body is reasserted as integral and necessary for experiencing the novel.

52. Peter Widdowson, "Introduction" to *Tess of the d'Urbervilles* (New Casebooks), ed. Widdowson (New York, 1993), p. 20.

53. Penny Boumelha, *Thomas Hardy and Women: Sexual Ideology and Narrative Form* (Brighton UK, 1992), p. 132.

54. *Ibid.*, p. 122. Feminist thinkers who have an interest in Dewey avoid these dualisms, but succeed in focusing critically upon women's issues and on biases stemming from unexamined gender distinctions. A new feminist approach to *Tess* could be developed from their work. See especially Charlene Haddock Seigfried, "Whose Experiences? Genderizing Pluralistic Experiences," in her *Pragmatism and Feminism: Reweaving the Social Fabric* (Chicago, 1996), pp. 142-73; and Gwen Hart Carrol, "'Power in the Service of Love': John Dewey's *Logic* and the Dream of a Common Language," *Hypatia* 8 (1993), pp. 190-214.

55. Andrew Enstice, *Thomas Hardy: Landscapes of the Mind* (New York, 1979), p. 144.

56. Roger Robinson, "Hardy and Darwin," pp. 147-8.

57. Bruce Johnson, "The Perfection of Species and Hardy's *Tess*," in *Thomas Hardy's Tess*, ed. Harold Bloom (New York, 1987), p. 35.

58. J. Hillis Miller, *Thomas Hardy: Distance and Desire*, p. 103.

59. John Sutherland, *Is Heathcliff a Murderer? Great Puzzles in Nineteenth-Century Literature* (Oxford, 1996), pp. 209-12.

60. Jim Garrison, *Dewey and Eros: Wisdom and Desire in the Art of Teaching* (New York, 1997), p. 64.

61. See Wayne Burns, *The Flesh and the Spirit in Seven Hardy Novels* (Alpine CA, 2002), p. 138.

62. See Burns, "The Panzaic Principle in Hardy's *Tess of the d'Urbervilles*," *Recovering Literature* 1 (1972), no. 1, pp. 26-41.

63. Burns, *The Flesh and the Spirit*, pp. 121-2.

64. *Ibid.*, p. 140.

65. *Ibid.*, p. 135.

66. *Ibid.*, pp. 133-4.

67. Jack Johnson, as quoted in Pamela Haag, *Consent: Sexual Rights and the Transformation of American Liberalism* (Ithaca NY, 1999), p. 26.

68. Burns, *The Flesh and the Spirit*, p. 132.

69. *Ibid.*, pp. 139-40.

70. Thomas Hardy, "The Profitable Reading of Fiction," in *Thomas Hardy's Personal Writings*, ed. Harold Orel (Lawrence KS, 1996), pp. 110-25.

71. Tony Tanner, "Colour and Movement in Hardy's *Tess of the d'Urbervilles*," in *Hardy's Tess*, ed. Harold Bloom, pp. 9-23. For an impassioned re-statement of Tanner's argument on Nature in Tess, see Philip M. Weinstein, *The Semantics of Desire: Changing Models of Identity from Dickens to Joyce* (Ithaca NY, 1984), pp. 108-24. Under this "stencil," Tess becomes an exemplary case of Hardy's attachment to "the Schopenhaurian ordeal" of Nature (*Ibid.*, p. 122).

72. Margaret Higonnet, "Introduction" to Thomas Hardy, *Tess of the d'Urbervilles* (London, 1998), pp. xix-xli.

73. Marlene Springer, *Hardy's Use of Allusion* (Lawrence KS, 1983), pp. 126-7. Compare John Goode, who finds that Tess, in the great scene of her being drawn through the overgrown garden toward Angel's music, when she is depicted as "crushing snails that were underfoot" (127), is exemplifying "the naturalist nature of Darwinist struggle." Goode, *Thomas Hardy: The Offensive Truth* (Oxford, 1988), p. 177. Goode, who seems to be writing in denial of the text, claims that "[T]he animus against nature spans the whole novel and it is real and no mere lament" (*Ibid.*, p. 112). The effect of such an approach upon experiencing the novel is largely one of massive distancing. "[P]redominantly," Goode claims, the theme of nature in the novel causes "us to stand away from the life portrayed." Goode, *Ibid.*, p. 121. Goode's account of *Tess* is a sobering example of a reader backing away from his own finest perceptions.

74. Dale Kramer, *Thomas Hardy: Tess of the d'Urbervilles* (Cambridge UK, 1991), p. 95.

75. Linda M. Shires, "The Radical Aesthetic of *Tess of the d'Urbervilles*," in *The Cambridge Companion to Thomas Hardy* (Cambridge UK, 1999), p. 161.

76. Higonnet, "Introduction," p. xxxii.

77. Higonnet, *Ibid.*, p. xxx.

78. Thomas Hardy, *The Life and Work*, ed. Millgate, p. 227.

79. Hardy, *Ibid.*

80. Lennart Björk, *Psychological Vision*, pp. 131-8.

81. Thomas Hardy, *The Collected Letters*, vol. 1, p. 190.

82. Stephen C. Pepper, *The Basis of Criticism in the Arts* (Cambridge MA, 1963), pp. 71-2.

83. Kristin Brady, "Thomas Hardy and Matters of Gender," in *The Cambridge Companion to Thomas Hardy*, ed. Dale Kramer (Cambridge UK, 1999), p. 101.

84. Peter Widdowson, "Hardy and Critical Theory," in *The Cambridge Companion to Thomas Hardy*, ed. Kramer, p. 82.

85. Brady, "Thomas Hardy and Matters of Gender," p. 101.

86. *Ibid.*, p. 108.

87. Havelock Ellis, quoted in Brady, "Thomas Hardy and Matters of Gender," p. 95.

88. Garrett Stewart, "'Driven Well-Home to the Reader's Heart': Hardy's Implicated Audience," in *Tess of the d'Urbervilles*, ed. Riquelme, pp. 537-51.

89. *Ibid.*, p. 550.

90. John Dewey, as cited in Edward Weeks, "Fifty Influential Books," *Publisher's Weekly* (March 23, 1935), pp. 1227-30.

91. Sheryl Gay Stolberg, "Grants Aid Abstinence-Only Initiative," *New York Times* (28 Feb. 2002). State governments in the U.S.A. provide still more funds to these programs, which deliver messages of shame and guilt; see Tamara Kreinin, "Message From the President," *SIECUS Developments* (Winter-Spring, 2002), p. 1.

92. Tamar Lewin, "Survey Shows Sex Practices of Boys," *New York Times*, 19 Dec. 2000.

93. Lynn Ponton, as quoted in Susan Gilbert, "An Expert's Eye on Teenage Sex, Risk and Abuse," *New York Times*, 15 Jan 2002.

94. W. P. Trent, "The Novels of Thomas Hardy, " in *Thomas Hardy: The Critical Heritage*, ed. R. G. Cox (New York, 1970), pp. 232.

95. *Ibid.*, pp. 232-3.

96. Peter Widdowson, "Hardy and Critical Theory," p. 79.

97. See as self-consciously up-to-date examples of new theoretical applications: an article by Adam Gussow, who expresses violent contempt for Hardy's narration and imposes his own authentic interpretation taken from Australian aboriginal ethnography, "Dreaming Holmberry-Lipped Tess: Aboriginal Reverie and Spectatorial Desire in *Tess of the d'Urbervilles*," *Studies in the Novel* 32 (2000), pp. 443-63; and D. E. Musselwhite, "Tess of the d'Urbervilles: 'A Becoming Woman' *or* Deleuze and Guattari Go to Wessex," *Textual Practice* 14 (2000), pp. 499-518. Contrast the sensitive use of Deleuze by John Hughes in *'Ecstatic Sound': Music and Individuality in the Work of Thomas Hardy* (Aldershot UK, 2003). Hughes is one of the few Hardy critics writing today who seem to stay in contact with the process of experiencing the novels while employing theoretical concepts. In Deweyan aesthetics, I would expect that virtually any critical theory can be used creatively, but only if the critic focuses on experiencing the work of art.

BIBLIOGRAPHY

Abercrombie, Lascelles. *Thomas Hardy: A Critical Study*. London: Martin Secker, 1912.

Ackerman, Diane. *A Natural History of the Senses*. New York: Vintage Books, 1990.

Aeschylus. "Prometheus Bound." Translated by David Grene. *Aeschylus II*. Edited by David Grene and Richmond Lattimore, 131-79. Chicago: University of Chicago Press, 1956.

Alexander, Thomas M. *John Dewey's Theory of Art, Experience and Nature: Horizons of Feeling*. Albany NY: State University of New York Press, 1987.

Angier, Natalie. "Author Offers Theory on Grey Matter of Love. "*New York Times*, 30 May, 2000.

Archer, William. *Real Conversations*. London: Heinemann, 1904.

Barrineau, Nancy. "Explanatory Notes." *Tess of the d'Urbervilles*, Edited by Juliet Grindle and Simon Gatrell, 385-410. Oxford-New York: 1988.

Bayley, John. *An Essay on Hardy*. Cambridge-New York: Cambridge University Press, 1978.

Beach, Joseph Warren. *The Technique of Thomas Hardy*. New York: Russell and Russell, 1962. (Original date, 1922).

Beer, Gillian. *Darwin's Plots: Evolutionary Narrative in Darwin, George Eliot and Nineteenth-Century Fiction*. London-Boston: Routledge & Kegan Paul, 1983.

Bernstein, Susan David. "Confessing and Editing: The Politics of Purity in Hardy's *Tess*." V*irginity: Sexuality and Textuality in Victorian Literature*. Edited by Lloyd Davis, 159-78, 242-46. Albany NY: State University of New York Press, 1993.

The Bible: Designed to Be Read as Living Literature. Edited by Ernest Sutherland Bates. New York: Simon and Schuster, 1936.

Björk, Lennart. *Psychological Vision and Social Criticism in the Novels of Thomas Hardy*. Stockholm: Almqvist & Wiksell International, 1987.

Blake, Kathleen. "Pure Tess: Hardy on Knowing a Woman." *Critical Essays on Thomas Hardy*. Edited by Dale Kramer assisted by Nancy Mark, 204-19. Boston: G. K. Hall, 1990.

Bleich, David. *Subjective Criticism*. Baltimore: John Hopkins University Press, 1978.

Bloom, Harold, ed. *Thomas Hardy's Tess of the D'Urbervilles: Modern Critical Interpretations*. New York-New Haven: Chelsea House Publishers, 1987.

Boone, Joseph Allen. *Tradition Counter Tradition: Love and the Form of Fiction*. Chicago-London: University of Chicago Press, 1987.

Boumelha, Penny. *Thomas Hardy and Women: Sexual Ideology and Narrative Form*. Brighton, Sussex; Totowa NJ: Harvester Press; Barnes & Noble, 1982.

Bradley, A. C. "Poetry for Poetry's Sake." *Oxford Lectures on Poetry*. 1-34. London: Macmillan, 1965.

Brady, Kristin. "Tess and Alec: Rape or Seduction?" *Thomas Hardy Annual* 4 (1986):127-47.

_____."Thomas Hardy and Matters of Gender." *The Cambridge Companion to Thomas Hardy*. Edited by Dale Kramer, 93-111. Cambridge-New York: Cambridge University Press, 1999.

Bron, Eleanor, reader. Thomas Hardy, *Tess of the d'Urbervilles*. Abridged audio version. London: Penguin Books, 1994.

Bronfen, Elisabeth. *Over Her Dead Body: Death, Femininity and the Aesthetic*. New York: Routledge, 1992.

Brooks, Jean. *Thomas Hardy: The Poetic Structure*. Ithaca: Cornell University Press, 1971.

Brooks, Peter. *Reading for the Plot: Design and Intention in Narrative*. New York: Vintage Books, 1985.

Bullen, J. B. *The Expressive Eye: Fiction and Perception in the Work of Thomas Hardy*. Oxford: Clarendon Press, 1986.

Bullough, Edward. "'Psychical Distance' as a Factor in Art and as an Esthetic Principle." *A Modern Book of Aesthetics: An Anthology*. Edited by Melvin M. Rader,315-42. New York: Henry Holt, 1935.

Burns, Wayne. *The Flesh and the Spirit in Seven Hardy Novels*. Alpine, CA: Blue Daylight Books, 2002.

_____. "The Panzaic Principle in Hardy's *Tess of the d'Urbervilles*." *Recovering Literature* 1 (1972) no.1:26-41.

_____. "*The Woodlanders* as Love Story." *Recovering Literature* 5 (1976) no.3: 21-51.

Caird, Mona. "The Morality of Marriage." *Fortnightly Review* 53 (1890):310-30.

Carrol, Gwen Hart. "'Power in the Service of Love': John Dewey's *Logic* and the Dream of a Common Language." *Hypatia: A Journal of Feminist Philosophy* 8 (1992): 190-214.

Carpenter, Richard. *Thomas Hardy*. New York: Twayne, 1964.

Casagrande, Peter J. *Tess of the d'Urbervilles: Unorthodox Beauty*. New York: Twayne, 1982.

Claridge, Laura. "Tess: A Less Than Pure Woman Ambivalently Presented." *Tess of the d'Urbervilles*. Edited by Peter Widdowson, 63-79. New York: St. Martin's Press, 1993.

Colapietro, Vincent M. "Embodied, Enculturated Agents." *Dewey Reconfigured: Essays in Deweyan Pragmatism*. Edited by Casey Haskins and David I. Seiple, 63-84. Albany NY: State University of New York Press, 1999.

Cunningham, Gail. *The New Woman and the Victorian Novel*. London-Basingstoke: Macmillan, 1978.

Daleski, H. M. *Thomas Hardy and the Paradoxes of Love*. Columbia MO-London: University of Missouri Press, 1997.

Davis, W. Eugene. "*Tess of the d'Urbervilles*: Some Ambiguities About a Pure Woman." *Nineteenth Century Fiction* 22 (1968):397-401.

Davis, Jr., William A. "The Rape of Tess, English Law, and the Case of Sexual Assault." *Nineteenth Century Literature* 52 (1997):221-31.

Derrida, Jacques. "Structure, Sign and Play in the Discourse of the Human Sciences." *The Structuralist Controversy: The Languages of Criticism and the Sciences of Man.* Edited by Richard Macksey and Eugenio Donato, 140-72. Baltimore-London: Johns Hopkins University Press, 1972.

Dewey, John. *Human Nature and Conduct.* (*The Middle Works*, vol. 14). Edited by Jo Ann Boydston. Carbondale, IL: Southern Illinois University, Press, 1988.

_____. *Experience and Nature.* (*The Later Works*, vol. 1). Edited by Jo Ann Boydston. Carbondale, IL: Southern Illinois University Press, 1981.

_____. "From Absolutism to Experimentalism." (*The Later Works*, vol. 5). Edited by Jo Ann Boydston, 147-60. Carbondale, IL: Southern Illinois University Press, 1984.

_____. "Context and Thought." (*The Later Works*, vol. 6). Edited by Jo Ann Boydston, 3-21. Carbondale, IL: Southern Illinois University Press, 1985.

_____. *Art as Experience.* (*The Later Works*, vol.10). Edited by Jo Ann Boydston. Carbondale, IL: Southern Illinois University Press, 1987.

_____. "Foreword to Henry Schaefer-Simmern's *The Unfolding of Artistic Activity*." (*The Later Works*, vol. 15). Edited by Jo Ann Boydston, 315-17. Carbondale, IL: Southern Illinois University Press, 1989.

_____, and James Tufts. *Ethics.* (Second Edition) (*The Later Works*, vol. 7.) Edited by Jo Ann Boydston. Carbondale, IL: Southern Illinois University Press, 1985.

Dolin, Tim. "Notes." *Tess of the d'Urbervilles.* Edited by Tim Dolin, 399-461, 466-75, 510-18. London-New York: Penguin Books, 1998.

Ebbatson, Roger. *The Evolutionary Self: Hardy, Forster, Lawrence.* Harvester Press-Barnes and Noble: Brighton UK-Totowa NJ, 1982.

Efron, Arthur. "The Tale, the Teller and Sexuality in *Tess of the d'Urbervilles.*" *Paunch* (Feb., 1967) no. 28: 55-80.

_____. "Perspectivism and the Nature of Fiction: *Don Quixote* and Borges." *Thought* 50 (1975): 148-175.

_____. "The Novel From the Western World: An Instrument for the Criticism of Civilizations." *Works & Days: Essays in the Socio-Historical Dimensions of the Arts* 3 (1985): 29-52.

Enstice, Andrew. *Thomas Hardy: Landscapes of the Mind.* New York: St. Martin's Press, 1979.

Fels, Anna. "Mind Fills the Need to Explain." *New York Times,* 17 Dec., 2002.

Forster, E. M. *Aspects of the Novel.* New York: Harcourt, 1927.

Freud, Sigmund. "The Taboo of Virginity." *Standard Edition of the Complete Psychological Works of Sigmund Freud.* vol. 11. Edited by James Strachey, 181-208. London: Hogarth Press and Institute of Psycho-Analysis, 1953-74.

Frueh, Joanna. *Erotic Faculties.* Berkeley-Los Angeles: University of California Press, 1996.

Gallagher, Catherine. "*Tess of the d'Urbervilles*: Hardy's Anthropology of the Novel." *Tess of the d'Urbervilles.* Edited by John Paul Riquelme, 422-40. Boston-New York: Bedford Books, 1998.

Garrison, Jim. *Dewey and Eros: Wisdom and Desire in the Art of Teaching.* New York-London: Teacher's College Press, 1997.

Garson, Marjorie. *Hardy's Fables of Integrity: Woman, Body, Text.* Oxford-New York: Clarendon Press, 1991.

Gibson, James. *Thomas Hardy: A Literary Life.* New York: St. Martin's Press, 1996.

Gilbert, Susan. "An Expert's Eye on Teenage Sex, Risk and Abuse." *New York Times* 15 Jan., (2002).

Giordano, Jr., Frank R. *"I'd Have My Life Unbe"*: *Thomas Hardy's Self-Destructive Characters*. University AL: University of Alabama Press, 1984.

Goode, John. *Thomas Hardy: The Offensive Truth*. Oxford-New York: Blackwell, 1988.

Gose, Elliot B., Jr. "Psychic Evolution: Darwinism and Initiation in *Tess of the d'Urbervilles*." *Tess of the d'Urbervilles*. Edited by Scott Elledge, 422-32. New York-London: W. W. Norton, 1991.

Granger, David A. "Expression, Imagination and Organic Unity: Remarks on Deciphering John Dewey's Relationship to Romanticism." *Proceedings of the Midwest Philosophy of Education Society, 1999-2000*. 218-32. Chicago: The Society, 2001.

Green, Paul J. "Tess, Memory, and Trauma." Eugene, OR: unpublished manuscript, 2002.

Greenslade, William. *Degeneration, Culture and the Novel 1880-1940*. Cambridge-New York: Cambridge University Press, 1994.

_____. "Rediscovering Thomas Hardy's 'Facts' Notebook." In *The Achievement of Thomas Hardy*. Edited by Phillip Mallett. London-New York: Macmillan, St. Martin's Press, 2000.171-86.

Gregor, Ian. *The Great Web: The Form of Hardy's Major Fiction*. London: Faber and Faber, 1974.

Grundy, Joan. *Hardy and the Sister Arts*. London: Macmillan, 1979.

Gussow, Adam. "Dreaming Holmberry-Lipped Tess: Aboriginal Reverie and Spectatorial Desire in *Tess of the d'Urbervilles*." *Studies in the Novel* 32 (2000):443-63.

Haag, Pamela. *Consent: Sexual Rights and the Transformation of American Liberalism*. Ithaca-London: Cornell University Press, 1999.

Hardy, Thomas. *The Collected Letters of Thomas Hardy*. vol.1. Edited by Richard Little Purdy and Michael Millgate. Oxford: Clarendon Press, 1978.

_____. *The Collected Letters of Thomas Hardy*. vol. 2. Edited by Richard Little Purdy and Michael Millgate. Oxford: Clarendon Press, 1978.

_____. *The Complete Poems*. Edited by James Gibson. London-New York: Macmillan, 1976.

_____. *Desperate Remedies*. Introduction by C. J. P. Beatty. Macmillan: London, 1975.

_____. *The Life and Work of Thomas Hardy*. Edited by Michael Millgate. London-Basingstoke: Macmillan, 1984.

_____. *The Literary Notes of Thomas Hardy*. vol. 1. Edited by Lennart A. Björk. Goteborg, Sweden: Gothenburg Studies in English 29, 1974.

_____. *Tess of the d'Urbervilles*. Edited by Juliet Grindle and Simon Gatrell. Oxford: Clarendon Press, 1983. *Note*: this is the definitive scholarly edition.

_____. *Tess of the d'Urbervilles*. Edited by Juliet Grindle and Simon Gatrell. (Oxford World Classics). Oxford-New York: Oxford University Press, 1988. *Note*: all unidentified parenthetical page references to *Tess* in the present book are to this edition.

_____. *Tess of the d'Urbervilles*. 3rd edition. Edited by Scott Elledge. New York: W. W. Norton, 1991.

_____. *Tess of the d'Urbervilles*. Edited by John Paul Riquelme. Boston-New York: Bedford Books, 1998.

_____. *Tess of the d'Urbervilles* Edited by Tim Dolin. London-New York: Penguin Books, 1998.(The 1891 text).

_____. *Two on a Tower*. Edited by F. B. Pinion. Macmillan: London, 1975.

_____. *The Woodlanders*. Edited by Dale Kramer. Oxford-New York: 1985.

Harvey, A.D. *Sex in Georgian England*. New York: St. Martin's Press, 1994.

Hawkins, Desmond. *Hardy the Novelist*. Newton Abbot: David & Charles, 1950.

_____. *Hardy: Novelist and Poet.* Newton Abbot: David and Charles; New York: Barnes and Noble, 1976.

Herold, John. "'Winking Toads' and 'Beatific Intervals': From Contextualism to a Pluralistic Reading of *Tess of the d'Urbervilles.*" Paper given at conference on Critical Pluralism, University of Nebraska at Lincoln, 1990. (Unpublished).

Hickman, Larry A. *John Dewey's Pragmatic Technology.* Bloomington-Indianapolis: Indiana University Press, 1990.

Higonnet, Margaret R. "A Woman's Story: Tess and the Problem of Voice." *The Sense of Sex: Feminist Perspectives on Hardy.* Edited Margaret R. Higonnet, 14-31. Urbana-Chicago: University of Illinois Press, 1993.

_____. "Introduction." *Tess of the d'Urbervilles.* Edited by Tim Dolin, xix-xli. London-New York: Penguin, 1998.

_____, ed. *The Sense of Sex: Feminist Perspectives on Hardy.* Urbana-Chicago: University of Illinois Press, 1993.

Holland, Norman N. "Unity Identity Text Self." *PMLA* 90 (1975): 813-22.

Howe, Irving. *Thomas Hardy.* New York: Macmillan, 1967.

Hughes, John. *"Ecstatic Sound": Music and Individuality in the Works of Thomas Hardy.* Aldershot UK-Burlington USA: Ashgate, 2001.

Ingham, Patricia. *Thomas Hardy (Feminist Readings).* Hemel Hempstead: Harvester Wheatsheaf, 1989.

Irwin, Michael. "Readings of Melodrama." *Reading the Victorian Novel: Detail into Form.* Edited by Ian Gregor, 5-31. New-York-London: Barnes & Noble; Vision Press, 1980.

Iser, Wolfgang. *The Act of Reading: A Theory of Aesthetic Response.* Baltimore: Johns Hopkins University Press, 1978.

Jacobus, Mary. "Tess: The Making of a Pure Woman." *Thomas Hardy's Tess: Modern Critical Perspectives.* Edited by Harold Bloom, 45-60. New York; New Haven: Chelsea House Publishers, 1987.

Jackson, Philip. *John Dewey and the Lessons of Art.* New Haven-London: Yale University Press, 1998.

Johnson, Bruce. "The Perfection of Species and Hardy's *Tess.*" *Thomas Hardy's Tess: Modern Critical Perspectives.* Edited by Harold Bloom, 25-43. New York-New Haven; Chelsea House Publishers, 1987.

Johnson, Lionel. "The Argument." *Tess of the d'Urbervilles.* 3rd. Edition. Edited by Scott Elledge, 390-400. New York W. W. Norton, 1991.(Reprint from *The Art of Thomas Hardy.* London, 1894).

Kettle, Arnold. "Introduction." Thomas Hardy, *Tess of the d'Urbervilles,* vii-xxiii. New York: Harper and Row, 1966.

Kincaid, James. *Child-Loving: The Erotic Child and Victorian Culture.* New York-London: Routledge, 1992.

Knight, Deborah. "Why We Enjoy Condemning Sentimentality: A Meta-Aesthetic Perspective." *Journal of Aesthetics and Art Criticism* 57 (1999):411-20.

Kramer, Dale. *Thomas Hardy: The Forms of Tragedy.* London: Macmillan, 1975.

_____. *Thomas Hardy: Tess of the d'Urbervilles.* Cambridge: Cambridge University Press, 1991.

_____, ed. *The Cambridge Companion to Thomas Hardy.* Cambridge-New York: Cambridge University Press, 1999.

Kramer, Dale, ed., assisted by Nancy Marck. *Critical Essays on Thomas Hardy: The Novels.* Boston: G. K. Hall, 1990.

Kreinin, Tamara. "Message from the President." *SIECUS Developments* (Winter-Spring, 2002): 1. (Sex Information and Education Council of the United States).

Law, Jules David. "Sleeping Figures: Hardy, History, and the Gendered Body." *ELH* 65 (1998): 223-57.

Lawrence, D. H. *Study of Thomas Hardy and Other Essays.* Edited by Bruce Steele. Cambridge-New York: Cambridge University Press, 1985.

Levin, Jonathan. *The Poetics of Transition: Emerson, Pragmatism, and American Literary Modernism*. Durham-London: Duke University Press, 1999.

Lewin, Tamar. "Survey Shows Sex Practices of Boys." *New York Times*, 19 Dec., 2000.

Lopate, Phillip. "'Breathless' Turns 40, Its Youthful Impudence Intact." *New York Times*, 16 Jan., 2000.

Martin, Jay. *The Education of John Dewey: A Biography*. New York-Chichester UK: Columbia University Press, 2002.

McInerney, Peter. "Conceptions of Persons and Persons Through Time." *American Philosophical Review*. 37:2 (April 2000): 121-33.

McLauchlan, Juliet. *Tess of the d'Urbervilles (Thomas Hardy)*. Oxford: Basil Blackwell, 1971. (Notes on English Literature).

Miller, Geoffrey F. *The Mating Mind: How Sexual Choice Shaped the Evolution of Human Nature*. New York: Doubleday, 2000.

Miller, J. Hillis. *Thomas Hardy: Distance and Desire*. Cambridge MA: Harvard University Press, 1970.

_____. *Fiction and Repetition: Seven English Novels*. Cambridge MA: Harvard University Press, 1982.

Millgate, Michael. *Thomas Hardy: A Biography*. New York: Random House, 1982.

Morgan, Rosemarie. *Women and Sexuality in the Novels of Thomas Hardy*. London-New York: Routledge, 1988.

Murphy, Patricia. *Time is of the Essence: Temporality, Gender, and the New Woman*. Albany, NY: State University of New York Press, 2000.

Musselwhite, D. E. "Tess of the D'Urbervilles: 'A Becoming Woman' *or* Deleuze and Guattari Go to Wessex." *Textual Practice* 14 (2000): 499-518.

Oberndorf, Clarence P. *A History of Psychoanalysis in America*. New York: Harper & Row, 1964.

Orel, Harold (ed.). *Thomas Hardy's Personal Writings*. Lawrence, KS: University of Kansas Press, 1966.

Ormond, Leonée. "Painting and Sculpture." *Oxford Reader's Companion to Hardy*. Edited by Norman Page, 295-97. Oxford-New York: Oxford University Press, 2000.

Padian, Kevin. "'A Daughter of the Soil': Themes of Deep Time and Evolution in Thomas Hardy's *Tess of the d'Urbervilles*." *Thomas Hardy Journal* 13 (1997): 65-81.

Page, Norman. "Art and Aesthetics." *The Cambridge Companion to Thomas Hardy*. Edited by Dale Kramer, 38-53. Cambridge-New York: Cambridge University Press, 1999.

Paris, Bernard J. "'A Confusion of Many Standards': Conflicting Value Standards in *Tess of the d'Urbervilles*." *Nineteenth Century Fiction* 24 (June 1969): 57-79.

_____. "Experiences of Thomas Hardy." *The Victorian Experience*. Edited by Richard A. Levine, 203-37. Athens GA: Ohio University Press, 1976.

Pepper, Stephen C. *Aesthetic Quality: A Contextualistic Theory of Beauty*. New York: Charles Scribner's Sons, 1937.

_____. "Some Questions on Dewey's Esthetics." *The Philosophy of John Dewey*. Edited by Paul A. Schilpp, 371-89. Evanston, IL: Northwestern University Press, 1939.

_____. *World Hypotheses: A Study in Evidence*. Berkeley-Los Angeles: University of California Press, 1961.

_____. *The Basis of Criticism in the Arts*. Cambridge: Harvard University Press, 1945.

_____. "Emotional Distance in Art. "*Journal of Aesthetics and Art Criticism* 4 (1946): 235-39.

_____. *The Work of Art*. Bloomington: Indiana University Press, 1955.

Ragussis, Michael. *Acts of Naming: The Family Plot in Fiction.* New York-Oxford: Oxford University Press, 1986.

Reich, Wilhelm. *The Function of the Orgasm: Sex-Economic Problems of Biological Energy.* Translated by Theodore P. Wolfe. Cleveland: World Publishing, 1971.

Riquelme, John P. "Echoic Language, Uncertainty, and Freedom in *Tess of the d'Urbervilles.*" *Tess of the d'Urbervilles.* Edited by John Paul Riquelme. Boston-New York: Bedford Books, 1998. 506-520.

Robinson, Jenefer. "*Languages of Art* at the Turn of the Century." *Journal of Aesthetics and Art Criticism* 58 (2000): 213-18.

Robinson, Roger. "Hardy and Darwin." In *Thomas Hardy: The Writer and his Work.* Edited by Norman Page, 128-49. New York St. Martin's Press, 1980.

Rooney, Ellen. "Tess and the Subject of Sexual Violence: Reading, Rape, Seduction." *Tess of the d'Urbervilles.* Edited by John Paul Riquelme, 462-83. Boston-New York: Bedford Books, 1998.

Rosenblatt, Louise M. *Literature as Exploration,* 5th edn. New York: Modern Language Association, 1995.

_____. *The Reader, the Text, the Poem: the Transactional Theory of the Literary Work.* Carbondale-Edwardsville, IL: Southern Illinois University Press, 1978.

_____. "Readers, Texts, Authors." *Transactions of the Charles S. Peirce Society* 34(1998): 885-921.

Scarry, Elaine. "Work and Body in Hardy and Other Nineteenth-Century Novelists." *Representations* 3(1983): 90-123.

Schweik, Robert C. "Moral Perspective in *Tess of the d'Urbervilles.*" *College English* 24 (1962): 14-18.

_____. "A Commentary on F. R. Southerington's Critique of Gittings'*Young Thomas Hardy.*" *Paunch,* no. 51 (1978):42-48.

_____. "Less Than Faithfully Presented: Fictions in Modern Commentaries on Hardy's *Tess of the d'Urbervilles.*" *Reading Thomas Hardy.* Edited by Charles P. C. Pettit, 33-56. New York: St. Martin's Press, 1998.

Seigfried, Charlene Haddock. *Pragmatism and Feminism: Reweaving the Social Fabric.* Chicago-London: University of Chicago Press, 1996.

Serres, Michel. *The Natural Contract.* Translated by Elizabeth MacArthur and William Paulson. Ann Arbor: University of Michigan Press, 1995.

Shires, Linda M. "The Radical Aesthetic of *Tess of the d'Urbervilles.*" *The Cambridge Companion to Thomas Hardy.* Edited by Dale Kramer, 145-63. Cambridge-New York: Cambridge University Press, 1999.

Shusterman, Richard. *Pragmatist Aesthetics: Living Beauty, Re-thinking Art.* Oxford-Cambridge MA: Blackwell, 1992.

_____. "Art as Dramatization." *Journal of Aesthetics and Art Criticism* 59 (2001): 363-72.

Silverman, Kaja. "History, Figuration and Female Subjectivity in *Tess of the d'Urbervilles.*" *Novel: A Forum on Fiction* 18 (1984): 5-28.

Smith, Roberta. "Conjurer of Ethereal Mysteries." *New York Times,* 1 March, 2002.

Southerington, F. R. *Hardy's Vision of Man.* New York: Barnes and Noble, 1971.

_____. "Young Thomas Hardy." *Paunch,* no. 51 (1978):29-41.

Springer, Marlene. *Hardy's Use of Allusion.* Lawrence KS: University Press of Kansas,1983.

Stave, Shirley A. *The Decline of the Goddess: Nature, Culture, and Women in Thomas Hardy's Fiction.* Westport CT-London: Greenwood Press, 1995.

Stewart, Garrett. "'Driven Well Home to the Reader's Heart': *Tess*'s Implicated Audience." *Tess of the d'Urbervilles.* Edited by John Paul Riquelme, 537-51. Boston-New York: Bedford Books, 1998.

Stewart, J. I. M. *Thomas Hardy: A Critical Biography*. New York: Dodd, Mead and Co., 1971.

Steig, Michael. *Stories of Reading: Subjectivity and Literary Understanding*. Baltimore-London: Johns Hopkins University Press, 1989.

Sternlieb, Lisa. "'Three Leahs to Get One Rachel': Redundant Women in *Tess of the d'Urbervilles*." *Dickens Studies Annual: Essays on Victorian Fiction*. 29 (2000):351-65.

Stolberg, Sheryl Gay. "Grants Aid Abstinence-Only Initiative." *New York Times* 28 Feb., 2002.

Stott, Rebecca. "'Something More to Be Said': Hardy's *Tess*." In *The Fabrication of the Late-Victorian Femme Fatal*." 163-199, 229-32. Houndmill-Basingstoke: Macmillan, 1992.

Sumner, Rosemary. *Thomas Hardy: Psychological Novelist*. New York: St. Martin's Press, 1981.

Sutherland, John. *Is Heathcliff a Murderer? Great Puzzles in Nineteenth-Century Literature*. Oxford-New York: Oxford University Press, 1996.

Tanner, Tony. "Colour and Movement in Hardy's *Tess of the d'Urbervilles*." In *Thomas Hardy's Tess of the d'Urbervilles: Modern Critical Interpretations*. Edited by Harold Bloom, 9-23. New York-New Haven: Chelsea House, 1987.

Tennov, Dorothy. *Love and Limerance: The Experience of Being in Love*. New York: Stein and Day, 1979.

Trent, W. P. "The Novels of Thomas Hardy." *Thomas Hardy: The Critical Heritage*. Edited by R. G. Cox, 221-37. New York: Barnes & Noble, 1970.

Turner, Paul. *The Life of Thomas Hardy: A Critical Biography*. Oxford-Malden MA: Blackwell, 1998.

Waks, Leonard J. "The Means-End Continuum and the Reconciliation of Science and Art in the Later Works of John Dewey." *Transactions of the Charles S. Peirce Society*, 35 (1999): 595-611.

Watson, William. *Tess of the d'Urbervilles*. 3rd Edition. Edited by Scott Elledge, 386-7. New York: W. W. Norton, 1991. (Reprint from *The Academy*, Feb. 6, 1892).

Webster, Harvey Curtis. *On a Darkling Plain: The Art and Thought of Thomas Hardy*. Chicago: University of Chicago Press, 1947.

Weeks, Edward. "Fifty Influential Books." *Publisher's Weekly*, 23 March, 1935: 1227-29; 1230.

Weinstein, Philip M. *The Semantics of Desire: Changing Models of Identity From Dickens to Joyce*. Princeton NJ: Princeton University Press, 1984.

Widdowson, Peter, ed. *Tess of the d'Urbervilles*. New York: St. Martin's Press, 1993 (New Casebooks).

_____. "Hardy and Critical Theory." *The Cambridge Companion to Thomas Hardy*. Edited by Dale Kramer, 73-92. Cambridge-New York: Cambridge University Press, 1999.

_____, ed. *Thomas Hardy: Selected Poetry and Non-Fictional Prose*. New York: St Martin's Press, 1997.

Williams, Melanie. "'Sensitive as Gossamer'—Law and Sexual Encounter in *Tess of the d'Urbervilles*." *Thomas Hardy Journal* 17 (2001): 54-60.

Williams, Raymond. "Love and Work." *Tess of the d'Urbervilles*. 3rd Edition. Edited by Scott Elledge, 460-71. New York: W. W. Norton, 1991. 460-71.

Williams, Merryn, and Raymond Williams. "Hardy and Social Class." In *Tess of the d'Urbervilles*. Edited by Peter Widdowson, 24-32. New York: St. Martin's Press, 1993.

Wilshire, Bruce. "Body-Mind and Subconsciousness: Tragedy in Dewey's Life and Work." *Philosophy and the Reconstruction of Culture: Pragmatic Essays After Dewey*. Edited by John J. Stuhr, 257-72. Albany NY: State University of New York Press, 1993.

Wright, T. R. *Hardy and the Erotic*. Houndmills-London: Macmillan, 1989.

ABOUT THE AUTHOR

Arthur Efron has taught for four decades in the Department of English at the University at Buffalo, SUNY, where he has offered courses on The Novel, Literature and Anarchist Thought, Literature and the Body, Literature and Psychology, and especially since 1990, on Dewey's *Art as Experience* and Literature. The authors he has been back to repeatedly are Cervantes, Thomas Hardy, D.H. Lawrence, and Virginia Woolf. Currently he teaches a graduate seminar on Studies in the Novel. Efron edited and published his own journal of criticism, *Paunch*, named after Sancho Panza, from 1963 to 1999. His book, *Don Quixote and the Dulcineated World*, came out in 1971. Efron draws upon the philosophical writings of John Dewey and Stephen C. Pepper in *The Sexual Body: An Interdisciplinary Perspective*, published in 1985 as a double issue of the *Journal of Mind and Behavior*. His monograph, also using Dewey, on Melville's *Billy Budd, Sailor (an Inside Narrative)* appeared in 1993, in *REAL*. His monograph on an anarchist interpretation of *Henry the Fourth, Part One*, appeared in *Works & Days: Essays in the Socio-Historical Dimensions of Literature and the Arts* (vol. 10, 1992); to this, there were five critical responses and a rejoinder. Efron's *Life-Energy Reading: Wilhelm Reich and Literature* (*Paunch*, no. 67-68, 1993), contains studies of *Wuthering Heights, The Blithedale Romance, One Hundred Years of Solitude, Story of O*, and *Jude the Obscure*. His article, "D. H. Lawrence, John Dewey and Democracy," was published in *D. H. Lawrence Studies* (Seoul), in 1999.

INDEX

Abercrombie, Lascelles, 214
abstinence, 191-2, 220-1
Ackerman, Diane, 85, 207
active equilibrium, 55
Aeschylus, 214
aesthetic object, 8-9, 17
aesthetic theory, xiii, xiv, 5, 8-20
aesthetic work of art, 7, 8-9, 181
Alexander, Thomas M., 15, 18, 39,
    199, 203, 213
agricultural work, 30, 44-5, 120-1
allusion, Hardy's use of, 33-4, 72,
    81, 106, 146, 208, 219
anger, 33, 48, 50, 53
Angier, Natalie, 217
animal life, 16-7, 60-1, 99-100
Archer, William, 170-1, 217
armor, 80
Arnold, Matthew, 188
art-centered experience, 6, 57
Arthurian legend, Tess and, 93
author's self, 1

Barrineau, Nancy, 195, 206, 211
Baudrillard, Jean, 63
Bayley, John, 41, 204
Beach, Joseph Warren, 195, 208
beauty of Tess, 160-1
Beer, Gillian, 69, 169, 205, 217
Bernstein, Susan David, 207
Bible, allusions to, 33-4, 70, 83,
    85, 87, 89, 92-3, 98, 99, 106
    B. and Tess, 177
Björk, Lennart, 82, 170-1, 188
Blake, Kathleen, 90, 157, 207, 214
Bleich, David, 198
"blighted or splendid" worlds, 40
body, 39-40, 80, 90-1, 94, 101,
    102, 111, 117-8, 127, 203

b. in Dewey's aesthetics, 16-
    20
b. in Hardy's novels, 40, 202
b. of Tess, 29-30, 40, 47-8,
    50-1, 54, 56-7, 68, 76, 84-
    5, 87, 92, 93, 94, 101,
    102, 127
"body's cry of 'Where?'," xiii,
    36, 88, 164, 174
body-mind, 39-40, 53, 60-1, 67,
    70, 87, 89-93, 111, 129, 137-
    8, 144, 148, 151
Boone, Joseph Allen, 208
Boumelha, Penny, 176, 207, 209,
    211, 218
Bowen, Priscilla, xiii
Bradley, A.C., 7, 198
Brady, Kristin, 45, 189-90, 204,
    209-10, 220
Bron, Eleanor, 155, 213
Bronfen, Elisabeth, 199
Brooks, Jean, 203, 204
Brooks, Peter, 40, 203
Browning, Robert, 107
Bullen, J.B., 196
Bullough, Edward, 133-4, 211
Burns, Wayne, 62, 154, 183-5,
    191, 205, 210-3, 216, 219

Caird, Mona, 163, 166, 216
Car Darch, 44-5
Carrol, Gwen Hart, 218
Carpenter, Richard, 208
Casagrande, Peter J., 200, 204
change, 130-1, 150-3, 182
Chant, Mercy, 113
character in fiction, 177, 189, 204
Clare, Angel
    complexity of C., 26-8

illness of C., 110, 130, 134-5, 142, 148, 151
intuitive side of C., 95-6
process of change of C., 130-6, 150-3
visits to parents by C., 80-3, 86, 110
Clare house, Tess turns from, 113-5
Clare, Rev., 79-83, 109, 114-5, 132
Clare, Mrs., wife of Rev., 114-5
Claridge, Laura, 162, 215
Colapietro, Vincent M., 211
"common" as shared interest, 158
communication as miracle, 70
confession scene, 95-9
    ethical core of c., 99, 100-1, 191
consent, sexual, 32, 202
consummation, wish for, 76-7
consummative phase and endings, 153-6
context, 4-5, 91, 207
    versus verbal linkage, 35-6
"Context and Thought" (Dewey), 4-5, 66
contextualistic criticism, 3
contextualism, 7, 57, 152, 201-2
control object, 8, 188
cow culture, 66, 73, 149-51
craftsmanship as loving, 55
Crick, Richard, "Dairyman," 68, 120
Crick, Mrs., 74
Cunningham, Gail, 205

Daleski, H.M., 34, 203, 212, 216
Darwin, Charles, 172, 218-9
Davis, W. Eugene, 161-2, 207, 215
Davis, Jr., William, 202

Deceased Wife's Sister Acts, 154, 213
Deleuze, Gilles, 221
"deliberate openness to life itself," 13
Derrida, Jacques, 9, 199
desire, 32, 48, 111-4, 145-50, 165, 209, 210-1
Desperate Remedies (Hardy), x, 209
Dewey, John, early realization of the body, 17-18
disgust, quality of, 117-8
Dolin, Tim, 196, 201, 204, 207, 213, 214
doubt, as quality, 33
Durbeyfield, Joan, 48, 52, 64, 80, 100, 135, 172-3
Durbeyfield, John, 12-3, 76-7, 127
    death of D., 129-33
Durbeyfield, Liza-lu, 154-6
Durbeyfield, Tess,
    melting into environment by D., 177
    mind of D., 40-2, 51, 52-3, 64-5, 71, 87, 94, 112-3, 123, 125, 143, 148, 150, 151, 158, 165, 177
    pathological development of D., 89-92, 123, 145-6, 174
    self and identity of D., 1, 52, 57, 166
    voice of D., 2, 41, 67, 134, 143-4, 167, 183, 216

Ebbatson, Roger, 217
Efron, Arthur, 207, 208, 209, 214
Ellis, Havelock, 190
embodiment of ideas, 127-8
Emerson, Ralph Waldo, 63

emotion, 5, 11-2, 17, 66-7, 77, 79, 88, 95-105, 129, 186, 202, 206
Hardy's view of e., 187-8
retroactive action of e., 12-3, 95
emotion in aesthetic experience, 11-3, 79, 80, 145
end-in-view, 14, 26, 87, 118, 193
ending of *Tess*, 152
endings, 153-6
Victorian e. rejected, 104
energy, 13-5, 29-30, 37, 73-6, 75-8, 82-3, 88-9, 90, 97, 105, 135, 177
Enstice, Andrew, 178, 218
erection, 116, 155
ethics, 51, 53, 87, 100-1, 166-7, 191
ethical intelligence, 52-4, 59-60, 64-5, 100-1, 166, 167
Ethics (Dewey), 1-2, 27
experience, 5-15, 69, 168-9, 181-2, 188-93
experience blockers, 19-20, 25-8, 31, 41, 49-50, 62-3, 72-3, 83, 84, 96-7, 103, 147-8, 157-8, 166, 176, 185, 188, 193
experiencing versus image-matching, 35-6
experimental quality in aesthetic creation, 2, 162
expulsion of the Durbeyfields, 127-8
extra-aesthetic factor, 183-5

family, criticism of, 38-9, 41, 45-6, 56, 71, 93-4, 172-3
"fear of what life may bring forth," 19, 211
Fels, Anna, 212
feminist approaches, 22-3, 84, 85, 157, 158, 163, 175-7, 218

"field woman" remark, 177
"Foreword" (Dewey) to *The Unfolding of Artistic Activity* (Schaefer-Simmern), 42
Forster, E.M., 98, 208
Freud, Sigmund, 3, 154, 196, 213
"From Absolutism to Experimentalism" (Dewey), 17
Frueh, Joanna, 149, 161
fulfillment, 137-9, 159-60, 165, 177, 168-9
fusion, aesthetic, x, 29-30, 37, 86, 130-1, 201-2

Gallagher, Catherine, 202-3
Garrison, Jim, 33, 182, 202, 218
Garson, Marjorie, 200-1, 209
gaze, male, 176, 189, 212
gender, 175-7
gender bias, 41, 75-6, 85, 106, 114, 175-7
Gibson, James, 201
Gilbert, Susan, 221
Giordano, Jr., Frank, 216
"gleaning of her grapes" allusion, 133-4
good and evil, 167-8
Goode, John, 154, 163, 200, 211, 213, 216, 219
Gose, Jr., Elliot, 40, 203, 215
Gothic novel, 104
Granger, David, 11, 199
Greece, meaning for Hardy, 82, 188
Green, Paul, 35, 199
Greenslade, William, 210, 217
Gregor, Ian, 2, 77, 195, 206, 214
growth, 61, 124, 151, 168
Grundy, Joan, 196
Gussow, Adam, 221

Haag, Pamela, 202, 219
habit, 12, 16-7

Haldane, J.B.S., 3
hanging of Tess, 154-6
"hard-logical deposit," 95, 101-2,
    125, 131, 165, 177
Hardy, Thomas
    Alec and Angel within
        himself, 159
    conscious inhibition in his
        writing, 54, 65, 73, 74,
        113, 117
    descent of, 2
    disturbance during writing
        Tess, 109-15
    personal involvement in
        Tess, 2-3, 37, 49, 55, 97,
        110, 128, 153, 177
Hare, Peter, xiv-xv
Harvey, A.D., 209
Hawkins, Desmond, 208, 215
hayrick scene, 121-3, 143, 178,
    210
Herold, John, 208
heterosexual relationships, 30-1,
    44, 175
Hickman, Larry, 17, 199
"higher passions," versus
    "inferior," 112
Higonnet, Margaret, 41, 186-7,
    196, 202, 204, 209-11, 219-
    20
Holland, Norman, 198
homo-erotic suggestions, 175
Horney, Karen, 90, 199
"hour for loving," 3, 174-5
Howe, Irving, 157-8, 214
Hudson, W.H., 63
Huett, Izz, 74, 82, 90-1, 106, 117,
    121, 128, 132, 170, 177
Hughes, John, 205, 221
Human Nature and Conduct
    (Dewey), 20-1
husband in Nature, 91, 128-9, 142
Huxley, Thomas H., 17

ideal reader, 6
identity in change, 1, 126-7, 135,
    136, 160
"immortal puzzle," the sexual
    relation, 60, 204-5
individuality, 43
Ingham, Patricia, 84, 206
inner experience, 105
inquiry, 7, 32-3, 38, 49, 98, 117-9,
    162
    i. by Tess, 49
intelligence, 180
intervening periods of discrimi-
    nation, 142
Irwin, Michael, 104, 208
Iser, Wolfgang, 197

Jacobus, Mary, 22-3, 25-7, 200-1
Jackson, Philip W., 6, 12, 197,
    199, 204
James, William, 69
Jewish identity, author's, 191
Johnson, Bruce, 216, 218
Johnson, Jack, 184, 219
Johnson, Lionel, 4-5, 196-7
Johnson, Samuel, 3
Jude the Obscure (Hardy), 100,
    150

Kettle, Arnold, 169, 216
killer, Tess as, 23-4, 141-2, 144,
    178
Kincaid, James, 204
Knight, Deborah, 211
Kramer, Dale, 4, 186, 196, 200,
    205, 207-8, 214, 200
Kreinin, Tamara, 220

Lacanian approach, 176
Law, Jules David, 203, 218
Lawrence, D.H., 5, 27, 37, 40,
    101-3, 201, 207, 208
Leopardi, Giacomo, 81

lesbian intimations, 175, 209
letters by Tess, 121, 123-4, 210
Levin, Jonathan, 197
Lewin, Tamar, 221
love interlude of Tess and Angel, 146-50
love-philosophy, 36-7, 71
love relationship, Tess and Alec, 48-52, 144-5, 161, 162
loyalty, Tess toward Angel, 157-8

Marian, 69, 76-7, 90-1, 121, 128, 161, 170
marital fighting, ix, 104-5
Martin, Jay, 9, 199
masculine typology, 158
masculinity of Angel, 75, 76, 80, 101, 105, 107, 109
The Mayor of Casterbridge (Hardy), 62
McInerney, Peter, 124, 211
McLauchlan, Juliet, 197, 215
Melchester, 213
melodramatic aspects, 106, 142, 184
Miller, Geoffrey, 172, 217
Miller, J. Hillis, 2, 35, 62, 157-8, 178, 195, 199-200, 203, 205, 214-6, 218
Millgate, Michael, 159, 195-6, 215, 220
Milton, John, 155, 164, 214
moralists as critics, 19
Morgan, Rosemarie, 205, 210, 216
mounting Alec's gig, 46-7
Murphy, Patricia, 217
music, 29, 63, 205
Musselwhite, D.E., 221

naiveté, cultivated, 13, 34, 88, 192
narration and self, 1-2, 3
narrator, Hardy as, xiii-xiv, 1-4,

23-4, 29-30, 33-4, 38, 50, 54-7, 60, 91, 92, 99, 103, 113, 131, 155, 176, 184-5, 210-1, 221
contempt for n., xiv, 4-5, 38, 50, 115, 171, 210-1, 212, 221
n. distracts from defects of Angel, 23-4
nature, ix, 1, 29, 30, 56, 60-74, 80, 103,, 111-2, 122, 149-50, 159, 169-70, 186-7
n. de-natured, 93-4, 95
n. unconstrained, 84
n. as valid concept, 62-3, 219-20
New Criticism, 6, 201
New Forest, 146
novel, theory of, 105, 157, 214

Oberndorf, Clarence, 196
omens, 93-6, 179-80
"once a victim" speech, 121-5, 210
One Hundred Years of Solitude (García Márquez), 121
Orel, Harold, 209, 213, 216, 219
Ormond, Leonée, 196

Padian, Kevin, 217
Page, Norman, 86, 196, 208, 217
Paris, Bernard, 90, 199, 204, 207, 212
passivity of Tess, 174
Pepper, Stephen C., 3, 7-8, 37, 57, 69, 79, 152, 175, 181, 183, 188-9, 199, 201-2, 204-6, 218, 220
perception, 9-11, 14, 18-9, 84, 119
p. and moral systems, 18
p. versus recognition, 10-2
perceptive series, 7, 44, 91, 209

perplexity in experience, 32-3, 134, 152
pessimism, 31, 57, 64, 168-71, 174, 187-8, 214, 217-8
p. regarding sex, 170-1
pheasants, killing of, 113-4
pleasure, 59, 81, 137, 149, 162
p. and "self-delight," 170
p. as "inherent will to enjoy," 171
pragmatist aesthetics, 6
"precarious promises of good," 181
predilection of the critic, 191
President of the Immortals, 155, 214
Priddle, Retty, 72, 90-1, 161, 170
"The Profitable Reading of Fiction" (Hardy), 112, 185, 219
pure, as term, 149-50
pure reason, 102
"pure woman," 161-7

quality, 9, 31, 119
emotional q. versus sentimentality, 135
erotic q., 149
q. in scene of Alec's murder, 141-2
q. of final sentence in *Tess*, 155

radical empiricism, 9
Ragussis, Michael, 199
rape, problem of, 31-4, 97-8, 117-9, 127-8, 167, 184, 203, 209-10
reader-response criticism, x, 8, 198
realism, 163
recognition, 9-10

Reconstruction in Philosophy (Dewey), xiii
red color, 35-6, 203, 207
Reich, Wilhelm, 156, 191, 206, 214
religions, 5-6, 54, 72, 75, 81-2, 85, 129, 158, 159
resistance and tension, 5, 63-4
Riquelme, John, 169, 201-3, 207, 209, 217, 220
Robinson, Jenefer, 206
Robinson, Roger, 217-8
Rooney, Ellen, 203, 208-9, 211
Rosenblatt, Louise, 197-9

sadistic action, 90-2, 158, 165-6
Scarry, Elaine, 40, 203
Schopenhauer, Arthur, 81
S. as key to *Tess*, 219
Schweik, Robert, 195, 212, 218
Seigfried, Charlene Haddock, 203, 218
seizure, total, 180
self-delight, need for, 59, 170
sentimental quality, 39, 133
Serres, Michel, 62, 205
sex, Dewey on, 20-2, 172
s., denial by critics, 199-200
s. impulse as overwhelming, 75, 170, 171-2
s. as indiscriminate drive, 172
s. as subject-matter, 10, 20-2, 60, 61-74, 86, 133-4
s. as target of repression, 172
sex education, Hardy on, 172
sex, genital, 37, 95
sexual body, 80, 111, 117-8
"sexual chaos," 156
sexual ethic, 51, 53, 100
sexual experience, quality of, 43-5, 51, 133-4, 136-9, 146-50
s. at Sandbourne, 136-9

s. at Tantridge, 183-4
s., Tess with Angel, 146-50
sexual experimentation, of Tess, 51
sexual instinct, 170-2, 189-90
sexual self, of Tess, 32, 88, 100
sexual thinking of Angel, 66-7, 98, 106-7, 145-6, 150-1, 179, 212-3
Shelley, Percy Bysshe, 107
Shires, Linda, 220
Shusterman, Richard, 6-7, 15, 17, 197, 199, 202
Silverman, Kaja, 176, 206-7, 211, 218
sin, 34, 161, 176
sleepwalking of Angel, 103-4, 208
Smith, Roberta, 196
sociologist, Hardy as, 1, 127-8, 172, 174
soul of Tess, 60, 68
sound, role of, 30, 59
Southerington, F.R., 195
Sparks, Tryphena, 2, 195
split-brain effect, 144, 212
spread, 12-3, 57, 132
Springer, Marlene, 219
stability of meaning, 182-3
Stave, Shirley, 202
Stewart, Garrett, 190, 220
Stewart, J.I.M., 5, 197
Steig, Michael, 198
stencil, 10-11, 28, 193, 207
Sternlieb, Lisa, 213
Stolberg, Sheryl Gay, 220
Stonehenge, 153, 165
Stott, Rebecca, 214
strained passages, 110-1, 115-6, 132, 178
strawberry scene, 46-7
"structure of sensations," 56-7
suffering, of Tess, 111-2, 123

Sumner, Rosemary, 27, 103, 201, 208
Sutherland, John, 178, 218
Symonds, John Addington, 188
synesthesia, 16

tale versus teller, xiii, 5, 207
Tanner, Tony, 186, 203, 207, 219
Tennov, Dorothy, 72, 205
Tess of the d'Urbervilles
    audio version, 154-5
    manuscript, 23-6, 103, 122
    plot, 20, 110, 116
    revisions, Hardy's, 23-6, 50, 54, 103, 122, 147
    unity, 3, 192-3
theory, critical, 184-5
tragedy, Hardy on, 156, 160, 168, 169, 188
tragic qualities, 11-2
Trent, W.P., 192, 221
Turner, Paul, 3, 68, 196, 205, 215
Two on a Tower (Hardy), 116

undeniable qualities, 26-7, 48, 64, 83, 89-90, 95, 101, 105, 122-3, 175-6, 182, 185-7
undergoing, 10, 11, 190
unified body-mind experience, 70
unifying ideas, 182
UR sound, 30-1
d'Urberville, Alec
    complexity of d., 26-8, 30
    development of d., 28, 119, 126, 128, 164
    killing of d., 22-3, 27-8, 142-3
    potential for fulfillment of d., 137-9, 159-60
    terrifying Tess d., 163
d'Urberville theme, 178-81
    portraits of d., 94, 102, 179

validity of reference in literature,
    180
value questions, 175
Van Gogh, Vincent, 11
virginity, ideal of, 97, 98, 101,
    131, 138, 147, 151, 191-2,
    209
voyeurism, 148-9, 176

Waks, Leonard J., 201
Watson, William, 27, 201
"we," editorial, 8
Webster, Harvey Curtis, 19, 217
Weeks, Edward, 220
Weinstein, Philip, 219
western civilization, 82
whole, unified qualitative, 181-3
Widdowson, Peter, 148, 163, 176,
    189, 211-2, 215, 218, 220-1
Williams, Melanie, 202
Williams, Merryn, 211
Williams, Raymond, 127, 169,
    211, 216
Wilshire, Bruce, 39, 203
Wintoncester, 155
Wordsworth, William, 62, 173
woman, as term 1, 157-9, 214
    strong w., Tess as, 215
    Tess as w., 157-9
women "advancing with the bold
    grace of wild animals," 86
work, as part of reading, 13
work of art, completion of, 23-4
world as unstable, 181
Wright, T.R., 201

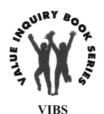

VIBS

The **Value Inquiry Book Series** is co-sponsored by:

Titles Published

1. Noel Balzer, *The Human Being as a Logical Thinker*

2. Archie J. Bahm, *Axiology: The Science of Values*

3. H. P. P. (Hennie) Lötter, *Justice for an Unjust Society*

4. H. G. Callaway, *Context for Meaning and Analysis: A Critical Study in the Philosophy of Language*

5. Benjamin S. Llamzon, *A Humane Case for Moral Intuition*

6. James R. Watson, *Between Auschwitz and Tradition: Postmodern Reflections on the Task of Thinking*. A volume in **Holocaust and Genocide Studies**

7. Robert S. Hartman, *Freedom to Live: The Robert Hartman Story*, Edited by Arthur R. Ellis. A volume in **Hartman Institute Axiology Studies**

8. Archie J. Bahm, *Ethics: The Science of Oughtness*

9. George David Miller, *An Idiosyncratic Ethics; Or, the Lauramachean Ethics*

10. Joseph P. DeMarco, *A Coherence Theory in Ethics*

11. Frank G. Forrest, *Valuemetrics⁸: The Science of Personal and Professional Ethics*. A volume in **Hartman Institute Axiology Studies**

12. William Gerber, *The Meaning of Life: Insights of the World's Great Thinkers*

13. Richard T. Hull, Editor, *A Quarter Century of Value Inquiry: Presidential Addresses of the American Society for Value Inquiry*. A volume in **Histories and Addresses of Philosophical Societies**

14. William Gerber, *Nuggets of Wisdom from Great Jewish Thinkers: From Biblical Times to the Present*

15. Sidney Axinn, *The Logic of Hope: Extensions of Kant's View of Religion*

16. Messay Kebede, *Meaning and Development*

17. Amihud Gilead, *The Platonic Odyssey: A Philosophical-Literary Inquiry into the Phaedo*

18. Necip Fikri Alican, *Mill's Principle of Utility: A Defense of John Stuart Mill's Notorious Proof.* A volume in **Universal Justice**

19. Michael H. Mitias, Editor, *Philosophy and Architecture.*

20. Roger T. Simonds, *Rational Individualism: The Perennial Philosophy of Legal Interpretation.* A volume in **Natural Law Studies**

21. William Pencak, The Conflict of Law and Justice in the Icelandic Sagas

22. Samuel M. Natale and Brian M. Rothschild, Editors, *Values, Work, Education: The Meanings of Work*

23. N. Georgopoulos and Michael Heim, Editors, *Being Human in the Ultimate: Studies in the Thought of John M. Anderson*

24. Robert Wesson and Patricia A. Williams, Editors, *Evolution and Human Values*

25. Wim J. van der Steen, *Facts, Values, and Methodology: A New Approach to Ethics*

26. Avi Sagi and Daniel Statman, *Religion and Morality*

27. Albert William Levi, *The High Road of Humanity: The Seven Ethical Ages of Western Man*, Edited by Donald Phillip Verene and Molly Black Verene

28. Samuel M. Natale and Brian M. Rothschild, Editors, *Work Values: Education, Organization, and Religious Concerns*

29. Laurence F. Bove and Laura Duhan Kaplan, Editors*, From the Eye of the Storm: Regional Conflicts and the Philosophy of Peace.* A volume in **Philosophy of Peace**

30. Robin Attfield, *Value, Obligation, and Meta-Ethics*

31.   William Gerber, *The Deepest Questions You Can Ask About God: As Answered by the World's Great Thinkers*

32.   Daniel Statman, *Moral Dilemmas*

33.   Rem B. Edwards, Editor, *Formal Axiology and Its Critics*. A volume in **Hartman Institute Axiology Studies**

34.   George David Miller and Conrad P. Pritscher, *On Education and Values: In Praise of Pariahs and Nomads*. A volume in **Philosophy of Education**

35.   Paul S. Penner, *Altruistic Behavior: An Inquiry into Motivation*

36.   Corbin Fowler, *Morality for Moderns*

37.   Giambattista Vico, *The Art of Rhetoric* (*Institutiones Oratoriae*, 1711–1741), from the definitive Latin text and notes, Italian commentary and introduction byGiuliano Crifò.Translated and Edited by Giorgio A. Pinton and Arthur W. Shippee. A volume in **Values in Italian Philosophy**

38.   W. H. Werkmeister, *Martin Heidegger on the Way*. Edited by Richard T. Hull. A volume in **Werkmeister Studies**

39.   Phillip Stambovsky, *Myth and the Limits of Reason*

40.   Samantha Brennan, Tracy Isaacs, and Michael Milde, Editors, *A Question of Values: New Canadian Perspectives in Ethics and Political Philosophy*

41.   Peter A. Redpath, *Cartesian Nightmare: An Introduction to Transcendental Sophistry*. A volume in **Studies in the History of Western Philosophy**

42.   Clark Butler, *History as the Story of Freedom: Philosophy in InterculturalContext*, with responses by sixteen scholars

43.   Dennis Rohatyn, *Philosophy History Sophistry*

44.   Leon Shaskolsky Sheleff, *Social Cohesion and Legal Coercion: A Critique of Weber, Durkheim, and Marx*. Afterword by Virginia Black

45.   Alan Soble, Editor, *Sex, Love, and Friendship: Studies of the Society for the Philosophy of Sex and Love, 1977–1992.* A volume in **Histories and Addresses of Philosophical Societies**

46.   Peter A. Redpath, *Wisdom's Odyssey: From Philosophy to Transcendental Sophistry.* A volume in **Studies in the History of Western Philosophy**

47.   Albert A. Anderson, *Universal Justice: A Dialectical Approach.* A volume in **Universal Justice**

48.   Pio Colonnello, *The Philosophy of José Gaos.* Translated from Italian by Peter Cocozzella. Edited by Myra Moss. Introduction by Giovanni Gullace. A volume in **Values in Italian Philosophy**

49.   Laura Duhan Kaplan and Laurence F. Bove, Editors, *Philosophical Perspectives on Power and Domination: Theories and Practices.* A volume in **Philosophy of Peace**

50.   Gregory F. Mellema, *Collective Responsibility*

51.   Josef Seifert, *What Is Life? The Originality, Irreducibility, and Value of Life.* A volume in **Central-European Value Studies**

52.   William Gerber, *Anatomy of What We Value Most*

53.   Armando Molina, *Our Ways: Values and Character*, Edited by Rem B. Edwards. A volume in **Hartman Institute Axiology Studies**

54.   Kathleen J. Wininger, *Nietzsche's Reclamation of Philosophy.* A volume in **Central-European Value Studies**

55.   Thomas Magnell, Editor, *Explorations of Value*

56.   HPP (Hennie) Lötter, *Injustice, Violence, and Peace: The Case of South Africa.* A volume in **Philosophy of Peace**

57.   Lennart Nordenfelt, *Talking About Health: A Philosophical Dialogue.* A volume in **Nordic Value Studies**

58.   Jon Mills and Janusz A. Polanowski, *The Ontology of Prejudice.* A volume in **Philosophy and Psychology**

59.   Leena Vilkka, *The Intrinsic Value of Nature*

60.   Palmer Talbutt, Jr., Rough Dialectics: *Sorokin's Philosophy of Value*, with contributions by Lawrence T. Nichols and Pitirim A. Sorokin

61.   C. L. Sheng, *A Utilitarian General Theory of Value*

62.   George David Miller, *Negotiating Toward Truth: The Extinction of Teachers and Students*. Epilogue by Mark Roelof Eleveld. A volume in **Philosophy of Education**

63.   William Gerber, *Love, Poetry, and Immortality: Luminous Insights of the World's Great Thinkers*

64.   Dane R. Gordon, Editor, *Philosophy in Post-Communist Europe.* A volume in **Post-Communist European Thought**

65.   Dane R. Gordon and Józef Niznik, Editors, *Criticism and Defense of Rationality in Contemporary Philosophy*. A volume in **Post-Communist European Thought**

66.   John R. Shook, *Pragmatism: An Annotated Bibliography, 1898-1940.* With contributions by E. Paul Colella, Lesley Friedman, Frank X. Ryan, and Ignas K. Skrupskelis

67.   Lansana Keita, *The Human Project and the Temptations of Science*

68.   Michael M. Kazanjian, *Phenomenology and Education: Cosmology, Co-Being, and Core Curriculum*. A volume in **Philosophy of Education**

69.   James W. Vice, *The Reopening of the American Mind: On Skepticism and Constitutionalism*

70.   Sarah Bishop Merrill, *Defining Personhood: Toward the Ethics of Quality in Clinical Care*

71.   Dane R. Gordon, *Philosophy and Vision*

72.   Alan Milchman and Alan Rosenberg, Editors, *Postmodernism and the Holocaust*. A volume in **Holocaust and Genocide Studies**

73.   Peter A. Redpath, *Masquerade of the Dream Walkers: Prophetic Theology from the Cartesians to Hegel*. A volume in **Studies in the History of Western Philosophy**

74.   Malcolm D. Evans, *Whitehead and Philosophy of Education: The Seamless Coat of Learning*. A volume in **Philosophy of Education**

75.   Warren E. Steinkraus, *Taking Religious Claims Seriously: A Philosophy of Religion*, Edited by Michael H. Mitias. A volume in **Universal Justice**

76.   Thomas Magnell, Editor, *Values and Education*

77.   Kenneth A. Bryson, *Persons and Immortality*. A volume in **Natural Law Studies**

78.   Steven V. Hicks, *International Law and the Possibility of a Just World Order: An Essay on Hegel's Universalism*. A volume in **Universal Justice**

79.   E. F. Kaelin, *Texts on Texts and Textuality: A Phenomenology of Literary Art*, Edited by Ellen J. Burns

80.   Amihud Gilead, *Saving Possibilities: A Study in Philosophical Psychology*. A volume in Philosophy and Psychology

81.   André Mineau, *The Making of the Holocaust: Ideology and Ethics in the Systems Perspective*. A volume in **Holocaust and Genocide Studies**

82.   Howard P. Kainz, *Politically Incorrect Dialogues: Topics Not Discussed in Polite Circles*

83.   Veikko Launis, Juhani Pietarinen, and Juha Räikkä, Editors, *Genes and Morality: New Essays*. A volume in **Nordic Value Studies**

84.   Steven Schroeder, *The Metaphysics of Cooperation: A Study of F. D. Maurice*

85.   Caroline Joan ("Kay") S. Picart, *Thomas Mann and Friedrich Nietzsche: Eroticism, Death, Music, and Laughter*. A volume in **Central-European Value Studies**

86.   G. John M. Abbarno, Editor, *The Ethics of Homelessness: Philosophical Perspectives*

87.   James Giles, Editor, *French Existentialism: Consciousness, Ethics, and Relations with Others*. A volume in **Nordic Value Studies**

88.   Deane Curtin and Robert Litke, Editors, *Institutional Violence*. A volume in **Philosophy of Peace**

89.   Yuval Lurie, *Cultural Beings: Reading the Philosophers of Genesis*

90.   Sandra A. Wawrytko, Editor, *The Problem of Evil: An Intercultural Exploration*. A volume in **Philosophy and Psychology**

91.   Gary J. Acquaviva, *Values, Violence, and Our Future*. A volume in **Hartman Institute Axiology Studies**

92.   Michael R. Rhodes, *Coercion: A Nonevaluative Approach*

93.   Jacques Kriel, *Matter, Mind, and Medicine: Transforming the Clinical Method*

94.   Haim Gordon, *Dwelling Poetically: Educational Challenges in Heidegger's Thinking on Poetry*. A volume in **Philosophy of Education**

95.   Ludwig Grünberg, *The Mystery of Values: Studies in Axiology*, Edited by Cornelia Grünberg and Laura Grünberg

96.   Gerhold K. Becker, Editor, *The Moral Status of Persons: Perspectives on Bioethics*. A volume in **Studies in Applied Ethics**

97.   Roxanne Claire Farrar, *Sartrean Dialectics: A Method for Critical Discourse on Aesthetic Experience*

98.   Ugo Spirito, *Memoirs of the Twentieth Century*. Translated from Italian and Edited by Anthony G. Costantini. A volume in **Values in Italian Philosophy**

99.   Steven Schroeder, *Between Freedom and Necessity: An Essay on the Place of Value*

100.   Foster N. Walker, *Enjoyment and the Activity of Mind: Dialogues on Whitehead and Education*. A volume in **Philosophy of Education**

101.   Avi Sagi, Kierkegaard, *Religion, and Existence: The Voyage of the Self.* Translated from Hebrew by Batya Stein

102.   Bennie R. Crockett, Jr., Editor, *Addresses of the Mississippi Philosophical Association*. A volume in **Histories and Addresses of Philosophical Societies**

103.   Paul van Dijk, *Anthropology in the Age of Technology: The Philosophical Contribution of Günther Anders*

104.   Giambattista Vico, *Universal Right*. Translated from Latin and edited by Giorgio Pinton and Margaret Diehl. A volume in **Values in Italian Philosophy**

105.   Judith Presler and Sally J. Scholz, Editors, *Peacemaking: Lessons from the Past, Visions for the Future*. A volume in **Philosophy of Peace**

106.   Dennis Bonnette, *Origin of the Human Species*. A volume in **Studies in the History of Western Philosophy**

107.   Phyllis Chiasson, *Peirce's Pragmatism: The Design for Thinking*. A volume in **Studies in Pragmatism and Values**

108.   Dan Stone, Editor, *Theoretical Interpretations of the Holo*caust. A volume in **Holocaust and Genocide Studies**

109.   Raymond Angelo Belliotti, *What Is the Meaning of Human Life?*

110.   Lennart Nordenfelt, *Health, Science, and Ordinary Language*, with Contributions by George Khushf and K. W. M. Fulford

111.   Daryl Koehn, *Local Insights, Global Ethics for Business*. A volume in **Studies in Applied Ethics**

112.   Matti Häyry and Tuija Takala, Editors, *The Future of Value Inquiry*. A volume in **Nordic Value Studies**

113.   Conrad P. Pritscher, *Quantum Learning: Beyond Duality*

114.   Thomas M. Dicken and Rem B. Edwards, *Dialogues on Values and Centers of Value: Old Friends, New Thoughts*. A volume in **Hartman Institute Axiology Studies**

115.   Rem B. Edwards, *What Caused the Big Bang?* A volume in **Philosophy and Religion**

116.   Jon Mills, Editor, *A Pedagogy of Becoming*. A volume in **Philosophy of Education**

117.   Robert T. Radford, *Cicero: A Study in the Origins of Republican Philosophy*. A volume in **Studies in the History of Western Philosophy**

118.   Arleen L. F. Salles and María Julia Bertomeu, Editors, *Bioethics: Latin American Perspectives*. A volume in **Philosophy in Latin America**

119.   Nicola Abbagnano, *The Human Project: The Year 2000*, with an Interview by Guiseppe Grieco. Translated from Italian by Bruno Martini and Nino Langiulli. Edited with an introduction by Nino Langiulli. A volume in **Studies in the History of Western Philosophy**

120.   Daniel M. Haybron, Editor, *Earth's Abominations: Philosophical Studies of Evil*. A volume in **Personalist Studies**

121.   Anna T. Challenger, *Philosophy and Art in Gurdjieff's* Beelzebub*: A Modern Sufi Odyssey*

122.   George David Miller, *Peace, Value, and Wisdom: The Educational Philosophy of Daisaku Ikeda*. A volume in **Daisaku Ikeda Studies**

123.   Haim Gordon and Rivca Gordon, *Sophistry and Twentieth-Century Art*

124.   Thomas O. Buford and Harold H. Oliver, Editors *Personalism Revisited: Its Proponents and Critics*. A volume in **Histories and Addresses of Philosophical Societies**

125.   Avi Sagi, *Albert Camus and the Philosophy of the Absurd*. Translated from Hebrew by Batya Stein

126. Robert S. Hartman, *The Knowledge of Good: Critique of Axiological Reason*. Expanded translation from the Spanish by Robert S. Hartman. Edited by Arthur R. Ellis and Rem B. Edwards.A volume in **Hartman Institute Axiology Studies**

127. Alison Bailey and Paula J. Smithka, Editors. *Community, Diversity, and Difference: Implications for Peace*. A volume in **Philosophy of Peace**

128. Oscar Vilarroya, *The Dissolution of Mind: A Fable of How Experience Gives Rise to Cognition*. A volume in **Cognitive Science**

129. Paul Custodio Bube and Jeffery Geller, Editors, *Conversations with Pragmatism: A Multi-Disciplinary Study*. A volume in **Studies in Pragmatism and Values**

130. Richard Rumana, *Richard Rorty: An Annotated Bibliography of Secondary Literature*. A volume in **Studies in Pragmatism and Values**

131. Stephen Schneck, Editor, *Max Scheler's Acting Persons: New Perspectives* A volume in **Personalist Studies**

132. Michael Kazanjian, *Learning Values Lifelong: From Inert Ideas to Wholes*. A volume in **Philosophy of Education**

133. Rudolph Alexander Kofi Cain, Alain Leroy Locke: *Race, Culture, and the Education of African American Adults*. A volume in **African American Philosophy**

134. Werner Krieglstein, *Compassion: A New Philosophy of the Other*

135. Robert N. Fisher, Daniel T. Primozic, Peter A. Day, and Joel A. Thompson, Editors, *Suffering, Death, and Identity*. A volume in **Personalist Studies**

136. Steven Schroeder, *Touching Philosophy, Sounding Religion, Placing Education*. A volume in **Philosophy of Education**

137. Guy DeBrock, *Process Pragmatism: Essays on a Quiet Philosophical Revolution*. A volume in **Studies in Pragmatism and Values**

138. Lennart Nordenfelt and Per-Erik Liss, Editors, *Dimensions of Health and Health Promotion*

139. Amihud Gilead, *Singularity and Other Possibilities: Panenmentalist Novelties*

140. Samantha Mei-che Pang, *Nursing Ethics in Modern China: Conflicting Values and Competing Role Requirements*. A volume in **Studies in Applied Ethics**

141. Christine M. Koggel, Allannah Furlong, and Charles Levin, Editors, *Confidential Relationships: Psychoanalytic, Ethical, and Legal Contexts*. A volume in **Philosophy and Psychology**

142. Peter A. Redpath, Editor, *A Thomistic Tapestry: Essays in Memory of Étienne Gilson*. A volume in **Gilson Studies**

143. Deane-Peter Baker and Patrick Maxwell, Editors, *Explorations in Contemporary Continental Philosophy of Religion*. A volume in **Philosophy and Religion**

144. Matti Häyry and Tuija Takala, Editors, *Scratching the Surface of Bioethics*. A volume in **Values in Bioethics**

145. Leonidas Donskis, *Forms of Hatred: The Troubled Imagination in Modern Philosophy and Literature*

146. Andreea Deciu Ritivoi, Editor, *Interpretation and Its Objects: Studies in the Philosophy of Michael Krausz*

147. Herman Stark, *A Fierce Little Tragedy: Thought, Passion, and Self-Formation in the Philosophy Classroom*. A volume in **Philosophy of Education**

148. William Gay and Tatiana Alekseeva, Editors, *Democracy and the Quest for Justice: Russian and American Perspectives*. A volume in **Contemporary Russian Philosophy**

149. Xunwu Chen, *Being and Authenticity*

150. Hugh P. McDonald, *Radical Axiology: A First Philosophy of Values*

151. Dane R. Gordon and David C. Durst, Editors, *Civil Society in Southeast Europe*. A volume in **Post-Communist European Thought**

152. John Ryder and Emil Višňovský, Editors, *Pragmatism and Values: The Central European Pragmatist Forum, Volume One*. A volume in **Studies in Pragmatism and Values**

153. Messay Kebede, *Africa's Quest for a Philosophy of Decolonization*

154. Steven M. Rosen, *Dimensions of Apeiron: A Topological Phenomenology of Space, Time, and Individuation*. A volume in **Philosophy and Psychology**

155. Albert A. Anderson, Steven V. Hicks, and Lech Witkowski, Editors, *Mythos and Logos: How to Regain the Love of Wisdom*. A volume in **Universal Justice**

156. John Ryder and Krystyna Wilkoszewska, Editors, *Deconstruction and Reconstruction: The Central European Pragmatist Forum, Volume Two*. A volume in **Studies in Pragmatism and Values**

157. Javier Muguerza, *Ethics and Perplexity: Toward a Critique of Dialogical Reason*. Translated from the Spanish by Jody L. Doran. Edited by John R. Welch. A volume in **Philosophy in Spain**

158. Gregory F. Mellema, *The Expectations of Morality*

159. Robert Ginsberg, *The Aesthetics of Ruins*

160. Stan van Hooft, *Life, Death, and Subjectivity: Moral Sources in Bioethics* A volume in **Values in Bioethics**

161. André Mineau, *Operation Barbarossa: Ideology and Ethics Against Human Dignity*

162. Arthur Efron, *Experiencing Tess of the D'Urbervilles: A Deweyan Account*. A volumein **Studies in Pragmatism and Values**